GREAT
NORTHERN
LOST MOOSE
CATALOGUE

WOOD ETCHING: JOHN STEINS

Published by Lost Moose, the Yukon Publishers
58 Kluane Crescent, Whitehorse, Yukon, Canada Y1A 3G7
*phone: 867-668-5076, fax: 867-668-6223, e-mail: lmoose@yknet.yk.ca
web site: http://www.yukonweb.com/business/lost_moose
*Prior to October 1997, area code is 403

Canadian Cataloguing in Publication Data
Main entry under title:
    Great northern lost moose catalogue

includes index.
ISBN 1-896758-02-9

1. Yukon Territory–Miscellaena.

FC4007.G73 1997   971.9'1002   C97-980157-5
F1091.G73 1997

Design by Mike Rice
Production by K-L Services, Whitehorse
Printed and bound in Canada

For information on ordering other fine Lost Moose titles, see pages 220-223.

Cover art: *Secret places*, 1997, by Janet Moore
Born in Ottawa, Janet Moore studied at the University of Waterloo and
Emily Carr College of Art and Design. Her work has been included in the
Canada Council Art Bank and the Yukon Permanent Art Collection and in
numerous private collections throughout Canada. Janet Moore lives and
works in Whitehorse, Yukon.

Inside front and back covers: Wood etchings by John Steins

97 98 99 00 01   5 4 3 2 1

PHOTO: JURI PEEPRE

CONTENTS

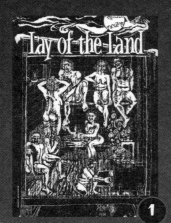

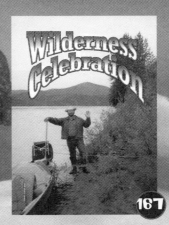
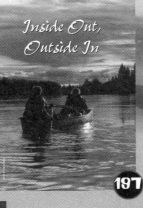

A TALE OF THREE MOOSE

How do you lose a moose? Simple. Tell it you have to powder your nose, and then hop in a cab. But lose a good idea? You can't do it; they just won't go away.

It's only now, looking back on the previous Lost Whole Moose Catalogues, that we see how good an idea it really was. A handful of enthusiasts from around the Yukon put together a collection of the things that made life in the north exciting. There were sled dogs, cabins, skinny dipping, forty below, wild meat, canoes, smoked fish, and above all, the resounding sense of the bush that is never quite absent in the north.

Open the original *Lost Whole Moose Catalogue* (1979) and you step into a piece of Yukon history, a chronicle of the days when Squatters' Road was a free place, when you needed a jeep to get to Annie Lake in April, when people tied reflective tape to their horses' tails so you wouldn't hit them on the highway.

Life was funky, and so was the catalogue. In its pages you can learn to make grouse fried rice, use pack dogs, and build a gravity-fed water system for your cabin.

By the time that *Another Lost Moose Whole Moose Catalogue* was published (1991), much had changed in the Yukon. The Whitehorse post ofice was gone, and with it the lawn, the mountain ash, and the Group W Bench. You could buy edible vegetables at the store, and most of the highways were paved. Fax machines were more common than pack-dogs. You could even watch a movie in the same year it was released.

This second catalogue was full of the things which still said "north" to us; the things we wanted to show each other, and say, "See, we are different. Our lives are unique, and this uniqueness is our compensation for forty below, mosquitoes, soft apples, high prices." *Another* did a roaring trade with those of us who had run out of gift ideas. What more could your mom want for Christmas than a book with a picture of her only son, stark naked, playing in the river with her infant grandson, similarly clad?

And here we are again, to say simply that—here we are.

In all our silly poems and our goofy pictures, in all our fine handcrafted easy chairs, filling our faces with rosehip jelly and lowbush cranberry tea, mushing our dogs or tapping at our computers, here is whatever the north means, at least to an ill-knit community, scattered around Canada and Alaska, in the hear and now.

Some of the naked or mud-flecked infants, some of the pregnant bellies, which graced the pages of *Another Lost Moose Whole Moose Catalogue* have grown into young authors, and this new generation of writers and artists is featured in the *Great Northern Lost Moose Catalogue*. Are they unique? Will we look back in twenty years and say, "Look, this was us, weren't we special, wasn't it worth it?"

I have no doubt we will. This book is our celebration of the north we know today. Whatever kind of thrown-together-and-scatttered-again-to-the-four-winds community we might have here, we have done what little we could to help stitch it together and show it off, in a land so big and wild you can lose a moose in it.

by Al Pope

Lay of the Land

Lay of the Land

Where there's more moose than people

by Max Fraser

HMMM...
Now Where
Am I?

The "land of the lost moose" is the part of the continent that contains, roughly, more moose than people. Except for a few major population centres, the north is a land of scattered small communities with much wildlife in between, particularly moose. This is the basis of a unique and great northern culture. In the Yukon, for example, there are 60,000 moose and 30,000 people. In the western NWT, there might be 25,000 people and 40,000 moose. In Northern B.C., about 70,000 moose populate the area north of Prince Rupert; north of this town there are about the same number of people. In Alaska, major population centres such as Anchorage, Fairbanks and Juneau, dominate, bringing the human population to over 400,000. In the eastern interior and southeastern part of Alaska(the Panhandle), 50,000 moose roam.

The moose, of course, are hardly lost. In Anchorage, where hunting is prohibited and much green space provides excellent habitat, moose are considered a wandering traffic hazard—especially when they cross roads in the winter. Most everywhere else, moose are spotted occasionally by people travelling through this great northern land. At hunting time, however, they somehow become more difficult to find, frustrating meat-seeking northerners.

That there are so many moose provides security to the persistent northerner who relies on the large creature for sustenance. That there are so many moose tells all others that we can take comfort knowing so much wild land and wildlife surrounds us. It's what makes living in the north so special.

PHOTO: FRANK PARHIZGAR/WWF-CANADA. ILLUSTRATIONS: (READING MOOSE) SCOTT BERDAHL. (SILHOUETTE MOOSE) JENNIFER STANIFORTH

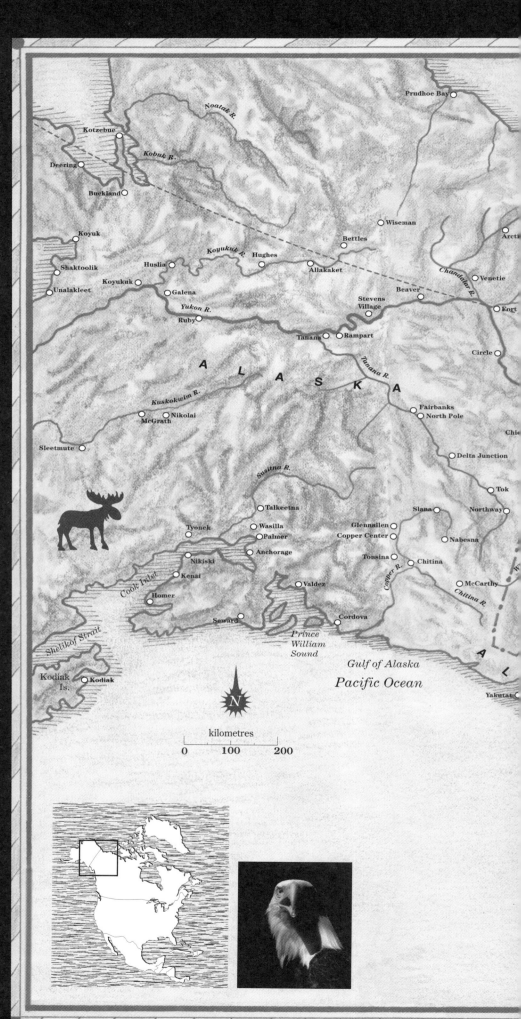

LOST MOOSE

Arctic Ocean

Beaufort Sea

Banks Island

Victoria Island

Sachs Harbour

Kaktovik

Herschel Is.

Cape Dalhousie

Cape Bathurst

Kuujjua R.

Holman

Amundsen Gulf

Tuktoyaktuk

Paulatuk

Coronation Gulf

rctic Village

Sheenjek R.

Horton R.

Anderson R.

Aklavik

Inuvik

Coppermine

Porcupine R.

Old Crow

Fort McPherson

Arctic Red River

Coppermine R.

ort Yukon

Eagle Plains

ARCTIC CIRCLE

Fort Good Hope

Great Bear Lake

Eagle

Peel R.

Snake R.

Chicken

Dawson City

Bonnet plume R.

Wind R.

Norman Wells
Fort Franklin

Fort Norman

k

Y U K O N

Elsa Keno

Stewart R.

N

N O R T H W E S T

Beaver Creek

Stewart Crossing

Mayo

Hess R.

O

Mackenzie R.

Fort Selkirk

Pelly Crossing

Macmillan R.

T E R R I T O R I E S

White R.

Carmacks

Faro *Pelly R.* Ross River

Yellowknife

South Nahanni R.

Fort Simpson

Great Slave Lake

Burwash

Haines Junction

Yukon R.

Teslin R.

Nisutlin R.

Liard R.

Liard R.

Fort Providence

Fort Resolution

Hay River

Whitehorse

Johnsons Crossing

A

tat

Carcross

Tagish

Teslin

Swift River

Upper Liard

Watson Lake

Fort Liard

L

Haines

Skagway

Atlin

Hay R.

A

Gustavus

Fort Nelson

L

Peace R.

Hoonah

Juneau

Stikine R.

Dease Lake

B

B

Chichagof Is.

Sitka

Telegraph Creek

E

R

Baranof Is.

Kake

Petersburg

R

I

Wrangell

Fort St. John

T

Prince of Wales Is.

Stewart

C O L U M B I A

T

Dawson Creek

I

Skeena R.

A

Ketchikan

Prince Rupert

JUST ANOTHER YUKON MORNING

by Skeeter Wright

A fine sunny morning dawned, a good one to spend drinking coffee with a friend. (The night was sunny too, but I had been asleep for that.) Qulan and I trudged up along the creek to Dave's cabin. Actually, I trudged; Qulan sniffed squirrel caches and pissed on trees. As we approached, I shouted a greeting and Qulan ran beyond the cabin.

Within a few minutes of my arrival, the coffee was brewed. Dave was about to begin a soliloquy on the relevance of Murray Bookchin's ecology-of-freedom-to-cabin-life when Qulan started barking. Apparently, something was up the hill beyond the cabin. I ran up the hill to investigate, following the trail through the spindly second growth pine, calling to my dog as I ran. But it seemed too early in the summer for bears to be in the neighbourhood and porcupine hadn't been around for years.

Within moments I could see a snow-white coat through the tree trunk maze and soon after I saw the long thin legs of a large beast. A horse—Katie's horse—must have gotten out and wandered downstream to here. Great, my dog was about to get his head kicked in by a horse. That would really ruin the morning.

As I ran closer I realized it was not Katie's horse at all. The legs I had seen between the tree trunks were those of a very large bull moose. It was browsing a stand of willows and apparently ignoring Qulan's annoying barks. Quickly grabbing and silencing the dog, I realized we were within 25 feet of an unperturbed bull moose. A truly Yukon event; the coffee could wait. Crouching, I kept my hold on Qulan and we watched the moose in all its splendour. I'd seen lots of moose, but never this close. The majesty of the big bull left me spellbound. The quality of the early summer willow sprouts clearly exceeded the distastefulness of a dog and human in close proximity. We squatted humbly in the presence of a wildness that would not deem to be annoyed by us domestics.

After a few minutes the moose turned to face us; I guess curiosity got the better of his aloofness. I wasn't too sure, but the reason he lowered his head to look at us may have been due to his nose being in the way. At least I figured that was probably the reason. On the other hand, maybe moose lower their head when they piss, because that's what he did next. I was taking careful note of these behaviours when I noticed one of his massive shoulder muscles tighten. The size and definition of that flexed muscle would have been the envy of any body builder.

My study of moose behaviour and anatomy was interrupted by the realization that the moose had lowered his head and urinated to signal his displeasure with my close presence. The tightening shoulder muscle was the prelude to the first step of a charge. The realization that I was about to get stomped into the early summer mud by a giant bull moose flashed into my brain as only a thought of an impending and painful death can. The whole chain of events— the lowered head, the urinating, the tightening shoulder muscle—had taken only seconds to occur.

I jumped up, letting go of Qulan; he could take care of himself. I turned to run, God knows where. You can't outrun a charging moose and even I could push over most of the second growth pine, so there was nothing to hide behind.

However, all those split-second thoughts of running and trees were quickly forgotten when my first step was a slip in the mud and a fall flat on my face. I remember hoping that the first stomp of those razor-sharp hooves with over a thousand pounds of weight above them would quickly crush through my skull so death would be swift.

It's really amazing how much thought can be squeezed into a split second. Images of a moose crushing a wolf's skull with a kick too quick to dodge and the surviving pack members limping off with crushed ribs, broken legs and cracked skulls came to mind. Then there was me, lying here on my stomach, waiting to be stomped into the ground.

My split-second reflection was suddenly interrupted by Qulan's barking. I looked up and there he was, chasing the moose toward the stream. I wasn't dead, the moose was not stomping me into the ground, and Qulan, who had started this adventure, was now ending it. I slowly pushed myself up, and then saw the tracks. There was a very large, deep impression of a moose's hoof in the ground just to my left. There was a second, even deeper impression of what seemed like an even bigger hoof on my right. He had run right over me. He charged and instead of stomping me into the ground, he had literally run right over me. He didn't even bother to give one life-ending or even crippling step on my terrified back.

When I returned with a glazed look and incoherent rambling about a moose and two big tracks in the mud, Dave knew something had happened. Qulan was nonchalant and busied himself with a nap.

Just another Yukon morning.

moose can reach a top speed of 56 km/hour but cruise at 32 km/hour over longer distances

Wonderful family traditions and their importance

by Gord Yakimow

Family traditions! How important are they? Well, if you ask me, I'd have to say that they are very important. It is "tradition" which defines what I am and where I have come from. But for the traditional practices I have been involved in, I would not be the complete person that I am today.

Let me illustrate. The name's Snowshoe. Sam Snowshoe. I was born and raised in the north—in the Yukon Territory. My Pa was one of seven, my Ma one of eleven. And in both families, they all survived. Me, I'm one of nine—five boys and four girls. And we all made it too. Tough bunch, us Snowshoes. So I've got a whole herd of aunts and uncles and in-laws and nieces and nephews. Spent my whole life up here, except for the past three years or so when my wife, God love her, dragged me down to the rain and the fog of Lotusland to have a stab at a new way of life. Said she was tired of the cold. Been trying to eke out a living down here ever since—competing with the slugs and the frogs and the damp. It ain't easy.

Up in the north we had about ten months of winter and two months of poor skating. Snow and ice—that's what I know. (Did you know that the Inuit have thirty-two different ways of saying "snow," each phrase describing a different snow condition?) And many of our key traditions in the north were associated with ice and snow. Let me tell you about one of them.

Each year, on January 31st, every young man in the family who has turned eighteen the previous year sets off on a dogsled trek from Whitehorse to Dawson City along the Yukon River. The trip usually takes five days. The average temperature in the first week of February in the Yukon is -45°C. Cold, you say? You bet that's cold. And why did we do it, you ask? Why, tradition, of course. The family's been doing it for generations.

My father did it when he was eighteen. Froze three toes off his left foot. That's why they call him "Hoppy." All those U.S. tourists nudge each other and point and wonder why the hell he walks so funny as he bobs along Main Street in Whitehorse. The locals, they know the story! And my grandfather before him was known as "Knot-nose." How'd he get that name, you wonder? The year he did the trek, the mercury dipped to -45°C as the mushers passed by Stewart Island. Froze his nose so bad they had to take it off his face when he got to Dawson. The doctors gave him a new wooden nose. Pine. With a knot on the right side.

As for me, if you look closely, you'll notice that I have rubber ears. Yup. Froze 'em both off. My wife loves to play with 'em. She'll bend 'em way over and let 'em go. "Broinnngggg!" She just loves that sound.

But what an experience that trip was! Fought off a pack of wolves one morning. Almost got trampled by a bull moose who wanted to warm up by my fire one evening. And then there was that night when I fell asleep and forgot to put on my earmuffs.

You say it's a family practice you think oughtta be stopped? Hell, no. It was good enough for my grandpa and good enough for my pa and good enough for me and it'll be good enough for my son…next year, when he turns eighteen. As a matter of fact, I'll be going back to the Yukon for the event to cheer him on.

A great place—the north. Wonderful family traditions!

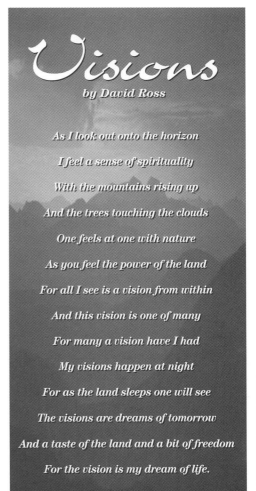

Visions
by David Ross

As I look out onto the horizon

I feel a sense of spirituality

With the mountains rising up

And the trees touching the clouds

One feels at one with nature

As you feel the power of the land

For all I see is a vision from within

And this vision is one of many

For many a vision have I had

My visions happen at night

For as the land sleeps one will see

The visions are dreams of tomorrow

And a taste of the land and a bit of freedom

For the vision is my dream of life.

The ballad of Dempster Dick

poem by Rob Mathewson

The gang was hanging around the fire
  Drinkin' away our cares.
We were here for the sun and the hills and the fun,
  And the chance to see some bears.

When Shell started fussin' and Will started cussin'
  And Tanya put on a scowl.
The fire went out, the wind came up,
  And the mutts began to howl.

A great truck of steel, with shining chrome wheels
  Drove in and a man swaggered forth
With a gun on each hip, and a sneer on his lip,
  We could tell it was "Dick of the North."

In these parts he was known for the seeds that he'd sown
  And the animals hung on his wall.
For his skill he was sought, and his Thirty Ought Ought
  That could make any critter fall.

Yes this was "Big Dick," and his gut was as thick
  As a sow with an unborn cub.
He'd bought it in town and guzzled it down
  In a dim-lit Dawson pub.

He sized up the camp by the light of the lamp
  And he let out a grunt like a boar.
"Yep there's two honeys here and only one steer
  So I've got a good chance for a score."

He mozied right up to the fire with his cup
  We could smell overflowing with rye.
"You folks be aware there's a ravenous bear
  That's caused thirteen Cheechakos to die."

"But you needn't be worried, or frightened or hurried,
  'Cuz Dick's got his Thirty Ought Ought
With a two hundred grain, it'll sever his brain,
  And he won't never know what he got."

Now Whitewater Will just hated to kill,
  A pacifist, dead against death.
He started to say, "There's a much better way,
  That will stop 'em, yet leave 'em with breath."

Just then a sound, made us all turn around
  To a grizz staring straight in our face.
Standing fourteen feet tall, tow'ring over us all,
  We could all feel our hearts start to race.

He surveyed the scene, (we could tell he was mean),
  And he gave Dick a long sideways glance
A frightening glare. We could all smell the air
  As Dick dumped his load in his pants.

Time stood still in the Tombstone Hills
  While Dick inched his hand t'ward his side.
He drew out the Ought and he fired a shot
  As the rest of us all ran to hide.

He fired five more at the monstrous boar,
  And he reached for his other side arm.
But it caught in his belt, and slowly he felt
  His life now in danger of harm.

As unreal as it sounds, the first six rounds
  Had missed by a country mile.
And odd tho' it seems, through Dick's blood-curdling screams
  We thought we could hear that bear smile.

Dick ran for his truck, but by a stroke of bad luck
  He tripped and he fell on his head.
When at first he awoke, to the fire's light and smoke,
  Poor ol' Dick thought for sure he was dead.

But tho' he'd been drinking Will had lightning-quick thinking,
  And he managed to save the day.
From where he was hiding as the monster was striding
  For Dick, he hit him with Spray.

Hit him square in the eyes, and no matter his size
  It stopped the gargantuan dead.
He turned on his tail and ran back down the trail,
  Just as Will turned to us and he said,

"I wouldn't have thunk, for as much as he stunk
  That I'd save that stupid bambino.
But it just needed provin', to stop Grizz a movin',
  Just hit 'em with ground jalepeno."

...a true story in the spirit of Robert Service

ILLUSTRATION: TANYA HANDLEY

PHOTO: MAX FRASER

Every summer thousands of southerners pack up their cars and campers for a vacation in the north. And every summer some of them get into trouble on the road. Fortunately, help is always close at hand because the first rule of northern driving is "never pass a motorist in distress." It's some of the other rules of the road that can be difficult for southerners to understand. So for the sake of these latitudinally-challenged travellers, here are some simple explanations of common northern road signs.

SPEED LIMIT: "Max. 80 km/h" doesn't mean 80 km/h is the maximum speed. It designates the "maximum compulsory tailgating speed" (MCTS). Below the MCTS, tailgating is compulsory. Above the MCTS, tailgating is, as always, optional.

BUMP: The presence or absence of a bump sign bears no relationship to the size of the bump. There are a limited number of bump signs available in the north, and every spring they are moved randomly from one set of bumps to another. Drivers are expected to remember where last year's bump signs used to be. They should slow down accordingly. This is a major part of the highway maintenance program. Moving bump signs around is a worthy source of employment in the north, and is therefore to be encouraged.

by Judith Quinlan

SMALL RED DIAMONDS: These are variations on the bump sign. They are smaller and more difficult to see. The general rule with small red diamonds is that once you see them, you've already hit the bump. These also create employment, primarily for auto body shops, which are the second biggest industry in the north.

STEEP SHOULDER: These signs are placed wherever there is no road shoulder and the ditch is a 60-foot cliff with a beaver swamp below—about 90% of northern roads.

SOFT SHOULDER: These signs mean that the road shoulder is made of quicksand, on the edge of a 60-foot cliff, with a beaver swamp below—the remaining 10% of northern roads.

MOOSE CROSSING: These signs are placed randomly along the highway for the purpose of creating photo opportunities for southerners. Moose can't read, and cross the road wherever and whenever they please.

NO HUNTING/NO SHOOTING: These signs are targets, provided for northerners who enjoy shooting holes in signs while driving by at high speed in pickup trucks.

DOTTED LINE: A dotted line down the centre of a highway means tailgate now.

SOLID LINE: A solid line down the centre of a highway means speed up and pass.

DOUBLE SOLID LINE ON A CURVE UP A STEEP HILL: This means that only loaded logging trucks may pass now.

Note about logging trucks: They always have the right of way. Logging trucks do not like to be passed. A loaded logging truck may look, to southern eyes, to be a slow and cumbersome vehicle, but this is deceptive. All logging trucks have jet propulsion and can accelerate from zero to 60 in six seconds, especially when trying to pass a Honda Civic on a steep hill with a curve and a double solid line.

I hope this introduction to northern road signs is helpful to our southern visitors. One more word of caution—northern wildlife has evolved a curious method for dealing with the hazards of highway crossing. What they do is wait behind any handy bush or roadside obstruction until a vehicle approaches. Then they hurl themselves at breakneck speed across its path. The only exception is the grouse which relies on camouflage to blend in with the road surface. When driving northern roads please respect this curious behaviour by slowing down whenever you approach a bush!

Thank you.

Northern road signs

A trading trip to Fort Selkirk

Looking for a Yukon identity

story and photos by
David Neufeld

The weekend of June 2-3, 1995, I travelled down the Yukon River to about 300 kilometres north of Whitehorse with my two children, Erin, 11 and Andrew, 8. It was a fascinating experience, and a privilege, to witness the first trading trip by the coastal Tlingits into Fort Selkirk in over a century.

The start of the boat trip was at Minto Landing. We unloaded our packs and carried everything down to the shore. Patty Van Bibber, Chief of the Selkirk First Nation and our river pilot, showed up and we piled everything helter skelter into his river boat. Patty's boat is a flat-bottomed shallow river scow, about 32-foot long and perhaps 62 feet across at the top of the hull. Built of plywood and reinforced with 2 x 4 ribs, it easily held twelve of us and our gear. Patty fired up the 50 hp motor, checked the 45 gallon drum for fuel and edged away from the shore.

Once clear he flipped us about and opened the throttles. The boat lifted out of the water and we travelled some 50 kilometres downriver. The water was low, signs of the spring breakup of ice still obvious. Uprooted trees, scarred banks and the odd piece of ice still lay along the shore. Near Fort Selkirk a curious brown bear sat on the bank and watched us go by. "Good country for bear," commented Patty. After an hour on the river we caught sight of the magnificent bluffs of basalt towering over the junction of the Pelly and Yukon rivers. Fort Selkirk lies just across from the bluffs.

Once we landed I set up camp and the kids went off to explore the restored buildings of the old community. By midafternoon a crowd began to gather along the riverbank, waiting for the Tlingit traders to arrive.

Standing on the bank of the river we all leaned cautiously over the edge. "Are they coming? Can you see them yet?" people asked. Straining to look upriver, wind in our face, we watched for the boat. But we heard them before we saw them. Snatches of song and the beating of skin drums blew to us through the air. Their boat drifted clear of the last bars at the mouth of the Pelly and now we could see the Tlingits coming.

The Chilkat Tlingit, the First Nation people of the Pacific coast, long ago traders of maritime goods for the furs and skins of the Yukon interior, were finally returning to Fort Selkirk. They came to celebrate the renewal of old trade and family connections linking the Northern Tutchone of the Pelly River with the people of Klukwan and Haines, Alaska.

Long ago, Chief Kohklux, of the Chilkat Tlingit, annually led groups of traders to the Yukon interior to trade. In 1852, he was one of the Tlingit party that travelled to Fort Selkirk. There, the party met Robert Campbell of the Hudson's Bay Company and visited his trading post. As Judson Brown, a Klukwan elder at the gathering, noted, "there was a small misunderstanding" and Campbell's post was ransacked. The Tlingit maintained their control of the Yukon trade for another half century. And the secret of the trade route between Klukwan and Fort Selkirk was one they kept as well, at least until 1869. At that time, Chief Kohklux prepared a map for an American scientist named George Davidson. This map has been preserved and is the oldest map of the southern Yukon in existence.

The drums and songs of the Tlingit were answered now by the Northern Tutchone. The boat landed amidst welcoming drumming. Judson Brown rose in the boat and in a strong voice gave a speech announcing the arrival of the Tlingit and their willingness to be friends and to trade with their hosts. A gift, a five-pound tin of Folger's coffee, was presented to Chief Van Bibber. He welcomed the visitors to Fort Selkirk and in turn offered hospitality, food and shelter. The Tlingit came ashore and boxes of trade goods, tents and other gear were unloaded and carried up the bank.

The Chilkat Tlingit dance group, wearing their traditional rich red and black or blue dance blankets decorated with shiny mother-of-pearl buttons, presented a series of dances and songs by the Stone house near the campground. Elders Clara Schinkel, Judson Brown, Albert Paddy and Stanley Jonathon gave speeches of welcome and celebration. A feast on the riverbank, of beef soup and barbecued salmon, was followed by more speeches and memories of meetings between families and friends of days gone by. Then came the trading.

Everyone crowded into the large Stone house. Tables were set up and in minutes, dried and smoked salmon, eulachon oil, tea, furs, beads and moccasins were laid out. Fort Selkirk was "open for business." Goods changed hands quickly and a general air of goodwill kept spirits high. Children traded homemade toys, ball caps and boxes of cereal.

Sally Buratin of Klukwan extolled the virtues of eulachon oil, "a spoonful cures stomach ache and it's wonderful on boiled potatoes. You can use it for anything." This clear oil is rendered from a small coastal fish, the eulachon. Also known as the candlefish, because of its ability to burn like a candle, the fish is rich in oil. Rendered by boiling the fish, the oil is a dietary staple among coastal Indians. Many Yukon Indians have lost their taste for it over the intervening years but all were willing to give it a go. A strong flavour, and a stronger odour. One person recommended that people open the jar outdoors.

Erin had a selection of necklaces decorated with tropical fruit ceramics which she used to garner a couple of strings of black and pearl white beads for sewing. She also assembled a collection of ball caps from the Champagne and Aishihik First Nation.

Andrew worked with his collection of homemade dinosaur models and some boxes of tea. After some haggling, the dinosaur market settled in at two dollars each while he used his tea to purchase a pint of eulachon oil for his mother. It is a

pungent brew to be sure.

After the trading, a Pelly trio including Franklin Roberts and Peter Johnie brought out their fiddle and guitars. Jigging, two steps and polkas polished up the floor of the Stone house and carried us all into the night. When we finally headed back to the tents the northern sky was already a rich pink as the sun began to rise again.

On Sunday morning Sally Buratin, Jonas and Lani Hotch and Lizzie Hager led a worship service featuring original gospel songs in Tlingit. Daniel Ashley and Joshua Hotch rang the old church bell at St. Andrews Anglican Church to signal the end of the gathering. Everyone bundled up their tents and belongings into boats for the trip upriver, relaxing and thinking about their new friends and having more such reunions in the future.

On the way home I talked with the kids about how the grandparents and great-grandparents of the people we had met had come together at Fort Selkirk to trade. I described the constancy of their presence in the land and the symbolic importance of the weekend gathering for those people. Erin remained unimpressed. "So what does that make us? Nothing?" she asked. A tough question. We're still immigrants, not only to the Yukon, but to North America. In the south we can ignore that tough question because we have made so much of North America European. In the north, however, it is still obvious who is the newcomer, the stranger. How do we come to belong to this place?

A memorable event

by Darryl James

My family used to go out camping a lot in the Indian summers. We have a fairly large trapline. Anytime our father would feel the pressures of everyday life or the high expense of living, he would pack up the family—even the dog would come along.

One time my father, my brother Wayne and I went goat hunting. My father spotted a few goats along the mountainside and decided that maybe we should go and get one.

Suddenly, we found ourselves packing some gear into the boat and heading across the river to the foot of the mountain. After landing and securing the boat, we started up the mountain. About halfway up the mountain we stopped for lunch and tea.

After eating, we rested for a bit before putting out the fire. Then we tackled the steepest part of the mountain. It seemed to take forever, but we finally reached the place where my father had spotted the herd of goats.

He told my brother and me to wait there and make as little noise as possible. We were quite exhausted so my brother and I decided to rest and keep warm. We each curled up into a little ball and managed to fall asleep on the side of the mountain.

My father attempted to go around the herd, but as he did so, the wind shifted and the goats smelled his scent. Suddenly, they took off to higher ground where they were out of immediate danger.

My father returned to where my brother and I were. Since it was getting late we decided to climb back down the mountain. After reaching the boat we headed back to camp. While eating supper that evening, I thought of what we could have had instead.

ILLUSTRATION: STEPHANIE VERHEYEN

THE HAPPY MINER • PLACER MINING

by Barbara Hanulik

Naming the Cookbook River

I loved William from our first conversation. We spoke in the back of a warehouse. I checked in hardware, matching up lists with screws, hammers, rods, nails. He moved freight—quietly, swiftly, with such precision sometimes I wouldn't notice him. Things just wound up in their place. William told stories of growing up in northwest Alaska, in Kotzebue, when summer visitors came through. Their frequent question: why would anyone name a river Cookbook? Some made up stories, some shook their heads. William would say, "It just is," smiling in his Eskimo way. "Cookbook" in Eskimo means piss.

William said he grew up next to a fox farm. "Next to" meant 15 miles away. His father worked delivering mail by dog sled. Describing his life as simple, he boasted of having no television, phone or automobile.

I loved him for his stories. William would tell me of growing up with the bootlegging bush pilots. (Some of the villages up north are "damp" or "dry," meaning alcohol can't be sold in some cases, or even possessed in others.) Archie Furguson was one of his favourites. He described Archie as a pudgy, squirrely bush pilot who flew by the seat of his pants and did everything else the same way. He and Joe Jenkins ran the area's whisky supply.

In one of Archie's bootlegging attempts, he lost a float balance mid-flight. He was almost out of gas and had to land, but couldn't land on water or land with only one float. At the last minute, a musher below looked up to see the one-legged float plane getting closer and closer, lowering onto his sled. The sled was crushed beyond repair and so was one dog, but the plane survived completely intact.

Sometimes the story changed, being retold in the warehouse again and again. But always William would follow with, "It's not like that down here in Juneau." It's different, not as reckless. The landscape, even the weather here, is more kind. "It's more like a suburb of Seattle than Alaska; only more bears and less people."

But I contend you can see glimpses around here—glimpses of what Alaska used to be like. You can look at the southeast villages of Hoonah, Angoon, Yakutat or many others that are hours, even days, from everyone else. In the phone book, the directories of these villages span one-half of a single-sided sheet of paper.

And here in Juneau you still see glimpses. I see them daily, taking the dogs out in the half-dark, half-light of winter's midmorning, ours being the only tracks in the snow except for a lone pair of hooves which you can follow until they disappear down the mountainside.

Then there are times when the airport is closed for more days than it is open in a week. Your mailbox is empty and who knows where your letters go after you put them in those blue boxes. They can't leave.

These are all glimpses of isolation. The isolation that is Alaska. When you take the glimpse, focus on it, hold it in, sit on the top of a mountain with just you and your canine friends. Sit and explore the inside while they run the ridges and discover the outside and soak it all in. It is the isolation that can drive you crazy or free your soul, and usually does a little of both; the isolation that William grew up with and loved.

by Lillian Seapy

ILLUSTRATION: STEVE SHEPHERD

11

Happy thoughts: FALL

by Ima Grump

Well, fall is finally here, and thank God for that. After the hottest summer since the last forest fire burned through town, I need a few weeks of rain-sopped boots and water dribbling through my leaky roof onto my pillow at night just to feel human enough not to take it out on every dog, cat and chicken from here to the Gobi desert. If I see one more kid with ice-cream slobbering down their face, I'm going to embed my head in the Llewelyn glacier.

Folks, with all that heat and happiness everywhere, I almost didn't make it. All them summertime baseball games on green grass, young sweethearts sippin' sodas by the lake, flowers, bicycles, smilin', suntanned people—it almost made me pack it in and head to Greenland. Instead, I spent the summer in my root-cellar.

And I tell ya folks, it was the best summer I've had in years. Sittin' in some dark, dank hole with a couple of sacks of old potatoes and a few dozen mice can make a fella commune with a whole 'nother side of life. Like some monk on a hill, it can bring a fella in tune with the higher reaches of himself and the universe. It can also make you kind of miserable.

Imagine not being able to leave your pit to go to the outhouse until the sun goes, 'cause its too much of a damn shock to your system after living in the dark so long. And what makes the problem even worse is the fact that the damn sun never goes down in the summer around here.

And if I ever did leave to challenge the melting sun, the first thing I'd see would be the face of my dog, Cementhead, drooling down on me as I tried to clammer out of my pit. Now they say that a dog doesn't perspire when it's hot, but instead they cool their whole body by panting out their mouth. So let's imagine for a minute, friends, some big, black, hairy mutt that's been lying in the sun all day because any sense they might have to lie in the shade has been baked out of their fat head weeks ago.

Picture as well, finally mustering the courage to leave my root cellar to make a dash for the outhouse, praying I don't see anybody in shorts along the way, and being greeted by Cementhead, the entire cooling mechanism of his body being limited to the few measly drops of boiling drool that is dripping off his tongue onto my forehead while his garbage breath wafts into my sacred dungeon where the only fresh air I got left is hardly enough to keep the mice alive, let alone the potatoes.

It's a darn good thing I had my radio with me in my hole or I might have really lost it that summer. The reception wasn't so good, but before the mice chewed through all the electronic circuitry, I was able to hear some fine radio programming on ol' CBC Yukon. It was only the eighteenth time I've heard the ten-part series on the old Yukon river paddleboats, so it was still fresh to me. It's a good thing something happened in this neck of the woods a hundred years ago, cause there sure as hell ain't nothin' happening now, I tell ya.

"In Yukon news today, Murray from the Forest Service in Mayo is changing a flat on the east side of town. He's only got two lugs off so far so drive carefully in Mayo everybody. More on that story on the noon show and Murray himself will be talking with us on Northern Light this afternoon from four to six, discussing tire hazards around Mayo and other parts of the Yukon as well." Why don't them CBC folks just go fishin' till the next gold rush and we'll be just fine occupying our time listening to static.

Maybe I shouldn't be too harsh on the ol' CBC 'cause I did manage to pick up one useful tidbit of information listening to that fine government programming during my summer hibernation underground. At least I thought it was useful information until the day I tried it out myself.

Seems as though they had some naturalist on there one day talking about edible plants in the north. She made it sound like fireweed, among other things, was downright tasty, nutritious, and no doubt plentiful. I filed that information under "Big Deal" in my mind until one day I got an inspiration to put it to use.

Opening the lid of my chamber-of-the-soul one evening in late summer, I gazed out into my yard and discovered my precious potato patch seared into the very soil that was supposed to give it life. I hadn't been watering it too regular

since my hibernation began, but I figured my own mutated genetic strain of potato could survive anything. No such luck.

Well, it wasn't going to be much of a winter ahead without something going rotten in my root cellar so I got to figurin' I'd give this fireweed idea a try. And if it turned out to be as tasty as they said, I could mow my lawn and just rake it all down my hole, and eat nice salads all winter instead of my bullet-proof potatoes that require too much damn time to deal with in the first place.

It took me a while to get around to trying out the fireweed, seeing as I was stuck in my hole finishin' off the last of my potatoes, but I finally did get around to it come September. I went out back of my cabin one day, looking for a place to harvest, preferably where ol' Cementhead hadn't been doing his business. I finally found a spot about a quarter-mile from my cabin and yanked me a fine bouquet of fireweed and headed back home for dinner. I don't know how to cook, so I figured a salad would be a fine way of doin' it, not to mention the least amount of work, so I put some on my plate and away I went.

Well!! Whoever the hell she was on the radio talkin' about eating fireweed, never said NOTHIN' about not eating it in the fall when it was seeding! So unsuspecting ol' me takes a bite of me fine, fireweed salad that day and it was like chewin' on an old, dusty feather pillow. Actually, it was worse. It was like being parched for thirst in the desert and THEN chewing on an old, dusty feather pillow. And making matters worse, when I immediately went to spit it out, nothin' happened cause it soaked up every last bit of moisture in my mouth and glued itself to the back of my throat.

So when I found myself in a bit of a panic not being able to breathe, I knocked my plate of fireweed salad into the air and all them snowflake seeds flew everywhere like a snowstorm in hell. Forgetting my respiratory emergency, I grabbed the first chunk of firewood I could lay my hands on and started smashing my radio to little bits.

Lord Almighty, it was a darn good thing them fall rains showed up to cool me down. If we EVER get another summer like that again, everybody around better watch out. There's gonna be a new ice-cream parlour in town and the only flavour I'm gonna have is sawdust.

Farewell, my friends

by Rick Charlebois

There is said to be a certain element of danger in extended solitude. Apparently, our civilized conditioning is not in tune with aloneness. There are many tales of psychological states that have visited hermits, miners, and trappers living alone for extended periods in the north.

It is believed that one begins to hallucinate, and life becomes distorted to the point where the mind is no longer able to distinguish between reality and imagination. Ultimately, the victim's survival instincts take a left turn and lead one to perish in some mysterious manner.

My name's John, by the way. Just John. Last names aren't important unless you want to add other names preceded with a title, and followed with abbreviated subtitles to denote your level of sophistication. I like to keep it simple…same as my shack. I call it a shack, but it's really a castle, my home in the woods. I get water from the creek, a woodstove keeps my blood from running slushy, a table sits under the bigger window, a counter surrounded with kitchen stuff under the smaller one, a plank bed in the far corner, lots of shelves for books and, of course, the AM radio. This is the essence of my fortress.

Sure, there are drawbacks. One who lives removed from the noise and confusion of city life must sacrifice the luxuries that accompany it. Running water, electricity, laundry machine, furnace, to name a few, are left behind at great expense to one's leisure time.

I've been living like this for about four years now, or is it forty? No, I don't even have as many under my belt, it must be four. I haven't been totally alone though, in a sense. I've had many friends and acquaintances guarding my sanity. For a while, there were some I could only see, as those appearing in my dreams, who never spoke. Others I could only hear, through distant sound waves. Then there were those I could neither hear nor see, like Dostoyevsky, Ramacharaka, and all the rest.

Over the course of my stay, I have come to see and hear them all. I can almost touch them. They have become an integral part of my little world…a world that has, by necessity,

taken on a new meaning. I have become quite attached to these friends, as one does after living with the same spouse for twenty years. It is easy to imagine the great sadness one might feel if this spouse unexpectedly vanished forever. This is how I have come to feel about some of those friends that have visited my little cabin almost daily.

I used to wonder why I chose to live this way. In the days when I could not answer my self–interrogations, I would say that I was simply following my intuition, for lack of a better understanding. It was Thoreau, an old acquaintance, who set me straight on that one when he said:

I went to the woods because
I wished to live deliberately,
to front only the essential facts of life,
and see if I could learn what it had to teach,
and not, when I come to die,
discover that I had not lived…

There is no greater feeling, in my mind, than to be able to bask in the luxury of putting chores aside. That sense of complete security when the survival instinct grasps your astral hand and says, "All is good. The cabin is built, the wood pile is high enough for two cold winters, moose meat is hanging on the cache, there's gold in the poke." That feeling of security is blissful in itself, but better yet, on a well-earned day of rest, one can have friends visiting to up the comfort level a notch.

When they visit, we usually tackle the world's problems and explore possible solutions. Most of the time we only end up making life more complicated. But a little metaphysics never hurt anyone, so it's allowed in my humble abode. We get to learn many things together, and have a lot of laughs, which Jay told us is good for the morale. I certainly had my laughs this morning when Peter was talking to some writer. Personally, I think Peter's brain is slightly polluted with P.C.B.—the Politically Correct Bullshit of the '90s involution—and after what seemed like five minutes of ugh, waaah, I, er…what… you…I felt obliged to inform him where the outhouse was. I couldn't tell whether he had to shit, puke, or talk!

Sometimes my friends piss me right off. The other day Vicky was talking with an

American astronomer. The subject was very interesting, but Vicky, in her usual way, would answer her own questions as he started speaking. While he was passionately involved with his theory of the origin of black holes, she interrupted again to ask how many astronomers worked in the various observatories across the United States. The scientist was getting so frustrated with her intrusions, he started answering her with a basic yes or no. I was so disgusted, I walked out to split some wood.

Arthur, well, there's a card. He covers all those topics from the simply bizarre to the absolutely unbelievable. Sometimes he reminds me of a tabloid journalist with a slant towards do-goodness. But Arthur is Arthur, and I kind of like his light-headedness and I really enjoy his wild comments on life in general.

Earlier tonight, Michael and Allen came over with some of their favourite pets from the political jungle. Michael set some of his traps and backed the beasts into a corner until they came out gnashing and slashing. It was better than the entertainment I usually get around here watching the grizzlies and marten and the other critters. Then Michael talked Al into telling me a story entitled, "Farewell, My Friends." He carried the oil lamp to the shelf behind the woodstove and sat on the stump.

His stories vary widely, from the philosophically-inclined to the humorously satirical. Tonight's story was one about the human condition. It told of a young boy who lost nine of his closest friends to a freak bus accident. Out of twenty-three students on this ill-fated bus, the boy had been the only survivor. It was a story of discovery that delved into all the gory details of the boy's experience and the giant steps needed for his recovery.

Al is incredibly gifted when it comes to reading a story. If you close your eyes, you can visualize the characters and setting like you were watching a film on TV.

When I opened my eyes, Allen and Michael were gone. Lister had appeared without my noticing, and he was going on

continued…

13

about death and dying. I excused myself and stepped out into the night, hoping the northern lights would cheer me up. Al's story gripped my heart with the fierceness of an eagle's talons. I watched the curtains of light shuffling across the November sky until I felt the familiar tingling in my spine that heralded reality. It seemed my extended bout with solitude had almost welded the imagined with the real…thoughts without expression surround the mind like a pack of wolves attacking a moose. All a moose needs to do is wield his antlers and chase them off, unless he's outnumbered. Once again, I felt invigorated by my wilderness hermitage. I turned to see the distant light of the oil lamp through the stretched–poly window. It glowed like a nugget ringed with black sand.

When I came in to sit by the stove, Lister was finishing his discourse. "'Impossible' is the word the intellect invariably comes up with when dealing with certain concepts such as death, the end of the world, or the permanent loss of a friend, or even one's sanity. Death of the body and death of the ego are equally unfathomable to the psyche…Good night."

There was a moment of silence after Lister's Amen. Then an unfamiliar, unfeeling voice bounced off the cabin walls, casually announcing its cold message:

"Due to federal cutbacks and the high cost of operation, CBC will no longer be broadcasting on AM. We are now switching to FM. Thank you."

ILLUSTRATION: WYATT TREMBLAY

PHOTO: ROBIN REID-FRASER

SNOWSUITS AND MUKLUKS

BY ALISON REID

I have two favourite pieces of winter clothing, winter being the season when I need to wear things I really like.

My snowsuit is actually an insulated coverall that Max bought for me at the closing-out sale of the Whitehorse Northern Store. Sizes were limited, so mine is large extra-long. It means the bum sags, but that is a minor fashion misstatement compared to the incredible amount of room there is for all kinds of layers. I can wear my snowsuit in temperatures that range from 0°C (one light layer) to -45°C (three underlayers, including my down vest), and feel safe and secure and comfortable.

Mostly I love my snowsuit for the same reason parents love their kids' snowsuits: no snow gets down the back or belly when we bumslide down slopes, or do angels and somersaults in the snow. When I'm out skiing or snowshoeing and I feel (or pretend I feel) the sun's heat, I don't have to be careful about how I flop down to enjoy it. And when I crash in a sudden loss of balance, there is one less thing to worry about.

My mukluks are even better; almost magical, I would say. How else can I express the incredible feeling of wanting to dance down the road at some paralysingly cold temperature? Or my certainty that I will return from my hour-long excursion in those temperatures with feet warmer than when I left? There is surely nothing rational about yearning for the temperature to *drop* to at least -15°C so that I can slide into that simple combination of moose hide and wool liner and once again feel so directly, yet so snuggly, the contours of the snow under my feet. (There is the risk of soggy mukluks and cold feet when it is any warmer.) I figure that it would take something incredibly high-tech (and expensive) to match my mukluks.

You'll know me when you see me on the trail, or lying on my back in a snowdrift, humming smugly, "I love my snowsuit, I love my mukluks, they are so wonder-ful-ly snuggly."

A song for a warrior

Once there was a special place for him
This brown man, with his brown grin
Stained by the things that pleasured him

There were days when the village people depended
On his perceptions, his visions and his deep wisdom
Until the day came, with a new way called Christian

It condemned his ancient power, "the work of the devil!"
Everything that he was, was now to no avail

Healing was his speciality, as was his ability to "see"
Was the ice safe, would it be a good season and was there
To be good moose-hunting?

Thrown to the wayside, man without purpose or identity
Alcohol consoled your pain and softened the blows
Filled the empty spaces of being helpful and needed
The pollutants were not heeded

But could it be, that you did see your future wrapped up in the
Soft white blanket of winter, ending before the New Year.
Conjured up with that one last beer?

And when you became weary, did you just stop for a rest
Knowing full well that it would be the earth's final test?
Cold at first then oh, so warm, like the spring

My old friend of a spiritual affinity
My heart goes out to you now, as are my prayers
They go out for you on your long last journey
To the place where there is someone who cares
And eternity is warm

No more can I ask those questions
That you pretended not to know
Questions that only life itself can answer
Questions that were unanswerable
Questions that were
Questions that
Questions

by Louise Profeit-Leblanc

THE SORROWING MAID

by Arlin McFarlane

When I tell this story I usually bring along the rock from the Tombstone Mountains that gave me the story, for though I wrote it, I don't feel it is my story. And I hold up the rock for the audience to see and tell them that I believe that rocks hold the history of the world and that at the end of one particular day I held this very rock up to my ear and after a long time I started to see a long valley and I heard a voice which said:

Touch me gently, for though I am now rock, once I was of human form. See these lines, they were once bone. What you have here is my foot, the part where the bones spread out into toes. Once I walked where you now stand, followed Tuktu trails high on mountain face. I was well loved by my people. Now I am a scatter of rocks. Look over there, part of my shoulder. No need to gather my parts though, for I can tell you the story of that summer, that beautiful summer.

We all had clothes made of Tuktu, golden, soft, warm. We followed Tuktu and they allowed us to take them. Gently they would come down and wait, eyes quiet, bright, and our eyes staring into their eyes and we would take them, with a sharp stone and them never moving. Gentle spirit of Tuktu.

That was the year I was with child. Summer life was easy but winter life was cold and hard. Rock caves lined with Tuktu and bear. Bear did not give herself to us freely as did Tuktu. For bear we had to fight. But bear kept our rock caves warm. I was with child. We had not seen bear that summer and the journey back to our winter home with our winter food was long. My mate knew he must get me a bear skin.

He prepared to go. I did not want him to go. I wanted his warm arms, not a bear skin. But he was far wiser than I and he left by that pass over there. Do you see it, the steep one?

I waited. We all waited. Oh we dried Tuktu and made clothes and slippers for our feet, but I waited. Everyday I would climb to the pass and sit on the rock and look out to the west. I loved the west, soft and golden like Tuktu. The pass was very steep. Even I was afraid to cross there, down into the dark valley of trees. It was hard to kill a bear.

At night I dreamed of warm arms and woke to empty cold. Yet, everyday, late in the day I would climb to the pass and sit. Summer was passing. My people watched me and I watched the west. Soon it would be time to leave.

It happened slowly at first, soft moss growing up my foot, cool, like hands, caressing, promising peace. And there I set to rest. My people came to me but my ears no longer listened and my lips no longer spoke and slowly, very slowly, the mountain rock crawled inside my skin shutting out all pain.

It was winter when my mate returned. He saw me immediately and put his warm arms around me, put my bear skin around me, tried to feed me bear fat and meat but my lips no longer moved and my tears no longer fell. He was too wise to stay with me, a frozen stone wife, with or without child. He did grieve, long and loud, so the mountains shook and the snow and rocks fell. And he left me my bear skin, though the other animals took it to line their caves. I was glad, what need had cold stone for warmth.

Centuries passed and there I sat. The Sorrowing Maid they called me. Many more people came by, in clothes not made of Tuktu. They touched my face and looked along with me out to the west.

One season a family of gulls nested in my lap where the female would watch for her mate who always came home.

I don't know how I came to be a small fragment in your hand. The wearing away of soil perhaps. I do know I have lived in the moss for a long time. Perhaps the moss people brought me here to rest. Touch me gently, for I am old and weary, though now that I have told my story I am sorrowing no more.

PHOTO: KEN MADSEN

ANNIE NED

by Yvonne Harris

Many nights I walked by the old folks home
Not knowing you were there,
The old wise woman whose words I cherish,
Whose memories are rooted in the distant past.

And how I wish I could have talked to you,
Asked about your childhood,
About your young loves and when you first got smart;
Stories from that world a century ago.

Before you left us I was comforted,
Knowing such a living treasure walked among us.
The day you died my heart cried out
To lose those memories, that voice from the past.

But you are not gone from us;
Your words remain and bring us strength;
Annie, the hunter, the trapper, the provider,
Left a message of courage for those who follow.

Sleep now you wise old woman.

Annie Ned was born in Hutshi Village in the 1880s and later trapped and hunted in the Kusawa Lake area. She never sat back waiting to have work done by men; she was a strong woman admired by all. Annie Ned died in September 1995.

PHOTO COURTESY OF KWANLIN DUIN FIRST NATION

STICK GAMBLING

by Pat Moore

Left and right hands of the people (Xs) hiding the object are indicated for each call from the perspective of the person hiding.

All that way (right hands)

```
X X X X   X X X X

R R R R   R R R R
```

Furthest from this point (between two players)

```
X X X X   X X X X

L L L L   R R R R
```

Closest to this point (between two players)

```
X X X X   X X X X

R R R R   L L L L
```

One right, the rest left

```
X X X X   X X X X

R L L L   L L L L
```

All that way (left hands)

```
X X X X   X X X X

L L L L   L L L L
```

One right , the rest left

```
X X X X   X X X X

L L L L   L L L R
```

Stick gambling–also called hand games–requires many skills. In essence, it is a guessing game in which all the members of one team hide an object while the captain, or shooter, of the other team attempts to guess in which hand each of the opposing team members is holding an object. The objects which are hidden in the hand are usually a coin or some small object such as a small stone or .22 shell. There are many other skills as well which may come into play and influence the outcome of the game. All the players move to the beat of the drumming, using their fluid motions to conceal any expression which would reveal the hand where they hold the object. As one team wins more of the sticks they may gain a psychological momentum which will carry them to victory unless the opposing team rallies. Traditionally, some exceptionally successful players were reputed to have the ability to use magical powers to either perceive where all the opposing players had concealed their objects, or to be able to so cloud the mind of the opposing captain that the captain would be unable to make a correct call.

Opposing teams usually have the same number of players, but the number of players on the teams is variable. Teams of four to six players are common in the Yukon, but in the Northwest Territories teams of as many as 16 players might compete on special occasions. Traditionally, men were the main stick gamblers, but in recent times women have also become adept stick gamblers.

The name "stick gambling" makes reference to the counter sticks which are placed in the centre between the two opposing teams at the start of the game. There are usually two more sticks than the total number of players on both teams. For example, for teams of six players each there would be 14 sticks in the middle at the beginning of play.

The two teams are usually seated or kneeling on the ground in two lines facing each other. A blanket or coat is often placed in front of a team to conceal the hands of the players while they decide in which hand to keep the object. They may also hide their hands behind their back while they move the object from hand to hand. Once the object is in place the players bring their hands up in front of them. If they want to cross their arms they have to hit their hands down on the ground in front of them and call out loudly "Diya" or some similar call to announce that they are crossing their arms. Players cannot cross and uncross their arms. A team wins counter sticks from the centre only when the opposing captain is unable to guess where a player has concealed an object.

Play begins with the two captains playing against each other to determine which team will be the first to hide their objects. Both captains hide an object in their hands simultaneously and then sit up and call the opposing captain. They make a simple hand signal, or use their little finger to signal, while keeping their hand closed. If one captain guesses correctly and the other captain does not, the team of the one who was correct is able to hide first. That captain also wins one stick from the centre pile for their team because they were missed by the opposing captain. If neither captain guesses successfully, or if both captains guess correctly, play continues through additional turns until one misses and one hits.

The team of the successful captain all

PHOTO: ANGELA WHEELOCK

hide their objects and quickly sit up ready for the opposing captain's hand signal or call. A team is supported by a number of drummers who provide a rhythm for play and also express the strength of the team by playing loudly. A team may also sing challenge songs themselves, or the drummers may sing challenge songs for the team as they drum. The captain indicates in which hand each player on the opposing team has concealed their object with a single hand signal.

Several of the more common hand signals are illustrated by Louison Ahkimatchie on the opposite page. In some areas there are specific hand signals for any combination of right and left hands for up to 16 players. Since most competitions in the Yukon have a maximum of only six players, a much smaller set of hand signals is adequate for these small teams. One common signal is simply pointing, either with the index finger or the whole hand to indicate all right hands or all left hands. A slight variation made by raising the thumb, indicates all right hands with one on the near end to the left, or all left hands, with one on the near end to the right. Yet another signal which is made with the hand pointing between two players of the opposing team indicates all hands closest to that point, left hands to the left, right hands to the right.

After the call is made those players who were caught show their object and are eliminated from further play in that round.

They may dramatically collapse as they are caught as if they have been wounded by the opposing shooter's call. Those who are missed win a counter stick from the middle and continue to play another round. Very successful players may be almost impossible to eliminate from play before winning a pile of sticks. These players are given encouragement by the other players, the drummers and the crowd. Once all the sticks have been won from the centre pile a team will also take sticks from the pile amassed by the opposing team. Play continues in one round until one team has won all the sticks.

When one team has won all the sticks one player from the winning team hides an object to determine which team will start the next round as the team hiding their objects. This is called "twenty one," an apparent reference to the card game "twenty one" where the last card is a make or break call. If the opposing captain makes a successful call, their team will start the next round by hiding. If not, the team which won the first round will start the second round. When either team wins all the sticks twice they are the winners of that game. There may also be special game counter sticks which a referee places beside them to keep track of which teams have won all the sticks once.

In the past, stick gamblers often bet money, food, or other goods on the outcome of a game. Today, players commonly bet only small amounts of money, typically quarters, on

each game. In some organized competitions, such as the Yukon Stick Gambling Championships, there are entry fees and teams compete for first prizes of thousands of dollars. Because of these organized competitions, and an increasing sense of cultural awareness, there has been growing interest in this recreational activity among Yukon First Nations.

DISCOGRAPHY
SOME STICK GAMBLING MUSIC

Jerry Alfred and the Medicine Beat

Etsi Shon–Grandfather's Song
(1995 Juno Award winner)
"Caribou Stick Gambling"
"Beginners Stick Gambling"

Nendaa–Go Back
(1996 Juno Award nominee)
"McQueston River Stick Gambling"

available from
Caribou Records, Whitehorse
403-633-5063

Festival Distribution, Vancouver
1-800-633-8282

COLOURS CHANGE

by Judith Quinlan

*O*ne of the things I love the most about living in the north is the way colours change through the seasons. Each season has its own palette, and like perfume or fine wine, there are different flavours or tones that make up that season's colour array. There's a strong middle note that dominates the landscape with its combinations of colour. There's a bottom note, more subtle, and denser, like a bass drum, a memory of the season just passed. And there's a top note, thin and reedy, an overtone of colours still to come.

In early fall, the dominant colours are oranges, reds and yellows—the colours of autumn leaves, drying fireweed, newly exposed berries and late summer flowers. The multicoloured array of summer remains, as tender flower heads die in night-time frosts, but they are muted now as their once green leaves compete, turning to yellow radiance. The top note is brown. Exposed branches, dried grasses and patches of earth begin to appear. Eventually, the oranges and yellows begin to fade to various shades of brown. The middle note becomes an amazing palette of browns, brown mixed with every possible colour, brown in various dull or brilliant tones. Tree trunks against the pale sky. Long dead wildflowers. Large rocks and open patches of earth, no longer camouflaged with greenery. Fencelines and roadways exposed. And as autumn moves slowly into winter, a silvery white top note appears. Hoarfrost in the mornings, or late into the day in shady spots. Snow on the mountaintops that make up the horizon. Silvery wetness as the frost melts on the last clinging leaves, on the metal of gate hinges and barn roofs.

The first snows fall, and eventually they stay. The browns begin to disappear beneath them, until they become only a faint reminder of autumn. Small patches of earth and rock in sunny places. The brown of the densest forest, where evergreen canopies still protect the earth.

But by midwinter, white is the dominant colour. White that reflects sunlight so intensely that sunglasses, perhaps ignored all summer, now are a necessity. The white changes hue according to the time of day, the weather, the temperature, the dryness or humidity. It can be golden white, or silvery white, or milky white, or eggshell white, or the furry white of ice crystals on top of snow. Now the top note becomes a palette of blues. Early in the winter, before the snow is very deep, the blue shades are only visible when the moon shines, or when the sky is thick with ice crystals on a sunny day.

But as the snowpack builds, it becomes more translucent; the light seems to shine through it as much as it reflects off it. And as whiteness dominates the landscape, even in places that were protected from falling snow, but have no armour against windblown drifts, the blue sky takes over. In every other season the sky can't compete with Gaia's glory, but in the deep of winter all is blue. Soft whites and deep, startling blues. At this time, the top note, the colour of approaching spring, is very faint. It is a tiny greyness at the edges of the blue. Shadows on snowdrifts. The walls of the shed. Gravel on the snowpacked roads.

By late winter, though, the palette of greys and blacks begins to dominate. Snow melts on the roads, exposing wet black mud. Melting snow on dried wood turns it black. Shadows deepen in the forest as the snow thins and the overstory becomes clear of snow. The deep blues begin to fade and darker colours dominate. As spring progresses, more and more of winter's damage is revealed—blackened grasses, water-filled ditches, greying slush at the side of roads and trails. On the frozen lakes, patches of snowmelt appear in shades of grey and brown. The top note now is a new palette of browns. Spring browns, paler and more yellow than autumn browns. The brown of new

willow shoots and sediment-filled creeks. Browns created by a warmer, more golden sunshine. Even the browns of returning birds, the picnic table once again visible, the mulch on the vegetable garden. And finally, in the latter days of spring, a new top note arrives—green.

Green tips on the conifers, and the tiny seedling trees that were buried all winter. The fuzzy green corona of poplar buds emerging. Lime greens and yellow greens that will deepen as the summer progresses. Green grass blades emerging above the matted remnants of last year's hay. Tips of spring bulbs in the flowerbeds. And as green takes over in late spring, a multicoloured top note carries with it the promise of summer's abundance. Small alpine flowers in blues and yellows and reds and purples. Crocuses on the lawn like tiny constellations of colour. Bright red rhubarb shoots. The blue waters of ice-cleared lakes. Dandelions and daisies and cornflowers. All through the summer, the colour palette runs riot, changing with each new bloom of different wildflowers. Early in the summer, the yellows and whites dominate. Later on the pinks of wild roses and reds of elderberries and wild raspberries begin to appear. Through it all, the strong bass note of green can afford to ring loudly beneath such a cacophony of colour. Even the sky provides rainbows and multicoloured sunsets and the vibrant blacks of thunderstorms.

And just when we feel as if we will become giddy and foolish amid all these colours, they start to change again, turning gradually back to a domain of yellows and oranges. The earlier-setting sun sends golden tendrils across the fields. The grasses yellow, and leaves begin to pale. Orange tarpaulins appear on bales of hay and boats pulled out of the water. The fireweed turns again into purplish-red patches along the paths. The light gets thinner, draining colour out of all but the most vibrant summer hues—the red/orange palette has returned.

CHRISTIAN
Steam Bath

by Dan Branch

Don rents a cabin from the Kiruna fundamentalist church. Use of a little steam bath comes with the cabin. Since the minister doesn't steam, Don has almost exclusive use of the bath.

The little building was not always a steam bath. It once served as a man's house. The tenant was a member of the flock who tried to honour the church ban on drinking intoxicants but was not always up to the challenge. He hated to drink alone and his resulting parties created an embarrassment for the church elders.

Village etiquette would not permit an eviction. In Kiruna it is impolite to openly punish someone for their indiscretions. The minister had to come up with another use for the building. His wife suggested that he turn the place into a rabbit hutch but the minister rejected the idea. Forcing someone out of his home to make room for domestic animals would be politically risky.

Don suggested that the minister turn the shack into a steam bath. He was tired of walking over to the high school for showers. Later in the week the cleric presented the idea to his church council. Soon Don had permission to convert the little cabin into a steamer.

A few months after the conversion, a Bethel friend and I took steam with Don. The friend, James, had just returned from Berkeley, California where he had attended a seminar entitled, "Men Exploring Their Female Self." He told me about the trip during dinner.

I looked forward to an interesting time in the Christian steam bath. After all, Don had grown up in a conservative midwest family. Lack of meat and potatoes on the supper table still made him nervous. He calls California the land of fruits and nuts. James's description of the seminar would do little to change his opinion about the golden state.

After filling plastic milk jugs with water at Don's house, we entered the steam bath changing room, stripped, and crawled on hands and knees through a tiny opening into the bath itself.

Don liked hot steams so we found the woodstove inside the steam bath glowing cherry red. Rocks held in place with chicken wire sat on the stove. A metal bucket full of water fizzled on top of the rocks. At first we just sat in a daze on the cedar benches, waiting to sweat. Then, Don made steam. Dipping a ladle into the water bucket, he slowly poured its contents over the hot rocks. A blast of steam followed to take the experience to another level.

With the room filled with steam James launched into a vivid description of his California seminar. He talked about male repression and how men need to be more like women. He urged us to let our feelings out and get rid of all the emotional baggage we carry around.

Don's eyes grew large as James made this pitch for new awareness. When James explained that even manly men have a female side, his host did everything but produce pictures of his children to establish his heterosexuality. James claimed that the seminar would enhance his chances with women. Don remained unconvinced and gradually increased the amount of steam in the room.

At first I shared Don's skepticism, however, slowly James won me over. I had felt bottled up lately. A snag on the Owhat River claimed my lucky lure last week and the new bird dog puppy was not working out. For some reason my wife couldn't grasp the gravity of these problems. Sharing with the guys would

lessen the pain. But James wouldn't give me a chance. He held the floor, sharing the wealth of his new knowledge with Don.

Don had by now moved into the extreme corner of the steam bath. His efforts to drive out James with steam hadn't worked and he was heading for the door when I jumped up to share.

I told James that he was right. Men should take a lesson from women and share things. "We have to trust our emotions," I told them. Don froze in his tracks. Taking this as a sign of agreement, I continued my speech. First, I told them about my fishing and dog problems and then shared a plan. This was state fair weekend, I told them, and Ohmar and Buck were due to set off the annual fireworks display in a few minutes. We could all go out to watch the show. We needed to cool off anyway and the light rain falling outside would provide a sensual bonus.

That is when Don blocked the door. Taking a good look at him for the first time since James began his speech, I saw a man in full blown panic. I asked if there was anything wrong. Don responded with a list of reasons why we shouldn't watch fireworks in the rain. The mosquitos, he said, would eat us alive. Dogs, he claimed, used the area around the steamer as a bathroom. It was too cold, he pleaded. When none of these arguments bore fruit he came clean. "It's the minister's wife," he explained. "She keeps a pair of binoculars on the window sill. If she saw the three of us standing buck naked in the rain there would be an eviction notice tacked to my door before I could reach for a towel." James wasn't going along with my plan either. He had lost interest when Don mentioned the mosquitos. Deflated I sulked around the changing room for awhile and went home, waving to the minister's wife on the way.

A WALKING TOUR OF WHITEHORSE

Through the eyes of a street kid

by SharonAnne LaDue

As a street kid in Whitehorse during the early '80s, I remember how we solved some of our needs. Housing was always a big problem. Staying out of sight from police and vigilant social workers was a major problem. We needed "cool" hangouts.

I think we were pretty ingenious, even though, during the winter months, most of us stayed in horrible situations. Sometimes with families who didn't give a damn, or we crashed with friends until parents asked us to leave. Then there were always the government-operated youth centres and group homes. I had been on the streets living day-to-day and when I moved into a group home, things changed dramatically. I felt as though my independence had been taken away and I was cooped up, watched and told how to think, act and feel. But it was better than freezing or starving.

During the summer months we had more options. There were several small tent villages in the Whitehorse area, the main one located on top of the clay cliffs behind the incinerator and another across the Alaska Highway from the Kopper King. Those tent villages were not weatherproof; ofttimes the tents were old, ripped, and mouldy. But just the same, I felt secure. I managed to rip off a new tent and sleeping bag. I treasured these stolen items, because they kept me warm and dry.

At times in the summer we would crash parties and sleep there. I often stayed with older guys, not because I was into sex with them, but because they had things I needed: warm beds, showers and food. Such simple, everyday items cost so much for a fourteen-year-old runaway.

Where did we hang out? You know where the Talisman Cafe is? It's quite a successful little establishment now, isn't it? In the early '80s, half of the building was an arcade called New York, New York. It was a scuzzy, dark, rundown building. I loved it there because I was surrounded by others wanting to be anonymous, tough and without pain.

On Main Street there is a quaint, quiet restaurant called Pasta Palace. Before, there used to be a restaurant called Christies. It also was run down and lots of tough, streetwise people visited the place. The atmosphere was pretty harsh. The owners didn't mind us hanging out as long as we were quiet. When we entered, the owner would say, "You kids come in. No haywire business."

The "sniffers" hide out: a place to disappear in. Y'know where McDonalds and Tags are? In the '80s there was a white army barrack building there. The first time I entered I was shocked! There were thousands of old bottles of nail polish, pam, whiteout and baggies, evidence of the sniffers. Besides the sniffers' paraphernalia there were hundreds of broken bottles of cheap wine. Villa. It was overwhelming. I was astounded at the mess, the layers of garbage, the sadness that enshrouded the whole area. The inner walls of the building were being ripped apart by age, by weather and by cold hands in need of a fire. There were fire pits. Someone was smart, the fire pits were made from large tin cans set in the corners. There were several battered, torn, stained, rotting mattresses. I itch just thinking of those old mattresses.

Today, if you want to go for a nice walk along the river, go to the boardwalk and bridge going to Kishwoot Island. In the '80s we would walk or swim across the Yukon River to Kishwoot Island. Hanging around the river was freaky, because of the down-and-outers. They were very scary. I think sometimes we felt scared of them because they represented one of our possible futures.

My favourite hangouts were the Pioneer Graveyard and the clay cliffs. Why? Because I was alone. No one was abusing me, conning me out of my precious belongings. No one was telling me how rotten I was. I could dream of my future, I could dream dreams of how my life would be if adults would stop intervening "for the best interests of the child."

Nowadays, I am happy they intervened. My dreams are coming true.

Friend-ship

by Serena Lee Mis.Ta-Nash

The twenty-mile drive to work, down Flat Mountain toward the Yukon River, is a fine start for a June day. The mountainsides glow gold, topped by white glaciers, our year-round friends. Poplar and willow leaves are nearly full; the ground cover is rich with new life, fireweed already a foot high and reaching for evermore sun.

Ground squirrels stand tall and send high pitched, side-of-road greetings; some make out-of-control dashes to the other side. Where they haven't made it, ravens feed at new food sites until the last possible second, then fly up squawking as I whizz past.

It is eight on the nose as I walk in the door at work and I can smell the coffee brewing. As I go to fill my cup a voice warns, "Not quite ready yet." "If it's warm and brown it's good enough for me," one of the guys pipes up. Already, the couches and benches of the drop-in centre are filling.

The pot finishes perking and we fill our cups. We sip away, words not necessary; the silence communicates. I glance over at a man across the room. He's slumped down in the chair, one leg crossed over the other, cup balanced on his knee. His baseball cap is pulled low over his face, the deep breathing a sure sign of sleep.

He knows he can't sleep here at the drop-in centre and I wonder if I should wake him. I don't want to. He's probably been walking around all night, surviving; he needs some rest. Yesterday, he told me that he had been beaten and robbed the night before.

Two guys had found him passed out on the riverbank. They had all been drinking together earlier. They knew he had some money left; they took it all, 60 bucks. He tried to defend himself, then just gave in. I asked if he had told the police. "No, what's the use of that? I'll look after it myself."

He's not so young anymore; the scars of survival line his brown face. He's been on the streets for the whole time I've been here, 14 years. Once again people move around to refill coffee cups. Our friend's eyes slowly open. "Have a good snooze," I ask. "Yeah, thanks, sis," he answers. A smile spreads over his face and he winks.

Filling his cup he comes to sit closer. "How are things today?" I ask, not sure I want an answer. He takes his time, sips his coffee, then talks, head down, voice muffled. I listen hard. "Sure was a pretty sunrise. The mountains turned gold." He lifts his face, the crowsfeet around his eyes move up, his mouth widens, and warmed by his smile, I nod in agreement.

It's a doggone shame

by Dan Davidson

"**M**an's" best friend sits on the steps of the drugstore, sniffing hopefully at the passers-by. His eyes are sad but trusting. In spite of his recent betrayal, he is willing to place himself in human hands once again. An hour or so before, he had arrived at the store with his master to meet the bus. We can imagine him strolling along in perfect contentment, much as he had been doing all summer around the town. The man, whether he carried a pack or not, was good to be with. This was just another walk.

But it wasn't. At the end of this walk, the man found a bus, got on it and drove out of the dog's life, probably forever. When I meet him, the dog hasn't figured that out yet, but the people who had watched it all from inside the store have.

It's easy to figure it out, from the man's point of view. This is a large dog, not a puppy. He eats a lot; he will make apartment hunting in the south difficult; he's an outdoor dog who will be able to fend for himself in Dawson and will be happier here.

The trouble with this line of reasoning is that it should have been completed a lot sooner, before he made a friend out of that stray and got him used to being with people. He should have resisted succumbing to the Klondike urge to have a big dog at your heels. He should have been able to see this far into the future without too much difficulty.

He isn't alone, of course. Dawson's streets are littered with the ragged remains of those fluffy puppies that folks just couldn't resist in April, May and June. Those cute little balls of fur got big and grew teeth. They turned out to be inconvenient to keep and impossible to travel with, something the superior human brain should have known from the beginning. Some give their short-term pets to friends or find other homes for them, but past history shows that a lot simply emulate the individual at the bus depot and walk away.

The dog thus abandoned quickly becomes a street animal. There are lots of them around and, following its natural instincts, the newcomer blends in with a pack and roams free, overturning garbage cans for sustenance, keeping the local cats in shape by conducting impromptu endurance runs, and holding nightly serenades for whatever ladies might happen to be in the mood to listen—there's always one somewhere in this community. Eventually, he becomes a nuisance, part of a pack that takes to following little kids home from school and pacing them as they run away. Just for the fun of it, of course. No harm intended.

Only trouble is that dogs in packs behave a lot like people in mobs, and often do things that would never have entered their minds when they were alone. The end of this sad tale might be that someone gets hurt. More likely, it will be that the dog gets picked up by a bylaw officer, taken to the lockup and put down when it remains unclaimed for the requisite period of time. Don't blame the person who pulls the trigger or presses the plunger on the syringe. This dog was destroyed when the person it trusted got on that bus.

There's no workable answer to this problem. People are to blame. In our throwaway world, it is all too common for them to come to Dawson with two suitcases, acquire all sorts of things during their time here, and simply leave them behind at the end of the season. If we had the option of forcing potential pet owners to post a bond or something before they could satisfy their cravings, we would at least be better able to deal with the messes they leave behind them. As it is, we'll just have to keep pleading for common sense.

Oh, and the dog? I hope he gets lucky.

PHOTO: PETER LONG

Silver–Bellied Cloudsucker

by Rick Charlebois

Earlier today, I heard a muffled noise and ran out to investigate. I pointed my best ear in the general direction of the annoyance and cupped my right hand around the lobe. It was one of the daily flights of the great Silver-Breasted Cloudsucker singing its rumbling notes with an earthshaking roar.

The intrusive song always seems to be magnified by the formation of the mountains as the vibrations bounce off the peaks and are carried down the slopes by a gentle breeze. It often catches me off guard, sounding more like the distant snarl of an animal than the blustery symbol of civilization that it is. Perhaps its secret mission is to remind me of the race to which I sometimes belong, something I have all but forgotten in my remote workshop. It is that time of year when the long summer days, filled with unending physical labour and the inner pressures of survival, have paved the way for the long winter nights of reading and philosophical reverie.

The silvery bird has long since flown off to roost in its concrete eyrie, but I can still see beneath its steely-white feathers, travellers peering out from under its wings, mesmerized by the purpose of their journey. I waved as they passed, but the distance was too great; nor could they see, through the haze of their gaze, past the immediate space encircling them. Had they been closer, they still would not have had time to see me standing on this desolate spot as they raced on, hugging the speed of sound to meet their goals.

This, the morning bird, carried passengers east over the Arctic to Europe; the evening bird carries its burden to our country. All these travellers always coming and going, here and there, many of whom are searching for that happiness we all seek. Some have found it, some are on their way, others would traverse infinite space and eternal time in their fruitless search. Everyday, hundreds of these searching souls glide past in the giant metal birds, and I wave with a happy smile from a hermitage which most choose to consider uncivilized, primitive, barbaric.

As I write, I can hear the song of the evening bird carrying the representatives of society in its belly…and I can almost hear their thoughts on trapping, the savagery of my lifestyle, and their accusations of its destructiveness to the environment. Though it is too dark to see, I know the great Silver-Breasted Cloudsucker leaves behind it a trail of poisonous gas—the excrement of civilization—for a track, a mark of its passage etched across the heavens.

An overture to the outpost outhouse

It's not as if I wasn't brought up with an outhouse, and not just the eastern Canadian cottage country version that was a seasonal novelty. No. We had a "true blue" dunny out behind the grape vine. Australians always did camouflage certain types of true blue.

My grandmother swept the gravel path to hers until it had the hard pack of concrete. My aunts cut newspaper into scalloped doilies that hung on a nail, and the place was as fragrant as honeysuckle vines and a tar can could make it.

Once a week Albert Fitzgibbons, shunned as tanners were of old, would come around the side of the house swinging a glistening black can in the same hand that would later deliver ice and apples, and would return with a full one on his padded left shoulder, bound for a multi-doored flatbed that a Yukoner would swear was built to house a couple of dozen dogteams. We girls would be hustled into the house, and a wide berth left for Albert. Albert wasn't high on the marriage stakes.

To encourage my father's murmurs about an indoor toilet, and to counteract his procrastinating nature, my mother handed out hammers and axes one day after school and we reduced the dunny to a polished limestone slab. For two weeks my dad did the rounds of the clubs and pubs with his unbelievable story, one foot on the rail and one hand on a beer. Men in passing pickup trucks would lean out and shout, "Bloody oath. Good on ya, love!" to my mortified mother.

Naturally, when I came north, out of a modern urbania of Italian ceramic toilets, Lysol and ensuite bathrooms, I expected the occasional outhouse. I sought a new life, fresh values. I hadn't expected to be thrown into the toilet roughhouse of the tourist guiding business, finding myself teaching paying southerners how to lift a divot of sphagnum, the virtues of a cup of warm water in the bush over a bidet in the city and the shortcomings of anal retentiveness for long distance canoeing.

I also had never expected such a wild and beautiful array of Yukon dunnies as friends had to offer. For every invitation to Sunday lunch, sauna and soup, ski and see, I could add another marvel to the outhouse list.

My best story involves little Levon, out on the Wheaton at Shiela's place. I was sitting there in the three-walled doll house, gingham curtains, good reading material, trapdoor for paper, birds, squirrels, and a view of wood heap and wild woods, rearranging my abstract kinship with potty

training and liberal theories of privacy when telltale noises indicated another being approaching my open air unit.

I hold to a private reality. No one will come near when I am here, hums my inbred vestal prudery. It feverishly drowns out the loudness of approaching sounds. Nope. Around the corner comes four-year-old Levon, buttons undone, braces trailing, eyes as luminescent as morning rain pools. He

PHOTO: CHRIS SCHERBARTH

PHOTO: MARLYNN BOURQUE

PHOTO: CHRIS SCHERBARTH

OUTHOUSE NUGGETS

T. Ruth McCullough

Outhouses are usually associated with a rural environment. Subsequently, stores are sometimes not in close proximity to the users of these facilities. A number of years ago, a gentleman decided he needed to order some toilet paper so he sat down and wrote a letter to Sears.

"Dear Sirs: Please send me a case of toilet paper." The response: "Please send us the catalogue number for the product you wish to order."

To which the gentleman replied: "If I had your catalogue, I wouldn't need to order the toilet paper."

OUTHOUSE NUGGETS

T. Ruth McCullough

In a remote service station, the owner became somewhat bored due to the significantly low number of visitors to that neck of the woods. He rigged up a speaker with a microphone beneath the floor of his customer outhouse. When a customer would retire to use the facilities, he would wait for a couple of minutes and then say into the microphone, "Excuse me, Madame, I'm working down here!" and then wait to see the look on their faces when they vacated.

climbs aboard the other half of the two-seater I have been denying as an aberration, an aeration device, a miscut, an alternate choice, and wriggles deep into the warm styrofoam, carefully laying his mitts on the side shelf and surveying the soft white world. When a requisite period of silence has been observed, he turns to me courteously.

"Are you going?" On my studied assent, he looks gently approving. "I'm going, too," and swings his heels once. And thus we know that the world is in good order at this moment. And thus do I learn the sacraments of the northern two-holer.

Of course, the very first outhouse visit was back in the early stages, during my first, test visit to the north. There we were, me and Dick, in his teepee camp out on Tagish, near Carcross. He showed me around. "Here's the big teepee, and, er… here's a tool tent, and the cook tent and Pete's tent is down that trail, and this here is the trail to the dock and ah…here are the shitter planks."

Never heard the word, except on a Sydney construction site, as a reaction to a misplaced plank, or a loose plank. Certainly never to describe two boards stretched over a musty lookin' dark hole, embedded in sweet smelling grasses and surrounded by fireweed, raspberries ready for picking and nodules of limey camomile.

What're they for? Could it be "splitter planks" maybe? Had heard of a crosscut saw, maybe in Harrowsmith. This rustic place could be using such a thing, but I thought one guy was up in a tree for that. "For shittin'." Holy!! Not for me. I'm a clean-living city woman, totally programmed for white walls and the blind slats snapped shut. Isn't this in the centre of camp? Isn't that the main fire pit just over the rose bushes? "Beautiful spot, isn't it?" he says. Seriously. He's eating a rosehip right about then.

The time had to come. I'd already scouted the place and figured out the exact timing. He'd gone for water. I went for water. Squatted carefully behind a willow clump, one eye on the trail, another on the teepee in case of surprise routes, I carefully clutched

PHOTO: LAURA PYKE

my linen pantsuit up out of the leaves. In the midstream of sheer relief, bottom bare to a mild fall breeze, eyes pinned to the faintest movement, I hear the unmistakable scuffings of boots on the open trail behind me, on that other intersecting trail, that trail to the nonexistent Pete's.

"Mornin," says a deep gentlemanly voice, as he passes 20 feet behind me, headed like clockwork for his morning tea in the teepee, toasty warm in his old wool plaid.

Since then I've become a connoisseur like the other folk up here. "Hey, great shitter you got," I say first off, so's they'll know I'm wearing shoepacks and carrying wholewheat muffins and crowberry jam under the hot tea towel as we clump up the porch steps.

continued…

PHOTO: MARIE CARR

PHOTO: JANNE HICKLIN

PHOTO: MARLYNN BOURQUE

Valuable

by S.D. Picot

"Have you ever dropped anything valuable
in the outhouse?" she asked him.
"No," he paused, "but once I was told I couldn't use
the bathroom at the gas station
unless I bought gas. So I pissed by the pumps.
I didn't need gas, I needed to relieve myself."
He was still perplexed.

FIRST PEE
INTO A CLEAN CAN

Moments earlier, a helicopter had made its way from Skagway, especially to take away the full can from this outhouse at the summit of the Chilkoot Trail, and to replace it with an empty one. Note the rails on the platform to slide the outhouse aside.

Lay of the Land

And they are. There's one on the Stikine that looks like a Jim Robb cartoon, lopsided, smoke stack askew with white multi-panes overlooking the pond where a

The Outhouse

by Karen Catlin

It is refreshing to sit
In my open air outhouse.
After dusting the seat of early morning snow,
I turn and aim myself down upon the icy cold ring shape,
Meshing my posterior to perfect fit.
The seat begins to warm.

Sipping coffee,
I gaze forward through the wooded landscape,
Listening to snow clumps melting and
Crashing down from tree boughs,
A squirrel hollers and a chickadee chirps from somewhere.
As the morning sun crawls high behind the clouds,
Moss which lives beneath the snow
Peeks brilliant green from the white undulating cover.

Suddenly, I am joined by my dear doggy.
Finished with her solitary walk about the yard,
She sits at my feet snuggled close against my legs.
I still sit; defecation long since complete
Perched on a warmed toilet seat,
Feeling the cold air rush at my exposed bottom.
Hoping as I sit, no creature exists
That might brave the methane gas oozing stalagmite;
To reach up with long claws and biting fangs.

Then, having only dressed myself in a robe and boots,
Goose bumps come and the dog whines in protest of the cold.
My ears consumed by the shrill,
Skin failing to brace against the chill,
I am driven up and away from my comfy perch
Over the dark hole.

As quickly as I had come;
down the uneven rootbound path,
I travel closer to warmth and safety.
With the trail at an end,
We slip behind the heavy cabin door,
Waiting until the next trip to
The Outhouse.

moose occasionally visits, occupied or not, to leave a tongue lick on the reflecting glass. Another is set with a rainproof slant to the seat between two colossal firs and a 360 degree view of old growth hemlock and devil's club. At Laberge, offcut pine slab makes one friend's look like an abandoned miner's coffin, and at Marsh Lake, a connecting door leads to the sauna and the half moon is a wind vane.

One is always a bit dubious about the condition of the styrofoam in these structures, strangely darkened, cracked and mended with a bead of silicone, or worn down to the plywood on the inner rim. Probably stored under the cabin for the summer. That could be it.

Shiela, meanwhile, has gone to serious instant composting with a pedestal affair behind the centre chimney and a bucket of enthusiastic microbes beside the seat. Her cabbages are the biggest in the Wheaton Valley. Levon loves the cabbages, too.

Our own is outfitted for summer with lodgepole boughs and a split-level doorway view of bearberry and kale, and for winter with two candles, and a see-through roof. In January, layered in down, with a two-way jacket zip for handy heat skirting, a mohair hat and mitts, there is no quieter place in the woods than our place, door open, the inside walls covered in an icy filigree of spider's webs, the outside a fantasyland of hoarfrost and snow eiderdowns.

I'm thinking of a mural for the ash can, and a better looking rock for propping the door, maybe a dutch door for windy days…and Albert. Albert was probably great marriage material.

OUTHOUSE NUGGETS

T. Ruth McCullough

Ever hear of a honeywagon? In my home town in northern Saskatchewan, this was a horse-drawn cart that emptied all the pots from the outhouses behind every house in the town. Biggest insult when I was growing up? Being invited to go for a ride on the honeywagon.

OUTHOUSE OUTLOOK

by Evie Estey

Alone and a-leaning on a knoll
A few hundred feet from the house
(In winter, a few hundred miles, it seems,
When snow trickles into my boots,
No chance to wait for "the last minute" then —
I must allow "travelling" time)
No door, just a few slats to bar
The Wilderness from my minute of solitude,
To read Elizabeth Browning's words
While squirrels chatter down
At me, and tease the dogs to barking.
A lonely vigil at the top of the hill
Where no soul intrudes while the open half-door
Signals my presence there.
Only the sweet words I am reading
And the wind chilling my exposed behind
Until the expected explosion
(aftermath of last night's beans!)
Frightens away the squirrels,
Who now cease their chatter.
Devils!
They got into the house again
and tore the bedsheets in my absence,
So I had to lie naked between
The mattress and blanket.
This is the stuff of stories to be told,
Not to be zippered on some book's pages
Or locked in only my mind
Where entry is prohibited to any except me.
My thoughts amble and stray from the book open on my lap.
Damn squirrels!
Nuisances, they are!
But their antics twig a memory long lost in my childhood,
Of children behaving like squirrels in trees,
Of hiding a marble from my brother
Who blanched when he discovered his best cat's-eye
In my possession,
Daring me to keep his prize
Till sheepishly I returned his orb,
An eye-shaped object
Like the eye of the squirrel still noisily scolding me
For disturbing its morning
With my LOUD FART.

OUTHOUSE NUGGETS

T. Ruth McCullough

I am as concerned about the environment as the next person and when I shop, I make sure that the products I select are of the recyclable nature. I do, however, almost draw the line at recycled toilet paper. It brings to mind a clothesline filled with bits of toilet paper swinging in a gentle breeze. My suspicion that this was actually occurring was confirmed the other day when I used an outhouse with a container in the corner labelled "used toilet paper."

Alaskan outdoor plumbing

POSTCARD: JEFF BROWN

Just how cold was it?

by Dan Davidson

I learned new ways to measure the cold one recent winter. Normally, I use degrees like everybody else, but circumstances introduced me to some new measures.

First there is coughing. Like half of the rest of Dawson, I had the flu—six weeks and going strong. It reached the point where I told people I felt fine, just to take my mind off it. They knew I was lying, but they were sick too and doing the same thing, so no one was hurt by it.

There were days when I had to lecture very quickly to get a few words in between the coughing spasms of my students. We took turns, partners in adversity.

Coughing. At 30 below, a deep breath hurts. I had to put a scarf over my nose and mouth and take off my glasses. (It's safer to be slightly myopic than to be blinded by the ice.) What with the general lack of wind chill here, I wouldn't normally do this until 40 below, but my agitated bronchial tubes fairly screamed when hit with unmuffled Arctic chill, so I altered my routine.

Going outside wasn't too bad, nor was walking from place to place, but the first breath of warmer air when I came back inside set off a burst of hacking. At 40 below, the coughing works in both directions and becomes more violent. Distinct shortness of breath is evident, and the scarf freezes quite quickly. By the time we hit minus 50, I'm in danger of coughing up whatever's in my stomach, a nasty thought when one's mouth is covered by a scarf.

The other measure is vehicle repair bills. The tab ran to a snapped alternator belt, several flat tires, a new battery, and new hose for the truck's power steering. The damage seemed substantially worse this year than last, which is a fair measure of the temperature. Rubber seemed more fragile than usual. The extension cord to the outside plug had some snow in it, and when I gave it a little rap on the fence before plugging the car in (just a small tap, really), it shattered on impact.

Other days, we got the hatchback open to pack in the groceries but couldn't get it to latch closed again. A cute trick, this. The hydraulic fluid in the lift arms was so cold that the hatch actually stayed closed the whole drive home unless we hit a bump at speed. (That didn't happen often, out of concern for the tires and the shocks.) We had to leave the car running, with the heater on full, for 20 minutes, to thaw out the locking mechanism so that we could shut it completely again.

It reached the point where the bright midafternoon sun seemed to be thumbing its nose at us. It looked lovely outside until you got there, and then you learned differently. Really, though, we love it, don't we? Someone who spent part of the winter in Mexico told me that, while there, he felt a kind of perverse pride at being able to say that he actually lived where it was as cold as the southern papers said it was. Not that he wasn't glad to miss most of the fun, but there was something special in the fact that he was going back to those temperatures—without flinching.

IT'S STILL SUMMER, RIGHT?

WYATT 8-96

AUGUST IN OLD CROW

How Ernie Lyall learned to control his bodily functions

by John McGrath

Ernie Lyall was a Labrador man who had come to the Arctic with the Hudson's Bay Company. He married an Inuk woman from a prominent Kingamiut family of Cape Dorset and they raised a large family, settling in Spence Bay. As a young man at Fort Ross and later at Spence Bay, he sometimes worked as a guide and interpreter for the RCMP on their winter patrols around Boothia Peninsula—from Gjoa Haven to Fort Ross and thence to Pelly Bay.

When travelling at -40, one of the most uncomfortable personal chores is that of excretion. There is no comfortable way to have a shit, and the usual practice is to put up a snow block for protection from the wind and get it over with as quickly as possible.

On one patrol, a young Mountie realized that, after a week on the trail, he never once noticed Ernie having a dump. He enquired as to how this seemingly impossible feat was accomplished. Ernie explained to him that during years of travel with his Inuk father-in-law, Kavavou, the old man, who was famous and wise among his people, had taught him many secrets of the Innumaruit or "real people," and that total control of the bowels was one of these secrets.

After this statement, the Mountie kept his trained investigator's eye on Ernie at all times, but never caught him with his pants down, either literally or figuratively. Were it not for the merry light in Ernie's eyes when he told me this story, I would have believed his tale myself, but as it was I pressed him for an explanation. It turned out that Ernie timed his "movements" to reflect those of the Mountie. When he was no longer able to hold it, the Mountie climbed out of his sleeping bag, put on his clothes—all unbuttoned to gain easy and quick access—and went outside to the snow block privy. Ernie would quickly climb out of his sleeping bag, use his snow-knife to cut out a snowblock from the floor of the Igloo, let go his load and quickly put the snowblock back in place. He then climbed back into the sleeping bag and feigned sleep as the Mountie returned, freezing and uncomfortable.

COLD AND THE METRIC WRONG

by Max Fraser

Northern literature is full of wild tales about the bone-chilling cold found in these extreme northern latitudes. While the tales may be exaggerated, the temperatures are not: they're a big part of northern historical mythology, and just as big a part of contemporary reality. A problem has arisen in Canada with the use of the metric system (Celsius scale of temperature). Because of it, we're losing touch with the roots of our literature. The mix of old-scale Fahrenheit and new-scale Celsius has brought confusion, and threatens to disconnect northerners, specifically Canadians, from our history, as well as our sense of what is real.

As with any good story, the harder things get, the better the story; in the case of northern literature, the colder it is, the better. Robert Service knew that. So did Jack London. Many of us grew up down south, shivering while we read verses of Robert Service.

You know what it's like in the Yukon
wild when it's sixty-nine below;
When the ice-worms wriggle their purple heads
through the crust of the pale blue snow;
When the pine-trees crack like little guns
in the silence of the wood,
And the icicles hang down like tusks
under the parka hood
– from The Ballad of Blasphemous Bill

I will never forget the severe impression made on me when I first read Jack London's *To Build a Fire*. (Just to think of it makes me cold.) The same impression is left with thousands of people from around the world who travel north every summer to see the Klondike goldfields, to see the land that God forgot, to see for themselves the place that birthed so much rich writing. (Few, however, visit in winter. Must be too risky, or is it just too cold?)

In *To Build a Fire*, London writes about a gold rush-era miner who heads out on a winter trail. It's colder than this person has ever experienced before. He's been warned by old-timers that no one should be out alone when it's colder than 50 below zero. It was so cold his dog became depressed. The dog…

…knew that it was no time for travelling. Its instinct told it a truer tale than was told to the man by the man's judgement. In reality, it was not merely colder than fifty below zero; it was colder than sixty below, than seventy below. It was seventy-five below zero. Since the freezing point is thirty-two above zero, it meant that one hundred and seven degrees of frost obtained.

The man believes he can make it, but in the end, does not. That experience, probably based on someone's real-life experience, contrasts with that of the more sensible Laura

Beatrice Berton, who arrived after the gold rush to teach in Dawson. She lived in a town where everything was a short walk away, rather than down some long, lonely and icy trail. In *I Married the Klondike*, Berton wrote:

On the night of the New Year's Eve Ball, it suddenly dropped to thirty below. Everybody laughed when I referred to this as the freeze. Wait until it gets down around fifty or sixty, they told me. A few days later, the thermometer of our little house showed fifty-five below, and when I put my nose outside that morning I felt as if I were pierced with hundreds of electric needles.

That's what Jack London called real cold. Hard to disagree with that kind of definition. Anything colder than 40 below has to fall into that category of real cold.

There's a problem with modern-day interpretations of olden-day stories about the frozen north. Consider that these stories originated around Dawson, a much colder place than Whitehorse, where this writer resides. I cannot claim to have experienced anything colder than minus 47(C) which is 50° below(F), and that was only for a day or two, not weeks on end. I wasn't tempted to stick my nose outside, though I did have to suit up to bring in more firewood, having wisely stacked ten cords no more than 20 feet from the back door.

During one recent winter, the radio reported every morning with dreary, claustrophobic, life-threatening pronouncements how much colder it was than the day before. In Dawson, it got down to something like minus 55°C. I couldn't believe it. That's like 67 below—a gold rush temperature if I ever heard one! The following summer, my Dawson friend John told me how much warmer minus 40 had felt when it warmed up from minus 50!

A major reality check takes place when temperatures drop below 40 below. That's the spot on the thermometer where the Celsius and Fahrenheit scales meet: 40 below is the same as minus 40. For every degree of Celsius lower than that, there's a greater number of Fahrenheit degrees. As a result, the Celsius scale reads lower, and fails to tell us how cold it actually is.

Take the coldest temperature ever recorded in North America, on February 3, 1947, at Snag, Yukon—83 below (later changed to 81.4 below). Heck, that's only minus 63°C. Somehow, that lower number just doesn't do justice to how cold it actually was. It was more than real cold. It was real, real cold…

We threw a dish of water high into the air, just to see what would happen.
Before it hit the ground, it made a hissing noise, froze and fell as tiny round pellets of ice the size of wheat kernels.
Spit also froze before hitting the ground.

– Weather observer Wilf Blezard, in Snag that day

In real, real cold, a person's breath leaves a vapour trail behind them and lingers in the atmosphere for minutes afterwards.

One Snag observer even found such a trail still marking his path when he returned 15 minutes later.

The Metric Wrong

The metric system—this Celsius scale—just rubs me the wrong way. While it's been around for 20 years or so, and while I've adjusted like most others to the temperatures, I still find myself converting from one scale to the next in my head, to adjust to how cold—or warm—it is. Especially when it gets cold. (You people in Alaska have not had to deal with this problem unless you drive through Canada.) Take minus 20. On the old scale, that was only zero—a nice, mild winter day. Not even cold enough to plug in your car. Great temperature for dogsledding, ice fishing, cross-country skiing, hitchhiking or walking downtown for a beer. You know, comfortable. Hardly even need to put on your parka, let alone that old toque.

On the old scale, 10 above was mild (now it's called minus 12). Ten below was not bad. Somehow minus 25 sounds a lot colder, but it's exactly the same temperature, just a different number.

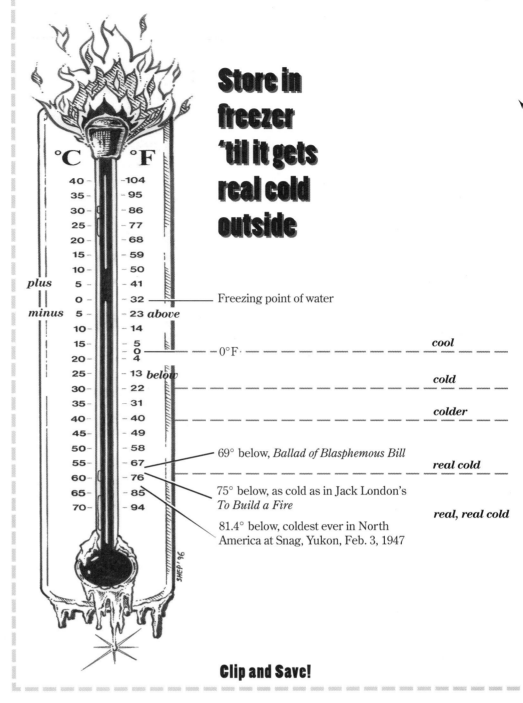

Store in freezer 'til it gets real cold outside

Freezing point of water

0°F ---- cool

cold

colder

69° below, *Ballad of Blasphemous Bill* — real cold

75° below, as cold as in Jack London's *To Build a Fire*

81.4° below, coldest ever in North America at Snag, Yukon, Feb. 3, 1947

real, real cold

Clip and Save!

Twenty below is good dog mushing weather. You must keep moving to stay warm. In Celsius, it's minus 30. 30 below and it's time to start being careful about how you manoeuvre your vehicle—let it warm up well, and go gently on the steering wheel and brakes for a while. Today, this is called minus 35.

I've also learned there's a big difference between 30 below and 40 below. There's a long way to go, in Fahrenheit, and for every degree there is a noticeable change in how cold it is and how you deal with it. Whitehorse hardly ever gets to 40 below, while that's a routine winter temperature for more central and northern Yukon communities. 35 below means one thing. Now it's called minus 38. This is the place on the thermometer where all those degrees get very crowded, and Fahrenheit serves no better than Celsius.

Some people tell me this is not a big deal, that cold is cold, that real cold is real cold, no matter what scale or what temperature. I can't agree.

These can be the same annoying people who take advantage of terms from the old scale and apply them to the new, and in so doing, get to boast about something that really isn't all it's cracked up to be. Allegedly-cold temperatures become the excuse to not do things. Community events are cancelled at 20 below, when really it's only zero Fahrenheit. Years ago, the same events wouldn't be jeopardized until the real 20 below, which turns out to be about minus 30 on the new scale.

After almost a generation of using the Celsius scale, many Canadians have yet to successfully adapt; it's clear that Fahrenheit is more familiar and more useful to many people, and will likely endure for years to come. It's in our literature, it's in our blood. And in the north, with Fahrenheit, people know how cold it really is!

ILLUSTRATION: STEVE SHEPHERD

It has been minus 40, or worse, now, for nearly ten days. Life just about stops. To go out anywhere means a major investment of time to get ready for the outdoors: wool socks, mukluks, ski pants, sweater, down-filled coat, a thin scarf inside your coat, hat big enough to cover your forehead and ears, heavy mitts, and a long scarf to wrap around your neck and face outside your coat to pre-warm the frigid air before you pull it into your lungs. All this is absolutely necessary; to omit any of this gear is to invite chill or even frostbite. (It has been said that in the Yukon in the winter there is no such thing as fashion; you simply wear everything you own.)

You assemble outside duties to be done in one outing, for the investment of time required to

The unwritten code is to always help someone in trouble from the cold. The cold can be a killer. Even when driving, you dress as though you are walking. For one thing, it is possible that you may end up hoofing it because of car failure. The other reason is that your car really is not warm. The engine needs all its heat to make sure it's warm enough to keep running; therefore you drain off only enough warmth to keep the windows clear.

Windows. Lots of people seal their house windows with plastic. Double panes are not enough. Frost grows ice fingers as you watch. My kitchen boasts the best "tame" glaciers in the neighbourhood.

We Whitehorse-Yukoners can take a few days of -40, but when it stretches to more than a

Minus 40
by Evie Estey

go out dictates that you make the most of it. You learn to recognize your friends by their coat, mitts and boots. Everyone has a distinctive dress, from the high-tech Gortex look to traditional bead-worked parka. The only visible part of a human is the eyes, for all flesh is by necessity covered, leaving only the peepers exposed. (The hat comes down to the eyelids, the outside scarf comes up to meet the lower eyelashes.)

Hoarfrost from one's breath wreaths about your head, "growing" from the little wool strands of your hat and scarf to freeze your eyelashes together. The cold stings your eyeballs. Your pace is determined by the fall in the mercury; the colder the air, the quicker your step. No dawdling at -40! The curious fact is that you overheat. I find the easiest cool-down is to take off my mitts. Steam escapes as my toasty hands meet the Arctic air. But not for long! Cool-down takes but a few brief seconds.

The city is very still; few cars run, the dogs are all curled inside their houses, ravens roost on the street lights to keep their feet warm. (Mother Nature neglected to give them feather "overshoes.") The city disappears in ice fog mixed with wood smoke and vehicle exhaust. These vapours do not dissipate during the cold due to an "inversion" where ground temperatures are warmer than that of the atmosphere; the river "steams" because the

water is warmer than the air. Ice crystals are frozen and suspended in the air, attaching themselves to everything not warm. In its heavy coat of frost, the outdoors is a fairyland.

As you open your door to this ice-shrouded realm, a dragon's breath of mist rolls across the floor. If this fog collides with a house plant, the leaf is wounded with brown frost spots. My cats retreat with repulsion from this arctic assault, wrinkling their noses in disgust. My first line of defence against the dragon, my outside door, wears a heavy skin of frost, as does any nail head on the outer wall.

The ice crystals in the air melt as you breathe them in; you can feel them thaw in your nose. In the daylight, often there are "sun dogs" or rainbows on either side of the sun caused by the sun's rays reflecting from the ice in the air.

The icy cold turns leather, rubber, plastic, and metal into brittle sticks. Cars become unreliable. (I simply leave mine alone and do a lot of walking.) Those whose cars do run waste time and gas with half-hour warm-ups. Now, that does not mean that the car is warm. It's merely not frozen! Tires stay "flat" on the bottom for the first five or ten minutes of the drive; "square" tires give a bumpy ride. Shock absorbers don't; they are frozen stiff. Many people carry survival gear of sleeping bag, extra clothing, shovel, tow chain, booster cables, fire starter, and gas line de-icer.

working week even the most hardy begin to complain and entertain ideas of a "sun and surf" vacation. The radio gives lists of meetings and events which are cancelled; messages are relayed to those without telephones, those on traplines, or those who shun community life and live beyond the settlements. Messages like: "John, your U.I.C. cheque is at Mom's," or "Tina, your skidoo part has arrived. Georgina will send it out on the next bus."

I am afraid this has created a skewed picture of our winter. It can be a magic time. I feel like a real pioneer in the isolation and hardship. The darkness and cold are the mysterious "heart" of our north. I really do not mind the freeze, but I do become frustrated with the inconveniences: the grocery trucks are often delayed, then arrive with frozen produce. I walk everywhere. And although I appreciate the calories that are consumed with the activity, I resent the time it takes! Take a taxi? You wait and wait and wait(!) for its arrival, if you ever feel rich enough to afford one.

I must confess that I take secret delight in scaring newcomers and tourists with horror stories of the winter. After all, anyone who has the stuff to stick out the true northern winter has earned the right to "embroider" the truths of the situation!

Spruce hate warm summers

by Ned Rozell
Geophysical Institute, University of Alaska Fairbanks

f Alaskans could choose the type of weather they lived in, I suspect most would pick a year like the interior had in 1995—one with a mild winter, an early, dry spring and a sunny summer.

One would think most living organisms would share our preference for warm and dry years, but a researcher recently found white spruce trees that thrive on the opposite.

Glenn Juday, an associate professor of forest sciences at the University of Alaska Fairbanks, studied the growth of two stands of trees about 30 miles down the Parks Highway from Fairbanks.

One stand, in Rosie Creek, was burned in 1983. The other was attacked by bark beetles in 1985 and sold to loggers in 1987.

By counting tree rings and measuring their width, Juday discovered the trees grew best in the coolest, wettest years.

Different tree ring studies done on isolated trees at high elevation show contrasting results: the warmer the temperature in any given year, the better the trees grow. That makes sense.

Look at trees on a sunny, south-facing slope and chances are they'll be a lot bigger than ones on a colder, north-facing slope.

The cold-loving white spruce in Juday's study differ from those sampled in previous tree ring studies because they grew in the upland, between rivers and mountain tops. They also grew close together, and competed against one another for moisture and sunlight.

Juday first noticed the upland white spruce's taste for cold weather when his son, Benjamin, did a high school science fair project.

Benjamin plotted yearly temperatures versus the thickness of tree rings from the stands his father studied. Positive spikes of years with beefy tree rings matched up with downward spikes that indicated low temperatures. Why do these trees prefer cold weather?

Juday thinks long, cold winters and cold, wet summers free up more water for trees to drink. In cooler years, less moisture is lost to

evaporation and through the leaves of trees than in warmer, drier years.

Juday's research shows more than upland white spruce's apparent preference for cold weather; it shows the trees are in trouble.

Because the white spruce he's studying have left a record of the past 200 years in their rings, Juday noticed a cycle of tree growth crashes and recoveries that correlates well with an index of local temperatures and precipitation.

The index, compiled from Fairbanks weather records from 1904 to the present, shows a trend of unprecedented high temperatures and low precipitation that began in the late 1970s. According to Juday, the recent warm, dry weather has hurt the upland white spruce. Spruce bark beetles, spruce budworms and other insects are attacking the stands.

Juday says the trees, stressed by the lack of moisture, are giving off chemical signals that draw insects like iron shavings to a magnet. Spruce budworms turn spruce needles brown, and bark beetles often kill spruce trees by tunnelling under the bark.

A change in the weather is needed for the trees to recover, says Juday. "What would really help right now are some cold, prolonged winters, and a few cool, rainy summers. All this wonderful weather we've been having in recent years has been coming at the expense of the trees."

The troubled white spruce mean more to Juday than just lines on a graph. He sees them as a tiny piece of the climate change puzzle.

When combined with other evidence, such as recent studies of disappearing permafrost, a picture of a warming world could come into focus.

While he's quick to point out that the change he sees is a very local one, it's a severe change from which white spruce trees may not recover unless things cool off a bit.

So the next time a few weeks of 30 below stall the car, or when waves of rain wash out a May canoe trip, think of how the weather is helping the spruce trees, and smile.

Heat wave

by Donna Pendziwol-MacMillan

The sun fire
Warmed the slumbering
August dragon
And woke him up
He flicked his tail
Sparks started to fly
Soon smoke from his flames
Obscured the sky
I smelled his breath
I felt his heat
I saw his reflection
In the sun's eye
That glowed orange red
While he scorched the earth
Turning yellow the foliage
The August dragon
Is putting me to sleep
In the days before winter
At my summer's end.

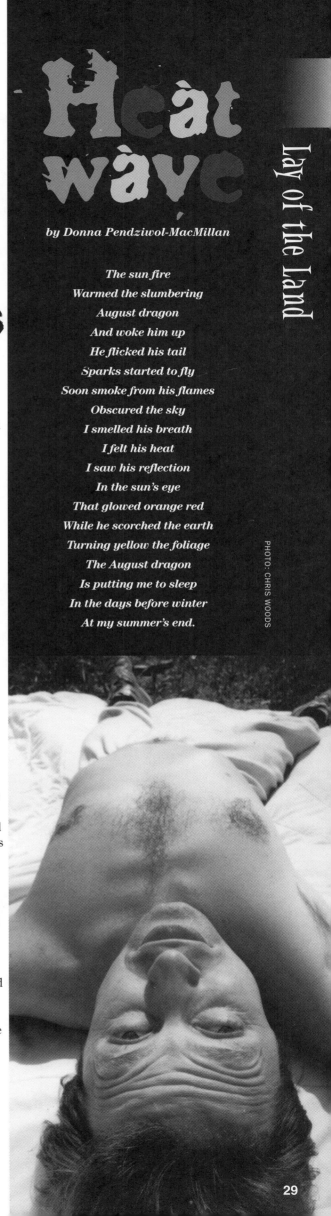

Subject: cold weather reports from whitehorse to victoria jan 96

by Yvonne Haist

The advent of e-mail means that some Yukoners can complain about how cold it is to their friends in Lotusland (Victoria, B.C.). Here is a collection of cold weather reports received by a pair of ex-Yukoners during the 1996 bout of extra-cold weather.

Rob and Helene

message one: Well it's been one of those weeks that make you feel like a real northerner. After a week of blizzards on and off closing every road into the Yukon, we hunkered down with a weekend of -45 weather.

message two: Today we surpassed the record for consecutive days below -40. Great eh? Don't you wish you were here enjoying it with us? Remember jumping into the car seat (if you can call it jumping with insulated pants and parka on) and landing on a block of concrete you do not remember putting on the driver's seat? Remember clunking off on square tires and the speedometer suddenly going berserk and a dreadful scream coming from under the dash? Or how about when you go outside for just a sec to dump the garbage and your bare hand freezes to the garbage can lid. Hey, best one yet. I put out a stock pot of chicken soup to cool. In the morning it had sunk four inches to the concrete of the back steps and formed its own little glacier. It took five minutes with a cleaver to free the thing. Snow drops eh? Who needs em? We have frost creeping across the floor from the picture window in the living room. We have nose hairs freezing to our scarves (saves one hauling around kleenex!). And best of all, none of the locks on our van open. But who gives a shit? You can't drive it anyway cause it's so cold you can't touch the steering wheel! Everyone is starting to snarl like the whole town has come down with PMS

simultaneously. No one meets at the Chocolate Claim (I think Josie left) or the No Pop (Arthur sold out). We meet at the video store where we stock up for the week so we don't have to talk to anyone for seven days. We are having a fine winter, how about you?

message three: The cold continues only now we have wind. Helene is off conducting a research course for Kwanlin Dun. I am hiding in the basement writing reports. My office is the warmest room in the house. Boy have we watched a lot of movies in the last two weeks. Mostly old favourites like Star Wars. Visual equivalent of comfort food.

Barb and Cam

message one: Okay. Ten plus days at -45 or less (or is it more?) is to be expected if you live up here, but still... We are surviving. Our home and vehicles are not. Water lines froze last week and cost $200 to thaw—had to take them apart and pour this weird "liquid plumber" type antifreeze stuff down them. Now we keep a tap running 24 hours. Thank goodness the water is not metered. The van froze up due to a faulty extension cord. When I went to crack the hood the release handle snapped off in my hands. Then I cracked the grill. Finally got it opened and thawed out. It could be worse. Actually, no it could not. Don't remember this much cold since 1982 or so. I thought we got through the '80s...but it's a dry cold....

message two:...Good movies: "Canadian Bacon" by Michael Moore ("Roger & Me") a goofy anti-USA anti-Canada satire worth checking out. "The English Man Who Went Up a Hill..." with Hugh-how-was-I-supposed-to-know-she...-Grant was fun. Right now Barb is watching "The Parent Trap" with Haley Mills. We've been renting mostly older films as the shelves have been almost empty due to everyone's huddling instincts.

Rehana

It's -40 odd here, yuck.

Wynne and Peter

message one: It is mighty cold here, -45 this morning. I even had to drive downtown which was quite the experience because you really could hardly see the car in front of you. My only hope was that everyone felt the same way I did and was therefore driving very slowly. Also, I was glad to know the twists and turns of the road.

This cold spell started last weekend and is expected to go into next week.

message two: We were talking tonite about recording the weather station...cold wave warning...wind warning...blizzard ...snow on the passes...bleak!!!

Joelle

It's so cold here that I can't even go to Brownies or skating. But of course I still have to go to school. Yuk!!

Yvonne

These are the e-mail reports thus far. Today it really does feel like Whitehorse in Victoria, with wind chill it is minus 20 which is mighty cold for this place. There go the rhododendrons, talk to you soon. Yvonne

SEASONAL IMPAIRMENTS

by Dan Davidson

ne of the annoying things about walking around outdoors at -42 is that you can't see your feet.

It's true. Put your hood up, fasten the flaps securely across your mouth, wrap around a scarf to protect your nose, and then try to look down. You'll have to bend over to do it.

If you're like me, this lack of peripheral vision comes at the time when you probably need it the most. I'm not planning to take on the job of shovelling out my front walk until things warm up later in the week. As a result, the boardwalk is an uneven jumble of drifted snow and footprints left over from the day before the temperature plummeted.

Between the stairs down from the front deck and the two smaller stairs at the gate, I begin to wonder if I will make it to the street. I have visions of completing the journey on my back, ending with a splitting headache. Maybe this is why the kids always want to slide down the stairs in the morning?

Somehow or other, without being really aware of it, I normally get subliminal visual clues as to where my legs are. But in this get-up, I always manage to feel like a video camera with the sound turned off. The world has a definite frame around it, and the hood muffles my hearing to the point where I generally can't hear the person next to me over the crunching sound my feet are making in the snow.

The two-block walk to the school is easy by comparison with my own yard, but my tunnel vision and diminished hearing are once again a nuisance at intersections. It seems unlikely that anything on wheels would be out on a day like this unless it is absolutely necessary. But I try to keep up the habit of looking both ways, so that I won't forget to when I'm walking with my kids. You other parents out there have probably noticed how many things you have to remember to do (or not do) when you're trying to set a good example.

So here I am at the corner. A quick turn to right and left and what do I see? The inside of my hood, that's what! I have to turn my upper body from the waist in order to check out the street. Nothing there. I haven't seen a vehicle moving since the garbage truck stopped in the back lane earlier in the day.

Onward I go and whoops! What was that? Bending over again, I find that I have stepped on a chunk of ice.

No more mishaps until I get to the school. It has an impressive-looking front facade, which features some big steps. I consider taking the handicapped ramp, but figure it might be slippery, so up the stairs I go. Not bad. I only trip once.

The trip back is a cinch. I've already done it in the other direction. I even miss the ice chunk. The only thing is, I left my gear on during the 10 minutes that I spent picking up the stack of papers I wanted to grade at home, and now I am what my grandmother used to call "a reek of sweat." She meant the condition of having perspiration running freely all over you, rather than the smell of it, as you might have assumed from the expression. In my case, there is a small river flowing down my spine, and another trickle on my forehead that seems to be freezing.

Steam is gushing from the scarf over my mouth and nose, and I am glad that I wore my contact lenses for this expedition or I'd be totally blind right now instead of just blinkered.

Home. Right. Now up the stairs and in the front door. Enough of this nonsense until tomorrow when I have to do it again. Sometime during the day, some youngster will ask me why we don't have a cut-off temperature for going to school. There is a good answer, but she or he won't like it any better than I do just now.

ILLUSTRATION: WYATT TREMBLAY

Blubber

by S.D. Picot

"Hey, let go
Of my blubber,
it's insulation
for the winter
ya know."

But she knew the extra layer around her gut was protection from other things, like boredom.

Entire dogteams succumb to cold

Yukon—An adverse event of considerable economic consequence attracted worldwide notoriety during the first quarter of 1947. A cold wave, beginning around the middle of January, blanketed the entire Yukon for almost four weeks, and at Snag the all-time North American minimum was shattered when a temperature of 84 degrees below zero was officially recorded. Game suffered considerably, a heavy toll being taken on rabbits and muskrats, while most predators holed up during the extreme weather. Reports reached the agency of entire dogteams succumbing to the unprecedented cold, leaving Indians without any means whatever of transportation. Trappers were unable to leave their cabins, while elderly indigent Indians were reduced to the lowest depths of sustenance.

• *Department of Mines & Resources, Indian Affairs Branch, 1946/47 Annual Report, p. 206*

ANOTHER DAY IN PARADISE

lyrics by Marty Waldman

It's freezing cold in bed, wake up you sleepy-head,
Go to the woodstove, and start another fire
Splitting kindling in your shorts and your rubber-boots,
Breathe out ice-clouds as you respire.
Boil some tea, and try to start the truck,
With your tiger-torch,
Blast of flame will melt the oil,
And bring icicles crashing down on the porch, and it's...

Another day in Paradise, the sun rises up through the ice fog.
Another day in Paradise, unfreeze that water line.
Another day in Paradise, listen to that chain saw choke at 50 below.
Another day in Paradise, a Yukon paradise, oh yeah!

And if Spring don't come too late this year,
We'll take the chains off when we go to town,
There's mud on the floor, wall, ceiling, and kids,
Hose the dog and the daughter down.
There's a pile of sawdust five feet high,
Blocking up the whole driveway,
How'd those mosquitoes get so big, rescue the cat, grab a baseball bat,
Drive them away, buzz, buzz, buzz...

Another day in Paradise, sawdust trail from the door.
Another day in Paradise, there's a hump in the living room floor.
Another day in Paradise, there's flooding on the Marsh Lake Road again.
Another day in Paradise, a Yukon paradise, oh yeah!

Hey, get that sunscreen on your body, man,
Where the hell do you think you are anyway, the Bahamas?

It's the middle of July and finally warm enough to sleep
Without five layers of pyjamas.
They finally got real good fruit at the grocery store,
No more smell, feel, taste, like wood,
Garden's finally growing and the backyard's full
Of every kid in the neighbourhood, and it's...

Another day in Paradise, where the sun shines day and night
Another day in Paradise, we're barbecuing everything in sight
Another day in Paradise, damn that blackfly bite
Another day in Paradise, a Yukon paradise, oh yeah!

Send the kids on back to school, it's time to start another year
Leaves come down, insulation goes up, time to start another beer
Time to pull out the snow-boots and the long underwear, order firewood
Just one more day in paradise, I tell you, man, this life is good, and it's...

Another day in Paradise, like a wheel going round and round,
Another day in Paradise, white snow on the sandy ground
Another day in Paradise, the Rendezvous can't come too soon
Another day in Paradise, a Yukon paradise, oh yeah, and it's...

Another day in Paradise, no more a city-living slob
Another day in Paradise, but I could use a better paying job
Another day in Paradise, the pickup finally died
Another day in Paradise, a Yukon paradise, oh yeah!

© 1991

PHOTO: SHELLEY GERBER

UNDER A SPREADING CEDAR TREE
THE WANING CHUM SALMON SAILS
HE ONCE WAS A MIGHTY FISH
WITH BRIGHT AND SHINY SCALES
AND THE MUSCLES IN HIS BRAWNY TAIL
WERE AS STRONG AS A TEN PENNY NAIL
BUT NOW HE FADES IN FLESH AND BLOOD
AS HIS MEAT IT TURNS TO MUD;
CALICO STRIPES OF GREEN AND RED
DECORATE THE DYING STUD;
HIS NOSE IS HOOKED AND NASTY
AND HIS MOUTH IS A TOOTHY MESS;
HE ONLY LONGS TO PROCREATE
BEFORE THE FINAL REST.
AHEAD HE SPOTS A TIRED HEN
HER BELLY THICK WITH ROE.
GALLANTLY, HE OFFERS TO
MAKE HIS FINS A GRAVEL HOE.
SHE ENCOURAGES HIM WITH HER POSTURE
AND AN INVITATION TO CALL HER KATE
BUT AFTER SMILING COYLY
SHE ACCEPTS ANOTHER DATE.
CRANKY FROM HIS JOURNEY,
HE STARTS A RUTTING WAR;
BUT THE DETAILS OF HIS BATTLE, GENTLE READERS WOULD DEPLORE.
TO FAVOR FISH DECORUM, I WILL SAY NO MORE.
NOR WILL I TELL OF THE ACTS THAT BENT
OUR BRAVE CHUM'S BACK.
LET'S JUST SAY HE FLOATED AWAY
WITH A SMILE AND AN EMPTY PACK.

DOG SALMON DOGGEREL
WORDS: DAN BRANCH ▲ ART: KAREN LYBRAND

MOOSE FACTS
Canadian alces

Moose are the largest deer in the world. Their humped shoulders, long gangly legs, stubby tail, huge nose, large ears and massive antlers (male) make these creatures look as if they were thrown together from "spare parts". Often larger than a horse, an angry or even irritated moose can cause harm or heavy damage. Females with calves are very protective and can charge with great speed. Rutting bulls have been known to charge people, horses, cars and even trains.

The moose usually avoids humans and is generally a "loner" but several may gather near streams and lakes to feed on willows or water lilies. They submerge themselves or roll in mud to find relief from the flies and mosquitoes that torment them. Moose migrate seasonally and may herd in winter, which helps to pack the deep snow making movement easier.

During mating season (September to October) bulls can be heard thrashing the brush with their antlers or bellowing loudly. Battles between males rarely cause death, but if the antlers interlock both may perish. Females usually bear one or two calves in the spring.

Moose are an important food source for people of the north and their numbers are protected to ensure their survival. Like other large animals, their ranges have been reduced in size but they flourish in sparsely populated areas of Alaska and Canada.

Remember, if you see any moose in the wild: Treat them with respect AND BE CAREFUL!

CONTENTS: ONE FUZZY MOOSE

7 72739 01200 4

NORTHERN GIFTS LTD.
1-800-665-0808

CANNED IN CANADA

CANNED MOOSE

These moose have been known to lie in wait under your covers and snuggle you to sleep.

CAN LABEL: NORTHERN GIFTS LTD.

A YEAR IN THE LIFE OF A MOOSE

Spring: As the snow cover begins to melt and flow downslope to the frozen stream beds, pregnant cow moose look for safe and secluded places to give birth. Calves are born from mid-May to mid-June. Some cows birth at tree line in the subalpine zone, while others birth at river level in the valley bottoms. In the southwest Yukon, grizzlies, which spend much of their time in the subalpine in spring, kill about 50 percent of each year's calves. Most of these kills are made before the calves reach eight weeks of age. Wolves take fewer newborns than grizzlies, but continue to prey on the older calves year-round.

Moose have a high reproductive rate. Many cows breed for the first time at one and a half years of age and every year or two afterwards. Where food is plentiful, twins are common and triplets are occasionally born. In the Yukon, about 30 percent of pregnant cows give birth to twins.

From late spring through summer, moose feed on the new buds and fresh growths of willow. Aquatic plants, like the yellow pond lily, draw the long-legged moose out into ponds and lakes.

Antler development begins in April or May, first in older bulls and last in yearlings. During the growth period, the soft spongy antlers are covered with a dark brown, velvety skin.

Summer: Waterways are important feeding areas for moose, but they also provide escape routes from the ever-present danger of predators. When pursued by wolves or bears, moose head for water where their long legs give them an advantage.

Moose are browsers; in a single day, adults can consume about 20 kilograms of twigs, leaves, shrubs and other land and water plants. A ruminant, like the domestic cow, they have a series of stomachs to help digest their woody diet and can sometimes be seen chewing their cud.

Calves that survive grow dramatically over their first summer. Adding as much as two kilograms per day, they weigh about 180 kilograms by autumn.

Fall: Cow moose can experience three estrous or breeding periods in the fall. The second estrous, which occurs between the last week of September and the first week of October, is the period of greatest fertility.

Rutting, which commonly occurs at treeline in the subalpine zone, brings new sounds to the landscape. The coughs, grunts, and bellows of bull moose are heard along with rubbing of antlers against trees and the calls of the cows. Finally, the clash of antler to antler resounds as two bulls collide and begin their shoving match.

Dominant bulls try to keep lesser bulls away from their group of cows, which can number up to ten or more. At the same time, the bulls continually monitor their cows, ready to mate with any that come into estrous. All in all, it's an incredibly demanding time for these bulls. They stop eating for a month or so during the rut, their necks swell and they become unusually aggressive. But it's short-lived power they wield. When the rut is over in October, many of the dominant bulls are exhausted, undernourished, and have lost up to 20 percent of their weight. Sometimes the price for perpetuating his genes is a weakened state that leaves the bull more vulnerable to potential causes of mortality.

Prime bulls drop their antlers from late November through February, while young bulls lag a month or more behind.

Winter: Winter is a season of reduced food supplies for moose, and increased predation by wolves.

Fresh willow buds, leaves and aquatic plants are no longer available. Forage is restricted to the woody twigs of poplar, birch, alder and willow. In late winter, when food supplies are at their lowest, some moose move into aspen stands and use their front teeth to scrape the bark down to the nutritious layer of cambium underneath. In parts of Kluane National Park and other areas of heavy snowfall, many moose will move down to the lower valleys as winter progresses.

An average Yukon wolf pack (seven to nine wolves) will kill one moose every five or six days through the winter. Although wolves tend to concentrate on calves and on older moose, any moose can be vulnerable to wolf predation, depending on the terrain, snow conditions, and its response to attack. By backing into a thicket of trees, a moose can fend off wolves with its powerful front hooves. Generally, a moose that remains stationary can successfully defend itself from wolves, while a moose that flees is attacked from the rear and often brought down.

by Yukon Government

ILLUSTRATION: JENNIFER STANIFORTH

34

MOST OF US, BUT NOT GORDIE

by Skeeter Wright

One of the advantages of working in the Yukon bush is having the chance to see the wildlife. Birds, moose, caribou and bear sightings are not rare. Most of us working for the mining exploration outfit that summer appreciated wildlife sightings. Most of us, but not Gordie.

When in camp, talk was usually about the staking job. That's when you're given a starting point, a particular compass bearing to follow and responsibility for bushwacking through dense bush for so many claim lengths of half a kilometre apiece before the helicopter meets you at a place in the bush marked on the map.

Anyway, our talk was about the job where you had to climb a rock face to avoid a multi-mile detour, or the stream you practically had to swim across because the trees were all too big to cut quickly enough to make a bridge, or the helicopter pilot who suggested letting you off on a tree top rather than trying to set down in a maze of spruce trees. Or the time you got chased by a mama grizzly and her cub.

Gord was one of the best with our outfit. He could cover more ground on a staking job or cut more line in a day with a bad chainsaw than any of us could with a good saw. He was good at his job and a nice guy as well. Maybe that's why the rest of us respected his fear of bears. We never told bear stories when Gord was around. Stories about the friend lost in a helicopter crash or the time Tony almost died when he fell down an ice chute to the rocks below were okay, but not bear stories. Our respect for Gordie was such that we avoided all the numerous bear stories that a bunch of bushers had in their repertoire.

I never did find out why Gord was so sensitive about bears, but what happened that one particular day of staking must have reinforced whatever had happened before.

As I said, Gord was one of the best. He could keep one eye on the compass and the other on the ground ahead while almost running through the bush, tying survey tape to branches and blazing trees with his axe to mark a clear trail. A good claimstaker can mark a straight trail and make up for the time lost cutting and writing the required information on claim posts every 500 metres.

That one day Gord was apparently doing really well. He had almost finished his numerous kilometres of claimstaking when he noticed a black bulky mass ahead. It was a black bear. He later said he didn't even think. He just dropped his axe and didn't waste time taking off his bulky staking vest. He grabbed the nearest tree and climbed. He said he never took his eyes off that bear. Not because he was afraid of losing sight of it. Just because he was so scared he couldn't pry his sight away from it.

Eventually, he climbed high enough up that spruce that he could take his eyes off the bear. Gord later explained he wasn't finished climbing. The tree trunk had thinned considerably and he just wanted to look up to see how much tree was left to climb. No reason to waste a good high spruce when there was a bear around. Use every last inch of that trunk.

Apparently the tree continued up a ways because Gord said he couldn't see the topmost branches. But what was interesting was that he saw more dark than light. He said he had expected to see blue sky in between the branches since he was so high. He wasn't sure how long it took, a minute or less maybe, until he realized it wasn't darkness up there. It was blackness. Black like black bear. Two black bear cubs. He had picked the tree up which mama black bear had sent her two cubs for safekeeping while she rummaged around for food or something near by.

Gord said he wasn't too sure if he climbed or fell, but he was on the ground mighty fast. Mama bear didn't seem to notice him until he was on the ground, but when she did, she moved fast. Gord said he was into the next tree in seconds, and she was at the base of the first one just as fast. She called the kids down and the three of them were gone in less time than it took the really scared Gordie to get anywhere near the top of the second tree.

That all happened years ago and most of us have gone on to spending our days in less dramatic and less story-producing endeavours. But I do wonder at times what it was that gave Gordie his very first bear scare.

ANIMALS

Bear Malling

Captivated by Caribou

e t c h i n g   a n d   s t o r y   b y   J o y c e   M a j i s k i

"So what is it about you and caribou anyway?" I often get asked. Well, it's like this. I feel a kindred spirit with them. Caribou are really curious animals—at times tending towards the goofy side with their antics. Longish legged, they hold their heads high and run with their legs flinging out in all directions. Now, I can't say I have ever seen myself run, but I am kind of leggy and some people have told me that I also fling my legs out in all directions when I run. Hmmm.

Caribou, like myself, also seem to like being on the move, especially the Porcupine caribou herd which migrates huge distances from their southern wintering areas to northern calving grounds. With a species name like Rangifer, what else could you do but roam the range? My north/south migration has become an annual affair as well, and I see no reason to fight a perfectly good natural inclination.

It seems that caribou like adventure. They will ride the spring ice floes if the river isn't completely clear of ice—even if it isn't

such a great idea—and they also spend a great deal of time milling about deciding which rapid is best to ford. I personally don't go about crossing ice-choked rivers, but I have often found myself on the bank, scouting some rapid, and I have also found myself in some rapids that weren't really such a great idea to run. Oops.

We also share a propensity for linguistics as I can snort, bark and grunt along with the best of them, although I do have the added advantage of being able to gesticulate in several other languages. Caribou also know how to have a good time and they take great delight in flying off at top speed in all directions just for the sheer fun of it. Now, I'm not as bad as my friend, Wendy, the "Whirling Dervish" of Banff, but a close second, I'm told.

There is a restlessness about caribou, as if they are afraid to sit still for too long. Constant movement helps to outfox the flies but it's hard to keep the pounds on. My excuse is outrunning the mosquitoes but it really is my secret fear of middle-

aged spread that keeps me on the move.

There are a few other things—like their huge feet and big noses—but I don't want this to get too personal. Nevertheless, it seems we have a few things in common, these caribou and I.

It's a cross between fascination and hilarity to watch caribou antics. Once, while working on the tundra, I watched a female make a huge circle downwind of me, stopping to stare and bob her head the whole time. When she finally caught my scent she did the characteristic caribou leap and snort, then took off like a shot (legs flying everywhere of course). Not more than five minutes later, she stopped and was back to replay the whole scene again—three times!

Caribou inspire me. Because of their nature and their migration, in essence, they represent to me the last vestiges of freedom and wilderness in the far north. So I will always have a spot in my heart, and on the page, for one of my favourite animals, the curious caribou.

Old Crow Flats a moose mecca

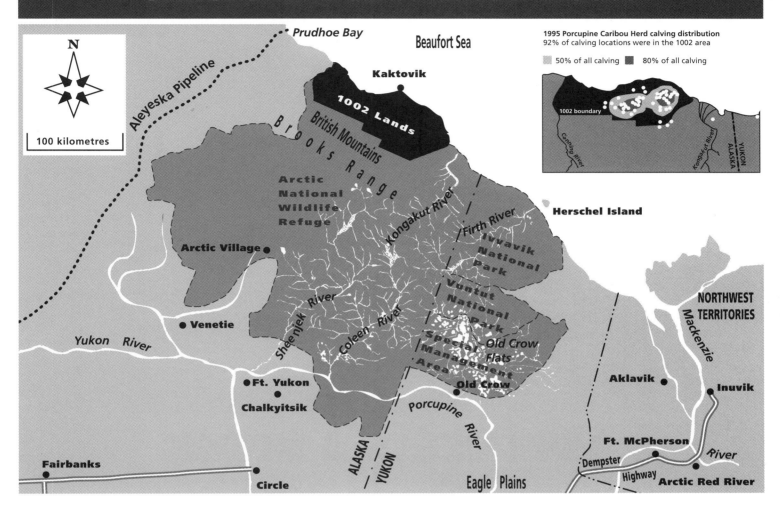

Prudhoe Bay
Beaufort Sea
Kaktovik
1002 Lands
British Mountains
Brooks Range
Arctic National Wildlife Refuge
Arctic Village
Firth River
Kongakut River
Ivvavik National Park
Herschel Island
Aleyeska Pipeline
N
100 kilometres
Venetie
Yukon River
Sheenjek River
Coleen River
Vuntut National Park
Special Management Area
Old Crow Flats
NORTHWEST TERRITORIES
Mackenzie
Ft. Yukon
Chalkyitsik
Old Crow
Porcupine River
Aklavik
Inuvik
Fairbanks
Circle
ALASKA / YUKON
Eagle Plains
Dempster Highway
Ft. McPherson
Arctic Red River
River

1995 Porcupine Caribou Herd calving distribution
92% of calving locations were in the 1002 area
■ 50% of all calving   ■ 80% of all calving
1002 boundary
Canning River
Kongakut River
YUKON / ALASKA

A N I M A L S

ran Mauer, a biologist with the United States Fish and Wildlife Service, has been documenting one of the most intriguing ecological discoveries in the history of northern wildlife.

It concerns the moose, of all species, about which almost everything appeared to be known, none of it very exciting.

As part of its mandate to manage wildlife in Alaska's Arctic National Wildlife Refuge, the service has been monitoring moose there since the early 1970s.

Through such studies, the service learned that moose become concentrated in valleys of Alaska's Brooks Range during winter. However, it also became apparent that these same valleys contained relatively few moose during the rest of the year.

Mauer wanted to know where the moose go in spring, so his interest was piqued when Yukon biologist Rick Farnell suggested that the Brooks Range moose were coming from the Yukon. In early April of 1995, Mauer radio-collared 57 moose (44 cows and 13 bulls) along the Sheenjek, Coleen and Kongakut rivers of the Arctic Refuge, as well as near the Firth River in Canada's Ivvavik National Park.

A week later, Mauer returned to check on the moose and found that most of them were gone. Of the 12 collared in the Kongakut, nine had already left. During May, Mauer tracked the movements of these and other moose, all of

which wound up in the Yukon's Old Crow Flats. A cautious scientist, Mauer discussed his findings with other biologists. He is now confident that these unusual moose are a bona fide migratory population.

He finds it very unusual that the majority of moose on the winter range are migratory. Migrating moose are a minority in other populations where this behaviour has been observed.

Of the 57 moose originally collared, 70 to 75 percent migrated. We're talking serious numbers here. In 1991, the U.S. Fish and Wildlife Service counted 722 moose in several of the major river drainages where the animals winter.

The length of this migration is also remarkable. The longest straight-line distance was about 200 kilometres for a moose which left the Sheenjek drainage and crossed the Coleen River Valley—not to mention the Continental Divide—to reach Old Crow Flats in the Yukon.

This far exceeds movements previously recorded for wandering moose. For example, on the Tanana River near Fairbanks, moose travel about 50 kilometres between the foothills of the Alaska Range and the White Mountains.

But why go to all this trouble to reach Old Crow Flats? Mauer calls the Flats a "moose mecca" because of the abundant food available there, both as aquatic vegetation in the numerous shallow lakes and luxuriant willow growth in partially drained lake beds. There may

also be other reasons known only to the moose, such as fewer predators or better escape habitat. Moose are typically considered a pretty stay-at-home species, so the astonishing distances travelled by these northern moose puts one in mind of the Porcupine caribou herd. In fact, the moose could be spring travelling companions of the caribou as they head to the 1002 section of the Arctic Refuge to bear their young.

The irony of this situation will not be lost on anyone familiar with the 1002 issue: the Yukon has the Alaskans' calving ground and the Alaskans have the Yukon's.

Fortunately, the calving grounds of the Alaskan moose in Old Crow Flats is protected by Vuntut National Park.

This park was created through the Vuntut Gwich'in land claims settlement and required six major oil companies to extinguish their leases in the Flats.

The opposite situation applies to the Porcupine caribou calving ground in the Arctic Refuge. There are no oil leases there now, but it could be blanketed with development in the near future if some Alaskans have their way.

But perhaps this revelation in the ever-expanding saga of the Arctic Refuge will encourage Canada and the U.S. to cut a deal. We'll tend your garden and you tend ours—migratory moose for migratory caribou.

by Doug Urquhart

MIKE MEETS A MOOSE

by Mike Hodgson

Canoeing in the early spring is a joy. Rivers are high and fast. The bush is fresh with new life. Insects are rare and so are the tourists.

Spring runoff makes rivers go where they usually don't. When the water volume triples, you get all sizes of channels looping away from the main river. When I see a tributary wide enough to take my canoe—off I go. I'm a sucker for them. It's like the opening of a door for a brief magical moment. Sometimes, however, this magic becomes a little too intense.

In the middle of May 1994, I had been paddling the upper Nisutlin for about three hours. This was a gentle paddle with no rapids or portages. It was my chance to do some exploring, some reading and to photograph some wildlife. It was closing on lunch when I saw a stream wandering into the willows. "Okay," I thought, "one last side trip before I stop and make tea."

The stream, though it appeared to run deep, was quite narrow. There was about a foot to spare on each side of the canoe. Sometimes these channels wither into nothing and you have to haul your canoe back upstream. This one, though, wandered into thick willows before breaking into an open area of grasses and reeds.

It was here that a big moose stood up about twenty yards in front of me. It looked straight at me and didn't run away. Now most of my moose photos involve a moose's butt-end disappearing into the bush. They get a whiff of me and bolt for the thick willows. This one didn't. It would be a terrific shot and I wasn't going to miss it. I slowly picked up my camera and took off the lens cap. Then I saw the calf. It was a newborn, bounding about, discovering the world. The first moose was no dullard without the wits to run away. This was Mama Moose, defending her babe from the world. As I drifted closer she stamped her front hooves as if to say "today, a man with glasses dies." The current, at about three miles an hour, would take me within two feet of her. Picture an average size man kneeling in a canoe. The top of my head is about four feet above the water line. An angry mother moose, standing on solid ground, could take off my head with an effortless flick of her hoof. The smart thing would have been to get out of the canoe and retreat to the main river. Unfortunately, I had been kneeling for most of the morning and my legs were asleep. Extracting them from under the seat would have involved some uncontrolled floundering about. In the meantime, Mama Moose would have decided that I was obviously a calf killer and crushed my spine. So, hoping her sense of smell had somehow short-circuited over the winter, I pretended to be a log. A sweating and quaking log—but a log all the same.

In the wild, making eye contact is considered a sign of aggression. So when meeting a potentially hostile creature, don't stare. I knew this. However, I wasn't going to take my eyes off her. If I was going to die, I wanted to stare death in the face. As the canoe glided by, my head turned on my shoulders. I could have been that kid in the Exorcist. I watched the moose and the moose watched me. I was close enough to count the individual hairs on her hide. I could see the season's first mosquitoes landing on her nose. I could smell her. I was that close.

All the while her calf was making calf noises and prancing around. Her new-born was having fun, and that's what probably saved me from becoming the headless canoeist. If the babe had made the wrong noise at the wrong time, the mother's primordial brain would have given her forelegs the clear message to "smash the log." She would have kicked a field goal with my head. I would have glided, headless, back onto the main river and slowly back to my home town. On the upside, I would be a part of Yukon mythology. Something to scare young children with for generations to come. On the down side, unfortunately, I would be quite dead.

In the end, I passed her without incident. My head, however, had rotated much further than it should have. A manoeuvre which, years later, still causes me pain. When I last saw Mama Moose, she was looking over her shoulder at me and urinating in the water. This seemed, somehow, appropriate. I put the lens cap back on the camera and continued my journey.

Walk through our backyard, pass the greenhouse and the vegetable garden, head down a short section of trail through aspen and pine forest and you come to Wolf Creek. The small clear stream lies about six metres below a steep bank. It runs over a cobbled bottom, threading its way through old beaver dams.

Wolf Creek is our connection with the wild, a corridor of life running behind our rural residential suburb in Whitehorse. We've seen moose, and plenty of moose droppings, in the meadow across the creek. Black bears have ambled through our yard, headed up from the creek. But we'd lived here for more than a year before we experienced what makes Wolf Creek truly remarkable.

Chinook salmon are spawning again in these waters. Just downstream of us, salmon end a 3,000-kilometre journey up the Yukon River from the Bering Sea. They're part of the longest chinook salmon river migration in the world.

Three thousand kilometres. That's the distance between San Francisco and Winnipeg. Imagine swimming against a strong current for that distance. Maybe a better analogy for humans would be running against a strong headwind between those two cities. Or maybe it's useless to look for analogies because humans can't fathom what drives a spawning salmon.

While swimming up the Yukon River, mature salmon must avoid the nets of Alaskan and Yukon fishers, the jaws of hungry bears and the hooks of avid anglers. Twenty kilometres downstream of here, they have to ascend the longest wooden fish ladder in the world. Along the way they pass innumerable small streams, but somehow they know to turn right at Wolf Creek. And, during this entire epic journey, they don't eat.

Now the fish were so close we could have scooped them up with our hands. And they were still pushing. It looked to me like there were many perfectly good spawning areas just below us. But these fish were going for broke. They were continuing their upstream struggle even though that effort required one last desperate leap up the fishway below the culvert.

The salmon would gather their strength in the calm waters at the sides of the pool before attempting the one-metre jump. Then they'd disappear in the foaming water underneath the spillway as they got into position. Suddenly, you'd see them rocketing straight up through the waterfall, powering their way with forceful strokes of their tails.

Chinook are the largest and strongest species of Pacific salmon, but this final jump was too much for most of these fish. It was agonizing to watch them try so hard, only to fall back into the lower pool. We

salmon in one short section of the creek.

We walked slowly down the creek, pointing out the salmon to our four-year-old son, trying to tell which ones were actively scooping out hollows for their eggs. A man standing on the opposite bank asked a few questions about the fish. His accent indicated that he was an American, probably a tourist staying overnight in the campground on his way back from Alaska.

Two school-age children were playing nearby. The man obviously knew the kids, but I wasn't sure if he was their father. But still I waited for him to play the parental role when the older child began picking up rocks.

The boy's intentions were obvious, but the man seemed unconcerned. Even when the boy began firing rocks at a salmon resting in the water, the man said nothing. When the boy began picking up more rocks, I intervened.

"Don't throw rocks at that fish. That salmon has swum all the way from the ocean to lay its eggs in this spot. It's not moving because it's exhausted. It deserves respect."

The boy looked surprised. The father registered little response of any kind. I could tell I wasn't going to get any backup from that quarter. The boy tried another tack.

"How about that dead one. Can I throw rocks at it?"

BACKYARD SALMON

by Sarah Locke

Salmon disappeared from Wolf Creek in the 1970s. In 1985, an ambitious restocking program was started. Every June, community members put on their gum boots and help release hatchery-raised fry into the creek. It's taken seven years of effort to bring mature fish back to this creek.

The very first time that my husband, son and I went to look for spawning salmon, we were treated to an amazing display.

Six bright-red salmon were swimming in a small pool below the highway culvert. The fish looked thoroughly bruised and battered, with scales ripped off their humped bodies and gashes on their snouts. They all looked like survivors that had beaten the odds.

Few bookies would care to lay odds on any particular fry returning to Wolf Creek. They have a one in four chance of surviving the downstream trip to the ocean and a one in a hundred chance of becoming an adult. Then the real challenge begins.

became streamside cheerleaders, applauding softly when one of them actually reached the upper pool. These were our hometown fish. We wanted them to succeed.

It's admittedly anthropocentric to feel possessive about members of a wild species because they're in your backyard. But I do. I want this salmon run to continue. The fish disappeared from Wolf Creek around the time our subdivision and the campground were built. It would be encouraging to think we could now co-exist with the salmon.

I didn't realize just how protective I felt about these fish until one incident last summer. We had a record run—242 fish went through the weir at the mouth of Wolf Creek, double the expected number.

We'd gone down to the campground during the height of the run, and couldn't believe the number of fish below the culvert. The shallow water was barely deep enough to cover the fish, but obviously it suited their purposes. We counted 15

After vetoing that idea as well, I tried explaining why these fish shouldn't be used for target practice. They were laying eggs; they were exhausted; they were part of a run just being re-established on this creek. I was trying to explain that he was witnessing a miracle, but I could tell that I was just another adult spoiling his fun.

The incident made me realize how vulnerable the fish are to people who don't know anything about them. Maybe they'd be more curious, more respectful, if they had any idea what these fish have been through.

In this small run, every single fish that returns to its spawning grounds is important. Every fish is a major success story.

So far this year we've spotted only one salmon in the creek behind our house. If we're lucky, my son will grow up watching wild salmon return to his backyard creek every summer. It's a gift I hope he never takes for granted.

Grizzly bears! Oh, no! The big bad wolf! Oh my! But what about the...

Dangers of the dark

It's dark out. We draw straws for first watch. None of us can sleep anyway, the tension is so great. The full moon climbs across the sky, silhouetting a breathtaking view of the mountains. Confrontation seems inevitable, but how can we protect ourselves?

Hours crawl by. Terrifying forest sounds reach our wooded wilderness abode—the rustling, murmuring, scratching, gnawing of unseen predators, waiting for the perfect moment to attack.

We are defenceless in the night and huddle together, periodically tossing firewood in the direction of the melee. Our circled wagons somehow keep us safe.

In the first light of dawn we take stock. Almost everything escaped injury and dismemberment. Unfortunately, the bottom half of the outhouse door had been chewed off, all the way up to the door handle. Facilities not for the shy and retiring.

The Yukon is fraught with danger at every fork in the trail. Weather. Wildlife. Geography. And porcupines!

On the trail to the biffie sits a quill pig, delicately clasping in her front paws a large bright yellow Arnica. Her lips curl around the flower top. Snap. Snip. Gone. Even though I weigh five times her weight, I am no match for her. Her lumpish body is protected by 30,000 needle-sharp quills which can flair up in a punk-like hairdo if she's threatened. Each quill tip has numerous barbs that quickly disappear in the flesh of its victim, making the most ferocious predator think twice about dinner.

A bushy brow seems to cock in my direction, beady rodent eyes squint at me. She's unafraid, but still this pokey, mild-mannered porcupine lumbers away, climbs the closest tree and sits there mumbling and grumbling.

Porkies are everywhere. In trees. Alpine meadows. Amongst the willows. They've even been seen crossing glaciers, and I have the photos to prove it. What it was doing there in high alpine country, clambering up a 35 degree slope, I don't know.

Where do they fit in really? There's been lots of research done on our big sexy Rocky Mountain mammals. We're starting to get a better handle on how they fit into the ecological balance. But the lowly quill pig? So far, most humans think they're just a nuisance!

When camping, the quill pig will find your improperly stored boots, pack or saltines. There's a reason for this. Sodium and teeth. Their taste for salt, coupled with long, continuously growing incisors, shortens the life span of our northern biffies. Any item touched by the salt from human perspiration can attract a porcupine.

Outhouse seats are favourites. Boots. Clothing. Aluminium boats. The rubber hoses in car engines. In the midst of porcupine country, gangs of marauding quill pigs can flatten all four of your truck tires, just like (bandits) punks in the inner city. In some parts of the mountainous west, people completely cover their vehicles with chicken wire before heading into the back country.

That's a scary amount of damage from a mammal that weighs between ten and thirty pounds and is mostly known for not looking both ways before crossing the street.

First Nations people used quills to finely decorate birch bark baskets and moccasins. Nowadays we still trade for this art form, using cash instead of Hudson's Bay blankets. On a fine summer evening in 1859, the first tourist to the Rockies, the Earl of Southesk, had porcupine for dinner. He remarked that "it tasted much like siffleur (gopher or marmot), too rich and fat."

Porkies are vegetarians, chewing bark from one tree to the next. I imagine that somehow this fits into the predator/prey concept in the great circle of life and helps keep the forest healthy, but I'm not quite sure how.

I lean back in the sun against a bark-stripped aspen poplar, squinting up at my gnawing buddy. I admire her piercingly particular personality. I am amazed by the porcupine's seeming impudence in the search for salt—trusting quill armour to protect life and limb from even semi-trucks, perambulating slowly about her business, merely blinking at interruption and, in the cover of darkness, not to be deterred.

story and illustrations by Wendy Bush

STRAIGHT TO THE POINT

by Wendy Bush

Cerebrally deficient. Motivationally challenged. Dull. Dimwitted. Lumpish. Witless. Slow. Hit 'em with a stick and they still come back to eat your boots. Mother evolution takes strange turns and this is one of them.

The porcupine's quills are hollow spears; a defence mechanism unequalled in the rodent kingdom. Approximately 30,000 barbs cover a porcupine's body.

The African porcupine has 16-inch quills, much like spears. When threatened, this animal abruptly stops and runs backwards, impaling the attacker. Serious business! None the less, bobcats, wolverines, fishers and great horned owls have managed to figure out a strategy. Grab 'er by the nose, flip 'er over, slash 'er stomach open. It's a myth that our North American species can throw quills. Not so. But those quills are so loosely attached to the skin that they separate on contact and embed themselves. Sometimes the quills work their way through muscles and flesh, penetrating the brain weeks later and killing the predator. Mostly though, porcupines are left alone and Ms. Quill Pig goes about her business unmolested.

The point is, the porcupine hasn't had to think about protecting itself over the last million years or so. The quills do it. Maybe that's not so stupid after all.

So drive carefully—protect a porcupine.
This message brought to you by: Canadian Porcupine Service • Bureau porc-pic canadien

THE SEX LIFE OF ERETHIZON DORSATUM

What did the male porcupine say to the female porcupine after they had an amorous adventure? "I'm stuck on you!"

Porcupines are solitary creatures by nature. They seldom get chummy enough to bunk two to a den. Snuggling up spoon-style isn't going to work with these guys!

So how do they do it? "Very carefully" is the typically glib answer. But the first obstacle is finding one another! These nocturnal beasts mainly rely on scent to find food. They're scarcely able to see groceries when they are right before their eyes.

Scooting the quiller

A N I M A L S

by Ginna Sue Copland

The Texas-style image grew as I drove home in the soft Alaskan dusk. A full-size pickup was parked along the road. A trim woman with shoulder-length blond hair, close-fitting jeans, and a snug T-shirt stood behind the pickup. A blond, a pickup, and a highway. She was bent over a dark-brown object the size of a gym bag, and held an empty plastic shopping bag. As I drove past, I realized she was trying to herd a porcupine off the road into the field.

I had migrated from the baked heat of the flat southwest to the cool Alaskan mountains. Automobiles had also roamed north and left pitiful road kills in their swath. Instead of slow tortoises and armadillos, the cars in the frontier state ambush poorly sighted porcupines.

I smiled. My lousy day was suddenly brighter. This time there would not be a flat pincushion. I thought of stopping, offering a hand, and telling her how she had made my day, but there were cars behind me. The farther I drove, the more I wondered. How could she move the porcupine with the flimsy plastic bag? It could rattle its quills and drive them through the bag with a power that has been known to drill through thick leather boots. When I could, I turned around and drove back to ask her, but the woman, the pickup and the porcupine were gone. Only a collapsed plastic bag lay on the side of the road. But it was all right; in fact, I preferred my mysterious image of the trim cowgirl guiding a porcupine with a flimsy plastic bag.

To return to a favourite browsing tree, a quill pig will mark her trail with the musky scent of porcupine urine. To a male porcupine, the odour of the female's urine is the ultimate aphrodisiac. If he finds a place wet by a female, he will snatch up a pawful of damp soil, hold it to his nose and amble around on his hind legs as if savouring the bouquet. Buddy tracks his "objet d'amour," and to add to the excitement, ritually "anoints" her with his own scent. The female generally gives this fountain of urine a somewhat frosty reception. She might flee, bite the male, strike at him with her paws or emit shrill, piercing whines. Really though, she finds his waterfall of perfume wonderfully stimulating.

So after a lot of wrestling, chasing, screaming and more urine showers, the male takes the active role. Contrary to folklore, he mounts from the rear, his belly resting against the female's upturned tail. Coital contact is brief. Afterward Hubby has the proverbial cigarette by grooming and cleaning himself. The happy couple may get lucky a few more times until one or the other climbs a tree and ends the contact by hostile screaming and lunging.

Aren't you glad you know all that now? But remember, all those funny porcupine noises you've heard while summer camping are not from amorous couples. Wrong season. Females come into heat in October or November.

Madame Porcupine, after a pregnancy of seven months, has a single cute-as-a-button pup. Quills are soft at birth but harden within five or six hours.

"OUR SIDE"

C'mon C'mon it's easy......

50 YEARS OF CARNAGE
ALASKA HIGHWAY

In Taosim, there is a yin-yang aspect to every phenomenon and hence the yin-yang will represent the female and male, up and down, night and day. It is the latter phenomena that will be considered here.

I am referring to sex, the aerial kind, and the two times of day that the most common insects of the north, the mosquito and blackfly, are in blood-letting modes.

In addition to different circadian rhythms, these insects also breed and develop in different aquatic habitats. The mosquito does it in still or stagnant water and the blackfly needs moving water to aerate its developmental stages.

The blackfly larvae attach themselves to rocks with silken threads, a sucker and hooks, and look like a moss-coating on the rocks when they are in high numbers.

Skeeters, on the other hand, lay single eggs on quiet water or in dampish places that are subject to flooding. Shortly after, they become larvae or "wrigglers," as they are commonly known. On sunny days they dance the hula just under the surface film, and can be easily observed.

Interestingly, most mosquito species produce only one, or at most two, generations per season. Most species live less than 30 days and don't disperse far from their hatching site, so it might seem reasonable to think that they would not be active for long. The complicating fact is that we are dealing with a large number of species which hatch at overlapping times.

For instance, early in the season the Unmarked Slender Mosquito (its official common name) of the genus Culiseta is abroad. It's the large slow one that allows its intended victim ample time to strike and kill.

An unusual feature of Culiseta is that it winters over as an adult under leaves and duff, and is the first mosquito active in the spring. Maybe it flies so slowly because of arthropodic arthritis acquired over the winter.

Before Culiseta has given up its ghost, a host of replacements have come on scene. I've been unable to locate any definitive studies for north of 60°, but B.C. has more than 45 different species and I doubt that more northerly areas are far behind.

That is a very brief semi-scientific profile of the creatures in question. Now, we must get to the meat of the problem—how to deal with the ornery critters. When I was in my middle teens, I worked for the forest service on the north shore of Lake Superior, where the density of mosquitoes and blackflies was phenomenal.

We wore thick wool shirts which they couldn't bite through (we were hot as hell) and there were times when one could hardly distinguish the black squares from the white on a buffalo plaid pattern! As one poured a cup of tea, its surface was immediately covered with blackflies.

On the bad days when it was hot and still, we wore head nets. They do work though they increase the sweating quotient considerably and the world is seen through a kind of "mesh haze."

On cooler days, or when breezes were blowing, we relied on skeeter "dope" (the term "repellent" came later) and a Foreign Legion-styled cap arrangement with cloth around the back and sides of the neck.

This was achieved by tying together adjacent corners of a large bandana, putting it over the head, and setting one's cap or hat over it. Liberally dosing it with dope made it quite effective and the same was applied to exposed skin. Citronella was once the most common mosquito dope. This volatile oil is derived from a southern Asiatic species of lemon grass.

If one is downwind of the wearer of this "perfume," it's not uncommon to pick up the odour from 50 yards away. It was once common practice to mix citronella with a liberal amount of castor oil or carbolated Vaseline. This made its effects last much longer. My favourite mix was one ounce of citronella, one ounce spirits of camphor and a half-ounce oil of

Pesky biters are in blood-letting modes

by Dick Person

cedar. This method may sound antiquated to a generation of spray-can users, but it is effective, biodegradable, concoctable by the average human and one's body is not subject to the toxic effects of current repellents. "Jungle juice" was developed by the U.S. military for soldiers fighting in the jungles of southeast Asia. It heralded a new age in keeping insects from attacking the exposed and delectable human body.

Regardless of the brand name, Cutters, Off or Muskol, the basic effective ingredient is diethyltoluamide or DEET. It's claimed that the higher the concentration of DEET, the more "bang for your buck." Percentages vary from 30 to 100.

People with sensitive skin or allergies are advised to use the lower levels of DEET concentration

if it's to be used on an extended basis.

So you've got a bottle of one of the 100-percenters—what now? Just decant your bottle into two others of the same size, leaving a third in each one.

Then fill your bottle with vegetable oil and a few drops of wintergreen, rosemary or lavender oil and you're all set. You now have three bottles for the price of one. This mix is also nicer smelling, longer lasting and less toxic to the body. I have done this regularly for years and it works well.

Let's look now at supplemental things we can do to reduce the insect problem. After extensive testing, the U.S. military found that lighter hues are less attractive to biters and stingers. They also learned that clothing should be worn loosely and that the fabric must be thick enough to prevent the proboscis from getting through. I've found that layers work especially well, as there tends to be some shifting between them. That action pinches off the fragile proboscis.

Blackflies present a somewhat different situation. If they don't get you on direct frontal attack, they crawl in under shirt cuffs, neck bands, hats and caps, under your beltline and around boot tops.

Since you can't feel them bite, they can inflict considerable damage before you are aware of it. As with mosquitoes, reactions vary widely. For some, the only result is a few minutes of itching, with just a mark at the bite site.

For others, swelling, reddening, a burning itch, and even festering occurs. Blackflies often do kamikaze dives into the eyes. If you have children, I suggest making head nets mandatory.

Application of repellent to clothing works well, especially around potential entry points. Wear pants long enough to easily tuck into boot tops. And don't forget to have gloves along for hand protection.

Frequently, I put a smear or two of repellent along the back section of my hat brim to protect the exposed neck and ears. I keep DEET away from my skin as much as possible. For me the ultimate mosquito garment is a hooded mesh jacket impregnated with repellent. It is extremely effective, light and compact. To renew its potency, just sprinkle it with more dope and then store it in a sealed bag.

Another tactic that works wonders, even at the height of the bug season, is to select good campsites. This includes pitching your tent well above water level, on points jutting into lakes and open to prevailing winds, or on non-brushy river gravel bars.

Winds approaching 15 kilometres an hour will absolutely squelch insect activity. And, of course, when the temperature falls to 4 or 5°C, the bugs disappear.

One last word as a survival note—if your repellent has been forgotten or lost and you are in bug-infested country, improvise!

Humans and other animals have gone out of their minds, or died of blood loss due to insect bites. Peeling strips of fresh bark off spruce trees and rubbing the sap on your face will repel insects, and thick mud, or even peanut butter smeared on is effective.

You may look pretty wild for a while but you will live through it.

GRIZZLY THOUGHTS

by Ken Madsen

"Y ou'll see grizzlies on the Nakina for sure," I said. "We saw five last time." Poco nodded skeptically. He had been looking for grizzlies unsuccessfully all summer. This river trip was his last chance before he drove home to California.

The Nakina flows into the Taku, an international river that empties into the Pacific just south of Juneau, Alaska. I had been along on the first descent of the Nakina two years earlier. We had encountered difficult rapids, deep canyons, rotting salmon—and sleek, well-fed grizzlies.

Poco and I paddled and portaged for five days, before the Nakina flushed us out of its canyon. Ragged-looking bald eagles launched from tree tops. They were moulting and their tails and wings had the jagged profile of a hockey player's teeth. Salmon darted under our kayaks. The rank smell of decaying fish rekindled visions of bears: muscular haunches, glistening eyes, strong jaws. We could see bear tracks on sandy beaches, winding between salmon carcasses. Around each corner I expected to see a grizzly blocking the narrow stream.

"We've probably passed a dozen grizzlies already," said Poco. "I bet they're all hiding in the woods."

At dusk we stopped at a gently sloping gravel beach. We carried our camping gear to a clearing in the forest. Poco was a snorer. Sleeping near him was like bedding down under a volcano—you never knew when he'd erupt in sleep-shattering grunts and moans. Since he valued his friendships, he always brought his own tent.

It was Poco's turn to cook supper. While he lit the stove and rummaged in plastic bags, I walked to the river for a pot of water. Salmon chased each other in the shallows. The river gurgled and plopped with frenzied spawners. A dead salmon stared at me with glassy eyes, one bite nibbled from its gut. It smelled fishy. It smelled like bears.

We were tired and went to bed as soon as it got dark. I wriggled into my sleeping bag and chucked my clothes to the foot of the tent. I switched on my headlamp and opened a book. Something moved down by the river. Something big.

"Poco," I whispered, "did you hear that?"

"Yeah." Then he yelled, "Come oooooon, sissy." Poco had bellowed this periodically during the summer—a joking machismo challenge for any grizzly that cared to listen.

It suddenly became eerily quiet. No snapping of twigs. No splashing of salmon. I imagined a bear, standing on its hind legs, trying

to remove the salmon stench from its nostrils, trying to catch our scent. Then the grizzly snarled. "Poco," I said urgently, "have you got the bear spray?" Our can of bear repellent, a toxic blend of capsicum and oil designed to spray in the face of an attacking bear, was outside his tent.

"Yeah…but I can't get the fucking lid off."

I unzipped my sleeping bag. I pulled a sweater over my head, put on pants and boots and crawled into the night. From Poco's tent came a loud hiss. He swore and rolled out of his tent in a spicy, orange cloud. Poco had removed the lid, but not in the manufacturer's recommended way.

Something crashed through the undergrowth. Something with deep-throated rhythmic breathing. I ran to a stand of cottonwoods. The branches were dead, brittle, untrustworthy, but two of the trunks grew close together. I braced my back against one tree,

pushed my feet against the other, and squirmed upwards, feeling grateful for my rock climbing experience. I found a branch strong enough to hold my weight. I hoped it was higher than a grizzly's reach.

"Poco," I shouted, "why don't you climb a tree?"

His back to a tree trunk, Poco stood like Clint Eastwood. The bear sprayer was his six-shooter. "I'd never get up one," he said calmly. "Besides, I'm covered in cayenne. I'm safe unless it's a grizzly with a taste for Mexican food."

I wondered if I should rejoin Poco on the ground in a display of solidarity. The grizzly roared. I stayed in the tree. I stood on my branch for a long time, until the rustling and cracking and deep-breathing faded.

"It's gone," said Poco. "Let's light a fire." My arms ached from clutching the tree, so I slid to the ground. I collected thin, dry twigs while Poco shredded cardboard from a box of pasta. Soon a crackling fire lit the ring of cottonwoods surrounding our clearing, but made the forest behind seem darker. The bear was nearby, somewhere in the darkness.

"My hands are burning," Poco said. "That spray is worse than jalepeño juice." I opened a water bottle and rinsed his hands. "Shit, I must have rubbed my eyes!" I grabbed another bottle and sluiced his eyes. The water cascaded over his face and dribbled onto his jacket. "It's getting worse." He ground his knuckles into his eyes. "Jesus, I can't see at all!"

"Maybe I should refill the water bottles," I said nervously, hoping he'd tell me not to bother. He didn't.

I picked up the bottles and the bear sprayer and tiptoed to the river. Every few steps I swung my headlamp in a semi-circle. No glowing eyes. I filled the bottles, jerking my head up each time a salmon jumped. I hurried to the fire, doused his eyes and pulled apart the first-aid kit looking for painkillers. I gave him a couple of capsules loaded with codeine and walked back to the river.

"I can see a little," said Poco after I'd made three harrowing trips for water. "It's blurry, but getting better."

"I'm going to bed," I told him.

"You'll never get to sleep," he warned.

I pulled up the stakes holding down my tent and dragged it closer to the fire. I crawled in. I left my clothes and boots on and pulled my sleeping bag around me like a shawl. The door was wide open. I lay awake, listening to Poco breaking twigs and feeding the fire. A throaty growl pulled me from the twilight world between consciousness and sleep. "It's back," yelled Poco.

I sprang from the tent, or tried to. The sleeping bag twisted around my legs like a boa constrictor and I toppled over in the dirt, struggling feebly. I kicked myself free, sprinted to the trees and climbed upwards. I waited until the rustling died out before returning to earth.

"This is ridiculous," said Poco. "I'm going to sleep." I tried too, listening to the normally soothing sounds of the river. Every splash was a heavy paw in the water. Every gurgle a wading grizzly. I gave up and returned to the fire. Another breaking branch propelled Poco from his tent and me up the tree.

The night stretched on, like an interminable B-movie. After a while we were too exhausted to care. We collapsed in our tents and slept fitfully until dawn. I felt awful, but Poco looked worse. The whites of his eyes were yellow and veined with blood. His face looked poached.

"I'm a wreck and I didn't even get to see the bear," he said. "I told you we wouldn't see any grizzlies on this trip."

Excerpt from Wild Rivers, Wild Lands, by Ken Madsen (Whitehorse, Lost Moose Publishing) 1996

Falcon on the wings

by Sheila Serup

While searching the cliff across the river with a spotting scope, we suddenly saw a peregrine falcon swoop into the air and swing below us. We quickly stretched out on the grassy ledge high in the Peel River canyon and leaned over the edge to watch him. He soared and arched through the sky, looping gracefully around, before settling down on the top of the cliff.

Through the lens he looked magnificent, with his striking white chest, black back and head. The light shone on every feature and marking. His profile was sharp and fierce. He was angrily squawking at us, annoyed at our intrusion into his domain. Finally, after days of searching, we had found a falcon. We scanned every ledge and crevice of that craggy rock face and did not find a nest. It seemed that he was alone, without a mate.

We were here as part of a Yukon-wide survey of peregrine falcon nesting sites. Volunteers teamed with biologists to form survey parties of four. The study covered 3,000 kilometres of Yukon waterways. This comprehensive study, part of a nation-wide survey, would determine the strength of the peregrine falcon population in the Yukon.

Our journey had started on the Bonnet Plume, my favourite river. Two years before, the clear turquoise waters, tumbling rapids and sprawling mountain ranges of this northern Yukon river had enchanted me. It's the perfect wilderness river with an exciting blend of whitewater and fabulous hiking.

The Bonnet Plume flows north for 250 kilometres through the heart of Tetlit Gwich'in traditional territory. After joining the Peel, the river winds its way another 280 kilometres to Fort McPherson, where our journey would end. During this sunny July, two other survey parties were canoeing the rivers on either side of the Bonnet Plume—the Snake on the east and Wind on the west. All three rivers drain into the Peel, a broad river which feeds the mighty Mackenzie.

This year the river didn't disappoint us. We landed on Bonnet Plume Lake after our flight from Mayo. When we left its calm, clear waters, we quickly

> The earth's plants and animals are going extinct at an alarming rate—a rate that some biologists have estimated at about 100 species everyday. Many more species are at risk, including some that live in the Yukon. Yukon species at risk have been identified by: the Committee on the Status of Endangered Species in Canada; the Convention on International Trade in Endangered Species, and the Yukon Wildlife Act.

encountered the fast and furious waters of the upper Bonnet Plume. The turbulent river was swollen and silty as it surged over rocks and through twisted gorges.

It was wet and wild as we dodged boulders in our heavily-laden canoe. Often waves crashed and spilled into our boat. Class III rapids were scouted and run. The high water level meant we could run them all, except for two congested falls. With only two canoes on a challenging river hundreds of kilometres deep in the wilderness, we were careful and conservative.

As the river descended into forested open valleys, we began scanning the cliffs for peregrine falcons. Graham Baird, at that time a biologist with the Yukon's Wildlife Viewing Program, explained that falcons were more likely to be found in wide valleys where there was more prey. With eyesight many times greater than that of our own, peregrines perch on cliffs and scan the land for small birds. We were looking for white streak marks on cliff faces which could indicate a nest site.

The mountain ranges slipped away as the river grew. In the haze of forest fire smoke, the ranges stood out as blue silhouettes, becoming lighter and further away.

The river quickened its pace on the last stretch to the Peel. Like a wild ravenous animal, it tore past gravel bars and uprooted trees. When we darted down a narrow channel, I heard my partner gasp. There on the bank at the water's edge was a huge bull moose, not more than three metres away. The animal was surprised and mad. He shook his massive head at us as we hustled downriver.

From a safe distance, we watched the moose

run up the bank and disappear into the brush. A second later, he leaped out into the river right in front of the next canoe. First we heard a tremendous splash as he bounded away, then we saw the astonished faces of James and Allison.

The Bonnet Plume enters the Peel at the beginning of a deep, curving canyon. After a hectic week of paddling, we spent two leisurely days exploring this sensuous canyon. Layers of rock and sediment sloped and angled upwards along the black walls. Long stony beaches lined the edges. The river moved slowly between them like a powerful mountain cat.

We hiked up one side to see if we could find an old trail once used by the Gwich'in people. Decades ago they travelled the Peel in moose skin boats. While the women and children walked around the rapids on the trail, the men steered their crafts through the canyon. Here we observed our first falcon.

A few days later, when we passed the mouth of the Snake River, we found our first pair. In the morning, we watched the falcons soar and streak through the air above the river, chasing each other. The way they fly is almost indescribable. One moment, they're weaving with outstretched wings; a second later, their wings are snug against their bodies in a searing dive. These birds of prey are the fastest birds in the world, often reaching speeds of up to 350 kilometres an hour

We thought they were playing until one streaked away like a meteor and made a kill over the trees behind our camp. James, also a biologist, was ecstatic when through his binoculars he saw the falcon snatch the bird out of the sky.

Graham's fascination with falcons began in childhood. He explained that because peregrines are moving so fast, they will strike and kill a bird with their talons before grabbing it out of the air. "Seeing them make a kill in the air is really something."

"A peregrine falcon diving on prey is the most exciting thing I have seen in nature," he said.

In the 1960s, the number of falcons in Canada crashed. Baby peregrines were not hatching because the shells on their eggs were breaking. Studies soon proved that pesticides such as DDT in the food chain

ANIMALS

were causing the thin shells. By the mid-1970s, peregrines were extinct in most of North America. The Yukon was one of the few places where some peregrines survived. For the last quarter of a century, there have been intensive efforts to reintroduce peregrines. Our survey helped to show that the total peregrine population has increased 30 percent over the last five years. Altogether, a record 121 nesting pairs were counted.

At our last campsite on the Peel, we heard falcons on the bank across the river. Through the scope, we could see two little chicks fighting over a chunk of meat. They were tearing at the meat, yanking shreds from each other. All of 12 days old, they pushed and shoved, little downy bodies scrambling about on the ledge.

I was struck by how closely, at such a young age, they bore the adult's distinct profile—the erect head with the downward curving beak and piercing, alert eyes. Not far away, their parent stood on a stump watching us in the drizzling rain. This was our first glimpse of peregrine falcon chicks. In the 10 days we spent on the two rivers, this discovery was the sweetest of all.

Patience is obviously a strong prerequisite in falcon watching; however, the rewards are tremendously satisfying. This was definitely the case as we stood in the grey rain watching the chicks squabbling in the nest and their mother flying low over the Trail River where it meets the Peel.

YUKON WILDLIFE SPECIES AT RISK

At risk in the Yukon and all of Canada
Identified by Committee on the Status of Endangered Species in Canada

Endangered
• bowhead whale
• peregrine falcon: anataum race

Threatened
• wood bison (also specifically protected by Yukon Wildlife Act)

Vulnerable
• grizzly bear (also identified by Convention on International Trade in Endangered Species)
• polar bear
• wolverine
• great grey owl
• short-eared owl
• trumpeter swan
• peregrine falcon: tundra race (also specifically protected by Yukon Wildlife Act)
• Squanga whitefish

At risk in the Yukon but not elsewhere
Identified by Yukon Wildlife Act

• mule deer
• muskox
• elk
• cougar

At risk elsewhere but not in the Yukon
Identified by Convention on International Trade in Endangered Species

• wolf
• black bear
• lynx
• river otter
• gyrfalcon (also specifically protected by Yukon Wildlife Act)
• all birds of prey

Recent worldwide declines in amphibian populations have led to concerns about the status of amphibians in Canada. The only amphibians known to live in the Yukon are the boreal toad, the northern wood frog and possibly the spotted frog.

MOST CREEPY CRITTERS ARE FULL OF ANTIFREEZE

by the Geophysical Institute, University of Alaska Fairbanks

Houseflies seem to have a mysterious power to transcend the cold. Give them a little heat, and they'll behave in January as if it were August.

One winter, an outbuilding that had been chilled to twenty below was heated up. Within just a few hours the place was buzzing with dozens of thawed-out flies.

Many northern buggy beasts can live in death-like dormancy through bitter cold, then thaw into pestiferous life as soon as the temperature permits.

Arctic woolly bear caterpillars can stay frozen solid at temperatures down to 50 below for as long as 10 months without damage.

Our multi-legged denizens aren't the only ones to master the freeze-thaw life cycle. It's possible to find frozen frogs, showing all the vital signs of granite, burrowed into the equally frozen mud in some interior Alaskan lakes.

Normally, freezing is deadly for living things. Ice crystals burst through cell and capillary walls, disrupting delicate structures at all levels from subcellular to whole organs.

Even when freezing doesn't rip and break an organism, it provides other stresses. No fluid flow means no transfer of oxygen and no disposal of wastes, problems that usually mean no life.

Some animals get around these problems by operating internal furnaces—the mammalian technique—and growing furry or fatty protections against the cold. Our so-called cold-blooded animals, the exotherms, don't have that option.

Instead, many use variants on the antifreeze theme, producing chemical protectants that keep ice from forming in their body fluids just as antifreeze keeps water from freezing in a car's cooling system.

Polar marine fishes are full of antifreeze, and so are many cold-adapted insects. This evolutionary adaptation means their life-sustaining fluids can be supercooled, staying liquid at temperatures below those at which they should freeze.

The antifreeze chemicals in fish and many northern spiders, mites and insects are proteins. They block the effects of ice

nucleators, particles that provide binding sites where water molecules begin the process of setting up the orderly lattices of ice crystals.

Nucleators turn out to be important also to the animals that get through the cold months by freezing solid. Their chances of surviving freezing are better if ice growth begins in the fluids not contained within cell membranes such as urine or blood plasma.

They are also better off if the freezing proceeds slowly and the crystals formed are small, as in good ice cream. To accomplish these ends, the animals synthesize nucleating agents when external cues, such as declining temperatures and length of day, trigger the process.

The nucleators provide binding sites for the ice-lattice formation to begin, and help set off the freezing process in the right places and at the right speeds to produce the safer kinds of crystals.

Little ice crystals tend to agglomerate into bigger ones, as happens when ice cream is stored too long. To prevent this effect, animals that freeze solid also produce enough antifreeze to block the refreezing of little crystals into bigger ones.

Many freeze-tolerant animals also produce other useful chemicals known as cryoprotectants. (This term is a fine technical cop-out. All it means is that these substances protect cell structures and membranes against various effects of chilling.)

The cryoprotectants regulate cell volume during freezing and also seem to protect vital proteins and enzymes from the denaturing effects of very low temperatures.

Finally, the cells and organs of frozen animals are capable of surviving for a long time without oxygen. As their metabolic rates drop to one to 10 percent of their normal resting rates, their needs for energy and waste removal drop accordingly.

So, our winter-surviving creepers and buzzers are little less than chemical and physical marvels, capable of survival feats well beyond human capacities. Swat we must, no doubt, but we should do so with a little more respect.

I never saw the point of moose hunting in Kiruna. There was too much salmon around to justify the purchase of a high calibre rifle. In the spring, when last season's catch started showing signs of freezer damage, a shirt-tail relative from across the slough would throw some moose meat our way.

Big game hunting on the river was just too much work. But one part of the actual hunt did really appeal to me—floating down clearwater streams in early September. The frosts of August yellow up the leaves of riverside birch trees and set the high bush cranberries to rot. These berries grow thick along the riverbanks where the moose browse. During moose season, skiffs full of hunters float through bends where the sweet smell of rotting berries hangs thick over the water.

Since everyone around Kiruna boat hunts,

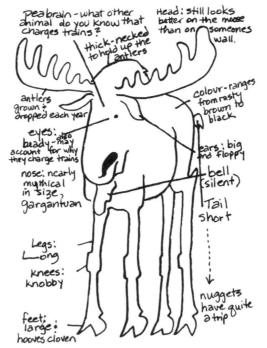

pea brain - what other animal do you know that charges trains?

thick-necked to hold up the antlers

Head: still looks better on the moose than on someones wall.

antlers grown & dropped each year

colour - ranges from rusty brown to black

eyes: also beady - may account for why they charge trains

nose: nearly mythical in size, gargantuan

ears: big and floppy

bell (silent)

Tail short

Legs: Long

knees: knobby

feet: large & hooves cloven

nuggets have quite a trip

the snag-ridden Big Grayling. Logs jammed two of the three channels but we were lucky enough to get through the one open route on the first try.

Twenty or thirty bends up the river we entered a big gravel bar area. Steve pointed out meat tripods put up by hunters who had already gotten their moose. After driving through the break in a partial log jam, I landed the skiff at the upriver end of a low gravel bar. No one had camped here before which meant there was no gut pile to attract brown bears.

We camped near a collection of white spruce drift logs and I started the fire while Steve set up our tent. We ate well that night— thick steaks and coal-baked potatoes. I wanted to stay up and enjoy the night, but Steve tossed water on the flames and climbed into his sleeping bag. There was nothing for it so I hit the sack.

STEVE'S MOOSE
by Dan Branch

on the good streams you are always within 30-06 range of another boat during moose season. I never wanted to chance catching a stray shot unless there was a good reason to gamble. If Steve hadn't called me from the airport one year at the end of August, I probably would have left Kiruna without ever trying for a moose.

"Dan," Steve shouted into the telephone receiver that day. "Can you bring your three wheeler over to the Friendship Air terminal and pick me up?"

"Well, ah, I'm kind of busy, ah, do you think maybe you could walk over to the slough so I can pick you up in the canoe?" I asked politely.

"You kidding me? I got several trailer loads of gear. Oh, by the by, you aren't doing anything for the next few days, are you?" he asked.

I saw the future and agreed to bring the skiff across the slough, fire up the three wheeler, and drive over to the terminal to pick him up. He was going moose hunting and I was going to take him. On the way to the airstrip I stopped by the store and picked up a moose tag. Two hours later, we were moving up the Kuskokwim towards the Valley of the Big Grayling River.

Susan didn't appreciate the rapid change of plans. She wanted to use the skiff to pick lingon berries on the bluffs lining Big Mamma Slough. As Steve and I walked out the door Susan smiled sweetly, but there was something about her demeanour that told me we had better bring home some meat.

We moved out into the Kuskokwim in front of Kiruna

MOOSE FOOD

TWIGS BARK Leaves Shrubs (Aquatic (Underwater) plants) Herbs

Moose can dive 5m under water for up to 30 seconds - looking for aquatic plants

and headed upriver. The Kuskokwim is still a big river when it passes the mouth of the Big Grayling. People measure distance on big rivers like this one in terms of cans of gas or miles.

I was changing to my second six-gallon can of gas when Steve spotted a small group of wolves moving along the willows on the opposite side of the river. The outboard stalled out before I could switch tanks. Startled by sudden silence, the wolves darted out of sight into the willows.

Twenty minutes later, we carefully entered

THE FIRST NATION PERSPECTIVE

When you ▢ something, the animal gives its life for you. So you've got to give thanks ▢ great spirit. Something had to die for you to continue with your life. That's the way I look at it.
– Art Johns, Carcross-Tagish First Nation

The hunting traditions of Yukon First Nation peoples have grown out of their intimate relationship with the natural world. Through wise use of local resources, the first people of the Yukon were able to feed, cloth and shelter themselves while developing rich communities and cultures. Moose and caribou in particular provided a bountiful source of food and raw material such as bone, hide and sinew.

Hours before first light, Steve burst out of the tent and fired up his Coleman camp stove. While the flames from the stove leaped high and yellow into the air, my partner filled my good cook pot with river water and set it on the burner. If I hadn't been in sleep deprivation shock, I would have told Steve that Coleman recommends waiting until the flames turn from orange to intense blue before using the stove for cooking. It would take me a day to clean soot off the pot.

While the pot blackened, Steve suggested loudly, in language not suitable for publication, that I get out of bed and make sure that the boat was ready for hunting. I stumbled into my clothes as he handed me a lukewarm mug of instant coffee. I tried to tell him about the danger of contracting beaver fever from the wild river water. "Steve," I pleaded, "Beavers piss in this water. If I drink it before it has been boiled for twenty minutes I'll get giardia."

Steve said that I was overly concerned with hygiene and passed me a cool bowl of instant oatmeal. "Here," he demanded, "choke this down and grab a chocolate toaster pastry. We got to go." While I checked over the skiff, Steve poured half a jar of instant coffee into his thermos and then filled it with the rest of the warmed-up river water.

I pull-started the outboard and tried to wake up. After floating forty-five minutes through the big gravel bar country, I asked Steve why he expected moose to be silly enough to come to the riverbank when even an idling engine could be heard for miles. "The big males were looking for a little action," he answered, "When the rut is on they get stupid." I guess they are a little like people.

We drifted the gravel bar section of the river three or four times before Steve began to lose hope. When he replaced his 30-06 with the coffee thermos, I was too beat to worry about beaver fever so I took the mug he handed me. We drank the strong brew while looking in opposite directions.

Steve looked with distraction downriver. I scanned upstream looking for low water. That's why I saw a bull swimming across the river first. I was already moving full throttle so there was nothing to do but warn Steve and watch the 2,000 pounds of meat stroll onto the beach and shake off river water like a bird dog. The law says your boat can't be moving under power when you shoot a moose, so I got ready to kick the boat out of gear as soon as Steve drew down on the animal. Since we were travelling upstream, we would move backwards as soon as I shut down the motor.

After seeing the moose, Steve tossed his mug over the side, spraying both of us with coffee. His rifle was cradled in the bow of the skiff. Grabbing it, he aimed and took it off safety.

Steve's moose watched all this with calm indifference. He was standing fully exposed on the beach now, a few feet away from the safety of a birch thicket. With one hand on the outboard kill switch and the other on the tiller, I waited for a sign from my friend.

The moose looked to be about three years old with a moderate rack. His meat would be tender and tasty. My share would contribute greatly to the quality of life next winter. Just as the boat moved within a hundred feet of our victim, he walked safely off into the woods. Steve went nuts. I went nuts. After landing the boat we chased through the woods, hoping to get Steve another chance. But it was gone.

Steve never saw another male moose during the trip. He drove me hard until the boat gas ran low. I pushed the little skiff fifty more bends up the river looking for another chance. One afternoon, with only an hour of light left in the day, we passed the place where the Big Grayling valley opens into a tundra plain. Steve hoped to spot something to kill. Tying the skiff to some scrub willow, we scrambled up a low bluff. Steve lit up one of his unfiltered cigarettes, sucked in several litres of foul smoke, and surveyed the scene.

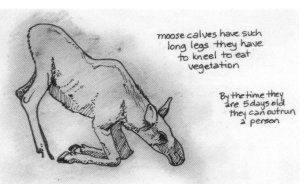

moose calves have such long legs they have to kneel to eat vegetation

By the time they are 5 days old they can outrun a person

You can make paper with moose nuggets — or sachets — and they are great for moose poop fights with your friends

The secret to really beautiful moose nugget jewellery is in the nuggets themselves... freshness, texture and size being among the more important considerations.

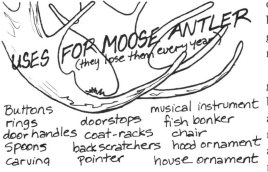

USES FOR MOOSE ANTLER (they lose them every year)

Buttons
rings
door handles
Spoons
carving

doorstops
coat-racks
backscratchers
Pointer

musical instrument
fish bonker
chair
hood ornament
house ornament

I'd like to think that my friend was moved to silence by the vista of broad tundra that reached the foothills of the Alaska Range. The

EAT THAT BLACK BEAR

The law does not require you to save the meat when you kill a black bear. But if you leave the meat in the bush, you're giving up a lot of decent meals. To eliminate the risk of trichinosis, just cook the meat well. If your black bear has a strong flavour, marinate the meat overnight.

Many hunters eat black bear meat. But we have yet to meet one who likes grizzly meat.

low afternoon light pulled colour out of the carpet of tundra plants making the brief transition to winter. While I studied the mix of light, shadow and colour, Steve ran the tundra with binoculars. "Get down," he shouted. I looked for moose until he handed me the binos with an order to search a low hill for caribou. There were six of them, grazing on a hilltop miles away.

Steve wanted to go after the caribou. Even the sweet flavour of their meat could not entice me to bounce across the five miles of wet tundra protecting the animals from Steve. He insisted on going so I set up camp and promised to wait.

He packed the coffee thermos, bullets and some dry fish, and headed toward his prey. I ate dinner and hit the sack. The next morning the sound of splashing brought me out of the tent. A nice bull moose was swimming across the Big Grayling.

Dressed only in underwear, I watched him pull out only fifty feet from the camp, climb the river bluff and stroll downriver. Steve had the only gun so the beast escaped unharmed. There was nothing for it. I made breakfast.

Fashioning a bucket from an empty white gas can, I spent the day picking low bush cranberries and trying to decide if I should tell Steve about the moose. It was a tough call. The information might help him find the guy. It would also bring Steve's anger to a boil. He would demand to know why I didn't run the moose to ground and then finish it off with my pocket knife. I decided to keep the moose a secret.

Steve returned after dark, packing the remains of a ptarmigan. He had bagged it with a head shot from the 30-06, leaving enough bird to eat. While I fried up the breast meat, Steve recapped his trip to the mountains.

After leaving me, he walked for a couple hours until it was too dark to take bearings. Huddling on a pile of lichen-covered rock, Steve then fought for sleep. At first light he set out for the hills. The caribou had moved off. He spent several hours trying to find them. When he failed, he ambushed the ptarmigan.

We hunted another day and then headed back to Kiruna. Susan accepted my lingon berry peace offering. Steve flew home to Bethel. Six months later he was back for the winter hunt. Borrowing my snowgo, he found his moose on the tractor trail. Susan and I enjoyed the machine's share until breakup.

ANIMALS

New wolf control program announced

Governor Tony Knows today announced a radical new method to control the wolf population in Alaska. According to a recent press release, local psychic Rudolph the Incredible has been appointed the "Commissioner Who Runs With The Wolves."

Although a specific plan has yet to be finalized, several initial concepts specify psychic thought control. Possibilities include rehabilitating the wolf population into a more docile one that would not threaten game animals such as moose, elk or possum; making the wolves just roll over and die; or convincing them that Alaska may not be that great a place to live after all. Maybe then the wolves would eventually migrate to southern California.

Rudolph, whose psychic powers have so far included key-bending and a variety of card effects, was apparently chosen by the new administration after a performance at a local restaurant. Officials were quick to point out that if the psychic control methods do not work, the Governor may change Rudolph's duties to include entertaining visiting dignitaries.

There was no stated salary, as Rudolph apparently is able to psychically will funds into his bank account.

Game Board officials, contemplating on which board they were playing a game, offered to physically control the Rudolph the Incredible population if methods do not prove successful.

by Jeff Brown

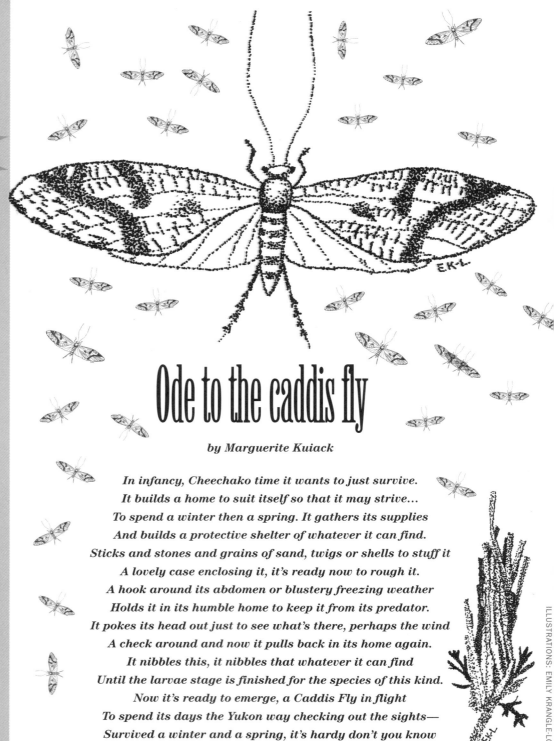

ILLUSTRATIONS: EMILY KRANGLE-LONG

Ode to the caddis fly

by Marguerite Kuiack

In infancy, Cheechako time it wants to just survive.
It builds a home to suit itself so that it may strive...
To spend a winter then a spring. It gathers its supplies
And builds a protective shelter of whatever it can find.
Sticks and stones and grains of sand, twigs or shells to stuff it
A lovely case enclosing it, it's ready now to rough it.
A hook around its abdomen or blustery freezing weather
Holds it in its humble home to keep it from its predator.
It pokes its head out just to see what's there, perhaps the wind
A check around and now it pulls back in its home again.
It nibbles this, it nibbles that whatever it can find
Until the larvae stage is finished for the species of this kind.
Now it's ready to emerge, a Caddis Fly in flight
To spend its days the Yukon way checking out the sights—
Survived a winter and a spring, it's hardy don't you know
And now we have a Caddis Fly, a bonified sourdough.

ILLUSTRATION: KIRK STEWART

Beavercide?

story and photo by Pete and Mary Beattie
Woodpecker Point, Yukon

The unfortunate fellow in the photo was found on our trapline last fall. Maybe he couldn't face the thought of another winter denned up in the riverbank? Or was another jealous beaver involved? Or just an accident? The possibilities and subplots go on and on. Imagine: the O.J. Beaver trial...the concept is enough to bring Gary Larsen out of retirement.

TOO CLOSE FOR COMFORT!

by Marcelle Dubé

A few years ago, Mark and I hiked the Slims River Valley in Kluane National Park. Five hours into what should have been a six-hour stroll, my feet grew the most amazing blisters. We decided to stop early and pitch the tent off the trail in a stand of trees. We enjoyed a meal of beans and salami before caching our food pack in a tree 50 metres from the tent.

In the morning, we left the pack outside the tent door while we breakfasted inside, protected from the buffeting of the wind. Then we

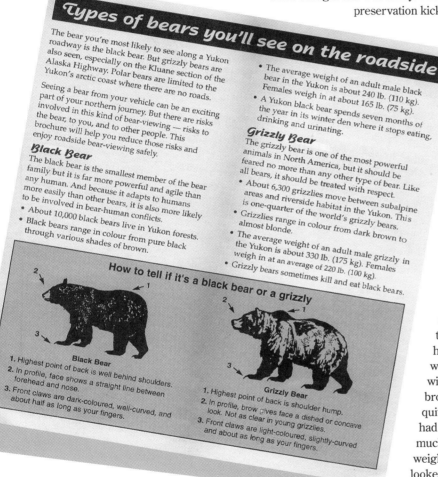

and seemed to consider Mark's invitation to take what it wanted as long as it wasn't us. Then it came to the front of the tent, near the food pack, and we got our first look through the mesh front flap.

"It's a sow," said Mark and in the same breath continued talking to the bear. Somewhere past the roaring in my ears (I eventually remembered to breathe), some part of me thought this was funny. Then self-preservation kicked in and I swallowed the hysteria. The sow stood on all fours, sideways to us, and looked us over out of the corner of her eye. She was young, with a reddish-brown coat—quite pretty. I had no idea how much she weighed, but she looked much, much bigger than me.

She must have decided that we were no threat, because she grunted and with one lightning swoop of her paw, caught the food pack and sent it flying ten metres. She followed it and settled down to some serious exploring.

Mark snapped into emergency mode. "Put your boots on," he ordered, donning his own. I never moved so fast in my life. "Out," he said, once we were shod, and headed for the front flap. At that point, my brain switched back on and I stopped him. "Back door," I whispered, indicating the flap furthest from the bear. Within seconds, we were walking quietly but quickly down the trail, away from the sow who was busy devouring our food.

lingered. We were so comfortable.

Suddenly, a twig snapped. We gave each other the I-wonder-what-that-was look. Something big brushed against a tree, heading toward the tent. We saw a dim outline through the translucent fabric of the tent and Mark said, "It's a bear." Then it came closer. "A grizzly bear."

The bear sniffed around our artificial eggshell. It pawed at the other pack leaning against the tent, but it contained no food. Then a big black muzzle pressed up against the tent, smearing the nylon, and I forgot to breathe. Mark began speaking softly and I couldn't tell if he was talking to me or the bear. It paused

Then Mark stopped. "We'll need water," he said, and my heart sank. The canteen was less than ten metres from the bear. I would have abandoned it cheerfully, but Mark headed back, keeping the bear in his line of sight. After coming close enough to smell her, he picked up the canteen and turned toward me. Then a funny look crossed his face. He slipped back into the tent, emerging a moment later with the binoculars and the camera. To my horror, he aimed the camera at the bear.

I could just see it—the click of the camera shutter would send the bear into a rage. There would be pieces of Mark all over the place, followed by pieces of me.

I said, as calmly as I could manage, "Don't even think about it." Mark hesitated, as the sow crunched noisily through containers. Then, with a reluctant sigh, he turned away from the prize-winning shot.

We headed for high ground and watched for any sign of the bear's departure, but our camp was too well hidden. All we got were glimpses of the trail as it wound its way through the trees creeping up the slope. We watched and waited, the adrenaline slowly subsiding.

An hour later, a lone hiker came striding down the trail. We waved at him furiously, trying to warn him of the potential danger, but he obviously thought we were just being friendly. When he finally reached us, unmolested, he looked at me strangely.

"Do you own a pair of yellow canvas shoes?"

He had come across our ransacked camp. When he found my shoes, he was terrified of stumbling across the body that belonged with them.

When we finally returned to the camp, we found the tent ripped to shreds. The sleeping bags were no longer identifiable as such. There was down everywhere. We cleaned up, packed the debris, and left. Then we found our can of insect repellent. There were big holes in it. We figured the sow had bitten into the can and it had exploded in her mouth, enraging her to this orgy of destruction.

As we hiked back, we came across the log we had used while having lunch the previous day. There were unmistakeable signs of the sow's presence. That's when we realized she had tracked us to our campsite. No doubt the salami had been too much to resist. Heading back to the car, we first had to cross an alluvial fan and its dozens of fast-flowing creeks all heading willy nilly for the Slims River. I fell into one and was carried thirty metres before I could free myself of the backpack and pull my soaking self out. We didn't stop until we reached the car and I could no longer feel that sow's breath on the back of my neck.

by Jim Erkiletian

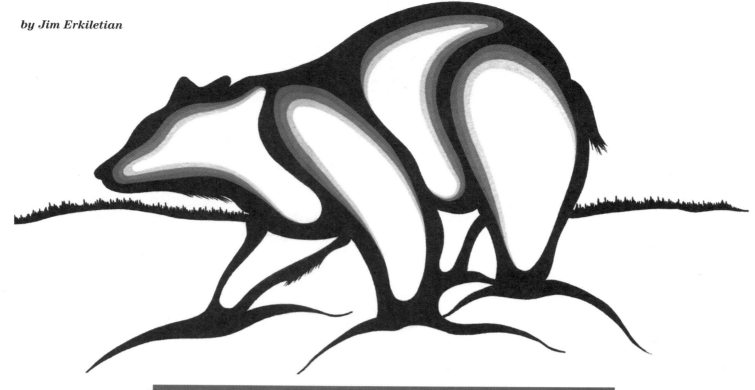

THE BEAVER AND THE BEAR

Scared? The worst I ever been scared was the time I was attacked by that danged beaver. It was out on the shore of Marsh Lake at the head of the Yukon River where I lived in a tent for a couple of years. Middle of the night, in the early fall, with no one and nothing within hearing distance. I was relaxing out by my fire in front of my teepee when I hear this terrible grr-roanching sound from way up the valley. I'd never heard a beaver before that time, and it set me to thinking real quick, "What in tarnation is that!?"

Then I didn't hear anything for fifteen minutes or so. Just long enough for me to relax and figure whatever it was had gone some other direction, and there it came again, GRONCH, only closer this time. Almost made me pee my pants.

For about an hour I keep hearing this sound out in the darkness, and it's getting closer every time I hear it. I was real spooked by the time it got within spittin' distance. The heebie-jeebies were crawling up and down my spine, and the hair was standing right out on the back of my neck. I had to pee bad, but wasn't brave enough to go far enough away from my fire. I could hear whatever it was rustling around through the dry leaves just over the riverbank. I'd swear I could hear big sharp teeth and claws clicking together.

I had to do something. I couldn't possibly sleep with that big ugly sucker tramping around out there gronching and rustling. There was a pile of dry spruce boughs by my fire, with the needles all turned brown. They don't burn for very long, but they crackle and flare up with a good bright light, so I tossed them on the fire and slipped the safety off my .303. Then, when there was plenty of light from those spruce needles burning and crackling away, I picked up a handful of little rocks and let fly in the general direction of the beast. I was shaking, waiting for a big hairy windigo with fire in its eyes to come charging over the bank at me, when I heard a last rustle of dry leaves, then a splat of a tail slapping on the water.

Made me feel kind of silly, all of a sudden, to get so spooked by a beaver. One of the reasons I'd come north in 1970 was because I was interested in studying beavers, in finding out how they go about constructing their dams. My information so far indicated it is a combination of learning and instinct. One trapper said she had seen mother beavers swatting the young ones around to get them to help build. Another said even very small beavers will start packing mud in response to the sound of running water. A good PhD thesis some day, I thought, and particularly Canadian.

I was attacked by a mad grizzly bear back in '73 or '74, hunting moose with Tlingit Elder John Joe from M'Clintok Bay. Since then I've learned most Canadians, and quite a few Americans, have bear stories of one sort or another. It's a good way to get to know people, get them started on their bear stories.

It was again in the early fall when the trees were turning colourful and there was a nip in the air all the time. We were out on the old trail that runs from Tagish over to Carcross, up on the first ridge above the Yukon River where it runs out of Marsh Lake. John was in the lead when we came out of the forest at the upper end of a valley that housed quite a bunch of beavers. From the ridge I could see six separate dams, each with its own lodge. Those beavers had that creek right down under their control from one end to another.

When beavers build a dam, they leave a low spot for the water to run out, a spillway. It's a good place to fish some times during the year, because the biggest fish will be strong enough to swim against the current, and the biggest of the big fish will make it all the way to the top beaver's dam. Salmon or dolly varden might be found either just below the spillway or trying to swim up the current.

That day, there were also bears, a mother and two nearly full-grown cubs. There was a light wind blowing in our faces, carrying our scent away from the bears fishing by the creek. They couldn't hear us either, because the creek was making such a racket.

Bears won't generally bother you in the bush, but they get awful touchy when they're minding their kids. And mean as hell, you better believe it.

The big sow reared up on her hind legs and looked right at us. And I thought, "Wow, a bear!" Then as she went back down on all fours and out of sight below the ridge I thought, "There's nothin' between her and us but that low bank." And I'd seen the backs of her cubs as they moved out of sight below the ridge, so I knew it was a volatile situation.

John hadn't seen them yet. He was a bit ahead of me on the trail, looking in another direction. So I clapped him on the shoulder and yelled "BEAR!" in his good ear and started running, looking for a tree to climb. After about ten or twenty paces I looked back and saw he had stopped dead still. Even his good ear was about eighty percent deaf, you see, and he hadn't made out there were bears in the vicinity. (Later he told me he thought I'd seen a moose and got overexcited.) Anyway, I stopped too.

I'd heard from elders that the grizzly will circle around to attack, so there is no way to know what direction she will be coming from. They're smart that way. I looked along the bank as I unslung my rifle.

There was a space of time where the adrenaline apparently hit my system and everything got real sharp and clear. I can still remember it today, and see it just like a picture if I close my eyes. It was like a real clear movie in slow motion, except I was inside looking out instead of outside looking in.

That real clear quiet space seemed to last a long time, then BANG! everything happened at once. Mama bear came steam-rolling over the ridge like a locomotive, heading right dead-on straight for John.

It must have been an incredible sight from straight on like that. I was seeing her from the side and she was huge. Even down on all fours, she was almost as tall as he was. He was looking her straight in the eye.

I had my rifle, a .303 Enfield John had lent me, the same one I had when the beaver almost got me. I'd slipped it off my shoulder and opened the bolt. We always hunted with the firing chamber empty. Lot safer that way. John was gazing off down the valley expecting to spot the "moose" that had got me so excited when he suddenly looked right in front to see that bear coming at him. He yelled, "Aha, you bugger!" and rolled his .270 Winchester off his shoulder, cocked, aimed and fired with less than ten metres between himself and the bear.

She stopped with one front paw still up in the air and her nose so close to his chest he could have poked her with the end of his rifle.

He may have hit her in the hump of bone bears have on their back. He said later he thought he saw some fur fly. Anyway, she decided not to kill him and turned toward me, probably because I was hopping around trying to get my rifle cocked and loaded while John was standing still. I was thinking that I'd have to shoot from a low-down position so as not to hit John if the bear knocked him over, so I was almost down on one knee. But when I saw her coming my way I stood back up and aimed.

Fortunately, by the time I had my rifle cocked and got a bead on her, she was going back toward the creek to look after her cubs, so I pulled my shot up just over her head. She stopped again and looked back over her shoulder at me, with a down right nasty look on her face. And if you care to know how many wrinkles there are on a mad mamma grizzly bear's nose, there are seven. Four down on the curved part and three more back by the eyes.

She decided not to kill me. I guess the thought of her cubs unprotected was first on her mind. Anyway, John fired again and I fired again, loose shots in the air to let the bears know we are the thunder gods. The mama bear ran back down by the creek and rounded up her cubs, bounded down the creek a ways, and then off into the bush.

John and I sat down and thought for a while. I saw him eject an empty cartridge from the chamber of his .270, and push the live shell back into the clip, so I did the same with my .303. Then, with a kind of wonder, John said, "I sure didn't expect to see no bear." He said that a couple of times as we sat there and let the adrenaline wash through our systems.

Then he built a fire. He was always building fires in the bush, every time he stopped for a rest. But he told me to get some green branches that time, which he piled on the fire to make lots of smoke. He had noticed the wind was blowing in the direction between our back trail and the way the bears had gone. Bears avoid smoke, because of forest fires, so he figured to lay on a little insurance that those bears wouldn't accidentally come around and meet us on the way back. I've always thought that was pretty together thinking for someone who five minutes before had stood nose-to-nose with a mad grizzly. After a few minutes we doused the fire and hiked back to his place. I was walking backwards most of the way, expecting a giant wounded bear to ambush us from behind a rock or something, but John was ambling along like nothing had happened, talking about this and that, occasionally reminding himself that "he sure didn't expect to see no bear."

We got back to the boat and motored across the lake. His wife, Julia, came down to meet us at the dock. We were back early, so she was expecting to help carry a load of moose meat up to the house.

She was kind of surprised when she saw nothing in the boat except our gear. John didn't say a word until we got back to the house and sat ourselves down at the kitchen table with some hot cups of tea. Then he waved his hand in the air toward the direction of the lake and said, "Big bear over there!"

Julia gasped. The other people in the kitchen—I think it was three elders and some grandkids—got real quiet. Elmer came in from the front room to hear.

"Came straight for me, then took after him," John explained. I nodded and took a sip of the beautiful hot tea. He related the tale with just enough dramatic touches to keep everyone interested. Years later I heard he was still telling that story.

That old bear must have weighed half-a-ton, but she was running and spinning around through the bush like a dancer. I can remember hearing the wind rustling through the dry leaves on the deciduous trees as she came over the hill, but not one sound from that bear. Not one leaf crumpling or anything as her big paws pounded down like giant feather-pillows. On tippy-toes, for a bear. And then the incredible shattering of the silence as the rifles fired.

And you know something? It's a pretty amazing experience having a mad bear come at you like that. But considering it in retrospect I wasn't really what you'd call scared that time. Nothing like I was with that durn beaver.

ILLUSTRATION: CHRISTIAN PAPEQUASH

Trapline cabin blues

by Peter Harms

"Loon Spirit"
C.P. 96

I met Kenny Nukon when I was teaching in Old Crow. He was an old, one-armed trapper who lived 20 miles upstream from the village. This song is dedicated to him. Thank you "Sit ya," for all the stories and laughs.

I've got those old trapline cabin blues
I miss the Old Crow Flats and caribou
Cause I love the life that's free…town life's not for me
I've got those old trapline cabin blues

Been hanging 'round this smoky town too long
I thought that I would like it here but now I know I'm wrong
A town is full of people, all jammed into one place.
But trapping camps are all spread out and in between is space

I've got those old trapline cabin blues
And now I know what life I'm gonna choose
Gonna head out to the flat, trap my lynx and fox and rat
I've got those old trapline cabin blues.

As a kid, to me the bush it was my home
As years went by folks left, and soon I was alone
The lure of town life caught them, they left for the easier way
I thought that I would try it too but here I cannot stay

I've got those old trapline cabin blues
Sure I don't have electric lights and stores and booze.
Life in the bush I find strengthens heart and soul and mind
I've got those old trapline cabin blues

I see what town life does to folks down here
They have lots of time to sit around, play cards, and guzzle beer.
I ain't gonna let it happen, I'm heading out and then.
I'll be walking living proof that the bush still turns out men.

I've got those old trapline cabin blues
My heritage and pride I will not lose
Smart as wolf and fast as hare, I can survive out there
I've got those old trapline cabin blues

ANIMALS

by Ned Rozell
Geophysical Institute,
University of Alaska Fairbanks

Their fair-weather cousins have long since departed, migrating for warmer climes and a more varied menu. They stay, appearing as little puff balls at Alaskan's birdfeeders even on the coldest days of the winter. Black-capped chickadees aren't built to take an Alaskan winter, but they thrive with unique adaptations to life in the north.

"Bigger is better when it comes to surviving an Alaska winter without artificial heat," says Pierre Deviche, an associate professor of animal physiology with the Institute of Arctic Biology at the University of Alaska Fairbanks (UAF). "Just like a large cup of coffee cools more slowly than a small one, a moose retains body heat more efficiently than a fox," Deviche says. "A fox needs to produce more heat relative to its body size to keep warm."

Weighing about as much as a handful of paper clips, chickadees overcome their size disadvantage with physical adaptations and by using their tiny, black-and-white heads. Susan Sharbaugh, a doctoral student at the UAF Department of Biology and Wildlife, says that in the interior, beginning in late July, chickadees begin wedging seeds, insects and other food into tree bark and other crevices.

Unlike squirrels, who create massive mounds of spruce cones for munching later, chickadees "scatter hoard," Sharbaugh says. Chickadees leave thousands of seeds cached throughout the half-mile range in which they spend their entire life. Later in the winter, perhaps when a birdfeeder runs out of sunflower seeds, a chickadee is somehow able to find seeds cached months earlier.

"These guys have a fantastic memory," Deviche says. "Studies of chickadee brains have revealed that the volume of the hippocampus, an area of the brain linked with memory, varies with the season. In fall, when a chickadee is

Busy, Brainy Chickadees Shun Snowbird Label

hiding food, the hippocampus expands. In the spring, when there's no more need to find cached food, it contracts."

In addition to brains that bulge with the season, chickadees physically adjust to a cold climate in many ways. In fall, they begin shivering. Although it's not visible at the birdfeeder, chickadees' chest muscles, called the pectoralis, repeatedly flex to generate heat. That heat is contained by the air trapped within a chickadee's downy coat.

A chickadee's feathers are amazingly efficient. Sharbaugh points out that when it's 40 below outside and a chickadee's feathers are

raised to create an inch-thick coat, the difference in temperature between the chickadee's body core and the environment an inch away is 148 degrees. Try standing outside at 40 below in an inch-thick coat. Brrr.

Unlike common redpolls, one of the other tiny species of songbirds that winters in Alaska, chickadees don't have an internal bag, called a crop, for storing food. Instead, chickadees must eat small meals, digest them, then eat again. Because they only feed in daylight, their window of opportunity is woefully small in winter.

To compensate, they eat as much as they can, adding fat each day that amounts to 10 percent of their body weight and burning it at night. This is like a 150-pound person eating enough to weigh 165 by day's end, then using enough energy at night to be back to 150 by the morning. "It's a huge physiological feat," Sharbaugh says.

Where Alaska chickadees spend the night is a mystery, but Deviche and Sharbaugh believe they ball themselves up in a crevice or cavity, alone, or perhaps roost in spruce branches. Once down for the night, chickadees turn down their internal thermostats to save energy, Sharbaugh says.

From a normal body temperature of about 108 degrees, chickadees cool down to around 90 degrees when roosting. Despite the energy savings of this method, Deviche says that on an early morning in winter it's almost impossible to find a fat chickadee.

During extreme cold snaps, researchers have found that birds show up less often at the feeder. Those that do don't spend any time messing around, concentrating solely on filling up rather than interacting socially.

Seems as though chickadees have a few traits in common with us humans, another organism that arguably wasn't built to survive an arctic winter.

The three gophers

by Peter Harms

nce upon a time in a land far away there lived three little gophers. They got sick of hanging around and went out into the wild, wild world looking for adventure. Their mother cried big salty tears when they left and told them to be careful, always change their socks at night, brush their teeth after each meal, and don't trust any animals with huge teeth.

Well, the first gopher hadn't gone 50 metres and she got tired. She found a big sandy cliff and started to dig her burrow into the soft sand. She went in about one metre and dug out a big room for her TV, her couch, her bed, her new compact disc player, and of course her Nintendo game. That evening along came a hungry coyote.

"Hey little gopher, can I drop by?" she asked.

"Poke a stick in your nose and throw sand in your eye!" shouted the cheeky little gopher.

"Ahh," said the coyote, "a smart aleck, ehhh? Then I'll claw and I'll paw and I'll cave your house in."

Well, she clawed and she pawed and the sandy hole caved in and the cheeky little gopher ran out of her house straight into a dark tunnel that had teeth on the top and the bottom. The coyote smacked her lips and with a little burp, was on her way.

The second little gopher had run up to the forest and found a big rotten log with a hole in one end. He thought that this would be a great place to live since he didn't have to dig any hole at all. He thought it was the best place in the world. Well, just as he got the Sega hooked up and the hot tub was warm, who should he see but a stranger with big teeth.

"Hey, Dude, how's life in the big forest?" asked the stranger.

"Take a hike, Spike," was the answer.

"Why don't you let me in and I can play you a few games on the Sega?" the kind-sounding coyote asked.

"Go away, you bug me," the little gopher said.

"Well, you leave me no choice but to claw and to paw and to cave your house in."

So she clawed and she pawed and the rotten log fell to pieces because of the ripping claws. The coyote got closer and closer to the shivering gopher until, SNAP! the second little gopher was history.

The last little gopher had always been a hard worker and she wanted a good safe house just like her mother had so she found the toughest, roughest, hardest dirt she could find. In fact, she didn't know it but she dug her burrow in the middle of the Robert Campbell Highway. Her little armpits sweated and her back hurt as she dug and dug and dug. Her little claws were bleeding by the time she dug through the gravel and rocks and she didn't stop until her burrow went down four metres.

She ordered out for some pizza and was just sitting down to watch some NHL play-off action on the tube when something was sniffing at the door.

"Little gopher, little gopher, won't you let me come in?"

"Look, rodent breath, why don't you go eat a porcupine or something?"

"Now little gopher, don't be so tough. I want you to know that your brother and your sister let me into their new houses and that we had a great party," the coyote chuckled.

"Well, all I can say is I hope you get sick. You're not eating me, not one little drumstick."

"Well, I'll paw and I'll claw and I'll cave your house in."

She pawed and she clawed and she pawed and she clawed and she tried and she cried, but the ground was too hard. The coyote got so mad that she didn't think of anything but getting that stupid little gopher and munching on her. But when you are a coyote and you are trying to dig a hole in the middle of a highway, there are a few things that you should always be thinking about.…

Well, after the Yukon Alaska ore truck went by, the gopher finished her pizza and had a nap on her water bed.

CATHERINE DEER 1989

by Jayne Fraser

In search of the perfect pet

For some strange reason human beings feel the need to take animals from their little worlds, and make them as content as possible within our own environment. We try to create near-perfect little ecosystems for them. In effect, we try to simulate the environments from which they were reluctantly plucked. The perfect pet, the way I see it, would be one that lived in its own environment (outside, for example, in its natural habitat), was able to feed, look after, and clean up after itself, and wanted only from me a bit of attention now and again. In other words, all of the benefits of a pet, but none of the bother.

The Gehrings had a pet like that. In the early sixties, the Gehring family, consisting of Bill and Doreen, and their children Curtis and Charmane, lived at Rock Creek, about 13 miles south of Dawson City on the Klondike Highway. In the spring of 1963, a two-day-old cow moose was found near Rock Creek by a family friend named Cameron Deeks. He ran a cafe across from the Dawson Airport. No one knows why the moose abandoned her calf. Perhaps the calf was born on the side of the road and people had a chance to pet it. Human smell would have confused the mother. Mr. Deeks kept track of the baby moose, and after two days the calf seemed in dire need of someone to take care of her. The mother had still not returned, so he offered the famished moose to the Gehrings.

The Gehrings had come to the Yukon hoping to farm. They were accustomed to hard work and wholeheartedly accepted the challenge of starting a dairy farm in the Klondike Valley. Over the years chickens, geese, turkeys—even a burro named Patrick—lived on the farm, along with opportunistic bears, foxes and wolves that hung out in the periphery. But in 1963, when they inadvertently inherited a moose, they had only a few cows grazing around their rented shack at Rock Creek.

Feeding the baby moose was a problem. The cows wouldn't allow her to nurse from them, so the Gehrings used a long-necked pop bottle to feed her cow's milk. After about two weeks, her health began to deteriorate. The moose was suffering from diarrhoea and losing weight. Her diet needed a change, so Bill ground up some willows, mixed them with eggs, and fed this concoction to her. Her health returned. In fact, she thrived, and claimed her place as part of the family. They named her Skookum.

Soon after acquiring Skookum, the Gehrings moved to a hay farm at Henderson Corner, 15 miles south of Dawson City. The turn-of- the-century operation was a perfect place for them to pursue their dream of northern farming. Bill was worried about how the moose would fare in her first winter. But by this time, Skookum was more like a cow than a moose. She spent the cold days quite comfortably right on top of the haystack, eating and sleeping at her leisure. She was becoming attached to the cows on the farm, although it seemed that the cows were more tolerant than affectionate with her. Neither Skookum nor the cows were ever penned up. When Bill acquired the moose, he said once, "I won't even try if she has to be penned up like in a zoo." The moose, along with the cows, roamed around Henderson Corner freely, and many tourists were taken aback when they came across the unlikely combination on the roadside.

Skookum also got along well with the Gehrings' dog. Moose grow a tuft of hair, known as a bell, below their throats. When Skookum was around a year old, the dog used to swing from this bell until it was torn off. This loss didn't seem to affect her any. She was later outfitted with a real bell so that hunters could hear her, and thus, would spare her during hunting season. You could hunt cow moose during that time. Bill actually took Skookum moose hunting with him once, hoping that the cow moose would attract a bull, but no luck there. Skookum was spooked by other moose, and bolted whenever another one was close by.

The Gehrings' young children treated the moose like any other pet. She was their friend. When the moose was down on her front legs, which is the only way a moose can "graze" a pasture, Curtis and Charmane were able to pet and play with her. She was gentle and affectionate, and not above licking the children's faces.

Skookum sometimes came right into the Gehring house, mistaking herself for a house pet. Once she was full-grown, getting her out of the house was no easy matter. Longtime Dawson residents remember visiting the Gehring farm and seeing Skookum help herself to the comfort of the indoors. She would also help herself to food in the kitchen, draining milk glasses and raiding frying pans. She jumped right through an open window one time, ran through the house, and jumped out another window.

Skookum became somewhat of a celebrity. Tourists often stopped at the farm to take pictures of her. Articles about her and the Gehrings appeared in various newspapers and magazines, including *Canada Weekly* and the July 1967, issue of *Alaska Sportsman*. One picture shows Skookum and Bill Gehring in the Discovery Day parade. Skookum is wearing a halter and a banner that reads "Dawson City Mule." Although Bill was able to halter-break the moose, and she could pack more than a hundred pounds, he wasn't able to ride her. Every time he got on, she would lie down.

In the summer, the cows would wander all the way to Lousetown to graze, a fifteen-mile trip to the west. This abandoned site at the confluence of the Klondike and Yukon rivers was officially known as Klondike City. It came by its more descriptive name after local prostitutes were forced to move there so that their business would not offend "proper" Dawsonites.

Skookum was becoming quite independent by this time and she didn't follow the herd. She wandered in the opposite direction to the North Fork of the Klondike, some fifteen miles east of the farm. But she always returned to Henderson Corner for the winter.

In 1967, Bill was working away from the area for the winter, so Doreen and the two children moved into Dawson. They saw or heard of Skookum only sporadically,

Occasionally, Doreen would visit the farm. If the moose was around, she would come up to Doreen for a dose of human affection.

The article in *Alaska Sportsman* concluded with a letter written by Doreen Gehring.

"Skookum spent the winter at home. Sometimes she went out in the afternoon for willows, but she was always home by dark.

"About two months ago, a cow was ready to calf. This cow took Skookum and another cow with her and started walking towards town. (Cows often wander away to have their calves.) They got as far as three or four miles out of town when the cow had her calf right beside the road. I didn't know about it until morning. Some motorists reported driving along the road and seeing our cow having its calf with Skookum standing beside her as though she were the midwife.

"I haven't seen Skookum lately. She should be having a calf this spring."

Skookum never did calf. The following winter she failed to return to the farm and some people, including Bill Gehring, speculated that Skookum was probably shot during hunting season. Doreen was never sure what happened to Skookum, but her time as part of their family made a lasting impression on her. Doreen still has Skookum's bell. In a letter to me she wrote about her years at Henderson Corner:

"It was a bit lonely. In the winter there was very little traffic on our road. Sometimes it was so quiet I almost felt like I was the only person left in the world. The cows and moose were a bit of company for me."

What more can you ask for in a pet? Perhaps only that it wasn't one that would quite so easily fill a freezer. When I moved to Henderson Corner in 1981, it was still operating as a hay farm. Since then the land has been subdivided into parcels and is a thriving community.

Recently, my attention was diverted by something moving outside of my window. I walked over, looked out, and there were two cow moose grazing right in my backyard. I went outside and approached them. I never actually touched them, but for a brief twenty minutes the pair seemed in my grasp. Watching them from just 15 feet away, I felt that they were indeed, for the pure enjoyment value of the moment, the perfect pets.

GLADYS LAVALLEE

by Karan Smith

I f you're going to make a moose tufting, don't shoot a summer moose. The dark hair of a summer moose is harder to dye, advises veteran moose hair-tufter Gladys Lavallee. "You can't dye it pink if it's black," she says sensibly.

Lavallee points to one of her tuftings that shows brown and grey flowers on a black velvet background. "That moose was shot in August," she states.

The lighter hides of winter moose are best for dyeing. The best hair for tufting comes from around the neck and the belly, or wherever it is long and white. Lavallee says the tips of the hairs are no good either because they're usually too wiry and don't bend into tufts very well.

Lavallee's glasses, dangling from a chain, rest against the front of her sweatshirt. The logo on it reads "The Yukon: The Last Frontier," but Lavallee did not learn her craft here. She learned tufting from a pamphlet when she was living in the Northwest Territories 25 or 30 years ago. After she sold her third tufting, a full-time career as a moose hair-tufter began.

"I wouldn't shoot one of those animals," laughs Lavallee. "After it's dead though, I might as well use the hair."

Seven days a week, sometimes ten hours a day, Lavallee moose tufts. In her home outside Carmacks, she dons her plastic apron and heads down to her basement. She says loose moose hairs are usually "flying all over the place" there.

She averages about 20 tuftings a week during the busy summer season, and her tuftings hang on walls all over the territory. She also has one in the National Gallery in Ottawa.

"When I started, it was a dying art. There was hardly anybody doing it," says Lavallee. "When I started you would have paid $165 for a tufting—they're not so rare anymore." Today, tuftings start at $50, unframed.

Upstairs, not one moose tufting hangs on Lavallee's wall. "After ten hours in my basement I don't want to look at the wall and see one."

Lavallee takes the moose hide, hair intact, and dyes it. Then she cuts a bundle of 15 to 20 hairs. "You bring the needle up and leave a loop of thread," she explains. "You stick the bundle in there (the loop) and pull the thread. One stitch for one petal." The stitch is knotted on the back of the material and the hair, standing in a tuft, is then sculpted with scissors.

Over the years, Lavallee has taught workshops on this traditional Athapaskan art form around the Yukon. Regalia, bags and belts were traditionally decorated with moose tufting.

Lavallee takes after her English father in looks, not her Cree mother. "People see me and say, 'You're not native.' I don't see why it should matter. It doesn't matter for me. People just like moose hair tuftings," says Lavallee. She was born and raised in northern Manitoba and moved to the Yukon in 1979.

Lavallee tufts freehand. Each tufting is unique because even similar looking flowers differ in the roundness of the petals, the space between them or the colour.

One of the marks of Lavallee's work is the shades of colour in her moose tuftings. Her trick is to use different parts of the long hairs, which dye lighter or darker. She points to the last of the garden flowers that fill a beer mug on the table. "See how the colour is darker here and lighter there," she says, her finger touching the petals.

"Everybody does something different," says Lavallee. "You can compare the cutting or shaping. Some make it maybe fluffier."

She also uses caribou and reindeer hides, shipped up along with her moose hides from the south. Any hair that is hollow is good for tufting, she says. Horse hair? Cow hair? "They're good for paintbrushes, not tufting."

Lavallee admits that sometimes she feels she's getting into a rut making flowers all the time. She tries to spice up the designs by adding birds or butterflies.

"It is messy and tedious and can be boring," warns Lavallee.

"I like doing artwork but I've never had any formal training. I really get into it because it's very relaxing…and you don't have to go out in -50 degrees Celsius."

That is, unless you're out hunting a winter moose.

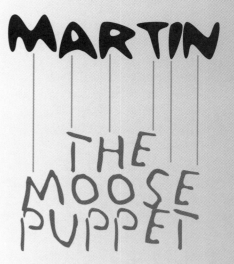

MARTIN THE MOOSE PUPPET

by Judith A. Speyers

Reprinted with permission from "Animal friends of the north," Highway Book Shop, Highway 11, Cobolt, Ontario, Canada P0J 1C0

Equipment needed: light cardboard, masking tape, brown and black felt pens or crayons, carbon paper, scissors, pencil, glue, paper clips, and yarn or string in the following lengths:

   12 pieces—10 inches long
   4 pieces—12 inches long
   2 pieces—4 inches long
   1 piece—6 inches long

1. Using the template on the opposite page, trace two body, four hoof and six rectangle shapes onto the cardboard, using carbon paper.

2. Colour body pieces brown. (Make sure you turn one body piece over before colouring it so when they are put together, the shapes match.) Colour hoof pieces black. Mark the eyes on the body pieces in black.

3. Cut out all shapes. Carefully poke a hole at the x marks.

4. Glue three rectangle shapes together to make a heavy stick. Repeat with the remaining three pieces. Place under a heavy weight while they dry so they will remain straight. When dry, glue the two resulting sticks at right angles to form an x. Make sure the holes line up.

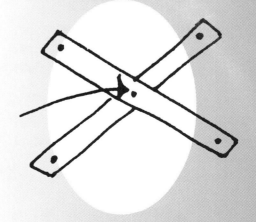

5. Thread the 6-inch piece of yarn through the centre hole of the glued strips and tie a knot.

6. Braid three of the 10-inch pieces of yarn together. Push the finished braid through the centre hole of the hoof and tie a knot so that the yarn won't slip through the hole. Repeat three more times with the remaining pieces of 10-inch yarn. This will give you four "legs" for your moose.

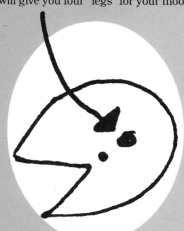

7. Tape the yarn "legs" to one of the body pieces at the o marks. Glue the two body pieces together, catching the "legs" between them. Hold the body pieces together with the paper clips until the glue is dry.

8. Poke the 4-inch pieces of yarn through the body piece at the x_1 and x_2 marks. Tie the knots close to the body.

9. Tie the two 4-inch pieces of yarn together as illustrated and then tie the 6-inch piece of yarn from the x-piece to the knotted 4-inch pieces.

10. Tie the 12-inch pieces of yarn to the x-piece of cardboard and to each of the hooves as illustrated.

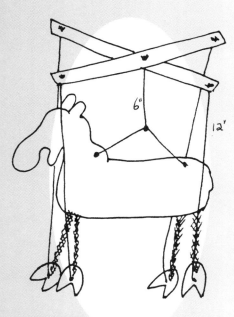

11. Hold the x piece in your hand and make the moose walk. This is difficult to do. If you move your hand in a back and forth and sideways rocking motion, with practice your moose should be able to move each foot separately.

HAVE FUN!!

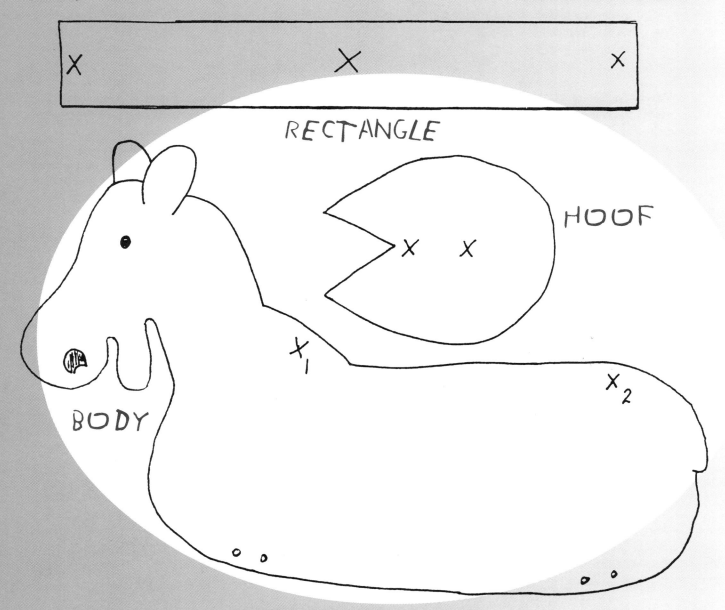

RECTANGLE

HOOF

BODY

BIRD WATCHING: A NORTHERN TREAT

by Pam Sinclair

It's May 23 and not cold, but the wind blowing across this wide-open landscape is relentless. A small bird is buffeted across the ridgetop where we're hiking, and disappears over the leeward side. Was that a flash of white on its tail? We scramble over loose rocks, escaping the wind just below the ridge to relocate the bird, and YES—it's a Northern Wheatear!

It seems miraculous that this delicate little bird, uttering metallic alarm calls as it bobs its striking white and black tail, has just arrived from Asia. We take a good look at its handsome black mask and other field marks, and quickly move on, leaving this remarkable bird to enjoy its respite from the wind.

For birders from around the world, the Dempster Highway is one of the Yukon's main attractions. It is enviable to have vast expanses of tundra, and the fascinating bird communities which make this landscape their home, just a few hours from the urban sophistication of Whitehorse. But you need not wait until tourist season to visit the Dempster! By mid to late May, most birds have returned. One of my favourite spring trips is visiting the Dempster for the long weekend in May. We usually camp at Tombstone Campground and take day-trips from there. Short excursions from Tombstone will take you to a variety of rich bird habitats, including Moose Lake and the surrounding tundra, the Blackstone River crossing and associated wetlands, and "Surfbird Mountain," a series of rounded hills to the east of the highway.

In terms of weather, anything can happen. You might have a gloriously warm, sunny weekend, or you might be scooping snow off your tent and chipping at blocks of ice for your morning coffee. But bad weather will not ruin your birding opportunities—on the contrary! Many migrants have already arrived, so a snowfall at this time of year will concentrate birds in areas of bare ground. You may not have your hike up Surfbird Mountain, but instead you have a chance of seeing Surfbirds, Northern Wheatears, Gray-crowned Rosy Finches, and other high-alpine birds right down near the highway.

At Tombstone you will wake up to a chorus of northern songbirds including the musical offerings of Varied Thrush, Ruby-crowned Kinglet, White-crowned, American Tree, and Fox Sparrows, and Orange-crowned, Wilson's, and Yellow-rumped Warblers. This sounds particularly melodious if you have chosen a campsite that was also claimed by a territorial male Willow Ptarmigan. The frenzies of goofiness that comprise this ptarmigan's courtship flight displays in the wee hours can't help but make you laugh. Due to the vagaries of late spring weather, the stage of moult the ptarmigan are in may make them very conspicuous. A late snowfall may suddenly make brown summer-plumaged birds stick out like sore thumbs. On the other hand, if the snow has melted off quickly, Rock Ptarmigan may be scurrying to bathe in any dirt or dust they can find to dim their dangerously bright white feathers. Like us, the ptarmigan always have one eye open for an approaching Gyrfalcon.

If the snow has melted then you will be able to hike up the mountains and hills beside the highway. Unless you like struggling through vast wet tangles of dense willows, you can easily gain good access to higher ground by using the communications tower road to the tower above, and head up to your left for a very pleasant walk along these rounded hills and ridges. Up top, you will have fantastic views of the landscape, and you will have a chance of encountering American Pipits, Horned Larks, Rock Ptarmigan, Northern Wheatears, and Surfbirds.

The Surfbird is a Yukon specialty. The Yukon is the only place in Canada where this species breeds. In fact, the world range of nesting Surfbirds is limited to the Yukon and central Alaska. The late Bob Frisch, who contributed an extraordinary amount to our knowledge of central Yukon birds, first confirmed that Surfbirds nest in Canada.

The Surfbird leads a curious dual life. In winter, large flocks frolic on rocky shores of the Pacific Ocean, dodging crashing waves and getting drenched in salt spray. Watching these wintering flocks, which share barnacle-speckled rocks with the likes of such ocean-loving birds as Black Turnstones, Rock Sandpipers, and Black Oystercatchers, it is difficult to imagine them more than a few metres from water. However, Surfbirds are very particular about their nesting habitat, and it has little to do with water. In summer, they seek out dry heath tundra on mountaintops many hundreds of miles from the sea. If you are lucky enough to see this enigmatic species on its nesting grounds along the Dempster, stop for a moment to ponder the strange life of this chunky shorebird.

SELF-SUFFICIENCY

On Willow Furniture

by Shiela Alexandrovich

I am primarily a basket maker, and have come to treat some of my favourite willow patches as my ritual grounds. But willows grow and change; soon my basket patch wanted to become tables and chairs. I took a good book out of the library, bought ten dollars worth of screws and nails, waited for a sunny, bug-free day in May, and built a table. Simple. I'm not as precise as some in my furniture, nor have I years of experience, but I make things I need, for free, that are sturdy and beautiful. I'll try to share my approach.

Willow, birch, alder, and poplar are all local materials that can find a place in rustic furniture. It does not take power tools to build rustic—and you can build just the thing for that funny little corner in the kitchen. There are few rules, and a piece will evolve as it is built—if you let it. Some of the finest wood workers have the hardest time with this. For me, it is a dance between design, materials, and the strength of the sunshine on that particular day.

on Gathering...

Sometimes I gather with a project in mind. Roadsides will give taller, straighter willow. Riverbanks or windblown ridges give more shapely stock. I may be looking for strong "Y" shapes for the table legs; after all, if two legs grow together then I don't have to fiddle about trying to join them. Often, shapes will catch my eye, and I have made it a personal rule always to bring these home. They will find a place, sometime.

I cut one to three-inch framing stock, usually shapely and solid. Benders are long, finer willow that bends to build backs, seats and arms of chairs or be the solidifying arches in tables and shelving.

Colour is a factor, although most willow will deepen into shades of red-brown. Alder is textured; birch white; young birch red. Some may be peeled, some painted.

I do some trimming on the spot, but I leave all the main branches on. It's hard to know when you might need a branch until you're working it into a piece, and you can always trim later.

I take a small, sharp handsaw, a pair of good garden shears, rope, and a thermos of tea. You can gather throughout the year, although spring and fall allow you to see what you are getting. A willow tree can be trimmed without killing it, but I take care how I leave an area. The trees have their own sort of dignity; just because they will grow back is no reason to leave a battlefield behind.

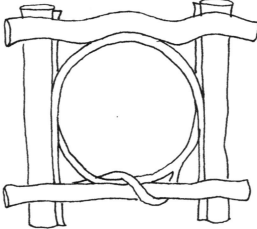

Arches and branches used to stabilize a table end.

Store gathered willow in the snow in winter, bringing it in to work. I build furniture in the spring, and I prop material up against my house with the butt ends in a big puddle I have until the puddle dries up.

on Design...

Define what sort of dimensions you want in a finished piece. There are basic measurements that will make a chair comfortable. I leave this type of information to books. I design chairs to include seat and back cushions, which usually get made from old futon cotton. If it is to be a plant table, I'll add a level or two to accommodate trailing plants. Or add a trellis at one end. I make what I need—my designs are defined by function. A bookshelf on my window ledge needs legs to keep the frost melt-down from soaking the books. A willow side-table needs at least one flat spot for my coffee cup. (The rest may heave and bend at will!)

I diagram the basic framework, writing myself a list of the number of pieces I need of 24 inches, 36 inches, etc., and then head out to the deck.

on Building...

Tools you will need include:
- screwdriver
- measuring tape
- small sharp handsaw
- good garden shears or clippers
- sharp knife
- round sided rasp

- hand drill—rechargeable or electric
- Phillips screwdriver bit (for drywall screws)
- assorted drywall screws, $1/4$ to $2^1/2$ inches
- panelling nails, different colours and lengths
- galvanized spiral nails $1^1/2$ to 2 inches
- a box of $3/4$ inch cigar-box brads for those fine tendrils
- lightweight hammer
- level
- twine or string for tying (I actually use a long silk scarf. It seems to tighten and hold well.)
- nail trimmers for trimming panelling nails that go right through
- a flat space to work on. In the winter, I use an old door, outside on the snow.

on Framing...

I will try to list some methods that work for me. Specific dimensions will come from your design. Or you can always find a project plan from a resource book.

Framing stock should be sturdy—$1^1/2$ to 2 inch diameter works well. Fit pieces together and mark them.

Use a round rasp to give a saddle for one piece to sit in. Two round pieces don't have a lot of contact. A saddle will greatly increase the strength of a joint.

Tie the two pieces together. Drill and then screw. Kneeling on two pieces often works well.

rasping out a saddle to fit two round pieces together

Balance as you build. Do two sides of a chair simultaneously, then put them together. Look at what you are building from all angles. A chair frame may need to be squared up. Give it a twist before adding diagonals and bracing. Bracing will solidify your frame; don't worry if it wiggles a bit at the beginning. I leave branches that will later wrap a chair leg, or help tie together an arm. If I know for sure I don't need a branch—snip!

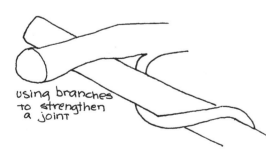

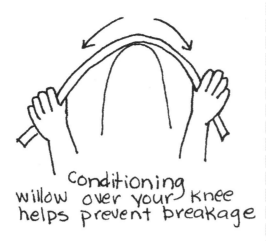

Conditioning willow over your knee helps prevent breakage

Tent Bower Construction

by Mike Wanner

ILLUSTRATION: HELEN O'CONNOR

The first summer I was here in the Yukon, I lived in a pup tent on a friend's property out in the Golden Horn subdivision. My tent site was located in a patch of very thick young pine trees. Now a pup tent can be uncomfortable when it gets hot, and miserable when it rains and we get enough of both here to cause unpleasantness.

So to relieve both problems, I built a bower to completely cover my tent.

First, I cleared the immediate area I had chosen for the tent site. I cut down the saplings at or below ground level.

Then I bent the tops of the saplings on the perimeter in to the centre and tied them together.

After that, I wove the saplings I had cut to clear the area, in and amongst the upright perimeter saplings. From then on, it was just like making a spruce bough lean-to. I kept on adding more and more boughs until I had plugged up all the holes.

It turned out to be quite waterproof and kept the sun from overheating my tent, and made me quite comfortable.

properly balanced. Being attacked by a nail-infested chair on the loose is not very funny.

As you add pieces, stop and look before you nail. Have enough material on hand that you can try out different pieces. Three six-inch pieces of willow can be very different. Certain bends and kinks in a willow will be a custom fit in the right place.

I spend more time fiddling around and finding the right piece for the right place than I spend on actually building. But then, I'm fond of the bent and twisted, rather than the straight. The grace in a piece often comes from the fine branches that curl and connect throughout. Each builder will develop their own eye, and if your taste runs to smoother, cleaner lines, then you won't need all the finer branches. Try to stay open to possibilities.

Arches make wonderful bracing. An arch facing upward, balanced by one facing down, will keep two table legs where they belong.

The Yukon grows some of the finest furniture willow, and has some wonderful rustic builders.

My kids and I have road-travelled extensively throughout North America, and never seen such a concentration of willow-workers as here in the Yukon. A toast to Yukon rustic builders, present and future!

using branches to strengthen a joint

on Benders...

Bend or condition the long willow over your knee, making sure it will indeed bend, and not break. Again, to achieve balance, add benders to one side, then the other. I use panelling nails for the benders, nailing from the butt end out. Keep the nails more than 1 inch from the butt, in case it splits. A willow bent to 180 degrees can spring apart with a lot of power if it isn't

Roughing it in the '90s

(with apologies to Susanna Moodie)

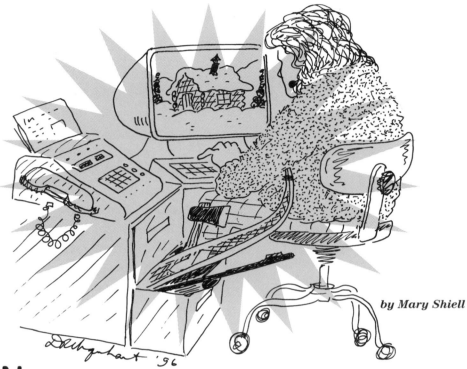

by Mary Shiell

No power. No plumbing. No phone/fax. No Mary.

Or at least that's the way I like to tell the story now as I sit smugly in my little corner of Canada's last frontier, officially dubbed Fawlty Acres, surrounded by all the modern conveniences. Not exactly fodder for a great pioneering epic, but hey, this is the '90s. Think of it as a kinder, gentler version of roughing it in the bush.

To be completely accurate, make that RESIDING in RURAL RESIDENTIAL. At least that's what the tax people call this little conglomeration of shacks, sheds, corrals and sled dog-lots. It certainly doesn't have the same ring to it, but in this day and age, precision seems to take precedence over panache. I still prefer BUSH. The very word conjures up images of Paul Bunyan-type men (and Lord knows we could use a whole lot more of them) and the courageous women who followed in their wake. You know those women. The ones who spent their days packing thousand-pound loads over high mountain passes and their nights turning moose turds into top quality jewellery. The ones who'd plug a charging grizzly full of lead and then go back to their cold, crude log cabin and calmly whip up a 10-layer chocolate cheesecake.

Things are slightly different these days.

It doesn't take a whole lot of gumption to drive the big, new 4 x 4 to town and back, with Johnny Cash belting out his top ten all the way.

But commandeering that truck around the drive-through at Tim Hortons Donuts, without bumping, scraping or scratching anything, is another story, one that takes a few years off my life each time I try it.

And what about when the fax goes on the fritz, taking incommunicado to a whole new level.

No more firing off snarky letters to editors in Toronto about the inherent bias against northern stories (like the subway crash is relevant here, nimb brain).

No more flogging dogmushing trips to the good denizens of Bermuda (it's not that cold here in the winter, REALLY).

And no more distributing 15 reasons to fly with MOE'S AIR SERVICE, not the least of which is the assurance that terrorists are afraid to fly with them.

Then, of course, there are the wolves at the door. Well, all right, they're not really at our door but they're too close for comfort, cruising through at all hours of the day or night en route to the nearby dump. Largely misunderstood, wolves are neither noble nor savage; they're simply bargain hunters like the rest of us.

When all things are considered, though, I probably run a greater risk of incapacitation from tapping too long on this damn keyboard than from anything life at Fawlty Acres throws my way.

Roughing it in the '90s. Not.

GETTING IN

(WRITTEN FOR AUNTIE)

by Louise Profeit-Leblanc

Whispy white hair
Draped over her naked
Body
Flanks and breasts sagging
Hanging
Hints of stretch marks
Childbirth
Belly flap conceals
And hides grey pubic
Hair

Toenails, thick, rigid almost
Grey
Tattooed on her hand is
Raven
Recollections of her childhood
Puberty
Charcoaled in forever

Loose skinfolds draping from arms
Which held her babies
Living and dead
Loving, tender embraces
With her spouse

She dips her toe into the water
Slowly, carefully, shaking
She lowers in the stiff legs and
Torso
Releases a long sigh, which denotes
Her fond appreciation of one of life's
Still lasting pleasures
The Bath!

Electricity

by Lona Hobbs

Electricity,
a commodity that holds us like a hostage
for without the pulsating voltage along wires
living becomes a stalemate.
Our electronic world is silent
daily routines dormant
vulnerability exposed.
Multiple Sclerosis
a disease that holds the body hostage
for without the neural transmission
to
muscles
living becomes a stalemate
our metabolism is altered
daily routines filibustered
vulnerability exposed.

BY JOYCE HAYDEN

Seeing Beyond Near Blindness

"If only I was perfect," or some version of this complaint, dominates our lives from childhood on. If only I was thinner, prettier, smarter, stronger or richer. We humans seem never to be satisfied with who we are. Our self-esteem is, for the most part, low. And low self-esteem is, after all, the greatest disability of all.

I've used my share of if-onlys in my life. Then, in 1983 I was given a gift, an opportunity to look inward, to change, and to grow. I was told I would be totally blind in three months, and that there was nothing that could be done.

At age 51, there was still much I wanted to accomplish. I was devastated, and I was angry. I set out on a get-healthy quest. We moved to the Queen Charlotte Islands, where the air is washed and dried each day. I ate natural foods, walked a lot, and began the soul-searching that eventually brought some understanding and meaning to what had, at first, seemed to be a major life disaster.

I had always believed in the concept that you get back, threefold, what you put out into the world. At least, superficially I had believed it. I briefly contemplated suicide, then decided that wasn't the answer.

My willpower strained to its limits as I tried to focus on finding something positive in near blindness. That was it! Near blindness—I still had some vision. I could see. Vaguely, of course, but I could still see. I began, slowly, and bit by bit, to focus on what I had, rather than on what I had lost. A small bubble of joy began to rise within me.

I had voluntarily turned in my driver's licence, and had given up, I thought, my independence. But I still knew how to drive. Earle drove me to North Beach, a long expanse of hard packed sand on the northern coast of the Charlottes. Here I rode a small motorcycle for hours, feeling the wind and spray in my face, and the release of self-directed speed. My soul felt cleansed. We dug for clams, bought crab off the dock, and beachcombed on those deserted northern beaches. I was beginning to find pleasure in small accomplishments. I learned to distinguish people by their shape, movement and voice. Now that I couldn't see facial expressions, I learned to read body language.

I began devising ways to cope with what had once been a disability, was next a challenge, and eventually became simply part of me, like the size of my feet. The slow pace of the Charlottes soon became boring and we moved back north. A lifetime fascination with politics re-surfaced. Disability be damned. I was going to run.

I sought, and won, a Whitehorse seat in the 1989 Yukon election. In 1991, I was appointed Minister of Health and Social Services, with responsibility for the Yukon Housing Corporation. It was an all-consuming job, and I both loved and hated it. Certainly, I was never bored.

I lost the next election, and we lost government. I had been the only cabinet minister in the country with a visual disability.

Next I was faced with a new challenge: that of retirement, and a scaled-down lifestyle.

It took almost two years to adjust. Now the bubble of joy grows ever larger, and my life is filled with very ordinary pleasures. Growing flowers, canning fruit and fish, and writing, add interest to my days. I've rediscovered needlework with the help of special glasses and I'm even enjoying cooking. (I still don't do coffee.)

I no longer expect perfection of myself or others. That, in itself, is a blessing.

I believe now that the loss of vision was a gift. It forced me to slow down, enjoy what I have and what I am, and look inward. I have learned to focus on what is joyful in my world. I gratefully use the tools that are available to me, like magnifying glasses, cassette books, the city bus system and other people's offered assistance.

Yes, I still get angry, and cranky, and frustrated. It just doesn't last as long and it's easier to laugh at myself. Will I always be able to see? I don't know, but I assume so, just as I assume my feet will stay the same size. And the challenges are still there. I started golfing recently (Earle watches where the ball lands) and I've just bought a computer.

I am content.

So

Do you know where there's any good berry patches?

by Anne Hargrave

ILLUSTRATIONS: HELEN O'CONNOR

This is the big question always asked of berry pickers, and we all know that berry pickers never divulge the locations of their favoured berry patches. Someone actually asked me once where my wild strawberry patch is, the one I spend two days wandering through to get enough of those wonderful little (perhaps even minuscule) flavour bursts to make one batch of jam. Needless to say, I was aghast and only managed to blurt out, "Are you serious?"

Well, the truth is that there are numerous enough berries throughout the Yukon that I have been tempted to respond by telling people to go for a walk in the woods and look at the ground. But that's not very nice, or very helpful. They really are easy to find once you get the hang of it, but there are a few rules.

The first one is not to be fussy about what kind of berry you want. Start with something simple and abundant, like lingon berries, also called low bush cranberries. They grow on creeping vine-like shrubs along the ground, and have green oblong, oval leaves. The berries are round and red. They look very similar to kinnikinnik, both as a plant

and as a berry. But the colour is slightly different. To learn the difference, break a berry open. If you are nervous, don't do it with your teeth. Use your fingers but don't worry, they aren't poisonous. If the berry is a dry whitish mealy thing inside with a brownish seed in the middle, you have kinnikinnik. If it isn't, but is instead a juicy, fruity interior, eureka! you have a cranberry. It will be a little bitter, but that's okay, because you won't eat them before you get them home.

Cranberries are the easiest berry to find. But, what if you went to pick cranberries and

Berry Liqueur

3 pounds berries
1 bottle (750 ml) Everclear or Alcool
6 cups sugar
3 cups water

Crush berries and let stand for 24 hours. (Put them through blender if you want.) Add Everclear and let stand another 24 hours. Then put the mixture through a juicer or cheese cloth so that it becomes a clear liquid. Boil sugar and water for five minutes. Cool. Add to juice mixture. It should stand three to six months before being used. Depending on the berry, it may take the full six months or more. It is cooked when the flavours don't separate out into a grain alcohol after-taste. I've made this with cloudberries and cranberries and found it a bit sweet, so you may want to cut back on the sugar.

you've found something else in abundance? Remember, the first rule—don't be picky, (no pun intended). Pick what you find, and take lots of plastic bags or pails to keep them separate. Maybe it's mossberries today; after all, they are often found in sort of the same place, under spruce tree forests.

The same place? Aha, now we are talking about habitat. (Habitat, according to the Concise Oxford, is an organism's natural home.) Just like other animals and plants, berry plants have specific conditions that they need for growing. To get better at finding berries, you have to figure out their specific habitats. For example, are they found in grassy open areas, in wet areas such as along shorelines and (heaven forbid) swamps, on the tundra, or in spruce forests? Starting with low bush cranberries and mossberries, look in spruce forests.

What's a mossberry, anyway? It is also called crowberry, and often grows in the moss. They are on long linear stems, which may be somewhat erect or grow along the ground, and have very straight, spiky deep green leaves that are reminiscent of tiny evergreen needles. The berries are a very dark purple or black, and are extremely juicy, with little seeds. Mossberries are also somewhat bitter and are better taken home for preparation. It only takes two cups of these to make a substantial batch of jam, and every one thinks you've been so industrious. (You can fool some of the people some of the time, etc.)

We've already covered the second rule—pay attention to habitat. Yes, there are other berries that are easy to find. Blueberries are extremely abundant and there is usually a mass exodus from Whitehorse to the White Pass during August.

Another excellent idea is to buy a berry or plant identification book to throw in your daypack. There are several paperback books that are relatively inexpensive and have good pictures and descriptions of the plants. Also, pay attention to what they look like when they are in blossom so you can be scouting for berry plants early in the season. Saskatoons, for example, are easier to find when in blossom, and very pretty, too.

Once you are out there wandering around, you'll find other berry plants. They may not have ripe berries yet, or they might already be past their prime. Never mind, just come back next weekend or next year to the same spot.

There are lots of other things to pick besides the three abundant types already discussed. Starting in late June (in the

Whitehorse area anyway) currants are ripe, followed by strawberries and raspberries, and if you are lucky, nagoon berries throughout July. Then, if you are a real dedicated berry picker, it's up the Dempster in late July, early August for cloudberries. Into August, it's Saskatoons and blueberries. Then, after our first frost and into September, it's mossberries, cranberries (high bush and low bush), and rosehips. This timetable varies, depending on the micro-climate of the particular patch, and what the weather has been like that season.

That's it. Wander around the Yukon, watch the plants, learn how to identify a few, and take lots of bags or buckets with you. When you have found a few patches yourself, you might have some information to trade with someone who then might tell you where that strawberry patch is.

What do you do with them once you get them home? If the weather is still nice and you are picking berries every other day, clean them and put them in the freezer until the weather is not so nice. That way you can also pick a little bit of one kind and keep adding to it until you have enough for a batch of jam or whatever it is you want to do.

There are lots of things to do with your berries once you have enough. Jams and jellies are a favourite, but you can also try pies, liqueurs, juices, muffins, various desserts and puddings. Or just throw some in your Sunday morning pancakes for a flavour treat.

Mossberry Jelly

2 cups mossberries
4 cups water
2 boxes powdered pectin
1/2 cup lemon juice
3/4 cup water
7 1/2 cups of sugar

Put mossberries and 4 cups of water in the blender and process until berries are pureed. Pour the mixture (most of the little seeds stay in the blender) into a heavy saucepan with pectin, lemon juice and 3/4 cup water. Boil rapidly, then add sugar. Boil hard for one minute. Be careful, for it boils over easily. Strain or skim, pour into sterilized jars and seal. Makes at least 8 cups of jam and tastes good on ice cream.

Happy picking!

by Judy Forrest

STEEL-TOED BOOTS

My first two pairs of steel-toed boots were purchased through the Whitehorse Copper mine store in 1977. They very kindly ordered the smallest pair of men's steel-toed boots available so we women folk could dress according to the safety code. I even purchased a pair of men's winter insulated steel-toed snowpacks, though they didn't quite fit, but I was able to minimize their flopping around with two pairs of wool socks. Those boots managed to see me through my year and a half of Hiab truck driving and mill operating at the mine.

I extended their life to get me through my stint at being the Jill of all trades during the construction of the Wolf Creek Subdivision in 1979. I was hired to shingle a roof of a log home, peel logs for another place and be the right-hand gal for a few other carpentry jobs.

My next pair of men's size 5 steel-toed boots were purchased at a western boot store in Victoria, B.C. for the 1980 work season. These boots protected my feet, and made them ache, while I was the bulldozer operator and prospector for an exploration company. I spent that summer in a fly-in bush camp in northern B.C. There I managed to acquire an 86-stitch chainsaw cut to my left thigh. When I was able to put weight on my leg again my boss sent me, and my boots, back out with the chainsaw to clear a helicopter pad on the side of a mountain. I had quite an argument with him as I didn't want to be using a chainsaw just yet. But he said I was the best chainsaw operator in camp, the job had to be done and I was the one going to do it. Needless to say, very pissed off, I went out (with safety pants on this time) and finished the job.

In 1981, my Victoria boots and I mucked through a summer of operating heavy equipment at a family-run gold mine on the Indian River, which is just off Hunker Creek near Dawson City. I was hired as the front-end loader operator, though I did run the bulldozer and buggy (scraper) when needed.

I managed to get those gold-laden babies to escort me through my 1982 job as the Wolf Creek campground attendant.

In 1983, for a spell, my poor abused feet got a break from the not-so-comfortable steel-toed boots. My partner, Bruce, and I, headed off on our South Pacific, New Zealand and Asia trip of a year and a half. Heaven: bare feet and sandals for months on end.

In 1985, I took a surveying course at Yukon College, so once again I was back in the steel-toed boots. I purchased my third—or is that fourth?—pair of steel-toed boots in Victoria at the Capital Iron Store on Wharf Street. I was thrilled that this pair was actually a women's size 7 1/2. That didn't make them any more comfortable in the long run. But they did seem to fit better.

After my surveying course, I was hired as an equipment operator at the historic town site of Fort Selkirk on the Yukon River. I ran the tractor for the summer, working with the restoration crew from the Selkirk First Nation doing a stabilization project on the buildings. Still in 1985, after a fantastic summer working at Fort Selkirk, my boots and I were hired on for highway surveying with the Yukon government on the Skagway Road. Shortly after I started on with Highways, the snow began to fly, so out came the old steel-toed snowpacks.

By chance, on another family visit to Victoria, I was wandering down Fisgard Street (between Douglas and Government) and found myself staring into a window display of handmade work boots. They had cleats, huge rubber soles and all sorts of bells and whistles for heavy bush work in the logging trade. There was something rather homespun about the place so I walked in to chat about boots. I told them my story of how my flat feet ached when I wore any steel-toed boots and that I often had to wear them for 10 hours a day or more. They were horrified at my discomfort and guaranteed I would have no problem with their handmade boots. We were measuring my feet, when they realized they had a pair just my size on hand. They whipped up a couple of leather inner soles shaped to my feet, and off I went with comfortable boots.

I didn't think it was possible.

I began the 1986 work season with those wonderful black boots. We trudged many a mile during my next few years of highway surveying.

After Highways, my boots and I spent three years on a Yukon government campground development crew. We travelled around the Yukon, building and repairing campgrounds. Here, I used a bobcat with lots of implements and the good old chainsaw.

My old leather buddies are now getting dried and cracked in a box downstairs. The last time I used them for work was 1991. A whiplash injury and the birth of our son Benjamin has caused me and my boots to go separate ways for now. Whenever we cross paths in the basement they stir up memories of the challenges and pleasures I experienced in my years of wearing steel-toed boots.

SELF-SUFFICIENCY

LOOK OUT FOR THAT AXE!

by Dick Person

The Yukon territory must be one of the highest per-home wood consumers anywhere in the world. This being so, it continually surprises me as I travel and visit about this country how many axes, saws and splitting implements are in a state of abuse or neglect.

This seems to be most common in the towns where another tool can be readily bought at the local hardware or general store. The person in the bush tends to maintain tools much better, either from necessity or habit, or both.

Let's consider the axe, which has been in continual use for over 100,000 years and may be our oldest tool. Today it's regarded by those who live in the bush as the most important all-around tool.

With it, shelters can be built, firewood gathered, snowshoes, paddles, and canoes constructed, deadfall traps made, animals dressed out—truly a versatile piece of gear.

There's not space here to consider the various kinds and styles and their different (but overlapping) uses, but I would like to look at a few simple things that can be done to keep an axe (or splitting maul) in usable and safe condition.

HEAD

Frequently, an axe head will be loose and this is potentially one of the most dangerous states it can be in. The axe head is in danger of flying off in the course of a swing while chopping and it is a missile that can kill or maim.

It also can shift its position on the handle, throwing off one's timing and point of impact and directing the blade toward some part of the user's body. The resulting blow can easily result in serious injury.

So, let's deal with the loose head first. Some use the quick-fix solution of immersing the head and handle in water. This will swell the wood in a couple hours or less and tighten the head, but it's a temporary fix. If repeated, it will cause dry rot in the wood and severely weaken the wood in the eye of the axe.

When it eventually breaks it will shear off right across the grain and there's no telling when it will happen or where you will be, or what may be in line with this IFO (Identified Flying Object).

Removing the axe head is the way to go and it may require repeated blows with a billet of wood on the underside of the head. Remove all old wedging devices from the handle.

Make a new wooded wedge from hardwood—a piece cut off from an old axe or hammer handle (hickory) is excellent—and fashion it one-half inch longer than appears necessary.

After it's driven into place, you can cut it off flush with the end of the handle.

It's very useful to have some metal axe wedges to accomplish the final tightening. I keep several sizes on hand and choose the correct one to drive.

UPPER HANDLE

Another part of the axe that takes a literal beating is the section of the handle for about three inches below the blade.

Poor accuracy in splitting, or a block that splits but also separates along the growth rings, allows the handle to smack the end of the block very hard and begin to splinter.

I've seen commercially-made hard rubber collars to cover this area. But it's also possible to protect the handle by wrapping it with soft steel wire and then coating this with a layer of epoxy. This is very durable and the epoxy can be renewed if necessary.

I've also used wet rawhide to do this job. When it dries it's on very tight and is tough!

EDGE

If the edge is badly burred over from hitting rocks, or needs a whole new profile ground into it, a power bench grinder is very useful.

However, two words of caution: *wear goggles.* Even if the grinder has a shield, a steel splinter in the eye could result. Make sure you have a good solid rest for the blade and keep the blade moving in a slow arc across the wheel. This will avoid burning (detempering). Steel iridescent blue marks are the sign you're using too much pressure, or moving the blade too slowly.

If you're out of reach of electricity but in the vicinity of a work bench or sturdy table you can use a C-clamp to hold the axe-head firmly in place, especially if you need to remove bad nicks and burrs.

In the bush, I just hold the blade forcefully against a flat stump to do the filing.

Learning to use a file well is one of the skills of axe (and saw) maintenance. If you are not practised with it, work at learning how to apply long smooth strokes to produce an evenly bevelled edge.

Filing into the edge is the most accurate and efficient way to do it and, in the beginning, it's recommended that you wear stout work gloves in case of a slip.

The best tool for the job is an axe file (its name in the hardware trade). It has an eight-inch blade and the tang drawn out into a handle.

One side of the blade is a coarse double-cut surface that removes steel quickly. The other face is a finer mill cut for finishing.

For a splitting axe, file the edge into a fairly abrupt wedge shape. This will quickly separate the end grain of your billet of firewood and cause the two halves to fly apart.

When the axe is to be used for hewing and chopping, as in cabin building, the edge should be filed thin and tapered evenly back in a crescent pattern.

This leaves the toe and the heel thicker. The axe will not bind in the cut and chips will spring out from the notch being chopped.

For a finely finished keen edge, I suggest using a rotary mower file, which has a much finer cut, or a round axe stone, which has a coarse and a fine side. Wet it with water or saliva for smooth fast cutting and use in a circular motion.

Any burr left from the initial filing work will be removed with the mower file or the stone and the resulting edge will be uniformly razor-sharp and a pleasure to use.

In low temperatures, before using your thin-edged hewing axe, warm the blade in your hands or slowly over a fire, as hard frozen knots may chip a super-cold edge.

Here's to safe and happy woodcuttings.

AS breath hangs in the frosty autumn air, thoughts turn to protecting home and body from the inevitable deep freeze of the coming season.

Many Alaskans choose wood heat to make the winter more bearable.

Burning firewood provides warmth by releasing stored energy from the sun—which has been converted by trees—to a mass we can use.

The energy provided by a certain species of wood is defined by British thermal units, or Btu, according to Jay Shelton's *Solid Fuels Encyclopedia.*

A Btu is the amount of energy it takes to increase the temperature of one pound (one pint) of water by one degree Fahrenheit.

For example, to bring a pint of water in a tea kettle from 60 degrees to a boil requires 152 Btu (212 degrees minus 60 degrees).

Firewood energy is measured in Btu per cord.

A cord is 128 cubic feet, which is a four-foot by four-foot by eight-foot pile of wood.

If a cord is cut in one-foot lengths to fit the stove, the resulting wood pile will be 32 feet long and four feet high.

New Englanders laugh at Alaskans for burning birch and spruce, but hickories and oaks, generally considered the best firewood, aren't hardy enough to survive our winters.

Hickory provides about 30-million Btu per cord.

The higher the Btu, the more heat burning wood provides to the living room.

Paper birch, the first choice of Alaskans who can get it, provides 25.4-million Btu per cord, according to a table on the energy content of interior Alaska trees prepared by George Sampson, a former Institute of Northern Forestry research forester.

Tamarack, a tree often mistaken for sickly spruce because of its spindly branches, provides 24.8-million Btu per cord, followed by black and white spruce at about 20.5-million Btu, aspen at 18.8-million Btu, and balsam poplar at 17.5-million Btu.

Sampson's measurements are for air-dry wood with a 20 percent moisture content. Wood is considered dry when it reaches a moisture content of 15 to 30 percent, according to Shelton. Freshly cut, green wood contains 30 to 60 percent moisture. Properly seasoned logs put off much more heat than wet wood.

When a log is placed inside a stove on other burning logs, it doesn't bring instant gratification.

First, the heat energy provided by the other logs drives off the moisture of the unburned log, and none of the heat from the reaction warms the room.

The wetter the log, the more energy that's used to dry it out. For that reason, and because dangerous creosote deposits increase when burning wet wood, Shelton recommends drying firewood for at least six months after it's cut live and split, which brings the moisture content down to an acceptable 25 percent.

Of Alaska woods, birch has the most Btu per cord because it's dense.

This means there's a lot more wood mass, and therefore energy, crammed into a birch log than the same-sized aspen log.

So, which puts off more heat: one pound of oven-dry birch, or one pound of oven-dry aspen?

It's a trick question, because all oven-dried woods have about the same energy content, 8,600 Btu per pound.

Oven-dried wood contains no moisture, an impossible feat to achieve without baking wood in an oven before burning it in a stove.

Therefore, if firewood were sold by the oven-dried pound instead of the cord, 10 pounds of aspen would be as valuable as 10 pounds of birch, but the aspen would take up twice as much room in the woodshed.

ILLUSTRATIONS: HELEN O'CONNOR

PAPER BIRCH BEST ON THE BTU SCALE
BY NED ROZELL
Geophysical Institute, University of Alaska Fairbanks

Sauna Comfort

Saunas have a wonderful effect on me. I have great conversations with people without the slightest concern about the shape of my body. I can't figure out why I seem less self-conscious without clothes, in saunas, than I often feel when I'm fully clothed.

I have only been a sauna buff since coming to the Yukon. Electric saunas had never attracted me much; it's the homemade wood-heated ones that I enjoy.

In the beginning, my lack of self-consciousness was at least partly due to taking off my glasses before I went in. Perhaps other short-sighted people have this same illusion—that if I can't see others well, they can't see me.

But even with contact lenses, I remain relaxed and comfortable with friends and strangers alike. It's a great way to meet people on a very nice level. Intimate without being sexual. In my experience, sexist men (the kind who ogle women on street corners) don't enter a sauna with naked women. I don't know why, but maybe they are uncomfortable for the same reason I am so comfortable. Good thing!

by Alison Reid

A Midwinter Night's Dream

by Al Pope

A veil of luminescent green against a background black
Drew spirals in the morning sky above my rustic shack,
As I tried to start the pickup truck at forty-five below,
And wondered why I'd left my home in south Ontar-eye-o.

For the tiger torch was grizzly and the tiger torch was loud
And it roared like burning thunder deep inside its stovepipe shroud.
But the bitter winter air fought back the heat of burning gasses
And kept the crankcase oil about the texture of molasses.

Back inside the cabin where the woodstove glowed and roared
In a losing battle with the frost on every log and board,
I poured a cup of Old Black Joe and took it to my lover,
Where she huddled down inside the bed with fourteen quilts above her.

Tell me again, my helpmeet sobbed, the memory I've lost,
Why we inhabit this poor shack encased in ice and frost?
It is the beauty, I replied, the glorious liberation.
It is the peace, the quiet, in a word, the isolation.

But I have a government job, she griped, from which I could be fired,
If you don't start that frozen truck and stoke that stinking fire,
And fill me full of coffee strong, and feed me breakfast too,
And get me rolling down the road before I'm frozen blue.

I love my wife above all else, her paycheque I admire,
And I love to fill her oil-lamp, and I love to stoke her fire,
But her patience is not endless, and I knew I had to go
To try and start her pickup truck at forty-five below.

Surely she will start, I prayed, the torch is underneath her,
Her rad is full of antifreeze, her carb is full of ether.
The motor gasped, it moaned, it stopped, I thought it had expired,
But then it coughed, and then it cranked, and finally it fired.

I held the throttle down till I was shrouded in blue smoke,
Then turned the heater on full blast, and let out on the choke.
I left the truck to idle, while like any mortal creature,
I took the opportunity to heed the call of nature.

As I undid my overalls I gazed on prospects bleak,
And even after twenty years I cannot bear to speak
Of the ghastly outhouse mountain jutting through the frozen seat:
Suffice to say I made it quick, and soon was on my feet.

Emerging from that awful box, I chanced to see a light,
And turning toward the source of it I saw a hideous sight.
For there, beyond the dog-lot, lit up like a Christmas card,
Stood a monstrous yuppie mansion, with a new car in the yard.

From in the house a man emerged, well in his middle years,
To start the car so casually, it brought me near to tears.
Impossible! Despicable! It sent me in a rage.
An overnight invasion of the dreaded modern age!

Hey, who are you, I called to him, what are you doing here?
How did you build this house so fast, why did you build so near?
How could you squat in my backyard and not ask my permission?
And even hook yourself up to the Northern Power Commission?

He looked at me indulgently, and gave a little smile,
And said, come on inside the house and warm yourself a while.
I need to run the mini-van, and you your pickup truck,
Before we send our wives to town, to earn the daily buck.

Awash with curiosity, I followed him inside,
And getting to the point at once, I said I'm mystified.
How did you know about my wife, and that she earns the dough?
He said, There's very little about you that I don't know.

I looked him in the schnozzle and I checked his balding spot.
You look just like my dad, I said, although I know you're not.
Are you my uncle? If so, I can tell you man to man,
I'm here for peace and quiet, not a gathering of the clan.

He said, Don't get excited, boy, you're acres off the mark,
And if you weren't dreaming you would know me in the dark.
For dad and son are nearest kin, but you and I are nearer,
As you shall see in twenty years when you look in your mirror.

A spiral green and luminous before a gibbous moon
Hovers in the morning sky above my cozy room.
From my window I can see a young man crouching in the snow
To tiger-torch his pickup truck at forty-five below.

FORTY BELOW

What do you do when it's forty below, you need to start your vehicle, and there's no place to plug it in? I've seen some innovative techniques over the years. A pan of hot coals out of the woodstove. Drain some of the oil, heat it on the stovetop, and return it to the engine. Make a flare out of a coffee can, pink insulation, and lamp-oil. Take the chimney out of an oil-lamp, and replace it with a tin can, and put that under the motor.

I've tried every one of these things, and they all work, sometimes. Then there are the times when they don't work, and the kids miss the school bus, and you're late for work, and you're all in the cabin together, sitting around the stove at forty below getting grumpier with each failed attempt to start the truck.

The most effective way of getting started without power is to use a tiger torch. For the uninitiated, a tiger torch is best described as the crudest propane device imaginable. It looks a bit like the Olympic torch, but with a twenty-pound propane bottle attached to it by a rubber hose, and it sends out a ragged flame up to about three feet long.

If it seems like an act of lunacy to set this raging fire under your vehicle, it is. Handled properly, though, there's at least a 60-40 chance that the torch will get you on the road, without melting any important parts.

Here's how it works.

You take a three-foot length of six-inch stovepipe with an elbow on the end, and set it up under the truck, with the elbow pointing up at the

BY AL POPE

centre of your oil pan. Do this before you go to bed. Take the torch, with the propane bottle, indoors for the night. In the morning, take the torch out, light it, and shove it inside the stovepipe. Don't put it all the way inside the pipe, though, because if you melt the rubber hose, you could find yourself in a very tricky situation. Check to make sure plenty of heat, but no flame, is reaching the oil pan. Adjust the torch accordingly.

If the tank is nearly full, you should be able to go away for twenty minutes, come back, and start the truck. If not, it's quite likely that the propane will soon stop coming out as a nice flow of gas, and begin to spurt liquid, which is both dangerous and ineffective.

The only solution I've found to this is to go out once in a while and turn the flame on the tank. This sounds suicidal, and probably isn't the safest procedure in the world, but it has proved effective in the past. Another idea is to have two tanks, and switch whenever one gets low.

The tiger torch plays an important role in the Yukon's ecology, as it weeds out unsuitably low vehicles, often burning them to the ground, and thus keeping the breeding stock strong. The biggest threat to the tiger torch, and therefore to the healthy maintenance of our '69 pickup population, is the Rural Electrification Plan. Warning: do not attempt to tiger torch a '94 Tercel.

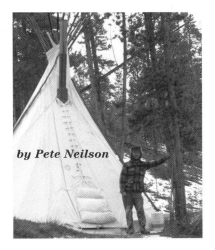

by Pete Neilson

24 Hours In A Teepee

After a busy day running errands in town, I finally point the truck towards home. It's just dusk as I park and take to the trail; the snow squeals under my feet as fresh snow starts to fall. Involuntarily, I quicken my pace. The fat, slow flakes tumble around me and the tensions of town seem to drain out through the ends of my limbs.

After toiling up the last hill, I pause to catch my breath, gazing back towards the distant mountains, now almost obscured by the thickening snow. Lights are beginning to come on down the valley and I turn to go.

Nestled in amongst the pines, my white teepee is hard to see in winter, but the woodpile offers a silent welcome. As I come around the final bend in the trail I'm glad to note a small column of smoke from the chimney; all is well, the stove is still going and the teepee will be warm. I've heard of people who use open fires in their teepees but I've never tried it myself, opting instead for the efficiency of the woodstove with an insulated chimney pipe through the smoke flaps.

Stooping through the doorway, I put down my pack. First, I light the kerosene lamp to brighten the gathering gloom. Next, some fresh wood for the fire and soon, supper is bubbling away on the stove. It's good to be home.

As I sit with my evening tea I absorb the northern silence. One of the first questions people ask me when they find out I live in a teepee is, "Don't you miss having windows?" The answer is no. The ability to hear what goes on around me has become an important aspect of how I relate to this earth. I miss it when I spend time in buildings; often I have trouble sleeping behind their walls.

In my teepee, I listen to the wind in the trees and the squirrels scurrying about. Before I open my eyes in the morning my ears give me a pretty good indication of the day's weather. Listening to the rain on the roof is an old pastime, but in a teepee you can hear it snow. If it has snowed overnight, all sound is muffled. If the trees are cracking, it is very cold and getting colder. If I hear the squirrels, it'll likely warm up a bit.

The wind is my primary aural companion. A significant change in wind velocity during the night, rising or falling, is enough to wake me.

I have never heard the Northern Lights hiss as some of my friends have, but I look forward to the day they rouse me from my snug refuge out into a cold, clear night to watch their compelling display. Tonight, however, I can hear the snow whispering down amidst the crackling of the fire.

In the morning, I awake to complete silence; the snow has stopped and the fire has died away to coals. I dash around the now cool teepee and soon the stove is sending out its heat again. I jump back under the blankets and listen to the portable radio while waiting for things to warm up.

After breakfast, I stroll out to the woodpile. The sky is blue and everything is shining white in the bright sun and new snow. I split some wood, then straighten and look around, enjoying myself on this crisp, clear day. Ravens fly by, croaking in their guttural voices. They always have something to say but I never know what it is.

Soon I'm surrounded by chickadees flitting back and forth. They often show up when I'm splitting wood. Aldo Leopold reports the same phenomenon in *A Sand County Almanac*. He speculates they respond to cracking wood in case it's caused by a newly downed tree with insects exposed for the taking.

In the afternoon, I take a short ski back to a small pond. Checking the fresh snow for tracks I see lots of snowshoe hare and squirrel, and once in a while those of a mouse or perhaps a shrew. I'm disappointed not to see the local lynx's tracks; maybe tomorrow.

As I'm getting supper I hear the wind sighing through the treetops. If it strengthens, it'll be warmer tomorrow. When I put out the lamp I discover the full moon. The pines cast their shadows over the canvas walls creating natural wallpaper. Later, I'm startled awake by coyotes howling. I lie back and listen to the wind.

SELF-SUFFICIENCY

PHOTOS: KAREN DIGBY

Building My Home In The Woods

by Helene Dobrowolsky

18 Sept. 1978: Got out to site, a feat in itself, with pile of gear, wall tent, cookpots, etc. Managed to put up tarp just before dark and rain.

21 Sept. 1978: More geese! Hauled 21 logs zip-zip with a slight delay at onset when I stepped into a hornet's nest. Escaped with only two stings due to much flailing and running and Brenda picking about a dozen out of my clothing.

While going to get the last log came within 30 feet of a beautiful huge bull moose trucking along the lake.

1 Nov. 1978: Hard to say which of the many jobs involved in cabin building has been most arduous, but cutting sods during a snowstorm certainly qualifies as dirtiest.... Snow keeps covering roof and ground. Avoid panic!

(Diary excerpts from my cabin log)

I was more than ready to build my own log cabin, or so I thought. During three years of living in cabins along the Carcross Road, I acquired distinct ideas of how my own home should look. No more shoeboxes! I was going to build a six-sided structure, more interesting. That way, the wall logs could be shorter so I could handle most of them myself. No power tools! Chainsaws terrified me and besides, this was the late 1970s. I was a purist. An axe, a swede saw, log dogs, a draw knife and level were all I needed. Not to mention many friends. My main expenses were food for volunteer workers and sharpening fees for borrowed tools. I became very friendly with the nice man at the sharpening service.

Building happened in two phases. In spring and early summer, I logged trees. The logs were debarked during a peeling party, then left to dry all summer. In September, my friend Brenda Barteski and I set up a wall tent and started hauling logs to the site. Jerry, a carpenter friend, made me a template for marking the 120 degree corners, and Peter Heebink gave me a quick lesson in building half lap notches. Off we went.

The next two months were amongst the most exhilarating of my life. Days began with oatmeal around the campfire watching vees of geese flying south and fresh snowfall slowly creeping down the mountains. Blackflies, blisters, splinters and new muscles on my back and upper arms. Evenings of rude, noisy card games around a kerosene lantern when my brothers came to visit. Awesome northern lights. A wonderful Thanksgiving potluck and roof-raising party. Sitting on top of a wall notching a roof support while watching frisbee and soccer games all around me on a sunny crisp autumn day. Digging sods during a snowstorm. Hearing, then seeing, seven swans a-swimming in the back slough. Laying down plastic on the icy roof at 20 below, with many stops to warm numb fingers.

The end result was small and crude. It was also cozy, easy to heat and if anything went wrong I could repair it myself. Sometimes it seems I've spent the last 19 years fixing all my original mistakes and still have a long way to go.

Much has changed. I now have a family and a town house, and computers are an integral part of my life. But the cabin remains the place where I am spiritually rooted. My husband and daughter share this feeling. The cabin has become a sanctuary for us all—a place for long hikes, many building projects and quiet, peaceful times. At the cabin, we are most ourselves.

PHOTO OF HELENE: MIKE RICE; CABIN PHOTOS: HELENE DOBROWOLSKY

Bluebird Wars

by Claire Eamer

The worst thing about working on my own, right now, is the bluebird. He's a workplace hazard.

For the past nine years, since my son was born, I have worked out of my home as a freelance writer and editor. I've written annual reports, economic plans, historical articles, newspaper stories, and book reviews, and I've edited everything from scientific studies to children's books. I've even compiled a college calendar and a couple of databases.

Flexibility is a prerequisite for this kind of work. It is also one of the major advantages, especially with a family. I can be home after school and during holidays, and we don't have to scramble to cover that working parent's nightmare—the teachers' professional day. We can also take vacations when my partner's job permits, without having to juggle the holiday requirements of another workplace.

A further advantage is simply staying home in the mornings. I am not a competent human being in the morning. In fact, I am barely human at all before nine o'clock.

Getting my son (who is also morning-challenged) fed and dressed and off to school stretches my abilities to the limit. Getting myself to an outside job decently groomed, reasonably awake, and worthy of my hire would be beyond me. Fortunately, all I have to do is pour another cup of coffee and stagger down the basement stairs to my computer.

The computer makes working at home far easier than in the 1970s, when I was a freelance journalist. Then I communicated with my clients by mail and the occasional phone call. Since many of them were based two time zones east of my home, the phone calls tended to come early in the morning. Over time, I developed the ability to sound articulate, competent, and wide awake, even while still dripping from the shower and trying to make coffee with my one free hand.

Now I can communicate and even submit my work by e-mail at a fraction of the cost and inconvenience. A well-constructed e-mail message conceals a multitude of sins, including my business wardrobe (venerable sweats), my state of consciousness (semi until the second cup of coffee), the condition of my desk (a disaster), and the fact that the dog is barking at the letter carrier, the washing machine is unbalanced and banging against the wall, and the breakfast dishes are still piled on the table.

Speaking of the dog and the washing machine brings me back to the bluebird. The hardest thing about working on your own is self-discipline—making yourself get down to work. I regret to admit that I'm not very good at self-discipline. Almost anything will distract me: an invitation out for coffee, a good book, the mail, surfing the Internet, walking the dog, even laundry. And the bluebird.

You see, our neighbourhood is besieged this spring by the Sylvester Stallone of the bluebird world. While his partner peacefully takes care of business in their nest on top of a streetlight, Sly Bluebird roams the block, flexing his wings and attacking windows, apparently assuming that his reflection is a rival male bluebird.

He flings his little blue body against the glass with a thud that, from my basement office, sounds like someone knocking at the door or moving around upstairs. When I go to check, I find not only a hormone-drugged bluebird but also a beautiful spring day, coffee in the pot, a dog desperate for a walk, and a dozen more things that should be taken care of before I get back to work. I scarcely get a stroke of work done these mornings. Personally, I blame the bluebird.

ILLUSTRATION: WENDY BUSH

THE OTHER SIDE

by Rodene Zimmer

Sometimes
I wish I were a man
so I could know the pleasure
of taking off my shirt
when I'm hot.
Sometimes
I'd like to pee in the bush
standing up.
Sometimes
I'd like to only carry a wallet.
Sometimes
I'd like to have a beer gut
and smoke cigars
and still think I was sexy.

WOODCUT: HEIDI MARION

HOW TO SURVIVE FORTY BELOW

Forty below. The beginning. The drone of the weather report on the radio had suddenly acquired greater significance with the prediction of a cold snap. It was, well, kind of exciting to think that we were about to be plunged into one of Mother Nature's cruellest lessons; slightly crueller, even, for us who live beyond the power line.

Things have a tendency to freeze at these temperatures; and not just the obvious ones you may think about, like water and lettuce and bread, but things like motor oil, and propane, and metal. My first introduction to forty below didn't hit me all at once, like a brick, but came in a series of shock waves. Like grabbing an icy door handle and finding my fingers stuck there, with just a split second to pull away before loss of flesh occurs. Or being alerted by startled grunts that my husband, who was repairing a dog-pen, had a metal fence-staple dangling from his lip, where he had stored it while hammering another into the post. Heroically, I swung my mitt, and swatted the staple away. His flesh went with it.

He could suddenly speak again, and they were not kind words. Lesson learned: at forty below, galvanized metal sticks like glue to human flesh.

Forty below may be miserable, but it is also a time of discovery. As the night-time temperature plunged to -45 and we pulled window quilts and shutters around the house for extra insulation, we realized that the propane lights were beginning to dim. Not to worry! After heaving the heavy cast iron kettle off the woodstove and setting it against the outside of the frozen tank, light was restored. Following the example of my neighbour, whose tank wears a stylish three-quarters length sheepskin coat, I found great entertainment in decking ours with down parka and toque. Instant snowperson!

Alas, I also discovered that my garden-grown potatoes had frozen on the inside porch. I slowly poured warm water over them, hoping for a gentle thaw, and soon had five pounds of frozen potatoes stuck to my fingers. One second to pull away without losing flesh! Another dose of warm water released my fingers, leaving potato peel stuck to the nails. Instant potato peeler!

Heavy frost had been creeping ominously up the windows with each corresponding drop in temperature, and I discovered that my phone bill, a stray Christmas ornament, and my mother's latest letter from Florida—with palm trees, just to remind us that, in some parts of the world, it was still above freezing—were now fixed features of the windowsill. Instant filing system.

Forty below is not the time for outdoor sleepovers (unless you are a crazed musher training for the Yukon Quest), hanging out the laundry, or changing a tire. It's a time for contemplating life, writing your first novel, cleaning out the junk drawer, renewing your sex life, eating, sleeping, re-reading your library, and sipping hot toddies by the woodstove—until the woodpile starts to look like a summer campfire. There is something humbling about getting to your last few sticks of heating fuel.

Life begins to revolve around the firewood: cutting wood, stacking wood, hauling wood, heaving wood into your stove. Instant workout!

Ah, the outhouse. No finer place to be at unbearably cold temperatures, except perhaps in a large steamy hot-tub. Our first encounter with forty below convinced us that plastic has no place in a northern outhouse, with wood coming a poor second. Styrofoam is the only outhouse seat for those who wish to escape injury and hypothermia. There is the added problem of dealing with the pyramid in the hole, because—remember?—everything freezes. If the pinnacle reaches the level of the seat, you have a problem. Hope for an early thaw.

Second week, forty below. No end in sight. When you breath in it feels like your nostril hairs are being tugged up through your sinuses, and if you happen to wear glasses, you will have the added challenge of tunnel vision every time you step outside. Count on at least 20 minutes to put on the minimum three layers of clothing you will need to travel to the outhouse or the woodpile.

A wonderful thing about forty below is that it's usually crystal clear outside, and if there's one thing that extreme cold does, it turns you into a sun worshipper. Odd to think of people sunbathing in a cold wave, but bundled up in long johns, thick wool sweater, insulated pants, double socks, down parka, fur hat, wool gloves, overmitts, and my heaviest, warmest, winter boots, I go out daily to get my dose of vitamin D. The four square inches of my face which remain exposed have to absorb enough UV to sustain the rest of me. I can visualize myself, basking on a tropical beach. Maybe I'm starting to hallucinate.

Yesterday, I lost part of the skin on my nose to frostbite. The zipper of my coat etched a brown mark onto my cheek. One of our sled dogs got frostbite on his penis sheath; I'll have to make him a fleece protector for his vital parts. Forty below can be very nasty if you don't pay attention.

Third week, forty below. We are hoping for a warming trend, but the weatherpeople say it is getting colder. We contemplate the meaning of colder. How can it get any colder? Forty-five, fifty, sixty below. How much colder is sixty below than forty below? Somewhere we have heard that if you throw a glass of water into the air at sixty below, it will instantly vaporize. If you stand a bottle of whisky outside, it will freeze, and if you try to drink it in this super-cooled state, it will freeze your gizzard. Amazing what will amuse a person after two weeks of forty below. I wonder at what temperature brain cells begin to freeze.

Since we haven't been to town, we're running low on food. Our neighbour has to go in, and is instantly swarmed with requests from everyone for fresh food, mail pick up, and toilet paper. You can count on your neighbours at forty below.

Finally, huddled around the woodstove with our fingers wrapped around steaming mugs of coffee, we hear the sweetest words we've heard in three weeks. The weatherpeople say temperatures are gradually warming; tomorrow will be thirty-five below, twenty below by the end of the week. Thirty below is balmy, twenty below is nirvana. I can go out with one less layer! I can wear my ski boots without freezing a toe. The outhouse is no longer an ordeal, and the dogs have come out of their houses to bask. I can walk over to my neighbour's to borrow an egg, and there is peace in the land as the chainsaws come to rest.

Forty below. It's something to say you've lived through, the sort of experience that brings people together, in a basic need for survival. It's a badge of honour that you bring out on sultry summer days when winter seems far away, or you want to impress southern visitors. You haven't lived until you've lived through forty below.

by Suzette Delmage

why sprout?

story and illustration by France Campagna

Sprouting your own food gives you complete control over the quality of what you eat. You will know exactly what seeds or beans you are using, and where they have come from. You know your water supply, plus you know that no strangers' hands have picked over your food. There are no pesticides, preservatives, or additives in your homegrown sprouts. They are the freshest, most alive food you can eat. Soaking seeds in water awakens the enzymes from their dormancy, and their nutritional value is increased from 10 to 2,000 times in some varieties. The sprouted seeds also become much more digestible. Vitamin B is increased and vitamin E increases by as much as twenty times, as does vitamin C. Sprouts are harvested at the point where the seed is manufacturing all those life-giving nutrients, but before the embryo has a chance to consume its vitamin-rich storehouse.

Dr. Bernard Jensen did a study on a group of African labourers who developed scurvy after switching to European beer. He found that the native beer was made from sprouted millet, which is very high in vitamin C, while the imported beer had none.

Another study, conducted by Dr. Cyrus French during World War One, studied two groups of troops suffering from scurvy. One group was fed lemon juice, the other sprouted beans. Within a month, over 70 percent of the bean eaters were free from symptoms of scurvy, as compared to only 53 percent of the juice drinkers.

Does this give you an idea of why to sprout? Do it for your health. Happily, there are so many varieties, each with their own texture and taste. If you enjoy fresh greens, you will love sprouts.

I like to sprout alfalfa, clover, millet, mustard and radish, all of which do well together.

I also use barley, rye, wheat, green lentils, mung beans, garbanzos (chick peas), soybeans, almond, buckwheat and sunflower seeds. You have to remove the hulls of these seeds before they are eaten or cooked.

You will need a large wide-mouthed jar, or a gallon crock, covered in cheesecloth, screen, or nylon stocking, secured by a rubber band. If you prefer to use a commercially-made sprouting kit, it will come with manufacturer's directions.

First, select the seeds of beans which you wish to sprout. One ounce of seeds will make about one cup of sprouts, or half a cup of seeds equals about four cups of sprouts. Using these figures, estimate the amount of seeds required to fill your jar with sprouts, and place them in the jar. Using twice as much water as seeds, soak overnight at room temperature. Next morning the water will be quite brown, and rich in nutrients. Some people drink it. I water the houseplants with it.

Keep the jar at about a 45 degree angle, to drain, but not to dry out. Rinse the seeds twice daily with tepid water. If the room is too warm, or the seeds are old, you may need to rinse three or four times.

On day three or four, you may put them in the light (not direct sunlight) for greening. If your seeds were the type with husks, you will first need to husk them. Immerse the seeds in tepid water in a large bowl. The husks will float to the top. Using your hands, or a small mesh strainer, remove as many as you can. Drain at this time.

There are no hard and fast rules about when to harvest your sprouts. They will taste different at different stages in their growth. I usually eat mine after one day of greening. You may store them in the fridge, or keep them in the jar, continuing to rinse, but now with cold water. They will keep for several days.

Even a young child can have a little sprout garden. It's a simple responsibility, which can give them a sense of achievement, while providing food for the whole family. With the trend toward the adulteration of foods, sprouting has become a necessity. Make sprouting a means of survival.

happy sprouting!

some sprouting references

The uncook book. Raw food adventures to a new health high by Elizabeth Baker and Dr. Elton Baker

The beansprout book by Gay Courter

Food healing for man by Bernard Jensen

GARDENING

WARMING TECHNIQUES FOR A COLD CLIMATE

by Marilyn Smith

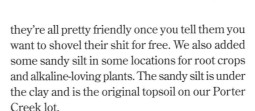

PHOTO: LYNDA EHRLICH

SELF–SUFFICIENCY

My partner enticed me to the Yukon with the line, "you can grow tomatoes here," conveniently omitting the fact that a greenhouse was required for their growth. Perhaps it was the low expectations I had that made my first crop in the Yukon so abundantly rewarding. Or perhaps it was the obvious success of Roy Ness (pictured at right with his pumpkin) that spurred me on. I'm not sure. One fact remains—with a bit of effort, my enjoyment of fresh garden produce is now satisfied for more of the year than I ever dreamt was possible five years ago.

My first exposure to the ropes of Yukon gardening techniques was the invaluable course given by Roy. He is an excellent resource on how to extend and improve the growth of plants by the most innovative and cheapest means possible. The *Yukon Garden Handbook* (Renewable Resources, free for the asking) was also helpful to expand my understanding of the challenge of gardening north of sixty.

I am amazed at how this community of gardeners shares their knowledge. As part of a gardening group of women, I get to ask questions of people with years of experience. We meet at each others' homes and, during the summer months, we visit gardens. A gardening group is a great way to cushion the ups and downs of what works and what doesn't.

Light, water, soil, and heat are the most important requirements for healthy plants. Fertilizing and pest control are the same here as anywhere else. Pest control is easier because we have fewer pests. The Yukon has a wonderful sterilizer and pesticide known as 40 below. This means no slugs—imported creepy crawlers are exterminated during the winter. We also have no problem with light. In fact, we get too much of it for some plants—like spinach—which tend to bolt in the midnight sun. However, low precipitation, poor soil and lack of heat can be problems.

WATER

Since this climate is very dry, a good automatic irrigation system can make gardening pure pleasure instead of sheer drudgery. Many excellent trickle and seeping systems are available. They have the distinct advantage over sprinkler systems of putting the water right where you want it—on the soil, not on the plants. "Irrigro" seeping lines made of Tyvek allow us to enjoy the peak of summer in a canoe rather than watering the garden.

This system required some initial plumbing to be done during the construction phase. Lines of poly-b pipes were laid underground to the

ends of each of the garden beds. The Irrigro system was installed to each of the outlets and since the lines are half-inch paper tubes, it was easy to customize the length of each line feeder by simply measuring and cutting the lines with scissors. A knot in the end of each tube was all that was needed to end each line. Most of the beds have two lines of watering tubes, although three lines is optimal for the four-foot width of our beds. This may sound like a lot of work, but with some initial investment of time and planning your reward is minimal maintenance and longer canoeing or hiking trips.

My philosophy is to make the work playful as well as minimal. To that end, I plant some of my crop in the fall to reduce the excessive workload of the spring. Root crops, lettuce, peas, chard, and garlic are planted in the fall and given lots of water early in the spring. Seeding needs to be shallower with this method as the seeds migrate down. My favourite crop of endives, radicchio, and chicories does very well in the Yukon summer since it is often a winter crop in Italy. These somewhat bitter greens withstand frost well and have phenomenal storage abilities. We are able to eat our radicchio, which has been stored in vegetable bags in the fridge, in December. Their vibrant variegated colours of red, yellow and green are an elegant addition to salads or soups.

Spring seeding begins, indoors, in March, using southeast and southwest facing windows. Our knockdown plant stand is on wheels which allows our seedlings to benefit from both morning and afternoon sun, with a minimum of fuss. Recently, we added grow lights to the seedling stand, but haven't used them yet. Growing your own seedlings can save you a lot of money, but it can turn your living room into a sauna and put a serious dent in your social life during the months of March, April, and May.

SOIL

Soil building is the first step to successful Yukon gardening. Most southern Yukon soils are very thin, excessively clayey or sandy, either too acid or too alkaline, and poor in organic matter. The central Yukon, on the other hand, never having been glaciated, can have excellent soil. Pictures of giant cabbages grown in Dawson City during the gold rush attest to this.

In the southern Yukon we have to create our own soil. The soil in our beds started with the poor clay topsoil brought in for the lawn by a previous owner. We amended the clay with truckloads of expensive peaty topsoil, lots of peat moss, and horse manure collected from a number of friendly horse owners. Actually,

they're all pretty friendly once you tell them you want to shovel their shit for free. We also added some sandy silt in some locations for root crops and alkaline-loving plants. The sandy silt is under the clay and is the original topsoil on our Porter Creek lot.

The first thing we constructed in the backyard was the compost bin. There are many designs around, but ours has three three-foot cube bins. It is framed out of old 2 x 4s and clad with plastic-coated chainlink fencing. We compost all our vegetable matter, and we ended up with so much that, after two years, we built another set of three bins. Composting is slow and dies out in the winter. We are lazy composters and only turn the bins once or twice a season. It seems to take about a year and a half to get good compost. If you turn more often, monitor the moisture or layer more carefully; then the breakdown of the organic material can occur in one season. The larger the bulk, the hotter the compost becomes and the faster the breakdown occurs. We also rent a shredder/chipper every autumn or spring and run the large stems through it, such as tomato vines, and small branches and woody stems. Breakdown is considerably accelerated this way, and we get a nice, finely textured compost.

Vermiculture in the basement also helps with composting vegetable scraps during the winter months. However, beware because the stuff can turn into an ugly, soggy, smelly mess that drowns the worms if you feed it too much, too fast. Extra vegetable scraps are stored in garbage bags outside and added to the compost heap in the spring when they melt.

HEAT

Since you usually have to create your soil, it pays to plan soil warming techniques into the process, as that can make the difference between a good crop and a poor one. First, we built raised beds on southern exposures, with the option of covers. The beds were constructed with 4 x 4s that were treated with a non-toxic preserver called "Once Over." The depth of the bed needs to be a minimum of one foot, but, the more soil the better. My beds are 18 inches deep.

The second warming technique we used was to insulate the bottom of the beds with heavy-duty blue styrofoam insulation, which allows the soil to thaw and warm up faster in the early growing season. A 1-inch layer of gravel for drainage and a 4-inch layer of manure for heat

PHOTO: MIKE THOMAS

and food was laid down. A good mixture of peat, composted manure and soil brought by the truckload completed the foundation.

The third important warming technique we used was to install hoops over the bed for "Remay" covers. This is a spun polyester blanket which allows sun to enter but prevents moisture from escaping the soil. Another advantage of row covers is that they prevent some pests from laying eggs on your crop. They also protect your plants from wind if your location is exposed. I believe this technique has given my plants at least a month's growing advantage.

The fourth, and final, warming technique that we planned into our system was an in-floor hot water heat pipe laid in the bottom of each bed and joined by underground insulated corridors. This was a way of feeding hot water to the soil in the spring to ensure early thawing. Our plan is to eventually link the tubes to an outdoor hot water boiler and connect this to a sauna hot tub system. (Hey, I need some reward system for my tight gardening muscles.)

One final word about warming. Look for existing micro-climates in your yard by planting next to the house, or in sheltered southern areas, or by creating them out of old tires, raised beds, or cold frames of plastic or windows.

GREENHOUSES

Greenhouse growing is, of course, the ultimate warming solution and is required for tomatoes, beans, squash, peppers, corn, cucumbers, eggplant and delicate herbs like basil. There are three basic types of greenhouses: attached to the house and heated; unattached and heated; and finally unattached and unheated. Attached, heated greenhouses allow garden production to start as early as January with harvesting of vegetables in June. With an unattached, heated greenhouse planting can begin in May and harvesting in July. The unattached, unheated greenhouse means planting in June and harvesting in August.

Greenhouse production can be simplified by automatic ventilation window openers and soaker irrigation systems which can be gravity fed or attached to the house water pressure. Water as a heat sink is a cheap and highly effective method for storing heat to moderate cooler night temperatures. Lots of water storage in the greenhouse also gives you the advantage of warm water for watering, which plants love. We have three raised 45 gallon drums for our soaker system. Milk and pop containers full of water are also stored under our raised

greenhouse beds. Raised beds in the greenhouse mean warmer soil and better air circulation.

We enhanced air circulation using a bathroom fan attached to dryer tubing which fed the warm air from the ceiling of the greenhouse to underneath the beds, thereby warming the soil. Warmth in the soil is critical to germination and maximizing passive heat collection is easier and cheaper than fuelling your stove on cool nights. Electric heater lines can be installed in the soil, but they are very expensive to operate.

Be careful. Too much of a good thing can be detrimental to growth. Ventilation during peak sun times is essential as greenhouse temperatures easily exceed 100 degrees Fahrenheit, damaging or killing most plants. Ideally, you want the temperature in the greenhouse to be between 60 and 80 degrees Fahrenheit. Automatic ventilators allow you to go canoeing during peak growing times. A minimum/maximum thermometer is also a useful addition to any greenhouse.

With enough water, good soil and warmth, incredible crops can be grown in the Yukon. If you set up the right systems you can go into the bush carefree while your garden takes care of itself.

by Peter Harms

Farming in the Yukon is not really that difficult. It is possible to lose large amounts of money and experience major disappointments and setbacks just like farmers farther south. I planted my 44-acre farm to oats this spring. The idea was that we would watch it grow rich and thick and then in fall spend an afternoon harvesting. It would be easy and even nostalgically fun.

Well, the rain fell in favourable non-agricultural areas like Crestview and the golf course, but precious little actually made it to Mile 8, Burma Road. My uncle from Alberta looked at my "spread" and figured that I should be able to comfortably run 20 to 30 head on this year's oat crop, providing I would run only geese. Perhaps if so many of my oats hadn't miraculously been converted into sweet clover and fireweed, we could have done better. Perhaps the rain we got during the harvest time could have fallen during the germinating time.

paddles parked in the poplars in his back field. Yes, it was a binder and, yes, it was for sale. I dragged it home and started guessing how to run it. Well, the cutting knife was dull so it was sharpened, the blades were loose so they were riveted, and the quick fix pine bushing was replaced with a beautiful oak piece. We pumped up the tire that held air and ran the other on the rim. Ready. I pulled down the gate and wondered why they made the binder larger than the opening in the fence. I really feel that the government should get a size-of-gate-opening inspector soon.

Ready to cut. I pushed the starter button and played with the choke, and optimistically, continued to try to start it. Then I filled the leaky tank with more gas. Then I walked to the house, got the truck and cables, and finally, with the extra juice, watched the old Ford

started wondering how to change the penal system so that work of this nature could perhaps be delegated to others.

We went another round and the blade supports snapped off so the large wooden paddle tried to beat the machine and the operators to death. I yelled at my wife to stop the tractor (very therapeutic at this particular time) and we enjoyed yet another breakdown to alleviate the boredom. This was a timely breakdown for it allowed us to get our rain jackets on and have rain run down our backs as we stooped over tying all the bundles with small pieces of twine.

That did it. I phoned around and found a functional binder a few miles down the road. This one worked the year before and needed only some minor canvas modification. This machine was a work of art. It was like driving a museum piece. It was beautifully painted in original John Deere colours and it did what it was supposed to. It took the grain and cut it off

Bringing in the sheaves

I realized my oat crop wouldn't be entered into the Harvest Fair when I could still see fat gophers sitting on their mounds at the end of July. My kids didn't play hide and seek in it this year either. It was a very beautiful oat field when the fireweed was in bloom.

Then it was harvest time. You know—get a binder, kids stooking, doing farm work like your parents did before you. How quaint! How exciting! How nostalgic! How labour intensive! Perhaps I shouldn't have tried farming on borrowed equipment alone. My neighbours must have wanted to run when they saw me coming. "What does he want now?"

I went to Joyce first to borrow her tractor. Well, I could borrow it if that pesky leak in the front bucket ram was repaired. No sweat. I phoned to Fort St. John for parts and they said they would have them up there in a few weeks, probably right after the first snow.

I went to my other neighbour and asked about the rusted metal with the large wooden

cough the black smoke from its lungs and run on its own power.

Ready to cut. The sharp blade hissed back and forth, the huge paddles flapped at the grain. The shear pin to the power takeoff snapped and the paddles stopped flapping. The smiling nostalgic hobby farmer chipped enamel off his teeth.

And so it was evening and night of the sixth day of perfect weather. I had borrowed a scythe from Steve Cooper but it didn't take me long to figure out why it and the push lawnmower are only seen in museums.

Ready to cut. The shear pin fit and away we went. The grain fell on the table and we would wait until the table was full and then stop the whole contraption and pull the oat-fireweed bundles off and lay them neatly on the ground. After the second round, we lay them even farther to one side so we wouldn't run them over with the tractor when we came past on the next round. After a few rounds I

close to the ground; the paddles paddled it onto the canvas; the canvas moved it up to the canvas elevators; these actually elevated it to the packy thingies; these packed the stems into bundles and hit a lever that told this magical machine to loop a piece of twine around the bundle and tie it into a knot. It was witchcraft.

The part that was truly incredible was that it went half a field before the packy thingies jammed up. The nice thing about the breakdowns is that you had plenty of time to stook the bundles. Stooking is the art of making three to six loosely tied bundles stand in a small pyramid so they can dry. Re-stooking is what you do after a wind.

What a harvest! No wonder farm kids move to the city. Mine didn't even thank me for the trip back in time. The field looks beautiful, the stooks in the evening sun are striking. It was an interesting experiment but I know that I'm not changing occupations.

Preserving the Yukon's Rich Harvest

 Summer in the Yukon brings a constant source of produce to harvest and preserve for the cold days of winter.

As soon as new vegetation starts, there are the tender fireweed stems to be picked before the green leaves open. This is delicious stir-fried or in salads. It freezes well, and added to soup or stew in the winter is a good source of vitamins and minerals.

Later, the fireweed blossoms can be picked and dried to make a delicately flavoured jelly.

Next, rose petals are great when picked and dried. Put about three cups in a jar and add one crushed cinnamon stick. Leave about two weeks and steep yourself a delicious cup of tea.

Dandelions are up now, too. The very small leaves are one of the first greens in spring and so delicious in salads. Time now to dig its roots. Strip them clean and they are very white. Dry them, grind them, then roast them in your oven, being careful not to burn them. Perk in your coffee pot and you have a delightful coffee to enjoy. The tedious work of cleaning the roots is well worth it.

Mid-July the berries start. The wild strawberries can be found along our highways. They are small, but the delicate flavour is one to enjoy. Put them on plastic covered trays to freeze, then put in plastic bags in your freezer.

Raspberries are found in many places. They are excellent frozen, easily canned for preserves, or made into jellies.

Black currants are plentiful along many creeks among the low willows. They make a uniquely flavoured jelly. Mix half and half with the plentiful mossberry. Bring to a boil, strain, add sugar to taste. Serve mixed with carbonated mineral water; it is great. The black currants freeze well. Use them instead of raisins in your butter tarts for a different flavoured tart.

Gooseberries with their prickly stems make an excellent jam; a gooseberry pie adds a unique dessert to your menu. The berry freezes well.

By mid-July, if rains are right, the mushrooms pop up every morning. These keep well, frozen, canned or pickled. The pickled ones are a great addition to dinner for company. Fresh, they go well in any salad. There are so many different varieties and the season extends to snowfall. You must rise early to pick these but early morning in the woods is so rich with the sounds of nature waking up, it's worth it.

Don't forget the cranberry season. The high bush cranberries give us a very uniquely flavoured jelly. The low bush cranberry freezes well for winter muffins, loaves and pies. Both cranberry sauce and jelly are delicious. Make your cranberry mincemeat while they are in season. In sealed jars, it ages well and provides you with goodies during the holiday season.

The mossberry is another great one. Try a raisin-mossberry pie. It is also good on cold winter days, used with rhubarb in a crisp or pie. With crushed pineapple, it makes a delicious jam. It also freezes well, just tied in a plastic bag.

Let's move now to our garden and greenhouse. Instead of that expensive lawn, you could use the land to provide you with a lot of your winter vegetables. A nice garden is great to see in the Yukon. Maybe the tourists would grasp the idea that we are not a land of ice and snow. Manure from the many goat, chicken and horse farmers, sawdust from your wood cutting and ashes from your stove are all you need to add to your soil each year. And now we are recycling so much.

Most basic vegetables grow well, and can be frozen or pickled. I only freeze a limited amount since vegetables lose a lot of goodness after a length of time in the freezer. With canning, you can keep them for years. Even very small baby potatoes can very well.

The greenhouse has its peppers and tomatoes. The early spring seeding of radishes gives you fresh goodies before other plants are ready. Tomatoes are so versatile. Peppers, like tomatoes, freeze well. Beans can be grown successfully in your greenhouse too.

Rhubarb is a good source of vitamins and roughage. Freeze it or cold pack it by putting it in sterile jars, cover with cold water and seal. Both ways it makes crisps, pies and muffins. With orange or lemon, you have a good marmalade. Chop, cook and strain. Bring to a boil, juice, add sugar to taste, then seal in sterilized jars. To serve, dilute with carbonated mineral water and what a delicious drink you will serve. Mixed with apple, strawberry or mossberry, you'll have a variety of desserts. It also makes a good relish to serve with your meats.

This sounds like a lot of work but what better way to spend the summer days than with a picnic lunch and the children in nature's garden. In the winter months you will have memories as you serve your harvest.

Many people are afraid of the bears. After 43 summers in the Yukon, spending many hours in the woods and along our highways, I have yet to face a bear. Take a few precautions. Talk at times or sing out loud. If you sing like I do, you will scare all the bears and many of the people out of your sight.

Your time spent harvesting and preserving the rich harvest of the land will enrich you and your family. Think of the clean food you'll be eating—no chemicals added for growth or preservation. Don't forget how it'll help your food budget. All in all, you collect rather a good salary, and teach your children how to enjoy the land.

by Bea Alexandrovich

Camping food

by Joyce Majiski

I got a call in January asking if I could come up with a good backpacking recipe for…say, day 5 of a trip, when the fresh food had run out. Since day 5 is not even halfway through most of our trips, I decided to go for day 11 of a 12 day trip, when the thought of one more lunch of salami, crackers and cheese is enough to do us all in.

I always find it a challenge to make up the menus. The goal is to create interesting meals, keeping the weight down, but making sure everyone gets enough to eat. Over the years, we've come up with a rough estimate of quantities for the staple items (pasta, rice, meats, oatmeal, cookies, etc.) on a per person basis. I often modify this estimate, so that a six-foot-four-inch man weighing 200 pounds and a five-foot-four-inch woman weighing 120 pounds aren't expected to either carry or eat the same amount.

The following meal has received rave reviews. It tastes great, and believe me, not everything you eat in the great outdoors tastes good just because you are hungry! This meal is simple to prepare, super lightweight and all of the ingredients can be purchased locally. If you have access to a food drier, you can also prepare the accompaniment to the main course in addition to drying your own tuna, onions and peas.

TUNA CAKES

- potato flakes (No-name will do)
- 1 can tuna for 3 people (can be dried; if not, clean and carry out the cans)
- 1 package dried peas or "Surprise" peas brand for 3-4 people (I use frozen peas and dry them)
- 60 grams cheese per person (your choice but old cheddar is my fav)
- 1-2 onions-worth of dried onion flakes
- lemon pepper to taste (in an old film canister)
- oil or lard to fry in

Directions

An hour before dinner, heat a bit of water and rehydrate the tuna, onions and peas. Add this and water to the potato flakes until you can make paddies that hold together. At this point add the finely sliced (or grated) cheese and the lemon pepper. Fry in a bit of oil until golden brown. Sometimes they stick to the pan, but even if they look disgusting, they will taste great!

An optional accompaniment, passed on to me by my friend Jodi Schick, is carrot and raisin salad. Grate and dry as many carrots as you want. To rehydrate, throw them into your water bottle, add water and let sit for a few hours. They miraculously appear as real carrots. Add raisins and spice with a bit of pre-spiced oil and vinegar dressing (in a handy nalgene bottle), and you have a refreshing, cool salad.

For those without food driers, you can buy pre-dried (commercial) tabouleh salad and rehydrate it in the plastic bag. For added effect, add some of the aforementioned salad dressing, and you have another great taste sensation.

PHOTOS: KEN MADSEN

On a Cold Winter's Day

by Brenda McClelland

On a cold winter's day, when ice fog obscures detail of the Yukon landscape and the morning is blurred by cloud, thoughts turn towards warmth and comfort.

On such a day my kitchen beckons me and I seek out ingredients that will sustain me through a cold morning and put a gentle warmth deep inside me.

And so it is then that I reach for my trusty oatmeal residing in a worn crockery holder. The top comes off and the small but mighty flakes of oatmeal tumble and cascade out. While the oatmeal is cooking and reaching its potential on my stove, I turn my attention to the details that make this a winter weekend morning "comfort" food.

Usually oatmeal becomes porridge with a sprinkle of brown sugar and sampling of raisins and a pouring of rice milk. On weekdays, it is hurriedly consumed as fuel before my walk to work in the cold and darkness. On weekends, as light hesitantly begins to come though my window and reaches further and further into my home, the oatmeal becomes part of a delicious repast.

On weekend mornings, the oatmeal that becomes a warm and welcoming porridge is greeted by dates cut in half and placed in a pinwheel design on the white background canvas of oatmeal.

Then, the smallest dab of fireweed honey is placed artistically in the middle of the pinwheel of dates. It looks inviting and decorative and it exudes a "slowing down" of time on this Saturday or Sunday morning. (Most often it is a Sunday morning.)

Finally, the "pièce de résistance" is added in a swirling pattern around the circle. The maple syrup reminds me of younger days and walks in the woods in spring.

It evokes memories of the smell and sound of the heaving sides of the big draft horses pulling through the maple sugar bush and the silver metal pails clinging to the trees. It is the excitement of spring when winter is still dominating but spring is pushing through and the smell in the air is unmistakable. It is one season becoming the next and so the cycle of life continues, and you are witness to the ebb of winter and the growth of spring.

This final ingredient, the maple syrup, is poured as a small rivulet of a creek, not a river. The scene is now complete and the bowl warms my hands quietly as I sit in the rocking chair and turn on the music of Loreena McKennitt and her sounds of "To Drive the Cold Winter Away." It doesn't feel cold anymore.

MY COOKSTOVE —OLYMPIA

by Shiela Alexandrovich

I sing a song to my cookstove tonight. A song full of sounds from my kitchen, my home.

*Through a hundred seasons
she's felt all the rhythms,
knowing full-well the time
of the year.
Neglected in summer and
covered with mail—
now shining again as
she calls me each morning,
offering coffee
steaming and strong;
she fills all the bowls of my
sleepy-eyed children,
all gathered around her,
their knees to their chins.*

*All through the day,
her duties now changing
from pickles and
baskets of greens cut to dry,
to ketchup and kettles
of cheese set to cheddar—
Past pots and the pans
and all the bathwater
to the sleepy-time treat
of cinnamon tea.*

*And the soft, dying crackles
that sing me to sleep
As we both settle in for our
well deserved rest.*

FROM MY COOKSTOVE

by Shiela Alexandrovich

It is January—we have friends for supper. Fish and turkey kabobs. My stove has a good bed of coals, and we decide to BBQ. Inside. In January. The original Jenn-air. Here's how.

With a good bed of coals, open the oven damper and chimney. Lift off the rounds, or the whole section over the firebox, and replace it with a rack. Voila. Rotate kabobs, drizzle marinade, crisp bread. All the smoke is sucked up the chimney. I always have willow around my house, so sometimes I add a large, oval roaster lid over whatever is grilling, and stuff a handful of green willow into the firebox. A touch of smoke—just what's needed!

What else could grill a fish, bake a baguette, keep tea hot and heat bathwater all at once?! I love my cookstove!

GOPHERS, A READY MEAL

by Glen Bunbury

An important skill one must learn when living on the land is the ability to provide sustenance for oneself. One of the most abundant food sources running around is the common ground squirrel or gopher. Many people may wince at the thought of eating one of these tunnel dwellers. However, if cleaned and cooked properly, they make an enjoyable meal that is quite high in food energy and protein. This is valuable information that everyone who travels in the outdoors should remember.

The first step is to find a need to eat a gopher. Extreme hunger may provide this incentive, although idle curiosity may substitute as the motivating factor. For others, it may be a cultural thing. First Nations people, for example, have been eating gophers on this continent for untold millennium and some consider the rodents to be a delicacy.

There are several ways to kill a gopher. Long ago, First Nations people used an eagle feather snare placed in the entrance of the gopher hole through the roof of the tunnel. This snare was connected to a willow. When the gopher stuck its head into the snare it was triggered and the willow sprung loose, tightening the snare and killing the gopher by strangulation. Today's methods are far more efficient. Nowadays, you can catch gophers with steel traps or shoot them with a rifle. A .22-calibre rifle is all the stopping power you would need on a gopher safari.

Once you have the gopher, it is up to you to decide how you want to cook it. Some people skin it, others singe it in an open fire. If you are feeling especially adventurous you may want to try boiling the gopher with its fur still on. Whatever way you decide, one thing is sure—you must gut it to remove the intestines.

For this example, we will say that you decide to singe the gopher and boil it. The first thing is to start a fire. Once the fire is going, turn your attention back to the gopher. Take a stick and sharpen one end of it. Then place it in the mouth of the gopher. Cut a hole in its cheek so the stick can poke through there. Place the gopher directly into the flames leaving it there for a few moments, turning it so that all of the fur is singed. Next, take the gopher out and, using a knife, scrape off the singed part of the fur. Repeat this process until all the fur has been singed and scraped off, to your satisfaction.

Once you are finished with this task, it's on to the gutting. This is fairly basic. Make a cut straight down the centre of the belly and pull the guts out. You can leave the liver in but you must remove the gall bladder from it. The guts of the gopher are also edible but you must take a bit of time and clean them. By this time, your pot of water should be boiling away on the campfire. Now, you simply place the gopher into the pot and let it boil for an hour. Enjoy.

MUM'S HUMMUS

by Mary El Kerr

I prepared hummus for my mother while she was visiting Whitehorse. I was so impressed with Mum liking my spicy food I named this for mums who are adventurous in their tasting. The fact that hummus is vegetarian and cholesterol-free should not discourage one with a taste for rich and creamy foods from trying it. Serve hummus with fresh chopped Italian parsley from the garden, Greek olives, fresh focaccia, vegetable crudite or biscuits.

*500 ml (2 cups) cooked garbanzo beans
juice of 1 fresh lemon
30 ml (2 tbsp) extra virgin olive oil
6 large cloves garlic
30 ml (2 tbsp) tahini
50-100 ml (¹/₃ to ¹/₂ cup) water
5 ml (1 tsp) coarse salt (or to taste)
.5 ml (¹/₈ tsp) cayenne pepper
10 ml (2 tsp) cumin seeds (fresh ground)
10 ml (2 tsp) coriander seeds (fresh ground)*

Heat olive oil in small skillet, add crushed garlic, cumin and coriander. Heat until it is hot. Do not brown. Remove from heat.

Place the garbanzo beans in a food processor with lemon juice. Add the oil/garlic mixture. Pulse until smooth.

Add the tahini, water, salt and cayenne to the processor and pulse again, until smooth. This should be a spreadable consistency. Add additional water if necessary.

Taste for seasoning. Place the hummus in serving bowls and serve immediately, or store in the refrigerator for up to one week. Do not freeze.

Cooked garbanzo beans freeze well, and may be kept on hand for a hummus emergency.

Rhubarb-strawberry meringue

by Vera Kirkwood

Atlin, B.C. must be a place where people live on rhubarb. If you ever have the chance to visit there, you'll notice its big broad leaves and bright red stems all around town.

750 ml (3 cups) rhubarb, cut up
45 ml (3 tbsp) flour
310 ml (1¼ cups) sugar
30 ml (2 tbsp) water
500 ml (1 pint) strawberries
2 eggs

Cut rhubarb into 2.5 cm (1 inch) lengths. Turn into a saucepan with the flour and 250 ml (1 cup) of the sugar. Blend together, add water, and simmer for 10 minutes, stirring frequently. Add the strawberries.

Remove from heat and stir in beaten egg yolks. Turn into a 20 cm (8 inch) square pan. Bake at 175°C (350°F) for 10 minutes.

Beat egg whites until stiff, adding the remaining sugar. Spread over pudding and return to 150°C (300°F) oven.

Bake another 15 minutes, or until meringue is delicately browned. Serves 6 to 8.

Rhubarb pork chop casserole

by Jackson Humphries

4 pork loin chops, 2 cm (¾ inch) thick
15 ml (1 tbsp) cooking oil
salt and pepper to taste
625-750 ml (2½ - 3 cups) bread crumbs
750 ml (3 cups) fresh or frozen rhubarb, cut into 2.5 cm (1 inch) lengths
125 ml (½ cup) packed brown sugar
60 ml (¼ cup) flour
5 ml (1 tsp) cinnamon

In a large skillet, brown chops in oil and season with salt and pepper. Remove to warm platter.

Mix 125 ml (½ cup) of pan drippings with 500 ml (2 cups) of bread crumbs.

Sprinkle 125 ml (½ cup) of crumbs into a 22 cm x 33 cm (9 inch x 13 inch) baking dish.

Combine rhubarb, sugar, flour and cinnamon. Spoon half over bread crumbs. Arrange pork chops on top.

Spoon remaining rhubarb mixture over chops. Cover with foil and bake at 175°C (350°F) for 30 to 45 minutes. Remove foil. Sprinkle with remaining bread crumbs and bake 10 to 15 minutes or until chops test done.

Rhubarb strawberry coffee cake

by Ilse Wohlfarth

When we immigrated to the Yukon in 1959, there were hardly any flowers, lawns or gardens. Gravel roads, pricklebushes and foxtails were the common sights. But then I discovered rhubarb. We had little garden space, so I took the wooden box off the sled, which the babies had been pulled in. There was my mini-rhubarb garden. It served as a great rhubarb patch for several years.

Filling
750 ml (3 cups) rhubarb, chopped into 2.5 cm (1 inch) pieces
1 litre (1 quart) fresh strawberries
30 ml (2 tbsp) lemon juice
250 ml (1 cup) sugar
80 ml (⅓ cup) cornstarch

Cake
750 ml (3 cups) flour
250 ml (1 cup) sugar
5 ml (1 tsp) baking powder
5 ml (1 tsp) baking soda
2.5 ml (½ tsp) salt
250 ml (1 cup) margarine, cut into pieces
375 ml (1½ cups) buttermilk
2 eggs
5 ml (1 tsp) vanilla

Topping
60 ml (¼ cup) margarine
185 ml (¾ cup) flour
185 ml (¾ cup) sugar

Prepare the filling in a saucepan. Combine rhubarb, strawberries and lemon juice. Cover and cook over medium heat for 5 minutes. Combine sugar and cornstarch; stir into saucepan. Bring to boil, stirring constantly, until thickened. Remove from heat and set aside.

Prepare the cake batter in a large bowl. Combine flour, sugar, baking powder, baking soda and salt. Cut in margarine until mixture resembles coarse crumbs. Beat buttermilk, eggs and vanilla; stir into crumb mixture.

Spread half of cake batter into greased 22 cm x 33 cm (9 inch x 13 inch) pan. Carefully spread the filling over the batter. Drop spoonfuls of remaining batter over the filling. Melt margarine, stir in flour and sugar. Sprinkle over batter.

Bake at 175°C (350°F) for 40 to 45 minutes. Cool in pan.

Rhubarb conserve

by Ev Church

1 litre (4 cups) diced rhubarb
2 oranges
1 tin pineapple tidbits (or crushed)
250 ml (1 cup) seedless raisins
1 litre (4 cups) sugar
125 ml (½ cup) walnuts, chopped

Wash and dice the unpeeled rhubarb. Grate rind of the oranges into long shreds. Remove the white membranes and with a sharp knife slice the pulp thinly. Drain pineapple. Place prepared fruits and orange rind in a large bowl. Add the raisins and sugar. Stir until well mixed. Cover with a cloth and let rest overnight.

The next day, rub a saucepan with salad oil. Add the fruit mixture. Bring to a boil, while stirring. Simmer until thick and transparent, about 90 minutes. Add the chopped walnuts and simmer 10 minutes. Pour into hot sterilized jars and seal. Wonderful!

Rhubarb dessert (an Estonian recipe)

by Lee Pugh

600 grams (1¼ pounds) fresh cut rhubarb
1 litre (4 cups) water
250 ml (1 cup) sugar
45 ml (3 tbsp) potato starch

Cut rhubarb fairly small. Put in saucepan with the water. Bring to a boil. Add sugar and potato starch that has been dissolved in a small amount of cold water. Bring to boil again. Pour fruit soup into bowl. Sprinkle with sugar to prevent crust from forming. Chill. Serve with dollop of whipped cream or ice cream.

Rhubarb and fig tea bread

by Jackson Humphries

250 ml (1 cup) diced rhubarb
435 ml (1³/₄ cups) flour
160 ml (²/₃ cup) packed brown sugar
125 ml (¹/₂ cup) thinly sliced figs
60 ml (¹/₄ cup) finely chopped, candied
    ginger
5 ml (1 tsp) grated lemon rind
15 ml (1 tbsp) lemon juice
125 ml (¹/₂ cup) butter
1 egg
7.5 ml (1¹/₂ tsp) baking powder
2 ml (¹/₄ tsp) salt
pinch of nutmeg
80 ml (¹/₃ cup) milk
10 ml (2 tsp) ground walnuts
15 ml (1 tbsp) granulated sugar

In a small bowl, combine rhubarb, 60 ml (¹/₄ cup) flour and 15 ml (1 tbsp) brown sugar.

In a separate mixing bowl, mix figs, ginger, lemon rind and lemon juice.

In a large bowl, cream butter with remaining brown sugar. Beat in egg. Combine baking powder, salt, nutmeg and remaining flour. Stir into butter mixture with milk. Blend in rhubarb mixture and fig mixture. Pour batter into greased 22 cm x 13 cm (9 inch x 5 inch) loaf pan. Stir together walnuts and granulated sugar. Sprinkle over batter.

Bake at 175°C (350°F) for 60 to 80 minutes, or until tester inserted in middle comes out clean.

Let cool in pan for 10 minutes. Turn out on rack to cool completely.

Rhubarb for supper

by Kate Buerge

2 eggs
  250 ml (1 cup) sugar
    30 ml (2 tbsp) flour
      750 ml (3 cups) rhubarb, cut in 1.25 cm
      (¹/₂ inch) pieces

    Topping
      250 ml (1 cup) flour
      125 ml (¹/₂ cup) brown sugar
      2 ml (¹/₂ tsp) salt
      5 ml (1 tsp) baking powder
      90 ml (6 tbsp) butter

Beat eggs, sugar and 30 ml (2 tbsp) flour. Pour over rhubarb in 20 cm or 22 cm (8 inch or 9 inch) pan.

Combine topping ingredients and sprinkle over top of the rhubarb mixture. Bake at 190°C (375°F) for 45 minutes.

Rhubarb muffins

by Judy Forrest

375 ml (1¹/₂ cups) rhubarb
10 ml (2 tsp) cinnamon
5 ml (1 tsp) baking soda
125 ml (¹/₂ cup) honey
1 egg
250 ml (1 cup) buttermilk
625 ml (2¹/₂ cups) spelt flour
5 ml (1 tsp) baking powder
125 ml (¹/₂ cup) oil
5 ml (1 tsp) vanilla

Mix dry items together. Mix liquids together. Mix both mixtures together. Bake at 200°C (400°F) for 20 minutes.

Rhubarb dessert

by Vera Kirkwood

625 ml (2¹/₂ cups) graham wafer crumbs
125 ml (¹/₂ cup) melted butter
60 ml (4 tbsp) sugar
1 litre (4 cups) chopped rhubarb
250 ml (1 cup) sugar
125 ml (¹/₂ cup) water
45 ml (3 tbsp) cornstarch
1 package Dreamwhip
500 ml (2 cups) miniature marshmallows
120 ml (4 oz) butterscotch instant pudding

Mix graham wafers, butter, and sugar. Save half for the topping. Put remainder in a 22 cm x 33 cm (9 inch x 13 inch) pan. Bake at 180°C (350°F) for 10 minutes.

Cook rhubarb, sugar and water. Thicken with cornstarch.

Prepare Dreamwhip as directed and add marshmallows. Spread rhubarb over the graham crust and Dreamwhip mixture over rhubarb. Prepare pudding and spread over Dreamwhip.

Top with remaining mixture of graham crumbs. Makes 12 servings.

Rhubarb "whine"

by Chris Scherbarth

I love rhubarb— not just for the pies and cobblers, but also for the way it thrives in my sub-arctic garden. I give plants away every year and still an embarrassing amount of rhubarb goes to waste.

This past summer I decided to waste less of the faithful perennial by chopping up 24 pounds of it to make two batches of rhubarb wine. For the first batch I followed the recipe carefully and, within 48 hours, I had 19 litres of "must" happily fermenting in a corner.

For the second batch, I substituted two litres of organic peach nectar for the (non-organic) white grape concentrate called for in the recipe. This way the must, squeezed from the rhubarb through a sterilized pillowcase, would be mostly organic. (Who knows what the sugar and wine additives lend to the mix?)

Batch #1 gurgled away for weeks and finished up as a dry, extremely tart brew. In fact, I couldn't even bear to swallow the portion that ended up in my mouth during siphoning. I was disappointed.

I had given Batch #2 extra sugar to make up for the drop in sweetness caused by my ingredient substitution. My doctoring of the recipe complicated fermentation, but things eventually got rolling. The final brew was more palatable, but too sweet for my tastes. Oops again.

I phoned the woman who had coached me through the "stuck ferment" crisis and explained my plight. Her response was music to my ears.

"God has blessed you," she told me. "You have one batch too tart and one too sweet. Blend them."

Blend them?! I hadn't thought of that.

Six months later, after the requisite "bulk aging," I blended and corked 50 bottles of my first non-u-brew wine. It's not bad either, once the taste buds have grappled with the initial, precocious tang of rhubarb. (My taste buds are rather accustomed to grape wine.)

Looking back, I find it ironic that what saved me from disaster was the fact I courted it twice. If I had made but one batch of wine, it would have ended up either too tart or too sweet. This way I have something I will proudly hand out at Christmas — if there's any left by then.

Yankee Bob's fruit stuffed grouse

For each person to be served, find, then head-shoot one grouse. Pick one-third of a cup of lowbush cranberries (lingon berries). Mossberries may be substituted, but don't have much flavour. Pluck the birds, being as careful as you can not to rip the skin, especially where the crop and the windpipe come out of the neck. You may cut the wings off at the last joint to save time and energy. Clean and save liver, gizzard, and heart for gravy.

Dice up one medium apple for each grouse. Mix apples and berries together with a liberal amount of cinnamon and a small amount of brown sugar. Stuff the fruit mixture into the birds. Don't forget to include the neck area, under the flap of skin where the crop was.

Carefully place them in a dutch oven or individually wrap in aluminum foil. Cook at medium to high heat for at least half an hour before checking to see if the leg moves freely and the apples are quite soft. It could take up to an hour, depending on how hot your oven is.

Boil giblets slowly in a saucepan for gravy, with onions, garlic, pepper, and celery, if available.

When birds are done, take out to cool. Thicken gravy with a paste of flour or cornstarch and water before adding to the cooled birds. Serve with mashed potatoes or rice.

by Bob Fink

Pickled Jack Fish

Mike Hodgson borrowed this recipe from Jack Warner who borrowed it from someone else who probably read it somewhere.

Scale and clean a good-sized pike. Cut it into bite-size chunks and don't worry about the bones. Place the chunks in a large earthen crock and cover with half a cup of coarse pickling salt for each quart of jackfish.

Cover the fish with white cider vinegar and leave in the refrigerator for five days. Stir each day.

After five days, drain and rinse with cold water. Let stand in ice water for 30 minutes. Drain and pack the pieces in jars, alternating layers of sliced onions and fish.

Boil one quart of white vinegar, two cups of sugar, and just over a half a cup of pickling spice. Allow this to cool and pour over the fish in the jars.

Keep in the refrigerator for one week before eating.

Now—everything has a downside. Pickled jack fish is terrific. However, don't kill off several jars at one sitting. You will get the trots. I have done this.

I drank beer, watched Saskatchewan destroy the Ti-Cats, ate two quarts of pickled pike and then sat in the outhouse for the latter part of an afternoon. I experimented on my friends—same effect.

CARIBOU HUNT

by Lisa Smith

It was a long philosophical as well as physical journey for me to go hunting caribou off the Dempster Highway. I had been a non-meat-eater for 10 years, including most of the time I've lived in the Yukon.

A few years ago, I decided to eat meat, but only good quality, ethically-raised meat. It was pretty expensive to buy that standard of meat. It also felt hypocritical, because I had always maintained that one of the reasons I did not eat meat was because I knew I could not do the killing, so I didn't deserve to eat it.

When I was invited to go hunting, I decided that perhaps this was my opportunity to put my money where my mouth was. I could help in the harvesting of local, high quality meat which I intended to eat. Even as I headed off in the truck with my hunting companions, I wasn't sure how I would feel about watching the kill, or shooting the rifle. At that point all I could commit to was helping with the butchering, the packing and the camp chores.

I have been hunting twice now, and have missed the kill both times, not on purpose, but simply because of where I was at the time. I am still not sure if I could shoot the rifle. The gutting and skinning were not as traumatic as I'd expected. I gave a silent thank you to the caribou, and then went to work methodically, without the kind of deep emotions over killing that I thought I would feel.

Butchering was a difficult time because I did not enjoy being around all the raw meat and blood. It was also a lot of hard work! By the end of the day, I wondered if I could eat the caribou—like making 50 dozen cookies. By the end, you don't want to see another one.

Well, I did eat that caribou, and I feel good about it. I feel that it is a renewable supply of healthy meat. The animal has had a good life. The meat is low fat, low chemical. If the herd is in danger from overhunting, I would, of course, rethink my position.

I eat meat everyday now, a situation I would not have imagined a couple of years ago. I feel healthier though, and get ill less often. I don't know if there is a connection.

What the Sears catalogue means to me

by Mary Shiell

I t happens every January. The mercury dives down into the ball of the thermometer. That means it's even colder than 40 below. But, by that time, a few degrees either way doesn't really make any difference.

The woodstove devours logs almost as quickly as you can put them in. The plumbing puts up a protest, requiring pampering.

And then there's the truck. Never mind the square tires, it doesn't even turn over. The sled dogs do. They thrive on the cold. It's getting them to stop that's the problem.

Just when I think I can't take the dark and the cold and the utter misery of it all anymore, salvation arrives with a capital S.

The Sears spring and summer catalogue. Page after beautiful page of healthy, tanned people lolly-gagging around in t-shirts and shorts under the hot sun.

When I was a kid I thought the Sears corporation was just horribly confused. Maybe they didn't have winter in Toronto, or they simply chose to ignore it.

Whatever the case, our family certainly appreciated the gesture. We turned it into a multi-purpose document. Sears became synonymous with entertainment as well as toilet paper.

Sometimes, out of sheer boredom on a cold winter's night (if for some asinine reason we weren't at the skating rink), we'd sit down with the Sears catalogue and an adding machine and see how much money we could spend. Pretending we were rich beyond our wildest dreams, we'd go through the catalogue and buy our favourite item from every page.

As I grew older and more cynical, I believed the arrival of the spring and summer edition in

the dead of winter was simply a cheap, crass marketing ploy. Consumer trickery. We're cold and miserable and we'll buy.

I have changed my thinking considerably since then.

Now I eagerly anticipate the day (it's always cold and it's always January) I get the crisp new edition.

Talk about a fix for cabin fever.

And perhaps that's what Sears had in mind all along. Sort of its corporate contribution to the mental well-being of all Canadians. And god bless 'em if it weren't for just one small detail.

It happens every July. The mercury soars to the top of the thermometer, making it a sweltering 30 degrees or more. Despite drawing the curtains, the heat penetrates every corner of the house.

The truck starts no problem. The sled dogs do not.

It's absolutely beautiful and you wonder why anyone would want to live anywhere else. And then it happens: the new Sears fall and winter catalogue rolls off the mail truck.

SOLITARY PARENTING *by Jay Cherian*

P arenthood is a big job, whether it be for a couple or a single parent. Community is a necessary ingredient in the raising of any child.

I am a single parent in that, at this point, I have ultimate responsibility for my child's care and well-being. My daughter spends most of her time in my company, and I am responsible for our finances. But my daughter has a few other significant caregivers.

We do childcare swaps. We have neighbours nearby with kids, whom we rely on. We have friends who call and say, "So when's the next time I get to play with your kid?" and who have more than average involvement in the parenting of my daughter.

It all adds up to being more than just me who cares about my kid. This makes me feel like the community around me has taken some responsibility for her care too.

To date, I have had a tough time with being a single parent. But it's only been a year and it seems that things might be getting easier. It's hard to dream when you're not quite sure where you're going to sleep at night, or whether or not you have enough food.

It's hard to carry food and laundry when you have only one bicycle to transport both you and your child.

It's hard to love when your heart is still icy with the anger, frustration, and sense of failure from a relationship that didn't work. It's hard to feel joy and pride in watching your child grow and learn, and have no one to share that with.

I have had some things going for me, too. I had a job that made some allowances for the fact that I was a single parent, and for my ideologies around parenting. For example, I was able to bring my daughter to work with me. And though my belief has wavered often, deep down I believe that in the long run things will work out just fine for us.

We're not through the tough times yet, but we've come a long way in the past year.

Still, my story doesn't come out easily. It's difficult

to explain what it means to me to be a single mother. I sat down one night and these thoughts jumped onto the page. They seem a bit dreary, but then for me, like I said, it hasn't been easy.

Things are getting better. My finances aren't so tight, my heart is warming up, and my daughter is healthy and happy. I know there are others that are worse off—and well, try me again in a year or so.

Nice looking, easy to build, strong:

Woodbox

instructions and illustrations by Norman McIntyre

This wood box can be moved to your door to load the firewood and wheeled back (full) without any effort. And it'll look good in your living room!

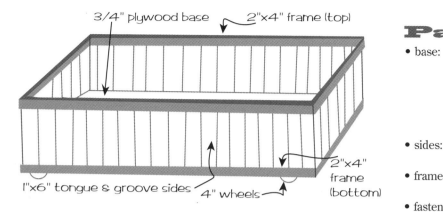

3/4" plywood base   2"x4" frame (top)

l"x6" tongue & groove sides   4" wheels

2"x4" frame (bottom)

Parts

- base: $^3/_4$ inch plywood (45 x 27$^1/_2$ inches)
  2, 2 x 4 braces (27$^1/_2$ inches long)
  4 inch diameter, industrial-strength castor wheels
- sides: 1 x 6 tongue and groove (or $^3/_4$ inch plywood)
- frame: 2 x 4 (top)
  2 x 4 (bottom)
- fasteners: large woodscrews

Tools

- drill
- skillsaw
- rubber mallet to knock wood into place
- screwdriver

Base

The base is made of a piece of $^3/_4$ inch plywood, 45 x 27$^1/_2$ inches wide. The width can be modified to allow pieces to fit your stove.

Two 2 x 4 braces run across the width of the bottom of the base. Screw through the base into the braces using large woodscrews.

3/4" plywood base 45"x27 1/2"

woodscrews

2"x4" brace 27 1/2" wide

Frame

The top and bottom frame pieces are made of 2 x 4s with a groove down the length of the 1$^1/_2$ inches edge to receive the tongue and groove pine ($^3/_4$ inch wide by 1$^1/_4$ inches deep). Use a skillsaw and chisel to make the groove before you cut the 2 x 4 into lengths.

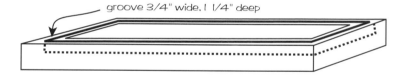

groove 3/4" wide, 1 1/4" deep

The 2 x 4 should measure 27$^1/_2$ inches long on the inside measurement for four of the sides and 45 inches long on the inside for the other four sides. The frames, when complete, should fit around the outside of the base.

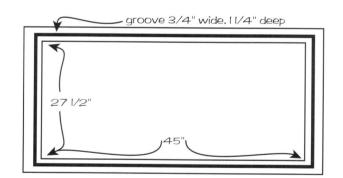

groove 3/4" wide, 1 1/4" deep

27 1/2"

45"

Screw the bottom frame onto the base (use a drill to pre-drill holes) through the side of the frame and into the 2 x 4 brace.

The top of the bottom frame should be level with the top of the base. Attach the four, 4-inch wheels to the corners of the plywood. The wheels should stick out about $^1/_4$ inch or so from the bottom of the frame, or a bit more if the box has to run over carpeting.

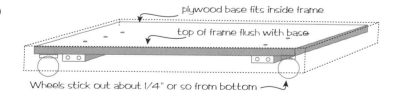

plywood base fits inside frame

top of frame flush with base

Wheels stick out about 1/4" or so from bottom

Sides

Cut enough 1 x 6s (finished $^3/_4$ inch thick) tongue and groove pine or spruce or poplar to make the walls. They should be about 24 inches high. You can use plywood instead of tongue and groove for extra strength on sides.

Stand the tongue and groove upright in the bottom frame. End pieces should be cut lengthwise at a 45 degree angle for a finished look. You can use piano hinges on the inside corners for extra strength.

Cap the tongue and groove walls with the top part of the frame.

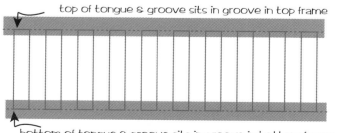

top of tongue & groove sits in groove in top frame

bottom of tongue & groove sits in groove in bottom frame

Growing Kids

The Far Side

A day on the Wheaton, Saturday, October 28, 1995

by Shiela Alexandrovich

ILLUSTRATION: JUDE LACOSTE

Welcome to the Far Side. My children, Jude Lacoste, 10, and Levon Lacoste, 7, and myself, make up our household. We live 40 miles from Whitehorse on a dirt road, beyond the reach of the powergrid. By choice. Our extended family includes two other households that hold this piece of land in common. There are no other children, but there are four other adults who are glad to make time and space for Jude and Levon in their lives. I'm glad, too!

My living comes from gathering and building artwork—mostly baskets and contemporary beading. I work here, we live here, Jude and Levon school here. Our days vary with the time of year. It is fall, and we have chosen a random day to share.

Jude's day
by Jude Lacoste

Yawn! I look around my room. I stare out my window and watch the frost drip down the pane. I'm awakened from my sleepiness by the sound of Levon's feet patting loudly up the stairs to the breakfast table. About five minutes later, Shiela yells up my stairs, "Jude! Breakfast!" I decide that I shouldn't starve my tummy, so I get out of my cozy blankets into the cold morning air. I put on a pair of pants and a sweatshirt. I rummage quickly through my sock basket and find a pair of red socks. Pulling on a pair of slippers, I race down my stairs. I enter the kitchen to the sound of the stove crackling. Porridge. Anyway, I gobble down my porridge. I didn't know I was so hungry! I shove my plate in the dishwater and gallop triumphantly towards my stairs. As soon as I reach the top, I take a sharp turn towards my desk. Grabbing a couple of books off the shelf, and snatching a pencil out of a can, I open a book and start my morning school. After an hour or so of math, socials and a couple of other things like doing craft work, I'm finished my work for the day. The rest of the day we play. We go exploring in the woods. About six o'clock, everyday, Shiela yells out the back

PHOTOS: MARLYNN BOURQUE

door, "Supper!" We race for the chow! We eat supper and play until bedtime. We brush our teeth and wash our faces. We all say goodnight to each other and go to bed. And that's a day on the Wheaton.

Levon's day
by Levon Lacoste

I got up this morning and came into the kitchen. Shiela made porridge for breakfast. I really like molasses, peanut butter, sometimes

banana and sometimes cranberry jam on my porridge. I played for a while, then I got dressed.

I went for a bike ride over to Chris's. Chris was holding the dogs by their collars and they danced on their back feet to get tied up. One dog, Blair I think, was loose. Everyone was jumping up and down after they had a run. I rode home and did some work on my fable book. I wish winter would come soon. The mountains are covered in snow today.

One of my work jobs today was pulling nails from boards from the old heat pen to burn in the kitchen fire. I also helped Jude and Shiela build the corral for a horse for Jude.

I took a break and made a smoothie from banana, milk, vanilla, and cocoa for Bob and Jude and me.

I pick up dog poo every three or four days. It's stinky. It goes in a bucket and after awhile Shiela takes it in the wheelbarrow to the big pile.

It normally takes two trips to fill the kitchen woodbox.

After my work, Bob and Shiela are going for a woodcut. Bob helped me load my bike in the back of the truck. We went down the Marsh Trail and I rode my bike back.

It was my turn after supper to do dishes and I took a long time.

I had a good day, and now I'm gonna eat some toast that Jude made.

Shiela's day
by Shiela Alexandrovich

8 a.m. Rise. Stoke the stove and set a pot of porridge to cook. Four big pike to fillet and grind—fish given to me for dog food is gonna detour through my freezer! Make a coffee, always a latté with fresh milk. Sip as I cut. Flesh the fish skins, set them to dry.

8:30 a.m. Kids up, eating, Jude starts her math. Answer a math question and try to keep track of what Goat, Turtle and Rat are up to in Levon's book. He reads aloud beside the stove as I clean up fish mess. Ten minutes to sit with a second cup.

10:30 a.m. Out to milk goats, feed dogs. Back in and set a batch of yogurt. I help Levon do a fable and colour. Sit for ten minutes and talk beads when Bob pops in. It's white on the mountains. Warm in the house. We eat lunch— dip and veggies, scones.

1:15 p.m. We are out putting rails up for a corral. A horse is coming! Hard to believe. Started a year ago—built a stall, put up corral posts, cleared. This fall we add rails and we are ready. Gonna board a pony for six months. Big nails, heavy hammer. The guy sold me the wrong bar for my chainsaw. Slowly I get to know the inside of these saws. Not what I want to know. No choice. I'm glad Chris is next door. He helps me pinpoint problems, offers solutions to try.

3:00 p.m. Marlynn comes for a visit. Coffee break. We talk dogs; Jude plays with her two boys. French and English. Everyone understands. We go for a quick load of wood before supper. Bob's truck—I don't have one. Borrow for wood and 100-pound propane tanks. Levon rides behind us on his bike.

Supper of potatoes and smoked fish, salad and fresh feta. As it happens—O.J. is acquitted. Discussion on justice and money. Jude doesn't understand how he could get off.

Levon does dishes. I vacuum out my big stone stove. Not in use yet. Kitchen stove is enough. Wonder if I've cut enough wood. Or got enough hay. Or enough money. Thoughts that pop in and out lots of days.

I take care of my animals; talk to the goats for a bit. The barn always smells good. Quiet munching.

I put the yogurt in a cloth bag to hang for cheese. Toast and teatime at the table. Help Jude with her world map project. Levon decides to "sleep over" in Jude's room. She reads to him.

10:30 p.m. I'm tired. Stoke the stove and go to bed to read a bit.

A full day, but then that's fall. Didn't fit in any artwork but by Saturday, I should be full into willow. Baskets and furniture. Jude needs a work space, a good desk. Winter will settle soon. Trying to keep track of what I have to do; when.

That's life on the Wheaton! Although we live closely, our days are often quite different. Levon visits more than anyone else here and probably holds the cookie consumption record. I don't sleep until 9 or 9:30 p.m; but then I am often the first to bed. There is room here. Room for us to live with our own rhythms, the daily rhythms, the seasonal rounds. Another day coming. Good night.

PLEIN AIR

PAR LEIGH MACMILLAN

*une expérience magnifique
une pas comme les autres
tu es seul avec la nature
le soleil qui brille
la neige qui miroite
une sensation pas ressentie par tous
des oiseaux qui dansent sur l'horizon
la silhouette de la montagne te surmonte
pas de civilisation à des kilomètres
tu es aux mains de la nature
ça te fait penser à l'environnement
c'est un équilibre facilement dérangé*

PRECIOUS LEARNING TIMES ON THE LAND

by Norma Kassi

My Indian name is Gwahtla Aaishih—I'm Gwich'in and from the Wolf Clan. I come from a nation that's about 7,000 strong. I was raised on the land for the first 16 years of my life. When I speak to people, I like to share some of my very precious times of learning.

My grandfather, Elias Gwahtlati, and my mother had taught me a lot. And those teachings I hold dear because it was what created the foundation for my life's endeavours. When I was growing up, every spring from April to June, we would hitch up our dogteams and head 40 miles on land over mountains and many lakes to our spring camp.

It was a beautiful and spiritual place, where there were a lot of animals and birds and our streams were full of fish. Only our language was spoken here. Everything we did, we did together; from the youngest to the oldest, we all had our chores to do.

When we got all settled then we began trapping for muskrats, which was our only income to buy the basic essentials we needed, like clothes and food. Nothing fancy: flour, sugar, tea, some rice and raisins. No such thing as candy—rice and raisins were our treats.

Everyday was hard work, from when we awoke, to when we went to bed. We loved every minute of it, too. As each day would go by and the snow began to melt, the spring animals and birds began to move and come back to us. The first times we heard the geese we'd all run outside, even if we had been sleeping. Grandpa would mumble something to them and so did my mom. We'd hear *Mahsi-cho*.

The most exciting time would be when the caribou were coming. My mom would always know where they would be and she'd send Grandfather, and later on my brothers, to a direction she'd point to. And sure enough, that night we'd eat and eat fresh meat, and my mom, my sister and I would start drying meat. We'd have huge caches just full of all kinds of goodies.

I've witnessed some very spiritual times being with my grandpa. I've seen him communicate with animals, something I later on learned to do. I've often wondered what would have become of my life if I did not have those teachings.

As aboriginal people we must maintain and practise our beliefs. We see an urgent need to renew indigenous thinking. Recognition and respect for the equality of all elements of life are necessary because it brings us into perspective as human beings. We believe that all life is equal because we are spiritual people. We are caretakers of our land and its animal kingdom. Our whole way of life, our cultures, our traditions derive from Mother Earth.

Our environment is precious to us. We believe that all life forms are of an equal balance. I was taught that every living being was of the same value as I was; that we must respect our animal world and be very grateful for all the basic essentials that we are offered everyday; to give something when we take. We cannot forget the blood connection we have with the earth.

You know, Mother Earth cannot sustain all this destruction to her body. It is up to us to do our part to keep her clean: her veins are the rivers, lakes, oceans; her breasts, the mountains, the land.

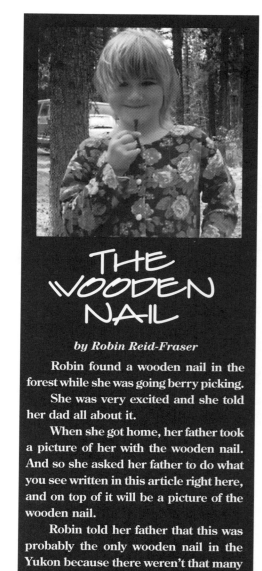

THE WOODEN NAIL

by Robin Reid-Fraser

Robin found a wooden nail in the forest while she was going berry picking.

She was very excited and she told her dad all about it.

When she got home, her father took a picture of her with the wooden nail. And so she asked her father to do what you see written in this article right here, and on top of it will be a picture of the wooden nail.

Robin told her father that this was probably the only wooden nail in the Yukon because there weren't that many around. And also because this was the first one she had ever seen. Usually, nails are made out of metal. So this was a very interesting kind.

Outside at Riverdale School

*I can smell the sweet grass,
almost taste,
as a gust of wind is rushing past.
Leaves,
falling gently,
the soft and satisfying, PLOP
as they fall to the ground.
The colour,
movement,
as life goes on.
Alone,
but not lonely.*

Caitlin Moorcroft

A modern legend

by SharonAnne LaDue

As a young child, I would stare at the northern lights in awe. The elders would always say, "Don't whistle, don't clap your hands. Stay quiet. Show respect." I would stand quiet and stare at the magical lights that danced across the sky. After the northern lights had faded I was left wondering 'Why can't I whistle or make noise?' The elders never answered my queries, even though I asked every time.

While attending F.H. Collins High School, my writing teacher gave us an assignment that made me think about the northern lights. I still didn't know why I shouldn't clap or whistle at the northern lights. So, given writer's freedom, I made up my own reasons why we should show respect and not whistle at the Northern Lights.

The Royal Elder entered the lodge wearing a warm cape made up of fine beaver pelts with a Crow Clan design in the back. The Royal Elder walked peacefully towards the warmest seat in the lodge which is given to the oldest member of the clan.

The Elder only spoke the language of the elders before, so her loving son interpreted the songs and words into English for the little eager ears listening to learn the old ways.

"My children, time marches on like that of the wolf, silently and never resting. My spiritmaker tells me it's soon time to join him in the moving spirits, the Northern Lights. So now I'll tell you why our spirits must go to the Northern Lights." The Elder stopped and looked around at the gleaming faces of the young ones, and at her loving son. "When my elders were just babies, the storyteller's son saved the Village-by-the-running-waters. 'How?' you ask.

"The storyteller's son was a brave man and an honourable son to the whole village. During his time-of-training he came upon a beautiful glowing apparition that told him that he was very strong and brave but soon his beloved village would perish."

The Elder stopped and looked around the cabin into the faces of the young and her loving son. "The young man said that this must not happen to his beloved village. The apparition told him, 'if you will honour me I can help save your village.' The young man implored the apparition to continue on. 'Ask for me on the darkest night in the next moon.' The apparition faded into the night.

"The young man returned to his beloved village and sat with the council for the first time and he listened to them rejoice over the goodness of the spirits. The spirits gave the village a warm fall, a longer time to get ready for the long cold dark winter. The brave young man felt a twinge of tension and curiosity. Did the beautiful apparition misguide the young man? No. No apparition would do that.

"Soon the ground was covered with deep piles of angelic snow, and the village was not prepared for the long cold winter. Now the council did not party foolishly. They knew that without the proper amount of food stored the village would die. No one would be able to save them." The Elder stopped and shook her head gently. "Not yet," she murmured quietly. "The young man knew that this was the darkest night of this, the eighth moon. He crept away from the villagers and went to a quiet grove to praise the beautiful apparition. 'What is it that you want, young one of the Village-by-running-waters?' questioned the glowing apparition.

"'I wish to praise you, Oh Great Glowing Apparition. What could I do to honour you so you will help?' The young man fell to his knees and praised the apparition with all his might.

"'I need the spirits of your people to paint my picture in the sky on long cold winter nights,' the glowing apparition said quietly.

"'Take my spirit please Oh Great One and the others after they have lived a long happy life. Please save my beloved village and I will be yours,' the young man promised. Racing back to the village, the young man told the council that they must get ready to hunt so they could save the village. The sky lit up with glowing greens, blues and pinks and the young man laid down on his death bed."

The Elder spoke quietly and looked at the young children and spoke again, "My spiritmaker has called for me. I told you this legend so you too will know what happens after you tire of this world and the spiritmaker calls for you. It is my time to paint the skies with the spiritmakers of our ancestors. Go outside and look to the sky," the Elder whispered and passed peacefully into the next world.

PAINTING: GLORIA ANDISON

Living in the Yukon

by Jovian Collins

When I come home on a frosty night
it's not too cold to my delight
and as I get into my old house
I see a scurrying little mouse
I'm not afraid and I'll tell you why
'cause in the Yukon we're not shy.

Now it's summer and I'm having fun
in the land of the midnight sun
and as I run so proud and free
I know this is where I want to be.

WHAT WOULD IT BE LIKE?

by Echo Peters

What would it be like to be born in the sky
Tell me please why oh why
What would it be like to live a long time ago?
To hear laughter and to see the snow
What would it be like to be able to write?
Or to stay way late into the night
But I do know what's it like to sing to the moon.
I'll show you how very soon.

Hunting a moose

by Roy Mervin

One day I was walking in the woods and I heard a roar. A black bear jumped out and it ran after me and I made it to camp. My grampa saw the bear and he shot at it and it ran up to a mountain.

Two days later, I saw the bear when I was with my uncle. We walked 10 miles and we saw sheep there. There were four rams and my uncle shot one so we cut it up. Then I packed some up and we had to carry it back. Then we saw two bull moose. One was big and the other one was small so I shot it. We cut it up and came back the next morning and packed out the moose. We had a lot of meat for the winter.

Growing kids

DÉCEMBRE AU YUKON

par Cécile Girard

Dans un territoire plus près d'ici qu'on ne le croit, en fait dans la partie nord-ouest du Canada, appelée le territoire du Yukon, vivait, il y a de cela pas très longtemps, en fait un an ou deux, un petit garçon nommé Décembre.

Décembre habitait une petite maison logée au fond d'une baie. Une rivière faisait mille détours devant chez lui. Derrière la maison, un sentier ombragé d'épinettes vêtues de lichen noirâtres conduisait à un lac minuscule. Quarante-sept canards sauvages et vingt et un rats musqués y passaient l'été.

Décembre aimait son entourage, sa famille ses chiens, ses chats et ses poules. Ce qu'il aimait moins, c'était la longueur de certaines saisons. Ainsi, dès que la première neige était tombée (habituellement en septembre), il demandait :

-Ma fête arrive-t-elle bientôt? Décembre était né la première journée du printemps.

Et l'attente commençait… dans ces jours obscurs d'automne où les heures de clarté fuyaient devant la nuit envahissante. Décembre pensait alors que l'hiver était éternel et que la date magique du 21 mars ne viendrait jamais. Que penser d'autre?

Après la première neige, tout devenait blanc pour les cent vingt-huit siècles suivants. Parfois il faisait même trop froid pour jouer dehors. Dans ce temps-là, ses parents discutaient de la température toute la journée. La maman prenait une petite voix inquiète et demandait fréquemment au papa de Décembre :

-Combien fait-il?

Ce dernier répondait presque gêné :

-C'est encore -44°C.

Ces jours-là, les chats Coton et Bouton demeuraient dans la maison. Les deux bêtes ronronnaient d'aise sous le poêle à bois. Décembre, lui, avait le droit de construire un fort dans le salon avec les coussins du divan. Ces derniers devenaient les murs, bien épais pour le protéger du froid. Une couverture de laine jetée sur la table à café lui servait de toit.

Au fur et à mesure que la journée passait, le fort s'agrandissait jusqu'à ce qu'un cri de sa mère en arrête la construction.

-C'est assez! disait-elle d'une voix forte et Décembre battait en retraite en protestant.

-Mais tu as dit que je pouvais!

-Oui mais tu es rendu dans la cuisine. Te rends-tu compte qu'il n'y a plus une seule couverture, ni un seul oreiller sur les lits?

-Oui mais maman, c'est parce que je voulais t'inviter à dîner avec moi à Fort -44° C.

Désarmée, sa maman riait. Décembre savait qu'elle aimerait le nom de son fort. C'était toujours comme ça. Quand Décembre utilisait des mots ou des bribes de conversation d'adultes, ceux-ci le trouvaient mignon.

-Fort-44°… Où prends-tu ces idées? Quelle imagination!

En fin de compte, les jours froids n'étaient pas si terribles, mais ils étaient très noirs et très nombreux.

«La noirceur colle comme de l'encre au paysage», se plaignaient les parents.

Pourtant Décembre les avait surpris souvent dans la nuit, le nez collé à la fenêtre, à admirer des aurores boréales, compagnes folâtres de l'obscurité.

-Qu'est-ce que vous faites? demandait-il.

-Nous assistons à un spectacle; c'est magnifique. Viens voir.

Quatre bras se tendaient vers lui. Niché entre ses parents, Décembre contemplait les faisceaux de lumière verte, rose et bleue qui dansaient dans la nuit. Le moment magique volé au sommeil s'éternisait souvent car Décembre s'endormait avant que la représentation ne soit terminée. Il est difficile de dire ce qui enchantait le plus le petit garçon lors de ces escapades nocturnes : entre lumière et tendresse, son cœur balançait.

Mais l'hiver il ne fait pas toujours froid et il fait souvent très beau. Le soleil qui brille et le ciel tout bleu invitent tout le monde dehors. Et cela devient vite une obligation. Alors qu'hier il n'avait pas le droit d'aller dehors, aujourd'hui, il n'a pas le droit de rester dans la maison.

-Est-ce que je peux regarder la télévision? demande Décembre.

-Avec ce beau soleil? Non! Ouste! Interdiction formelle de regarder la télévision aujourd'hui! Il fait trop beau, s'entend-il répondre. Il faut profiter de la journée, continuent ses parents.

-Mes parents sont des profiteurs, pense Décembre. Ils profitent de la journée, profitent de la fin de semaine, profitent du soleil, profitent du beau temps. Profiteurs! lance Décembre.

Mais sa mère l'ignore et continue à chantonner :

-Mon Dieu qu'il fait beau!

Juchées dans les trembles qui entourent la maison, trois perdrix grasses picochent des bourgeons sur les branches; des geais du Canada disputent la nourriture des chats. Des vols de passereaux voyagent d'une épinette à l'autre en piaillant. Dans la forêt, les lapins mâchonnent des branches de conifères abattus par des vents récents. Le long du sentier qui mène au lac, on peut voir les traces de festin laissées par les écureuils : des écales de cônes forment des petits monticules bruns sur la neige blanche.

Le printemps qui ramène la fête de Décembre finit toujours par arriver, les éternités ayant malgré tout une fin. Du jour au lendemain, les parents sont excités et ne parlent plus que des journées qui allongent. Ça devient le sujet de conversation préféré dans la voiture tous les soirs en rentrant du travail : «Regarde, il fait encore clair! On voit le sommet de la montagne. Les cygnes vont être bientôt là!» Ils se félicitent mutuellement comme s'ils en étaient responsables.

-As-tu vu le ciel? Il fait encore clair!

Décembre ne peut plus entendre cette remarque qui revient maintenant matin et soir. Les journées allongent. Mais comment peuvent-elles allonger?

Allongent-elles comme les sangsues qu'il attrappe en été? Penché au bout du quai, il les regarde nager les yeux mi-clos. Il est un monstre préhistorique et les sangsues sont ses ennemies jurées. Vivement avec un bâtonnet, il les sort de l'eau et les jette sur le quai. Les bestioles, conscientes du danger, rampent en s'étirant afin de rejoindre l'eau. Elles deviennent longues, longues, si longues. De véritables journées d'été. Décembre est magnanime et il laisse ses prisonnières s'enfuir non sans les avoir averties d'aller se balader ailleurs.

DECEMBER IN THE YUKON

by Cécile Girard

In a land near by—in fact, in the north-western part of Canada, called the Yukon Territory—there lived—not so very long ago, only a year or so—a little boy named December.

December lived in a small house at the far end of a bay. A river turned back upon itself a thousand times in front of his home. Behind the house, a path lined with lichen-clad pine trees led to a tiny lake. Forty-seven wild ducks and twenty-one muskrats spent their summers there.

December loved his home, his family, his dogs, his cats and his chickens. What he didn't like was the length of certain seasons. And so, as soon as the first snow fell (usually in September), he would ask: "When will it be my birthday?" He was born on the first day of spring.

And then the wait would begin during those dreary fall days when daylight fled the invading darkness. December came to believe that winter was endless and that the magic date of March 21st would never arrive. What else could he think?

With the first snow, everything turned white for the one hundred and twenty-eight centuries that followed. Sometimes, it was even too cold to play outside. On those days his parents talked about the weather all day long. Worriedly, his mother would ask his father, "How cold is it?"

And his father always replied, almost embarrassed, "It's still minus 44 degrees Celsius."

On those days, the cats—Cotton and Button—stayed inside. They purred in contentment under the woodstove. December

was allowed to build forts in the living room by using the cushions of the sofa. They became thick walls to protect him from the cold. A woollen blanket over the coffee table became the roof.

As the day wore on, the fort grew in size, until his mother put a stop to the construction. "That's enough!" she said loudly and December retreated, protesting.

"But you said I could!"

"Yes, but you're in the kitchen now. Do you realize there isn't a single pillow or blanket left on the beds?"

"Yes, but Mom, I wanted to invite you to dinner at Fort Minus 44 Degrees Celsius."

Taken aback, his mother laughed. December knew she would like the name of his fort. It was always like that. Adults were always charmed when he used words or phrases that he'd overheard them use.

"Fort Minus 44 Degrees Celsius. Where do you find your ideas? What an imagination!"

All in all, the cold days were not so terrible, except for being too dark, and too numerous.

"The dark clings like ink to the landscape," complained his parents. And yet, December would often catch them late at night, their noses pressed to the window, admiring the northern lights, the aurora, that flighty companion of the dark.

"What are you doing?" he would ask.

"We're watching the show. It's marvellous! Come see."

Four arms would reach for him. Nestled between his parents, December would admire the lights tinged in green, pink and blue that

danced in the night. The wonderful moment, stolen from sleep, would last longer than he did. December was often asleep before it ended. He didn't know what enchanted him most about these night-time adventures. His heart hovered between light and tenderness.

But winter was not always cold and it was often very beautiful. Bright sun and blue skies invited everyone to go outside, an invitation that soon became an order. Although yesterday he wasn't allowed outside, today he wasn't allowed inside.

"Can I watch television?" he asked.

"With that sun? No! Outside! No one watches television today! It's too beautiful out," was the answer he always got. "Take advantage of the nice weather," continued his parents.

My parents like to take advantage, thought December. They take advantage of the day, of the weekend, of the sun, of the beautiful weather. "Users!" he called out to them.

But his mother ignored him and continued to sing, "My God, it's so beautiful out!"

Perched in the aspens surrounding the house, three plump partridges pecked away at the buds; Canada jays argued over food with the cats. Sparrows wheeled in formation from one pine tree to another, calling to each other. In the forest, rabbits gnawed away at the branches of the coniferous trees felled by recent winds. All along the path leading to the lake were traces of the squirrels' feasting: pine cone scales formed little brown mounds in the white snow.

The spring, herald of December's birthday, always came. Eternity ended. Parents became excited and talked of nothing but the lengthening days. It became the favourite subject of conversation on the ride home at night. "Look, it's still light! We can see the mountain peak. The swans will soon be back!" They congratulated each other as though personally responsible.

"Look at that sky! It's still light!" December was getting tired of hearing the same refrain morning and night. The days *were* getting longer, but how was it possible?

Did they lengthen like the leeches he caught in the summer? Leaning over the edge of the dock, he would watch them swim, his eyes half-closed. He was a prehistoric monster, the leeches his sworn enemies. With a stick, he flicked them out of the water and dropped them on the dock. The creatures, aware of danger, crept toward the water by lengthening their bodies. They became long, long, incredibly long. Like summer days. December magnanimously allowed his prisoners to escape, but not before warning them to go play elsewhere.

Translated from French by Marcelle Dubé.

Growing kids

SILENCE

by Chad Francis

Silence fills the room

a sound of its own

a feeling of its own

a blanket thick, impenetrable

thin, weak

warm and cold all at once

stiffling, ominous

free, open

Wondrous!

Questions

by Amy Strachan

Are we real,

Is anything real?

Are we just characters in a play,

And everything is the setting?

Or people in someone's mind,

And our lives are an on-going dream?

Do we serve a purpose,

Or are we here just to occupy space?

Why do we live,

And why do we die,

Why do we love,

Why do we hate,

Why do we desire,

Despise,

Hurt,

Help,

Compliment and criticize?

Are we the way we appear,

Are we the dominant species?

Does anyone really care,

Or does no-one really mind?

How long will our society live,

If we're living at all?

Do the dead rest in peace,

Or do they truly have an afterlife?

Why do we sleep,

And why do we wake?

Why do we comprehend,

And still are so mystified?

Why do we think,

Create,

Listen,

Ignore,

Confront and avoid?

If all this is not important,

Then what is?

If there are so many questions,

Shouldn't we find answers?

Life

by Eliza Armstrong

Is reality a dream

if it is then why don't we wake up

living life in the shadows of others

watching them live their lives

running into a downward spiral

twisting round and round

falling into a new life

a quiet place

but still no different than the other

I'm a drifter

don't belong anywhere

and never will.

EARTH'S GREATEST CONTEST

by Angus Pope

I dreamt that all the Yukon men
the mushing mining lot
the trappers and the prospectors
the real old Klondike flock

took all their gear
packed for a year
and headed to the west
where they would rewrite history
with Earth's Greatest Contest

For all the cowboy guys and gals
the western dudes and duds
the gunslingers and sheriffs
the classic western studs
were coming out to meet them
and setting up their stuff.

The contest was quite simple
it may sound dumb at first
everything a team did
a new point their team pursed

For instance all the sourdough
that Yukon people made
and all the sparkling gold they mined
and every dogsled race
all made them one point richer
and closer to first place

And for every high stake poker game
held in some low down saloon
and every risky show-down
held with some greasy goon

and all the fancy riding tricks
and all the cattle herded
For all the tough old western types
another point was earned

The thing went on for days and days
with no one up or down
that's just the way the contest went
and then the news hit town

the people came from near and far
suspense and tension grew
a crowd swept up from all around
for the ultimate rendezvous

then something must have gone quite wrong
there was a change in score
the west was winning three eighty eighty-nine
to three eighty thirty-four

The Northerners were mourning
their hearts were quite dismayed
I guess that all the western guys
had easier cliches

But then a wrinkled stooped old man
whose eyes were soft and stunned
whispered in his softest tone
"don't lose your faith my sons"

There's one thing you've forgotten
that lies within us all
and if we were to use it
our opponents all would fall

Now one thing that you need to know
if you don't live way up here
It's deeper than our heart and soul
and our bottomless mugs of beer

Some things are too hard to explain
some things you have to know
more precious than anything
that can be mined
it's called True Northern Gold

The final contest then was held
And everyone was there
a cluster of excitement grew
as people stopped to stare

The scorekeeper half broke his wrist
the screaming crowd drew close
and the Klondikers had won
by thirteen grand
when the heavy dust cloud rose

The people carried them on their arms
and screamed in happy glee
as they said to one another
we'll have a jubilee!

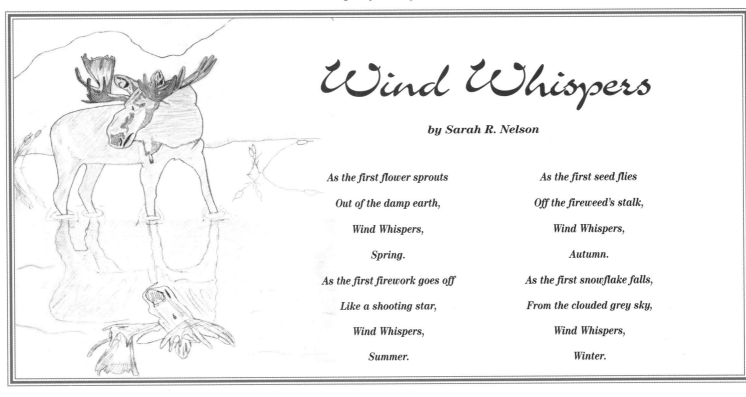

Wind Whispers

by Sarah R. Nelson

As the first flower sprouts

Out of the damp earth,

Wind Whispers,

Spring.

As the first firework goes off

Like a shooting star,

Wind Whispers,

Summer.

As the first seed flies

Off the fireweed's stalk,

Wind Whispers,

Autumn.

As the first snowflake falls,

From the clouded grey sky,

Wind Whispers,

Winter.

Answered prayers

School fire in Old Crow shocks the community

It was a typical January Tuesday afternoon in Old Crow—clear, sunny, quiet and cold. Forty below cold.

Unless you had happened to shut off the engine of your skidoo, or else turned down your office radio, you would not have heard anything out of the ordinary. But, if you had done either one of those things, then you would have heard a faint humming, almost buzzing, sound in the distance—a building's fire alarm. At about 1:00 p.m., just moments after this odd sound began, another joined it. One that you could not miss. Loud, piercing. The community's fire alarm.

Where is the fire?

At moments like this, if you're alone, you immediately scan the horizon for a blackish-brown column of smoke, mixed in with the white steam given off from a blaze. You look, praying that it's nothing serious.

The school is on fire.

You run for your skidoo, struggling with it as you try to start the damn thing in -40 degrees Celsius. All you think of is getting there, to the school. You pray for the skidoo to start.

Please, start! Damnit! Start!

It does. Your prayers are answered. You keep praying as you drive down Old Crow's "main street," staring straight ahead at the rising column of smoke and steam. You notice that the billowing tower is growing in width with each passing second. What could have started the fire? You envision an explosion…

Please! Please, let no one be hurt!

At times like this you really notice the difference between large, southern cities and small, northern communities. In a city, when tragedy strikes, you pray for the safety of your child, your partner, your family member, your friend. In a small community like Old Crow, you pray for the safety of everyone. Of every teacher, custodian and staff member. Of every single child.

The children! Please, please let them all be safe…

Tears well up in your eyes to accompany the lump already present in your throat as you drive up to Chief Zzeh Gittlit Elementary School, now completely engulfed in smoke. Parents, grandparents, cousins, aunts, uncles…all are

story and photos by Jacqueline Pruner

scrambling for their children. You see the principal, standing there, watching his school burn to the ground.

Is everybody safe?

Yes, everybody got out.

You feel like laughing out loud! Suddenly, the school, flames licking out of its main doors, doesn't matter as much, for there is no life within it. It becomes just a burning, empty building.

Empty. No one is hurt.

Some children were in shock. The fire began under the floorboards of the school (faulty heating tape), so the children had to be evacuated immediately. They had no time to gather up any of their coats, jackets or winter boots. One class was having gym when the alarm was pulled. Children and youth ran out into forty below temperatures wearing only their gym suits. They were immediately taken to the nursing station to warm up. Some continued shivering even after they were wrapped in blankets and warmed up. You assist in comforting them. To help keep them warm, you divide up your jacket, your neck-warmer, and your scarf among the children as you bundle them up before

transporting them home in the frigid cold.

"I never thought that'd be the last time I had gym class," one youth was rumoured to have whispered as he watched the fire. Although the children mourned the loss of the entire school, many have said they will miss the gymnasium the most.

Thirteen-year-old Tammy Josie was in the school when the fire began. She remembers the early moments of the fire quite vividly.

"It was very scary. When the fire started, I was in shop class. Steven Frost Sr. was teaching us how to skin a wolverine. Right when he was in the middle of skinning, we heard the fire alarm go off, and thought that it was just a practice test alarm. And then Mr. Burke, our principal, ran in, yelling, 'Quick, everyone out!' So everyone looked at each other and started running towards the door. Steven Frost Sr. dropped his good skinning knife and ran out behind us, after everyone else. I can remember wisps of black smoke rising from the floor. I panicked and ran out the door, forgetting everything. I lost my jacket, my boots, my mitts and my packsack, along with all my schoolwork and supplies."

The fire burned long into the night. Our volunteer firefighters tried to save the building, but couldn't. Everyone around here knows that the best way to start a fire on your woodstove is to build it from the bottom up, putting down fire starter first, then split logs, then logs. Fires burn best from the bottom up. So did our school, from the floorboards up.

The exhausted firefighters kept a night-long vigil around the blaze to ensure that no power lines or gas tanks were reached by the heat and flames.

By 11:00 a.m. the next morning, all that was left was a pile of black, charred wood, hot-white ash, and a few tongues of fire, licking at the air.

You lick your lips and let out a whistle, all the while shaking your head as you look at the empty space that was once the school.

I can't believe it's gone…

Now the children often sit at kitchen tables, over soda pop, glasses of juice or tea, and reminisce, through stories and humour, about the school. They are now older and wiser, in appearance and words; they've experienced a tragedy and survived to tell the tale.

"We've got a lot of good memories from that school," they often say. "We had some good times there."

"I'm just glad that no one was hurt in that fire." The children always end their school tales and jokes with some comment such as this, like an Amen at the end of a prayer.

Me, too.

You smile as you feel those tears and lumps welling up again in your eyes and throat, as they did that January 28 afternoon when you first arrived at that fiery scene.

You are thankful that your prayers were answered.

The response from the Yukon, and other parts of Canada, was phenomenal. A plea went out on the radio that night for donations of winter clothes for the kids and school supplies. The Department of Education building in Whitehorse became the drop-off point and hundreds of boxes quickly piled up. After word of the fire was on the national news, one teacher in Brampton, Ontario wisely used news of the tragedy as a "teachable moment," after which the kids in the class collected books and money to send to the kids in Old Crow.

Flames

by Brianne Meister

The flames are demons,
Jumping, racing, sweeping across the land.
The blazing colours of red and orange,
Leave behind only black.

The demons lead a path of destruction,
As they roar with rage.
Leaving their haunting silence,
And footprints of smouldering ash.

ILLUSTRATION: CHRIS SCHERBARTH

Growing up ON THE streets OF Whitehorse

by SharonAnne LaDue

I consider myself an ex-street kid. I spent time living on the streets of Whitehorse, sort of. I always had somewhere to sleep. Sometimes, someone felt sorry for me, so it was a good place to crash. Sometimes it was not a good place, like the one time when I stayed at a place in Porter Creek. To sleep on the floor in the basement, the guy there made me go to bed with him. I hated it, I hated him for taking advantage of me. But I refused to stay at the Youth Centre. That place scared me. All those kids—all angry—all troubled. I figured my only option was to periodically run away and stay with wolves like the guy in Porter Creek. You are probably wondering what makes a kid leave home and live so precariously?

For me, it was not an easy decision, but at the time I knew of no other way than to leave my abusive mother. Surviving by my wits on the streets was easier than living with her. Being in that abusive, mother-daughter relationship my wits were pretty sharp, but my feelings for myself were, well, in the gutter. All the negative past experiences caused a lot of pain. Being so young and without much guidance I did what most street kids do. I turned to drugs, alcohol and sex. Those harmful things made me feel safe. Even for a minute—that was better than another day of pain.

In my life it was the mental and emotional

anguish I experienced at the hands of my adoptive mother that drove me to run away at the young age of fourteen. She made me feel so unwanted, so ugly, and so unloved. I truly believe my mother adopted me because she wanted a cute little girl she could dress up, and treat like a little doll. I do not know if she ever considered the fact that I would have a will of my own.

After fourteen years, each worse than the one before, I could no longer stand the barrage of spiteful comments, so I ran away. I was screaming for help from every pore of my being, and that is why I chose to run and live on the streets.

To survive on the streets I learned how to con people, how to shop-lift and other illegal things. Like many of the street kids of the '80s, we did not break the law for kicks, we did not steal from individuals. Unfortunately, at the same time, we had to eat, we had to survive. That meant stealing, usually just what we needed and always from the bigger stores, never the little family-owned convenience stores. I guess we had a limited code of ethics.

For most people living on the streets would be abnormal; for me, I felt like a normal kid. Living moment to moment, it was fun and hard. We found fun in being silly, for just the simple things. Things like singing the "Bear Necessities" from the Jungle Book cartoon down Main Street, or just feeling free of the abuse. We had control, or so we thought. Street life was harsh, nobody had anything for free. Everything had a price. Like finding a place to crash, finding a friend, everything had a price. Being a young woman, the price was the use of my body. That hurt, but it was better than hearing my mother screech on about my inferiority. Living on the streets, nothing lasts for long, not friendships, not friends, and not safe havens.

After about a year, I had found confidence and friendships that helped in my healing process. I left the streets. I still see some of the kids that I left there. They're struggling. They haven't found their way off the streets yet.

Yukon's Teen Parent Program grows up

by Joyce Hayden

Dreamed about in 1989, started in 1990 under the New Democratic Party government's "returning to learning" program, the Teen Parent Program was originally set up in portables near the Selkirk Elementary School in Whitehorse.

In the fall of 1995, it moved into a new home next to F.H. Collins Senior Secondary School, continuing its five-year history of providing education and support to young Yukon women who get pregnant before completing high school. It has been one of the government's, and the community's, success stories.

The education component of the program is funded by the Yukon Department of Education. The Department of Health and Social Services provides funding to a non-profit society for a child care centre, as well as supplying a family support worker for the young parents.

The program is operated by a four-corner partnership between the two

ILLUSTRATION: JANET MOORE

government departments, the Council for Yukon First Nations and a non-profit society, the Teen Parent Access Education Society, set up for that purpose. They work together to provide a supportive, non-judgmental environment where young parents can complete high school and learn parenting and general life skills while their babies and toddlers are cared for in an attached, professionally-run child care centre. When they reach grade ten, students take courses at the centre as well as attend F.H. Collins for some of their course work.

Participants come from around the territory and have ranged in age from fourteen- to nineteen-year-old young adults who have decided to return to school. The majority of the students are from Whitehorse, no doubt because the stress of moving to another community, looking for housing and coping with day-to-day living becomes overwhelming for young moms-to-be from rural communities.

The program opened with five to eight girls, and has grown to accommodate over twenty young women and their babies. The new facility provides space for 24 or 25 students and up to 28 children (16 infants and 12 toddlers). Enrolment seems to be divided equally between First Nation and non-First Nation teens. The personal support provided by the teacher/coordinator, a second teacher, the child care workers and the family support worker contributes greatly to the program's success.

The Teen Parent Program is a nurturing program that builds self-esteem and self-confidence, while providing skills necessary to cope as a parent. The women grow very close during their time at school, and provide a strong support group for one another. Many friendships made at the centre continue after the girls leave. Not all teens stay until graduation. Some leave, and some come back a second time. They are always welcomed.

Sylvia Neschokat, a member of the society, says, that "the challenge is to attract the 160 or so Yukon teen parents who could use the program. Forty to fifty of them live in Whitehorse." It's a big step, it seems, for young women who are pregnant, and who choose to have their baby, to return to school.

The new facility, next door to the high school, no doubt helps spread the word among teens. As the program matures, it is vital that it maintain its warm, homey, and caring component. That is obviously what makes it so special—that, and the willing support it receives from government and the community.

"There are similar programs across the country," Neschokat says, "but none that enjoy the kind of financial support that the Yukon program has." We can but hope that this support continues, providing new options and choices for young pregnant women, who are so often funnelled into a limiting life of poverty and low self-esteem.

Spirit of the past

by Denise McDiarmid

My spirit left my body and travelled to the place where I once lived. The place where the sun always shines and the moon always shows; a place where the water ripples with a little gust of wind. A cabin and cache stand tall, a little ways off shore. I float over there and see the place where my brother and I used to go sliding after I was finished my school work.

As I float onto the porch I remember one snowy afternoon when my brother and I were jumping into the deep snow; my parents came out and we had a snowball fight. Oh those were the days!

I start to enter the cabin and remember the Halloween when we went out on the porch and walked back and forth knocking on the door getting candy from our parents until they had given it all out.

Inside I see the table where we used to sit every night and eat dry meat. Then I see our bunk bed. I float over and look under the bed expecting to see our mice dolls in their box homes, but nothing was there. I lay my head down on my parents' bed. I think I hear the sound of dogs barking. My dad rushes outside. Thinking it's a bear he shoots the gun off, but then another gun shot comes in return. Half an hour later our friends from Woodpecker Point are inside talking and laughing with us. I open my eyes and realize it's only a memory.

I feel my spirit lifting and I know I must go back to my body, but I don't want to; I want to stay; I want to stay and remember. I grab the wall by the door. I thought I felt the chart where my mother would put a sticker by our names every time we wouldn't wet the bed, but the feeling was gone as fast as it had come.

Outside by the cache I thought I saw a moose hanging, but then it was gone. I travelled to the lake shore, then across the lake to where my father had shown me the native paintings on the rock wall, but later on I found out he had put them there.

I turned around and headed back to shore, then sat down and wept. I wish I could go back to those days, those happy times. Then my spirit lifted up, just as I saw the last sign of the shore I remember the first time I had come here. I had jumped off the plane and stayed by the shore picking up any pretty rocks I found; later that winter I lost them. They are gone just like those days; all that is left are the memories I have. I want to share them with others but they don't seem to be interested, so I keep them to myself.

My spirit travels over the river, over Mayo Caselot's and Vicki's, over the church and the administration building, then to the school. Just as we pass over it, I remember the Christmas when we came back from Edward's Lake, never to return. We went to the school Christmas concert and were all bushed, but one of my teachers grabbed me and put me on stage to sing with the rest of my class. They were all dressed nicely while I was in my bush clothes. Take me back, take me back, I'm torn between two worlds I love, then and now. But I know I cannot go back so I look ahead at the days to come, knowing I'll never lose the memories of Edward's Lake.

All these memories make me feel so old, yet I am still very young with lots more memories yet to come.

When I was about nine, a bunch of us kids got together and built a treehouse. I thought the treehouse was way better than the real house I lived in. The treehouse was just a bunch of 2 x 4s nailed to three spindly pine trees, with two pieces of rotting plywood nailed on the top for the floor. Then we built the walls using scraps from the lumberyard. Mr. Ambundson hated having us scrounge wood scraps from his lumberyard, but we always did. So the walls of our treehouse were pieces of wood that looked like they were really logs. After nailing the log pieces in place, I had

THE TREE FORT

by SharonAnne LaDue

because she pretended she was an archaeologist finding a forgotten city, or something. She was strange.

Micki, she got into the most trouble. Her parents were a little weird, so when they found out that Micki had brought the family "hairloom" to our fort, they got really upset. I don't know what a family hairloom is, but there wasn't any hair on it. The thing Micki brought to our fort was an old dull scratched silver tray. Us kids rigged up the tray as part of the elevator system. I guess Micki's mom was the most upset because we drilled holes in each corner. Unfortunately, the drill didn't work very well, so there are some

to steal my dad's jigsaw. I got the one that used batteries because we didn't have electricity at the treehouse. With the jigsaw we cut three windows in the walls, broke seven blades and wore out the batteries nine times. My dad sure was not impressed with us.

I think he locked up all of his tools, at least the ones he could find. When we finally finished the treehouse we had to lug home seven hammers, four pounds of nails—straight, bent and broken—three saws and a hand drill, a battery-operated jigsaw and two planers that never worked.

When my dad saw us lugging all this stuff from the cliff he slapped his forehead, probably wondering how much damage we had caused to his tools. We quickly dropped off the tools and all nine of us were talking to my dad at once, sort of like bees swarming around a flower. He was so overwhelmed he couldn't get a word in edgewise. Pretty smart, eh? He couldn't give us trouble. We dropped the tools off and ran as fast

as we could out of the yard. My dad foolishly yelled at us, "I hope you're having fun!" I don't think he knew what to do.

The next plan for our tree fort was to fix it up inside. That meant getting stuff from my mom's sewing room. You know, like a bolt of cloth to make curtains, pillows and coverings for the sofa that we "borrowed" from Daniel's family's guest house. I don't think they had many guests. Well, I chose this material that was really shiny and soft to touch. I found later it was silk. Ooops. How was I supposed to know?! It looked great in the tree fort. But my mom was so angry, us kids thought it would be best if we borrowed stuff from other parents for awhile.

Jimmy borrowed this waterjug off his parents. How were we supposed to know it was an antique worth thousands? That waterjug now has crazy glue stains and big chips missing and the handle is gone. I think Kyle got angry and threw that jug at Jimmy. The jug hit the wall and the top part shattered. Kathy thought it was great

new scratches added to the old ones that were all over the tray. Poor Micki, she had to go to summer school and she could only see us on the weekends. Bummer. Micki didn't know that the tray had been in the family for three "genderations." Whatever is a genderation?

Jamie, he almost got grounded for the whole summer. He brought out a case of jams and preserves that his mom had made. Most of the jams and preserves were made with "lickcurs." I think lickcurs were booze 'cause we all got feeling woozy after eating six jars of raspberries. Jamie's mom came to the fort screaming, "Those preserves and jams were entered in the annual fall fair! I wanted to win the contest! I could have won a thousand dollars!" She started to cry. You see, Jamie's folks were kind of poor. Ooops. We unanimously agreed she would have won, if we hadn't eaten most of the jams and broken the other jars.

Poor Jamie, he had to use all his allowance to replace all the busted jars. I think that of the

36 jars, only four made it back to his house. Jamie owed his mother seventy-two dollars. Us kids decided the best way to raise money to help Jamie was to have a garage sale. We figured if we went into our brothers' and sisters' closets as well as our parents' closets we could find lots of good stuff that they didn't want. That was the stuff we could sell.

We made lots of money at the garage sale, over $150. Then the long arm of the law stepped in and stopped us in our glorious tracks. All of our parents, 18 of them, and innumerable brothers and sisters, surrounded our tree fort.

"Enemies!" cried Jamie.

"Battle stations, everyone for themself!" screamed Daniel.

"Hey, this is fun!" whispered Micki.

"Sure," I agreed as we closed up the tree fort, knowing that none of the angry mob could touch us. We were safe in our fort, until we ran out of food and water, which was going to happen at about supper time.

"You know what we need? An escape route," said Daniel.

"That way the enemies would stay here yelling and we could be at home eating," Micki interrupted. She was always thinking of food

"Hey! I know! Let's use the rope swing!" yelled Jamie.

"Shuddup!" I screamed back. "If you holler, everyone is gonna know what we're doing. That ain't gonna be any good. Whisper, stupid!" I was getting a little scared. My parents and both my older brothers were in that angry mob. If they got a hold of me, I was toast. I had sold my mom's wedding dress. The way I figured, since she got married in 1970, and had three kids, she didn't need it anymore. Well, I guess I needed a lesson about "centimental" value. I know centi means 100, and mental has to do with the brain. I still don't get it: hundreds of mind value. It doesn't make sense. I couldn't figure it out.

Well, our parents hung around for a couple of minutes until most of the moms decided it was time to get supper ready. Then the fathers drifted off. I think they wanted to catch the last innings of the Blue Jays game. But, my dad and Micki's dad came back. They both had their axes. Then one dad said, "Okay, if you don't come out of that blasted tree fort, we are going to chop it down!" He sure was angry.

We basically ran around in circles, screaming our heads off, blaming each other. Thunk, thunk. The tree fort shook as the axes bit into the trees. I decided to send our white flag of surrender out the window, maybe they would stop chopping long enough to let us get down. Slowly, sheepishly we got out of the tree fort. We stood in a big clump, not wanting to separate the group. But the battle was lost and we were all going to be POWs (prisoners of war) for the rest of the summer.

WALKING ON THE MOON

by Jason Overbo

You know it's cold when exposed skin can freeze in less than sixty seconds. You also know it's cold when simply taking a brisk walk can freeze your lungs. Freeze your lungs? What the hell does that mean? Freeze your lungs. But when it's really cold, and I mean lock-your-doors-build-a-fire-and-don't-even-think-about-coming-out-till-spring cold—your spit actually freezes before it hits the ground. Think about that; you spit, and it takes what…less than a second to change it from liquid to solid?

Yes. That's the way it was. Granted, not everyday but, where I grew up it was known to happen. Imagine fingers so numb you can't even tell if they're still there—and you're only halfway home from school. Picture spending thirty minutes just to dress to go outside. That, my southern friend, is practically a story in itself.

First, there was the white, waffle-knit long johns, followed by two pairs of the thickest, homemade wool socks you could get your hands on, then the pants, undershirt, overshirt, and turtleneck sweater. (Northern moms

…continued on page 101

Why Charlie?

by SharonAnne LaDue

I sort of slid down the door, crying. Tears rolled down my cheeks. I felt faint. "Why Charlie, why?" I murmured. I composed myself, brain off, feelings off. Had to do what had to be done.

Charlie was my friend. We were both 16, in grade ten and considered good kids. Neither of us got any attention. I guess that's what happens when you are too good. I lived in a group home. Charlie lived with his dad.

Charlie was funny, he could make jokes about everything. Charlie was sensitive, but he was not happy. Not really happy. Charlie's dad was a sonofabitch; he was mean and cruel. Nobody knew what happened at that house, except maybe me. And I cared.

I remember the last time I saw Charlie. He was frail, the burden was getting too heavy. I could see it. When we went out, it seemed to help lighten his mood. We had fun.

We got home before curfew. Charlie told me to come over in the morning, maybe we could go for a hike to Miles Canyon. I agreed to be over before 11 the next morning. Charlie smiled his sad smile and said that'd be great.

I went over the next morning. Charlie was still in his room. I went to his door yelling, "Hey, Charlie, let's go!" I touched the door knob and heard the loudest bang ever. I didn't open the door. I knew what he had done. I wanted to remember Charlie as a fun loving kid with a great sense of humour.

I don't know where Charlie's dad was, but there were seven or eight little kids swarming around me, crying, "What did Charlie do? Where's Charlie?" I gathered all those kids and told them we were going to play a game at the group home. I got them over to the group home, no questions asked. I think they were in shock. My group home worker tried to calm me. My mind was full of confusing thoughts rebounding off each other. She didn't believe me right away. I asked a couple of the boys to watch the little kids for 20 dollars. Completely ignoring her, I phoned the cops and explained the situation. I'm sure I was a couple of shades paler than before, because the worker jumped into action and phoned everyone else. I got angry. Those people didn't need to know. They did not know Charlie or care for him. They didn't know what Charlie had been through.

Whenever I had asked Charlie how he was, he almost always said, "I'm okay. I hate my dad. I hate what he did." For Charlie, he needed to say that, it helped him know it was okay to hate his dad. I told him that I hated my mom and it was okay. You see, Charlie and I were abuse victims. I got help because I demanded it. Charlie tried to be the perfect kid so his dad wouldn't beat up on him so much. Charlie tried, only once, to tell his side of the story. No one listened.

DOG SLEDDING

by Jodi Harms

Wow, can four dogs ever make a lot of noise, especially when they see their harnesses!

It is 20 degrees below zero (Celsius) and the sun is shining way up there in the sky. It is a beautiful day for a dogsled ride down the Yukon River. I live down by the river and today I planned to go on a long ride all the way to Lake Laberge.

I have taken out the sled and hooked up the gang line for my four dogs, so now I can hitch them up. My lead dogs are the ones I hitch up first, and then my wheel dogs. The two dogs I use for lead are Spirit, who has blue eyes, and Midnight, who is all black. I hitch them up first because they keep the line tight so I can hook up Nikkie and Rocky (my wheel dogs) more easily.

Out of my four dogs, Spirit is the only one not really barking. She is whining a little but compared to the other guys it is nothing. They are making me go deaf!!

Finally, I get Rocky's harness on and get her hooked up behind Midnight. It always takes a while because she is shy.

I bring the bag of booties out from the folds of the sled bag and start to put the colourful little things on their feet. When putting on the booties I always have to put Nikkie's booties on last or else she will chew them off. She isn't quite used to them yet but when she is running she is fine.

Finally, all the booties are on and now I can get going. At the back of the sled I untie the thick yellow rope that holds the sled back, pull up the snow hook and we are gone!

Once out on the river, Midnight starts goofing off. As we slow down, he jumps over Spirit. He has chewed the velcro on his front booties so that as we speed up they come flying off. Luckily, I am able to scoop them both up out of the snow as I go by.

We are trotting along the left side of the river and Midnight sees a little tree on the snow-covered sand bar off the edge of the island. He dives off the trail and heads for it. Midnight's jolt sends me off balance and I fall off the sled and into the snow. I am able to grab the end of the sled and my dragging slows the dogs down until they stop. I take a

while to get back up onto the sled, and as I do, I look at the team, who are almost up to their chests in snow. By the time I have the team back on the trail Midnight has changed places with Spirit, and has also succeeded in chewing his other two booties!

Finally, we are blazing across the glinting, snowblown surface of Lake Laberge. The lake is shining and sparkling as we trot on. We sometimes skim over paths of snow, the dogs scooping it up to wet their throats. The sun is high in the sky, chasing the clouds away and watching us go by. Spirit loses a bootie! I try to catch it as it comes under the sled but miss. Soon it is just a tiny little coloured speck on the glinting ice.

Halfway onto the lake we stop to have a break. I haul out some bowls and a special meat tea for the dogs and give them some. Midnight eats his the fastest.

Soon we are on the trail heading home.

There is just something about the stillness of the ice, the padding of the dogs' feet and the panting of their tongues that makes dogsledding so special to me.

PHOTOS: MARTEN BERKMAN

The Quest

by Kellie Sellars

PHOTO: MARTEN BERKMAN

*Your eyes are on the snowy track which
you have always loved. You see the last one go and
you know your time has come. The noise began
to soften, they seemed so much like stone,
as an icy wind blew by, and chilled you to the bone.*

*You take two breaths and get ready, as
you wait for the starter to say go. Then finally
your time has come. Your heart begins to pound
some, you then begin to wave, and you know
the dangers coming up could put you in the grave,
but it's the dogs' lives not yours
that you would rather save.*

*Your hands are getting cold, the dogs are
getting tired, but you urge them on for
another half a mile. You finally reach the checkpoint, the dogs seem almost dead, you know
just how they feel, but even though
you're tired, you've got to have a meal.*

*Your body aches from lack of sleep, and you
think you're going to die when you finally
reach the warm-up room with a bed a mile high.*

*You put racing from your mind, but think of
other things like a nice cozy fire and
what tomorrow brings. You get up next morning,
hitch the dogs to the sleigh, your object's
to get to Fairbanks today.*

*The wind's in your face, you feel chilled to
the bone, and you think any minute the
dogs will be stone. Then you finally cross
the finish line, and you come in first. Your
prizes are divine. So next year when it
comes time please ask me "are ya comin'?"
I'll say fine 'cause when I cross the finish line
the money will be mine!*

RUNNING THE NIGHT AWAY

by Aven Crawshay

Running in the gleaming night

Looking up to northern lights

Wind is howling it can blow

Yukon Quest is where we go.

Dogs are running

with the breeze

Songs are whispering

through the trees.

No one talks of unknown fear

Dangers are something far too clear

Dawn to dusk it's not the same

Yukon Quest is its name

Running on the frozen trail

Dogs run fast, they will not fail.

wrote the book on layering.) Then, you were ready for the snowpants. Of course, if you were cool, you didn't have to wear snowpants, because…you had a skidoo suit, which is basically ski pants and a jacket except it's all one piece (and it's black and has Skidoo embroidered in big white letters down one sleeve). First, it was laid face-up on the floor. You sat down and wriggled your toes down through the legs and out these little elastic sleeves sewn into the cuffs. Then you'd stand up and jump a couple of times to get it just right so you could pull the arms on, shrug into the shoulders, and finally close it with a zipper that starts down at your crotch and goes all the way up to your chin. Usually there was also a hood which, if it was a good suit, detached with a zipper so you could pull it off and stuff it in your pocket (as soon as you were out of mom's sight, of course).

Oh yes, heaven help you if you weren't cool, and all you owned were conventional pants. But if you were indeed inflicted with this foul misfor-tune, hopefully at least they were the same colour (black) as your jacket so from a distance you could maybe pass them off as a skidoo suit. My snow-pants were fire-engine red (probably so I wouldn't get run down by the crazy car with iced-up windows and only one headlight—more about this later). They were fire-engine red and they were HUGE (so I wouldn't grow out of them so fast); in fact, I'm almost certain that if I could dig up those bad guys right now, they'd still fit me. (And come to think of it, I'm sure they're tucked away somewhere.)

Yes, very few things on earth could exceed the hideousness of my snowpants, but the creature that was my parka did the job nicely. My parka was a khaki-green tent, stuffed (and I do mean stuffed) with feathers. (Picture blazing red pants and olive-green jacket—no danger of that combo being mistaken for a skidoo suit, no matter what the distance.) It came down past my knees, and had an enormous hood that could easily have fit two or maybe three of my heads inside of it (and I had a big head, even as a kid). And oh, almost forgot, the hood also had a long strip of coyote fur running all around its front edge.

We got these jackets from a mail order army surplus store. They were

…continued on page 103

Growing kids

IN THE YUKON

by Mandeep Sidhu

Strong beautiful and free

That's what Yukon's forests are to me

Vast, far, and large

From the Arctic Circle to Lake Laberge

The forests and the animals

Are listening to the great nature

As it lives

And most kids think of our forests as

trees and animals

But that's not all

There is the beauty of fall

As the leaves turn yellow, brown, and red

Then the leaves fall down dead

What about Christmas without a tree?

That would not be for me.

Balloons

instructions and illustrations by Jeff Brown

Although there are many different types of balloons, the ones used here are the Standard 260! This means that, when inflated, the balloon should be two inches across and 60 inches long. For most figures you will make, this will be all you ever need.

To get them inflated is a trick in itself, but once you've got the technique, a little practice will have you spewing as much hot air as any good politician.

As a joke, you can let it snap back and hit your hand. It won't hurt, and can help to start things out with a good laugh. If you're holding it correctly, you can also let it snap back in your face, letting it hit the inside of your hand, rather than your face.

First, stretch the balloon out a couple of times. Hold it lightly with each thumb and forefinger about an inch down from the nozzle. Get a big deep breath. I put the nozzle between my teeth to position it, then, as I start to blow, I let the nozzle move forward till it is held by the inside of my lips.

As air enters the balloon, it begins to straighten out. (When you blow up a regular balloon, the nozzle is larger, and your lips can be opened wider, but with these, the hole your lips make to force air into the balloon must be a lot smaller.)

Next, you'll want to force a bit of air inside to form a small bubble. For many, this is one of the hardest parts. Once you've got your small bubble, try to keep the momentum going and continue your inflation.

To keep my cheeks from doing a "dizzy" as I'm blowing, I angle back my hands and press them against my cheeks. This also helps me visualize the need to force a straight stream of air into the balloon.

Instead of blowing the balloon up all the way, leave a tail of uninflated balloon at the end. As a rule, for each twist in your balloon sculpture, you will need about half an inch of tail. This will give you a little room to work, without your balloon popping.

Another hint is to let a little bit of air out of the balloon right before you tie it. This makes the balloon a little softer and easier to work with.

It's not easy at first, which helps keep the field of balloon sculpturing a bit wider open, but you'll soon get the hang of it.

If inflating them continues to be a problem, do as the professionals do: get a pump! Your own experience and financial condition will help you determine what pump is best for you.

I have a small Qualatax pump which I only use sporadically because I feel that part of the magic for kids is to see the balloon being blown up right in front of them. (Adults are amazed too!) For a large event, consider a pump, or blowing up a number ahead of time and keeping them in a garbage bag.

Twist and lock

To create your balloon sculptures, you'll need to learn basic twists. First, if you have purchased professional balloons they will be made with quality rubber, and under normal use, will not pop when you twist them. (Well, okay, most of the time!) Balloons you buy in a drugstore will work in a pinch, but should be avoided if possible.

The basic twist is created by pinching off a section of balloon beginning at the nozzle end. This will be called a bubble and will be a variety of sizes, from half an inch to usually no more than eight inches. Once you've pinched it, twist it around several times. One source says eight twists is the minimum, but I usually can get by with less.

If you let the balloon go, the twist will unwind (a good visual gag!), so you'll have to hold it while making your next twist. Following this second twist, fold the balloon back over itself and pinch and twist it together with the first twist. This will lock the twists together, and prevent them from coming apart.

If you look at it with imagination, it can be the head and ears of a dog…or a cat…or a mouse…or a moose!

Moose

(Moose be time for a balloon!)

Inflate a balloon, leaving a six-inch tail. Form a three-inch bubble and stretch it a bit by pulling on the nozzle. Squeeze the middle of the bubble to form its own distinctive nose.

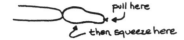

For each set of antlers (left and right), form a series of four half-inch bubbles (six for longer antlers), and twist together at the beginning and end of the series of bubbles.

When you have both sets of antlers complete, continue with neck, front legs, body, back legs and tail as with your standard animal.

Mosquito

Inflate one balloon and leave a three-inch tail. Make a four-inch bubble at the nozzle end and a one-inch bubble at the tail end (preceding the uninflated portion).

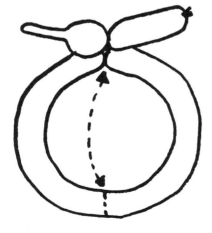

Holding the two twists together, form the balloon into a loop. Pinch and twist the aforementioned twists together with the opposite section of the loop.

Adjust for proper attack position.

Optional: Paint evil eye, sneer, black tip, or enemy aircraft markings on balloon.

Caribou

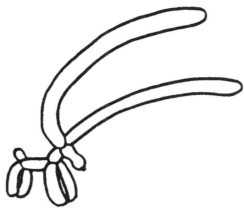

Inflate one balloon fully, leaving no tail. If it blows up into a curved shape…great. If not, you can help form it into a gentle curve by blowing a little hot air onto it. Place this aside. It will be your caribou's horns, or roof rack.

Inflate another balloon, leaving a three-inch tail. Form a four-inch bubble at the nozzle end. Stretch the bubble by gripping the nozzle and pulling. Now, give the middle section of the bubble a squeeze and you'll have given the nose a distinctive shape all its own.

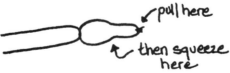

Attach the caribou's horns at this point, as you also twist in two one-inch bubbles for the ears. Form a three-inch bubble for the neck, followed by two five-inch bubbles for the front legs. Lock twist these together. Add a six-inch bubble for the body and two more five-inch bubbles for the rear legs. The tail, of course, remains at the end, where it belongs.

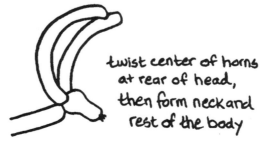

twist center of horns at rear of head, then form neck and rest of the body

highly touted by this fine company as field tested by the Canadian Army to seventy degrees below zero. This sounded pretty cool at first, or until I realized that what it really meant was that my jacket had probably been used for eight weeks straight by some nasty, sweaty, G.I. wanna be, who didn't shower and never once took it off the whole time they were gone! And another thing, it leaked feathers—all the time. If one of my buddies slapped me on the back I looked like an unlucky Canadian goose that just got popped by some trigger-happy hunter—feathers everywhere!

Next we had (again, only if you're cool) these funky, white, come-up-to-your-knee astronaut boots, with enormous rubber soles that made you about two inches taller (very important). Each boot weighed about the same as a small dog (and I'm not talking about no poodle or Shih Tzu here, I mean a DOG—husky or malamute). I wore mukluks, which is what the Inuit wear. They are extremely comfortable and incredibly warm, but hopelessly uncool. (And they definitely don't make you taller.)

Mukluks are made up of two separate pieces. First there's a brightly coloured duffel liner that you pull on. It's sort of like a stiff, loose-fitting sock, that comes up to just below the knee. Then comes the actual mukluk itself, which is basically a snug, ankle-high slipper made of soft caribou leather and flowers beaded onto the top. Sewn to this slipper is a loose-fitting canvas upper which also goes to just below the knee (usually leaving just a hint of colourful duffel liner peeking out over the top). To keep it from falling down there's a leather thong that ties around the top and another at the ankle. Walking in mukluks is like running around in your stocking feet because there's no heel or sole or anything; just this soft piece of caribou leather. You can feel every pebble and every bump, through the bottoms of your feet.

Now to keep your hands warm you added (again, only if you're, you know…) these huge monstrosities that looked like mutant welders' gloves, but in reality were nylon covered mitts (black of course) that came tight at your wrist then puffed out and extended almost to your elbow. They had a zipper down one side, so they fit over the sleeve of your skidoo suit, and then

…continued on page 105

I like to live in the Yukon

When Lorraine Cardin's grade 2 and 3 students at École Whitehorse Elementary School were asked, "What's so special about living in the Yukon?" this is what they had to show and tell.

In the Yukon, we have all the seasons—fall, winter, spring and summer. In the summer we have the sunshine all the time. In the winter we get to see the sunrise and sunset during the day.

In the summer we like to go canoeing, rafting and boating on lots of lakes and rivers in the Yukon—Tagish Lake, Takhini River, Echo Lake, Tatshenshini River, Braeburn Lake and the Chilkoot River.

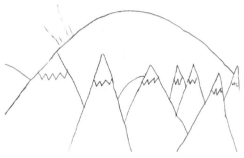

We go hiking on the Chilkoot Trail and meet friends along the way.

We go gold panning.

We do lots of things in the wintertime. We like to go skiing, skating, dogsledding, skijoring (our dogs pull us on skis!) and skidooing. We can go cross-country skiing and downhill skiing too!

We like living in the Yukon because that makes us Canadian.

Family winter clothing requirements

Kid age 12

- green coat is acceptable to -5°C
- green coat, polar fleece required between -5°C and -18°C
- winter coat required between -18°C and -25°C
- winter coat, polar fleece required below -25°C

* gloves and hat must be with you at all times

Kid age 9

- red coat is acceptable to -5°C
- winter coat is required between -5°C and -18°C
- winter coat and polar fleece or a sweater are required below -15°C
- snowpants are required below -15°C

* gloves and hat must be with you at all times

Love, your parents

P.S. Hey! Wind chill counts in figuring out temperatures.

by A. Nony Moose

PHOTO: WYNNE KRANGLE

PHOTO: CHRIS SCHERBARTH

ILLUSTRATION: EMILY KRANGLE-LONG

WINTER FAREWELL

by Donna Pendziwol-MacMillan

In the span of time
Before the Yukon's powder dry snow
Turns to mush
My northern children have
A unique spring ritual
They rush
To build snow figures!

you zipped them up tight so no snow would get in. The deluxe model also came with a circular lambskin pad on the back of the hand that you would wipe your nose on. Believe me, when it gets that cold your nose is leaking like a two-dollar faucet, all day long. Of course, wiping your constantly running nose on the back of your hand may sound a little nasty, but the truly disgusting part came when you got home from school, peeled off those wet gloves and left them on the heat register so they'd be dry by morning. Imagine what the register looked like, glazed as it was with several days worth of melted nose drippings. Nice!

Our heat register, on the other hand, was always whistle-clean since my Sears mail order mitties didn't come with the nose wipe feature. They were, however, the same colour as my snowpants (oh, joy), and further, had been fitted with a custom made set of idiot strings, made by sewing a long piece of yarn onto one mitten, running it up the inside of one sleeve, across your back, and then down to the other mitten, where it's sewn again. Idiot strings were the ultimate humiliation 'cause then when you didn't have your mitts on, they'd dangle from the end of your cuffs like two severed hands hanging onto your wrists by a feeble flap of skin. Of course, you rarely lost your mitts, but good Lord—at what price!

But I digress; we were talking about keeping the head warm and the ultimate tool for this very serious task was a black wool cap that clung to your head like a helmet. It was just long enough to cover your ears (when you pulled it down real tight), but if you didn't, you could still sort of look like Brando in Waterfront. The really good ones had a facemask that tucked up inside of the hat and if it got real cold, or you didn't want to be identified, you could pull it down and all that was exposed were these two little circles for your eyes. Then you could look like one of those incognito, bad-guy, professional wrestlers (so cool). I never once got to look like one of those incognito, bad-guy, professional wrestlers because I had an enormous, multi-coloured toque, with a pom pom (size of a small grapefruit) attached to a six-inch string coming straight out the top (it looked like a round, furry, soap-on-a-rope), and it would keep time with me when I walked, bouncing

...continued on page 107

Outdoor fun with families

by Leslie Knight

Yukon, the land of the great outdoors! Although it was the main reason for moving here, its true benefit has only been realized with the addition of little people to our household.

Once upon a time, wilderness adventures meant fly-in canoe and ski trips, long distance travels and adult company. Now, it includes a one-kilometre walk through the forest behind our home where we enjoy glimpses of rabbits, tracks of moose (and ATVs, unfortunately), raven caws and even an intimate exploration of the scat of grouse—not a delicacy we encourage.

Speaking of food, we enjoy edible wilds without venturing very far. Young children can discriminate between edibles and non-edibles. The fireweed and rosehips are edible; the purple larkspur and lupin are not. "Yuck scat" has become the alternate cry in the wilderness for our adventurous two-year-old.

So our wilderness travels have brought us closer to home. Although we look forward to a return to whitewater river trips and glacier ski trips, we now enjoy slowing down enough to smell the wild roses nearby.

5-star outdoor adventure

by Pam Glassby

A fun, relaxing trip is to hire a boat on either Tagish or Atlin lakes. Both lakes are beautiful and the family is able to visit many spots during a weekend (or longer) trip.

The houseboats come in various sizes and can sleep up to eight adults and kids quite comfortably. One doesn't have to be a sailor to be the skipper. These boats are basically RVs on floats!

All you need to bring are sleeping bags and food. If you're looking for the easy life, you'll be pleasantly surprised with the amenities on board, which include cooking equipment and running water complete with shower and toilet!

One tip: start looking for an overnight spot early. It's a challenge to reach a consensus with so many on board! For those who enjoy the outdoors, the campsites are wonderful so you don't all have to sleep on the boat.

Remember to find a spot far enough away from your best friends with young babies if you cherish an uninterrupted sleep.

Houseboating is also a great opportunity for those who enjoy hiking, swimming and windsurfing (in wetsuits as the waters are a little on the chilly side).

This is a 5-star outdoor adventure in our books.

Camping

by Jenny Cuthbertson

We've always enjoyed camping—the simplest of living. Exploring the open spaces and sleeping in a tent relaxes us. With the addition of a toddler, camping brings new focuses—watching the path made by an ant crawling across a stone or listening to a squirrel chattering angrily from branches above. Robin, our child, collects armfuls of pine cones and "icks" (sticks) for us to throw into the water. Our walks are slow and wandering and detailed.

It wasn't always so. When we first camped with our fifteen-month-old son we expected screaming protests at being put to bed in a strange new tent. But we didn't hear a peep. And so it went until the third night, when suddenly, for no reason that we could fathom, he gave us an epic struggle and left us wondering if camping was worth the effort.

Now, with a few experiences under our belt, we plan to do more camping. Robin continues his pattern of sometimes going to bed easily and sometimes not. We no longer worry or struggle with him. And we've learned on our camping trips that we don't need bags of entertaining toys, only a keen sense of discovery and exploration.

WINTER TRIPPING

by Wendy Nixon

The sun is shining on the snow and on our skis, the dogs are harnessed and hitched, and three little warmly-dressed people are being bundled into sleeping bags on the sleds. There are a few cries of resistance from the little bundles, but soon we are moving and the little people close their eyes and settle into the sleds for morning naps. Now the only challenge left to the parents is to keep dogs, sleds, ski poles and harness lines from getting tangled.

The real challenge comes later, in the cold, dark tent. Keeping a crawler in his lofty down sleeping bag when he is used to free ranging in his crib proves impossible. I resort to putting two layers of snowsuits over warm sleepers. Now he can't move even if he wants to, so he finally settles into the sleeping bag. His father suggests that he may be too warm with these multiple layers. I'm not convinced until a few hours later when our crawler wakes up with cries of discontent. I stick a finger through the multi-layers, and feel the rivers of sweat pouring down his neck. Definitely too many layers.

merrily from one side of my head to the other as I made my way to school. And finally (since I wasn't fortunate enough to have a tucked away facemask in the top of my huge, multi-coloured toque—though heaven knows, there was plenty of room for it up there)—we had the bane of northern children everywhere—the scarf. (Of course, mine was handmade and matched my toque and my socks.) Scarves are the easiest thing in the world to knit—I mean, think about it—and consequently mine was maybe ten or twelve inches wide and as long as, oh...I'd have to guess that baby was as long as, say, a mid-sized Chevrolet (and G.M. was still building a pretty big car back then). Mom would turn me around so my back was to her. (This is why I can't, to this day, say exactly how long that sucker was. I never actually saw the damn thing all laid out and business-like.) So, she'd turn me around, then she'd find the middle of the scarf and reaching both hands around me (I can still feel her warm bosom in the small of my back as she pulled me close to peer over my shoulder), she'd line it up so it covered all of my nose but not too much of my eyes (Lord knows I had to be able to see so I wouldn't get run down by that crazy car with the iced-up windshield and only one headlight), and then she'd just start wrapping me up like her little, dead Egyptian prince. When she got close to the end she'd tie a big granny knot and simple as that—I was ready for school.

Of course, by now I'd lost maybe three pounds just by sweating, so I was itching to roll. Mom would hand me my lunch. (It would be frozen by the time I got to school. By the way, we never used a freezer in winter; Mom would just store food out on the balcony). Anyway, she'd hand me my lunch and my books and trundle me out the door with a peck on my multi-layered forehead.

Outside it was black and I mean black, black. As black as the bottom of a witch's boot, black. Dark as a sinner's heart at midnight, black. You see, in the Yellowknife wintertime, the days are extremely short (being so close to the North Pole and all), and I can remember getting up and walking to school when it seemed like it was still night. All the street lamps were on and cars had to use their headlights. (Thus Mom's concern for the crazy

...continued on page 109

young family

by Heather Alton

Our young family has been lucky enough to have a riverside cabin to use as our outdoor retreat. But one particular summer was different. Our adventures had us out on the road.

Of course, it all started out with great enthusiasm and excitement (or we might never have left the driveway). Tent, sleeping bags, ensolites, pillows, baby doll, bedtime stories, two-year-old, four-year-old, parents—got it all! Off down the road. Five hours later, baskets full of stories, snacks, songs, toys, playdough and tapes (how many times did we listen to that ?X!O tape?), we made it to the campground.

All goes smoothly—up goes the tent, in go the sleeping bags (the arrangement of which is much debated), meals, trees and flowers examined, meet neighbours (Joe from South Carolina) with great enthusiasm. No problems. We've got this camping thing covered!

Then comes sleep time. It started with the usual rituals—8:30 washtime, snacktime, booktime—but then what happened to bedtime???

Somewhere between the wrestling match, endless examination of every detail of the tent's interior, rearranging of sleeping bags and "just one more drink" we had regressed to subtle (10:30), and not-so-subtle (11:30), threats. Who knows what Joe from South Carolina must have thought?

Fortunately, things got easier over the next two weeks. We all settled down and had our good nights and a few more horrible nights. Would I do it again? Sure, but I'd do a few things differently. Before departing, the children would have naps in the tent, play in the tent and sleep overnight in the tent, thereby making the tent seem routine and *boring*. It should be easier next year when the kids are a year older, but then, there's always the cabin.

PHOTO: KEN MADSEN

I WAS WALKING STRAIGHT... AND A MOSQUITO FLEW UP MY NOSE...

An average camping trip in the north

by Bhreagh Dabbs and Anna Krangle-Long

In the Yukon, our camping trips are never dull. We always end up with more company than we started out with—like mosquitoes and grey jays. The grey jays eat our food and the mosquitoes eat us. Occasionally, squirrels visit us too. We hope you like wildlife for you will see lots.

Be prepared for the unpleasant odour of the outhouses. The outhouses may not always have toilet paper so you may need to use the moss growing on the seat.

Always be careful of the berries you eat because they may be hazardous to your health.

Usually we end up quite dirty because in the campgrounds of the north there is no running water. A lot of people bring some soap or shampoo to clean themselves.

Our tips for having a safe and fun camping trip

- Always wear long pants; mosquitoes love shorts.
- Bring toilet paper; the outhouses don't always have enough.
- Put a tarp under your tent or you may wake up wet and cold.
- Always put your tent pegs in really deep otherwise you could get blown away.
- Bring a compass if the area you're camping in is new to you.
- Bring waterproof matches because normal ones may not work after they get wet.
- Bring a flashlight with you.
- Never bring scented stuff such as food, sunscreen and toothpaste into your tent because bears will smell it and come to check it out.

Growing kids

Tagish

by Angela Lane

There's a big lake in front of our house. There are two or three eagles at the beach and every morning one flies across. Our house has lots of room and big windows. In summer, we play at the beach and go canoeing. In winter, me and my brothers go tobogganing and downhill skiing and sometimes we go skating.

There are lots of kids. Sometimes the wind is very strong. We have a nice friend called Ed.

On the mountains all the leaves are pretty in the fall. We like to go exploring and play on the glass fort. We picked a whole bucketful of cranberries. We collect clay from under the water. We ride our bikes on the dirt road. We have a stinky outhouse. We get our water from the Tagish well. While we were looking for berries we found an old paddlewheel boat. We collect rocks and bones at the rocky beach. Mom collects driftwood.

We have lots of fun in Tagish.

The River

by Robyn Boss

The wind is a River,

Swiftly flowing through the trees,

causing them to dance and sway.

Rushing and diving to the ground,

soaring high above the trees,

above the mountains,

above the clouds

until the violent thrashing

slows to nothing.

Hear Yukon

by Naomi Brault

I awoke to the sound of birds talking
and leaves running.
The forest is so beautiful
with its own harmonic sounds,
so unlike in the city with the horns blowing
and the crows cawing.
It puts me to sleep at night,
where I dream
The trees are old and creaking,
the willows are round and snappy.
My dream goes on for hours on end,
when suddenly
I awoke to the sound of birds
talking and leaves running.

Le Yukon

par Anna Krangle-Long

Le Yukon c'est très beau,
des montagnes et de l'eau.
Pas beaucoup de pollution
et pas beaucoup de population.
Il y a beaucoup d'animaux,
et des poissons qui vivent dans l'eau.
Les quatre saisons
dans le Yukon sont très différentes.

La neige arrive quand il fait froid,
et s'empile sur les toits.
La neige tombe sur les enfants
qui jouent à saute-mouton.

Le soleil vient quand il fait chaud,
des fois c'est trop.
On enlève les épais vêtements,
et respire l'air du printemps.

Des adultes et des enfants
Des montagnes pointues
Des montagnes rondes
On trouve tout cela au Yukon

L'épilobe, c'est notre fleur.
Au Yukon tu n'a jamais peur.

Le Yukon, c'est notre maison
et on est content de vivre au Yukon!

My school

by Lindsey Edmunds

Birds singing
and lots of trees,
smell of wood
and rustling leaves!

Crickets chirping
and bouncy fences,
raindrops falling
and people's faces!

car.) In fact, by the time school let out, the sun was long gone and we were back to the sinner's heart, etc. The only time it got light out was for a little while over lunch hour. Anyway, it was still dark and beginning to get very, very, cold. That previous indoor sweat is now glacier-water against my young skin. The only warm spot is deep in my tummy where Mom's steaming porridge still simmers.

I don't really remember how far the actual walk to school was; I think it took about forty-five minutes but then young eyes see things differently and I could be wrong. I do know that the only sound on those frigid morns was the sharp crunch of fresh snow as I walked, and the swish-swish of red snowpants as my nylon thighs rubbed together. I felt like a stiff-legged zombie wandering aimlessly through town. I peered carefully around, and as my eyes adjusted to the darkness, I saw other child-zombies also making their way to school, looking eerie in the long shadows of the street lamps and occasional car. (Night of the Living Dead, Part 2: The Offspring)

As I turned to cross the street, I paused and looked both ways (crazy car) but it was difficult to see because the hood blocked my side view and that damn coyote fur kept getting in my eyes. I could only see straight ahead so I had to take these little-kid shuffle-steps to the left and then more little shuffle-steps to the right, to make sure there was no traffic. It was clear, and as I crossed I'd catch my languid shadow on the snow-covered road; from the side I looked like the Michelin tire person with a submarine periscope where the head should be. Or maybe I'd be an astronaut. Yeah, an astronaut—go to space, walk on the moon—that would be the coolest....

by Jessica Jobin
and Lindsay Sinclair

Seeing the spawning salmon at Wolf Creek was one of the most touching moments of our life. We mean, it may sound like one of those dull moments but believe us, it wasn't. It was one of the only times we have ever seen nature taking its course.

Sensational moments with salmon

As we walked through the bushes to the creek there were two gems of red in the crystal clear water. Scratched up but bold—two salmon. We assumed they were mates ready to spawn. It may be hard to believe but those two were the only living salmon we saw that day. We watched them for quite some time. The way they pushed themselves up the current fighting anything in their way is what convinced us to write this poem for all those strong surviving salmon.

I am a salmon strong and free
I avoid you killing me.
I am a salmon cold and bold
I am better than gold.
I am a salmon who lives to die
but believe me I never cry.
I am a salmon who's not afraid to fight a tidal wave.
I am a salmon ready to be washed away to the nearest bay
where the gulls will feed on my flesh everyday.

cleaning trout

by Peter Harms

It was fun to watch everyone take a turn at cleaning trout. Two girls had a hard time with this and this poem is dedicated to them, Jamie Williams and Jennifer Gonnet.

They stood there at the table
In their hands a sharpened knife
And lying on the table
Was a fish bereft of life

They twisted up their faces
When their hands contacted slime
Seemed scared to touch, like the fish was hot
Or covered with some grime.

Their voices proclaimed total disgust
With their "Oh gross, Yuck, and Uhhh"
When various orifices
Emitted milt, or eggs, or poo.

The sharp knife silently slit the meat
And with grinding, cut the head.
They winced and looked with pity
Even though the fish was dead

The long blade slid underneath the skin
You stick it in...you know where.
You slit it up the belly
And guess what came out there?

Many different coloured guts,
Bags of white and green
Like twisted globs of swollen worms
Enough to make you scream.

Their hands moved slowly to the blobs.
They hoped that they were able
To move this mess from inside the fish
And place it on the table.

With your thumb you push the blood out
That dark line on the spine
It was just as bad to feel its blood
As if it had been mine.

We washed it clean, we're finally done.
Our cowardice...yes, defeated!
It was gross, disgusting, really crude,
And now we're supposed to eat it?

It all started when Mr. Harms said, "Well, class, next week we are going to go camping at Rocks River." We all cheered and left for home. When we got home we started packing for camping. Finally, the week was over and on Monday we left for Rocks River.

CAMPING

by Pixie Ingram

Mr. Harms brought his guitar so we sang on the bus. We got there in an hour and we all cheered.

We helped get the things out of the bus and then we hiked a kilometre. It ended up that 23 people were allowed to go.

When we got to camp we set up our tents. Then we went for a long, two-hour hike and picked up some souvenirs like bear claws, fangs, skeletons of animals and a whole bunch of neat stuff like that. Then we went back to camp.

After that we stayed by the fire and had music. It was fun. Finally everybody got tired so we went to bed. When we woke up we got dressed, went to the fire and had breakfast.

In the middle of the afternoon, our teacher told us all to come to the fire. He was going to try to show us a moose call. He called loudly. It was so loud we all plugged our ears. Then, when all of us were talking to each other, we heard, way off in the distance, the real call of a moose. It sounded huge. We were kind of afraid but we were okay. That was all that happened. It was cool.

fish camp

by Blair Hubley

We walked to fish camp, about one kilometre. My bag was heavy. We had two resting points, one by the corner and one by the creek. Kids helped out other people with their bags.

Setting up the tents was hard because some people's tents ripped. It took some time.

After the tents were up we gutted trout. We untangled the nets to get them out. Gutting fish was cool. The knives were really sharp. Some people got trout with eggs in them. Some got sick when we cut off the heads. When we were done, we washed them and took them to smoke.

I liked Try Sticks because it helps me on my carving skills. Some people got cuts on their hands. We used poplar and followed patterns.

Later that day we went on a hike. The best part of the hike was that it was hard. Some people whined. We saw three big horses. I liked the first one the best. I loved the berries. We were so high that we were in sheep country. We saw lakes and alpine meadows. Kevin shot at a gopher but he missed. Then we walked down the mountain. Kevin shot at a grouse and got it.

For food we had bannock, Kraft dinner, caribou stew, fish and oatmeal. Mr. Harms

helped us make s'mores. They were delicious. Some were burned in the fire. We used chocolate chips, marshmallows, and graham crackers. We had storytime by the fire. It was smoky. There were four stories. One was about the small crow, one about the big worm, one on the salmon jump, and one on the north wind.

After storytime we had singing. We sang in the wall tent. It had a stove in it to keep us warm and a lantern to help us see. We sang a song called Horse so loudly that some people lost their voices. We sang for about one hour.

The next day we had to pack up and leave. We walked past the creek and stopped to play there. Joe saw a fish. We caught sticks and had water fights. After that we made banana boats. We made them ourselves. They were good.

ILLUSTRATION: JESSICA JOBIN AND LINDSAY SINCLAIR, PHOTO COURTESY OF HAZEL BUNBURY

Growing kids

YNAG

story and photos by Jacqueline Pruner

THE YOUTH GROUP THAT COULD, AND DID

It's amazing how sometimes the most unlikely people manage to turn a simple, honest idea into the most extraordinary of accomplishments.

This true story is dedicated to the children and youth, age two to 22, who live in the small remote Arctic community of Old Crow. Their strength, courage, hard work and dedication provided them with what they have always deserved—dreams that come true.

I n September 1995, I moved from Victoria, B.C.—an area often heralded as Canada's tropical lotus land—to take a two-month job in Canada's "great white north." Old Crow is the Yukon's most northerly community, located north of the Arctic Circle. My job was to work for the Vuntut Gwich'in First Nation (VGFN) of Old Crow as their Porcupine Caribou Lobby Coordinator. There, I found another paradise.

I viewed the opportunity to spend a couple of months in such a unique northern setting as an exciting adventure and an excellent chance to gain work experience, having recently graduated from university. I

don't really think I knew just how far "up north" was when I accepted this contract. I can recall expecting a community of about 800 to 1,000 people, a few stores and road access. What I got was Old Crow: 250 to 300 people, two stores, and fly-in service only. I moved into the community not knowing a soul. I had only names on paper—a few of them misspelled at that—to go by.

The first couple of months flew by as I got acquainted with my new neighbours. I'll never forget the night I had a knock at my door from a neighbour of mine, Peter Josie.

"Here, this is for you," he said, thrusting out a gift in his clenched fist.

It was a whole caribou shoulder and leg, freshly skinned, with the hairy ankle and hoof still intact!

"Uh, thank you—massi cho," I managed to stammer, gingerly accepting the neighbourly gift. In the past, I'd never been able to clean and stuff a chicken without feeling queasy! What was I to do with this—this carcass? In the end, I kept that shoulder in a clean garbage bag on my front porch, which acted as my freezer.

I lived in a three-room log cabin heated by a woodstove situated in the middle of the kitchen, the largest of the rooms. I learned to start a fire and keep it going throughout the night. I finally scrounged up enough courage to cut up the caribou shoulder and make a soup under the direction of my neighbours.

As I was really beginning to feel a part of Old Crow, I began to contemplate what I could give back to this community. And then an idea suddenly came to me.

Since I'd been a crisis line counsellor as well as a youth counsellor, I offered my services on a volunteer basis to the school. "Old Crow has some really troubled kids," I had heard once or twice, "who get in trouble with the law and don't listen to the elders."

Starting in early December, I listened to the children. The same general theme kept coming up: the children were bored and lacked a sense of empowerment. Old Crow, with all of its beauty, uniqueness and traditional activities, offered very little in the way of modern recreation for youth, aside from a skating rink and snow machines. For years now, the children and youth had spoken

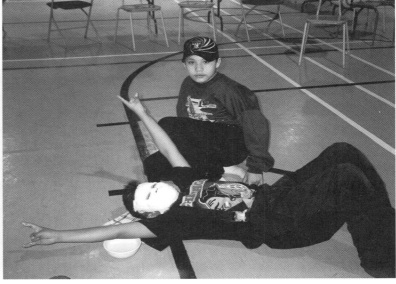

out at Tlo kut (Grassy Place)—the General Assembly of the Vuntut Gwich'in held each summer. Each time they had requested a youth centre—a place where, in a community with no restaurants, arcades or theatres, the youth could spend their time. Although many adults in the community supported this request, a youth centre had so far not been built. At one time an arcade was set up in an empty building, but this arrangement was only temporary—the building was reclaimed by the adults in order to establish a Vuntut Gwich'in government office. The kids were left feeling betrayed and marginalized by the community. They were frustrated; they felt that their voices were not being heard. As a result, they were experiencing feelings of low self-worth and helplessness.

In late January, during a counselling session with two boys from the intermediate class, an idea was born that, if successful, could help change those feelings of boredom and frustration felt by the children and youth of Old Crow. What if we started our own youth group with the aim of getting a youth centre finally built?

We held a meeting that Saturday evening. By 7 p.m., my three-room log cabin was brimming over with young people! I explained my offer to them.

"I think that we should form a youth group with a goal to build our own youth centre! I'm willing to work for you, just like I do for your government. Together, we'll lobby on behalf of the youth group and make sure we get ourselves a youth centre!"

"What's 'lobby' mean?" one of the younger children asked in a high-pitched, squeaky voice from among the dozen or so faces packed in the "living room"—the only room with enough furniture to comfortably, barely, hold them all.

"Well, lobbying," I began, not sure how to explain the term to a young child in a way that could be understood with certainty, "It's kind of like…well…like nagging."

"Would we have to pay you?" an older boy asked, his bright, sharp eyes narrowed with suspicion.

"Of course not—I'd work for you for free," I assured him.

"And we'd be your boss?" an outspoken girl by the name of Miranda asked as she pushed her way through the sea of young people to stand right in front of me. Her face lit up with excitement and astonishment.

"Uh, yes, that's right," I replied. At this point I began to wonder what exactly I was getting myself into. "So, what do you think?"

"Cool! Yeah!" was the unanimous reply from the now-members of the newly-born youth group.

"What are we going to call ourselves?" was my next question. After all, we had to have a name.

The next half-hour was spent batting around a wide assortment of possible names: Children of the Nation, Justice For All, and Children of the Grave. (There are several young heavy-metal fans in this community!) Yet none of these names seemed appropriate for the purpose of the group.

Not too long before this meeting, I had given a speech at their school, at which time I had taught them the word "acronym." Once one of the children recalled that word, names quickly followed: Youth Action Group (YAG), Native Action Group (NAG), Youth Native Action Group (YNAG). That was it: YNAG. Our motto (or battle cry, if you will) became "YNAG? Because we wanna!"

Over the next four months, YNAG began its fundraising and awareness campaign. If the adults weren't going to build an activity centre for the youth, then the children and youth would. Our first event was a sleepover-movie-party night, held at the community hall. Parents paid $10 per child, and from 7 p.m. to 9 a.m. the next morning, they did everything that's done at sleepover parties: watched movies, ate snacks, ran around, listened to music—everything but sleep, that is. As the appointed secretary-treasurer-lobbyist for YNAG (and, at the time, the only adult in the group), I acted as the adult supervisor for over 30 YNAG members who chose to attend. With about 60 children in the kindergarten to grade 9 school of Old Crow, that was quite a turnout.

I didn't sleep one wink all that night.

Our next event was a St. Patrick's Day buffet brunch. The kids helped set the tables and prepare the food. In the spirit of the holiday, the pancakes were dyed green with food colouring. YNAG members did a terrific job. Twelve-year-old Arthur Kendi alone cooked over six dozen eggs!

The events that followed—a spring market, at which YNAG members sold scented candles they'd made themselves out of beeswax and old baby food jars, a chocolate bar sale campaign, and yet another sleepover-movie-party—were all successful. Government agencies such as the VGFN's Land Claims and Social departments and the Women's Directorate of the Yukon government began approving funding grants to our group. Once YNAG found itself with money to spare, we opened our very own commercial account.

Without the constant worry of paying the bills, YNAG could afford to give something back to the community that had helped us to get ourselves established. We began a recycling program in Old Crow. Now, every Friday, 13-year-old Tammy Josie, YNAG's Youth Recycling Coordinator, organizes a door-to-door popcan pick up service. The cans are crushed by YNAG members, and flown to recycling facilities in Whitehorse. The refund—5 cents a can—goes towards funding our activities. Just six months after beginning this program, YNAG registered the abandoned post office as an official recycling depot. We call it the Caribou Canteen Recycling Depot. (Tammy, who came up with the name, asks, "Do you get it? "Caribou" because the caribou are so important, "can" because popcans were the first thing we started recycling, and "teen" because YNAG recycles and helps run the depot!")

From late May until the middle of June, YNAG rested—the secretary-treasurer-lobbyist (me) headed south for a week-long business trip, followed by a vacation. While on vacation, I received a telephone call from one of the VGFN councillors, informing me that there would be a meeting the following Tuesday with Bill Brewster, then Yukon Minister of Community and Transportation

Services. One of the items on the agenda was the outdoor swimming pool promised to the community the year before.

YNAG had voted unanimously for a youth centre. Members didn't want a swimming pool. Why? Because a swimming pool would be filled with chlorine—a chemical "that wouldn't be good for the land." Because "we have a river to swim in already." Because a youth centre could be used year-round, whereas an outdoor pool could not. Because the children and youth of this community had been promised a youth centre for years now.

On my way back north, instead of taking the regularly scheduled flight from Whitehorse to Old Crow, I ended up on a charter flight. The charter belonged to none other than the government officials who were flying up to attend the very same meeting I was returning for.

We passengers got to chatting with one another, as passengers of small northern airplanes tend to do. Within minutes, we were discussing one of the meeting's agenda items—the swimming pool versus the youth centre.

We arrived in Old Crow around 10:30 a.m. The meeting was scheduled to begin at 1 p.m. Since I had extra time, I went home to a cabin that had not been lived in for over a month. Before leaving for holidays I had packed up my belongings and stacked the boxes everywhere in anticipation of a spring flood that never happened. Now I spent the time unpacking.

By 1 p.m., just over a dozen children and youth, complete with baseball caps and bubble gum, were sitting in the community hall. The intent of the meeting was to deal with community and transportation services in general, so a number of items were on the agenda, including a new school and a proposed elder's home. Unfortunately, the

swimming pool versus youth centre was the second agenda item. This wouldn't have been so bad except that the first item was sewage. Not likely a subject that would keep the children on the edge of their seats.

Finally, after an hour, our agenda item was reached. By this time, YNAG had lost a few members because of the sewage item, the call of the outdoors and the lure of the candy counter at the local grocery store. But we still had enough kids left to leave an imprint on the Yukon government officials.

Noticing that the kids were beginning to show early symptoms of stage fright, I spoke first. I summarized YNAG's position and sat down. I hoped that the members, after seeing how easy it was to speak to a large group, would now volunteer to speak for themselves. I was wrong.

Community adults began to voice their opinions and concerns, most of them agreeing with our position. All this was well and good, but I really wanted those children and youth to speak up. The question was, how to do it? I was running out of time.

"Do any of the children wish to speak?" Bill Brewster finally asked the one question I was not prepared to answer.

Then, suddenly, an idea hit me.

"Everybody, stand up!" I half-whispered, half-shouted.

All the children rose from their seats. Now what? I thought.

"What does YNAG stand for?" I almost shouted with excitement, like a high school cheerleader getting the spectators to spell out the name of their home team.

"Youth Native Action Group!" they shouted back, just as excitedly.

"Are we working to get a youth centre?"
"YES!!!" they practically screamed.
"What do we want to have in it?"
"Videos! A pool table! Traditional crafts!

Painting! A weight room!" they replied, each of them shouting out different forms of recreation.

So far so good. Now it was time to ask the all-important question—the question that would make or break our chances of getting a youth centre instead of a swimming pool.

"Do we want a swimming pool or a youth centre?" I blurted out loudly. Then I held my breath.

The silence that followed was unbearable.

"A YOUTH CENTRE!" Every child and youth in the community hall shouted in unison.

I exhaled, smiled at the government officials, then sat down. My knees felt just like the half-melted freeze-pops some of the YNAG members were holding in their hands and periodically slurping.

We waited. The children slurped.

Within minutes, Minister Brewster agreed with our position.

"You just got yourself a youth centre."

"Did you hear that? WE GOT IT!" I shouted with joy and astonishment.

"Yaaaay!" was YNAG's unanimous reply.

The minister then began to outline the terms of the funding, but was interrupted with sporadic, but continuous, shouts of "Massi cho! Thank you," from the children.

That day was a wonderful one, one I will never forget as long as I live.

It was amazing how such an unlikely group of some 30-odd children and youth, aged two to 22 years, managed to turn a simple idea into the most extraordinary of accomplishments.

YNAG's youth centre is scheduled to be completed sometime in the fall of 1997. In the meantime, YNAG will continue to raise funds for the furnishings and equipment that will decorate Old Crow's new youth centre.

GETTING TO
the zone
by Ava Christl

Mornings start slowly. Even though the sun awakens me earlier and earlier these days, I rarely start my day any earlier. There is no real reason to—nothing urgent happens that early—the day will be long enough.

Art

I begin with a slow circuit around the house, checking the seedlings, poking into the studio to look at what I did the night before, plugging in the kettle, turning on the radio.

I go out for a pee—checking the sky as I go. Watching the weather, the cloud formations, the colours of the lightening sky. I scan the horizon, noting the receding snow line on the mountains and the buds greening on the trees.

Mornings are spent, coffee in hand, writing letters or proposals, paying bills, making phone calls. Taking care of the business of being an artist.

After lunch I settle into my studio. I approach the canvas slowly and with timidity—I'm edgy, tentative, nervous. I perform a kind of dance—in and out of the studio, brush poised. But I'm not quite ready, not yet. I have to wait awhile, so I read a bit, pace the floor, do the dishes. Sit at the table and watch the blank canvas. It would look like nothing is happening.

The images are ready, or so I think, fully laid out, fully composed in my head. But I seem not to be ready to make that first mark. I cannot tell you what I'm waiting for. But I know that if I just wait a bit, give it time, it will emerge. Without interference, without force, the painting will begin. And then I'll be sure, excited, confident. Fearless.

At that moment, I am "in" the painting, totally absorbed, not thinking anymore. My hand is on automatic pilot, the brush mixing and laying on colour after colour, each one relating to the last, yet maintaining the whole. I work quickly then, intensely. My heart rate goes up.

I am not wholly or consciously aware of what I am doing. The changes of direction, the mixing of colours, the ongoing analytical processes are all taking place on another plane. I am in a place known to psychologists as "the zone," a place of heightened awareness, heightened levels of energy and intensity of focus.

For me, attainment of that state requires solitude. I need to be alone to achieve that singularity of purpose. When I am in that state, I work quickly, time flies by, the work progresses. Between bursts of energy and activity, I eat or watch the painting from the kitchen. I'm analysing its progress, seeing where I need to make changes. I need to be alone then too, while I think about what I've done and what I'm about to do. And I need to be alone to develop the ideas that lead to the physical work in the first place.

Ideas are born, not of the conscious intellect but of a mind let free to wander. Imagination has to be loosened, dreams allowed to rise from the subconscious, fantasies pursued.

Most of my ideas arrive, unbidden, at night. Often I lie in bed reflecting on the day's work, coming down by watching the night sky, the stars, the northern lights. Suddenly out of my reverie will come the next image, a new approach, a solution to unresolved work.

I let the shapes and forms and colours roam freely around in my head. Like dreaming, the images develop, change and dissolve at will. Some of these ideas are ridiculous. Some are useful. Sometimes in this state, there are flashes of brilliance. Sometimes I wake up with the light still on and early Van Morrison playing on the radio, and I know that the next day will begin slowly too.

Not long after Joe Migwans drove up to the Yukon from Manitoulin Island, he was asked to drive a Champagne and Aishihik First Nation elder to a potlatch in Carmacks.

"They said, 'This guy needs a ride. Why don't you drive him?'"

So he went to pick up Sam Williams, who was in his 80s.

"And since that time," continues Migwans, "We did lots of stuff—hunting, fishing, making grub boxes. We became the best of friends."

One day, Migwans asked him, "Do you know how to make drums?"

"No," replied Williams, "But I've always wanted to know."

"What do you need?" pondered Migwans.

"We need some wood, some hide, something to tie it in the back," decided Williams.

"So we went into the bush, got a tree and started bending it," says Migwans, his story trailing off.

Now, five years later, Migwans is making drums and teaching drum-making workshops. The Ojibwa, his long hair pulled back, describes his life as "between jobs." Since coming to the Yukon in 1988 he has become involved in acting and a native parenthood program. Migwans, who first started drumming when he was 21, found making drums was something he wanted to try.

His description of how to make a drum isn't far off from Williams' first guess.

"You get some wood, get a circle, get some hide and lace it at the back. It's that simple," says Migwans. "But it's a lot of work," he adds.

He shuffles through photos. One is a drum he made for his two-year-old son. "He runs around banging it," smiles Migwans. Another is a picture of Migwans smiling, standing with his arm around Williams by a shelf piled with drums and tools. There is a close-up shot of a plywood mould that he and Williams devised.

Trial and error was their teacher, Migwans says. "We both carried on making them. And each time we got better and better. We'd talk to each other and share. We cracked a lot of wood at first," he laughs.

The soaked wood is left around the plywood mould for two to three days. After the circle is removed, holes are drilled at the joint, then wet rawhide is sewn through the holes to clasp the circle of wood tight. Then he puts a handle on and stretches wet hide over the wood frame. Sometimes he paints the inside of the drum.

"I can only teach you what I know," Migwans stresses. "It's not what the elders know."

"The traditional way, you sat and listened all day. You didn't ask any questions. You just sat there and watched and watched and watched. And listened."

Sam Williams died in September 1996.

JOE MIGWANS

by Karan Smith

PHOTO: OREIN CORBEIRER

VISUAL ARTS in the YUKON

by T. Ruth McCullough

One thing is for certain—there are more artists per capita in the Yukon than there are lost moose! Everybody I know, with the one possible exception of my husband—although he is a great patron—either plays an instrument, sings, dances, writes poems or stories, tells stories or performs. Think about it. I'm sure you will agree. And for anyone you can think of who doesn't do one of those things I've just mentioned, I'll bet you would agree that on occasion, they act like a darn fool!

Seriously though, there are a tremendous number of very talented people who live in the Yukon. The types of art that visual artists alone make, cover an immense variety including painting, sculpture, carving, pottery, photography, weaving, basketry, quilting, glass work, mixed media, and a whole variety of other crafts like moose hair tufting, quillwork, beading and sewing. The visual arts community is strong, vibrant and visible. You can view works by local artists in public collections located at the Yukon government administration building, the Andrew Philipsen Law Centre, city hall, Yukon College, the Workers' Compensation Board building and the Elijah Smith federal building. As well, there are a number of impressive corporate collections like those of Northwestel and several medical and legal outfits. Hardly a week passes without an exhibition of work by one of our local artists at some of the less likely venues such as restaurants, public building foyers and lately, the kiosks on Main Street. Of course, there are the more mainstream locations, the Yukon Arts Centre Gallery and the O.R. (Operating Room) at the Guild Hall.

How has this visual arts community developed over the years? There has been a tremendous amount of work by a small group of people, typical of any movement here in the Yukon. Over the years, highly qualified individuals have travelled north to provide inspiration, technical expertise and incentive to grow and search out new

...continued on page 119

Art

LET THE AMAZEMENT RUN WILD

DOUGLAS RAYMOND SMARCH
by Karan Smith

Douglas Raymond Smarch, Jr. doesn't consider himself an artist. It was only a few years ago that people started calling him that.

"Before that I was just liking beautiful things," says the 28-year-old, his black moustache feathering over his smile.

He was also making beautiful things:

antler carvings, birch wood flutes, bone bird whistles, net bags. "You name it, I'll try it," he explains.

As the youngest of five brothers growing up in Teslin, Smarch made his own toys. His first one was a miniature skidoo made by gluing two wood shavings onto a wedge of wood.

Smarch says he gets something out of everything he creates. "And every person I meet," he adds. "I hate losing friends." Sitting in a smoky coffee shop, he knows half the people travelling in and out the door. "Hi," smiles a tall man. "I'm buying a speaker from that guy," confides Smarch.

Bending a straw in his hands, Smarch leans against the wall. His curling black hair reaches down to his yellow and green plaid shirt.

"When I make something for my personal self, it's something that appeals to me—things that are unique and age well. Something I envision becoming a family heirloom."

"I'm afraid to contain it [his art] or define it," says Smarch. "I want it to be free. Let the amazement run wild. Let the uniqueness run wild."

Smarch slowly releases his thoughts on what he does. He double-checks my scribblings across the table, to make sure I copy his words correctly.

"I don't want to cut off initially what is important to me, to chase a career," he says. "It's important to me to feel whole. It makes me see more, appreciating being alive, taking things to heart. I've gone through some difficult things that I've had to resolve myself. But life always amazes me."

But by making what he creates from the heart, Smarch also feels his vulnerabilities are exposed.

A few years ago he made an intricate carving out of a Dall sheep horn. "The carving displayed my struggle. It was like taking who I am and exposing it and making it solid. Each carving I do has a little bit of me in it. This carving is about people—what's inside a person, the uniqueness of each person. It tells a story of what isn't seen by others."

This carving is probably the piece Smarch is best known for. Someone called it "Abundance" and it was bought by Ottawa as part of a Yukon First Nation contribution to the National Indian Art Collection. "It's one of the best he's ever made," says Linda Polyck, arts administrator for the Society of Yukon Artists of Native Ancestry. She describes the carving, inlaid with copper and abalone, as giving "the impression of being a fossil with a lot of open work. It looks almost like lacework."

In selling the piece, Smarch encountered new difficulties, as it was his first big piece to sell. "Just pricing it, I went through this whole battle trying to find out my value."

People give Smarch sheep horns, elephant skin and soft carving stones to make things and request informal commissions. In his blue gym bag on the seat, among a towel and crumpled clothes, rests a foot-long caribou antler. A woman he knows gave it to him to carve. Last year, someone gave him a beaver foot.

"I made a bag out of it," he says. "Our people traditionally made them to hold bullets when hunting."

Making traditional things and his Tlingit ancestry are important to Smarch. "I run across people who talk about it [traditional things]. It makes a picture in my head and I try to make it the best I can."

At a Whitehorse art gallery, two employees stand behind the counter, examining Smarch's work. "It took me a while to figure it out," says one, referring to Smarch's snowshoe weaver. "I've seen my grandmother use this," says the other picking up a four-inch hook made from a sheep horn. The first holds a smaller "shuttle," pierced with two holes to thread sinew, and makes a weaving motion in the air. A squirrel snare holder is also displayed. It is made from moose bone and sheep horn and is designed to hold snares when travelling so they don't tangle. "It's a good idea," comments one of them.

Smarch also makes instruments and plays flute in the band Sundog. A rattle made from deer bone rests on the store counter. Caribou hide is wrapped around one end where deer claws that look like hollow shells hang. Smarch's flutes are sometimes decorated with mineral inlay, beads and hide. He's made them from bone, birch wood, pine and bamboo.

"I'm trying hardwood now because with softwood the sound is more muffled, "he says.

Regularly, Smarch meets with the others in the band to practice. "We believe the music is given to us by the Spirit. People have to define what that means by themselves. That's what we sing about—the water, the fire—always giving unconditionally."

"For the native people to live in society these days, you have to live both ways and so today that's living traditionally," says Smarch. He adds, "And with your own standards."

"I wonder if I'm somewhat close to how people back then appreciated life," muses Smarch. "I like to stay in the mode of realizing how incredible it all is."

PHOTOS: YUKON GOVERNMENT (RICHARD HARTMIER)

Art

Carving whistles

by Dan Branch

For more than a decade Ketchikan's Totem Heritage Center has offered a place for people to learn the art of the northwest coast. Cultural skills are passed on and students learn about the heritage of southeast Alaska's first people. Artists from Canada and the lower 48 come there each year to teach. In the spring of 1994, Haida artist Reggie Davidson taught a class on traditional whistles.

These whistles, carved from red cedar, were traditionally used in ceremonies to rep-

resent a spiritual presence. During the class, students sought to understand the technology used by past master carvers.

The students started with a split of wet red cedar cut to rough dimensions

with a band saw. Planes and sharp straight knives then fashioned a small cylinder. Wet red cedar smells like a mix of perfume and turpentine. The scent filled the room and clung to the carver's hands. No one noticed after the first hour. They were too busy shaping the whistle.

Windows form two walls of the Totem Heritage classroom, allowing students a view of the totem poles brought in from abandoned village sites for protection. At the beginning, everyone's head was down, concentrating on their whistle blanks. Later, when they began carving stylized ravens and eagles on the whistles, some students checked their carving against the masterwork on the old poles.

Time passed without notice. Some students joked or told stories. Reggie explained how to process deer toes for use on dance robes. He passed on other information and advice. He told students that he never understood carving until he started taking part in traditional Haida dances. "I once made something I called a headdress," he explained, "but no one could dance in it so it was no good." After complaining about time pressures, he said, "a carver is like the carpenter without kitchen cabinets. He never has time to make his own regalia."

Always there was music or Haida story tapes playing on Reggie's portable stereo.

When students began fine tuning their whistle reeds, the room filled with the sound of futile blowing and frustration. They were pleased when the first whistle produced its deep sad tone.

After someone asked for a song, the teacher picked up a large deer hide drum decorated with an abstract frog design. Setting a heart beat rhythm with the drum, he sang in Haida. Some songs are known in Ketchikan. Others are not. The students carved while he sang. His last song was sad. Reggie explained that it was written after a group of children sent from the Queen Charlotte Islands to Victoria died from smallpox.

The class spanned four weekend days. During the week Reggie taught his art to students at Ketchikan, Alaska's Schoenbar Junior High. On the second Saturday the junior high art teacher visited with the whistle carvers. His reverence suggested that Reggie Davidson is a skilled teacher of children.

On the last class day, Reggie invited the students to watch two videotapes. The class moved upstairs to take seats arranged in front of a television. More ancient totem poles reclined on racks along the wall of the room.

The first tape documented the carving and raising of a 50-foot totem pole more than ten years ago. The students learned that Reggie served as an apprentice to his brother Robert who designed and carved the pole. The second tape showed Robert constructing a decorated deer hide drum. In each program, Robert told the viewers that the Haida artist stands on the edge of a sharp knife. The knife divides the corporal and spiritual worlds. Artists give a view of one world to the citizens of the other.

The students watched in silence and then returned for the last hour of carving. This class, like all the others, ended with cleanup. Garbage bags were filled with fragrant cedar chips. Reggie reminded his students to store their whistles in a plastic bag so the wood won't check. Students thanked their teacher and left.

After the class ended, Reggie Davidson returned to the Queen Charlottes to carve a large red cedar canoe.

VISUAL ARTS

from page 117

direction or approaches to making art. Some of these people include potter Luke Lindoe, printmaker Steve Mills, carver David General, weaver Brin Pinchin and painters Toni Onley, Gordon Smith and Landon Mackenzie.

It hasn't been easy for artists here. These workshops are generally short—one weekend in duration—and sporadic. But they have managed excellence in their production. Like everywhere else in Canada, visual artists can rarely support themselves by their art alone. This means a second occupation becomes mandatory. Visual artists can be found working in galleries (they have an excellent eye), restaurants (they provide a creative flair to your meal), daycares and schools (they are great at teaching kids art) or office jobs (they make sure the environment is flamboyant and visually stimulating). All this and they can still return home after putting in a full day of work and make wonderful works of art.

Who are some of the artists whose work you may have come to know? I will quickly walk you through a number of names whose works can be viewed in public places. This list is nowhere near complete but I hope it will give you an idea of the multitude and immense creativity of Yukon artists.

Of course there is Ted Harrison who has now retired from Yukon winters and resides in Victoria. Most Yukoners are familiar with his jolly summer and winter scenes of immense landscapes with brilliant skies, quaint figures, blue ravens and pink dogs. He works in acrylic paint on canvas.

Another well-known painter is Jim Robb. His watercolour renditions of slightly off-kilter cabins and skewed villages can be seen in many offices and homes throughout the Yukon. Jim is responsible for the *Colourful 5%* publications and I for one include him in that five percent!

There are many more artists whose work is not yet common place to the average Yukoner. Allan Edzerza meticulously carves bone and antler. His work includes traditional motifs and the birds, animals and human figures are exquisitely carved with incredible detail.

Another carver, whose work is hanging in the Visitor Reception Centre, Elijah Smith School and Yukon College, is Keith Wolfe Smarch. His work also employs traditional First Nations images. Following the customary Tlingit legends, his cedar masks and relief sculptures all have a story to tell.

...continued on page 121

Art

Weaving grandmother's time

by Karan Smith

Art

"Are your hands clean?" asks Ann Smith. "Yes," I say, nodding. She double-checks anyway as I hold my palms up.

"I have to do that," she says. And rightly so, as I grasp a corner of her beautiful Ravenstail dance robe. The rectangular robe is woven in a striking black and white design traditionally called "echo of the spirit voice of the trees reflected in shadow." "Wolf moss yellow" is woven into the robe for accent. Long tassels hang from the rows, reaching a "great fringe" along the bottom.

Grandmother's Time took a year to weave, thread by thread, with her fingers. The namesake is "in honour and respect for all the past weavers," says Smith. "Mmm hmm," she adds, accentuating her sentences.

It all started when Smith attended a weaving workshop about five years ago in Whitehorse.

"I guess I just wanted to try it out," says Smith, of Tutchone and Tlingit descent, who learned to sew, bead and tan from her mother. "I came to realize this was part of our culture and tradition. And then I just got very serious about it."

And now Smith is one of the leading full-time weavers and is reviving this Tlingit tradition in Canada.

Her work has not only been exhibited in the Yukon, but also in British Columbia, Ontario, and the United States, including a small commission for the United Nations in New York. Her work also travelled to Greenland, Russia,

Sweden and Japan as part of a touring international art exhibition.

Grandmother's Time is a "man's size" ceremonial robe and Smith points out a photo when it was first worn and danced in at a potlatch in Alert Bay. Smith shakes the robe a little to show the way the design and weaving contribute to the visual appearance of movement.

"The only place where you can find the old robes now is in museums or books. But to get the right information it's best to be next to the old robes."

Smith spent a week at the Royal Ontario Museum in Toronto examining the only historic Ravenstail robe in Canada. There are only 11 of these historic robes today, some only fragments, and half are in European museum collections. Smith's current work at home is inspired by the old robe she spent time with in Toronto. It is a transitional robe that combines the Ravenstail and Chilkat styles.

But Smith doesn't copy the old robes. "The old robes I used as my teachers, also to help guide me," says the petite weaver, her long black hair tied back and reaching her waist. "I look at their designs and I work with the old designs and from there, I make sure I don't do a complete copy. To work with the design, that's part of the skill."

"I have many teachers," says Smith. "That's why I mention I travelled a lot." She has been to British Columbia, Alaska and Colorado to share and learn the Ravenstail and Chilkat weaving techniques with other women who are aboriginal weavers.

Smith has also travelled to teach. She did a demonstration of the traditional weaving techniques in Victoria at the 1994 Commonwealth

Games. But she prefers teaching the art at the community level.

"I feel it's very important to pass on the knowledge," says Smith several times during our conversation. "I really feel it's important teaching the First Nation community. It has to be done."

Smith, who left school when she was 16, has worked in many fields including secretarial, radio broadcasting and as elected counsellor for the Kwanlin Dun First Nation in Whitehorse. But it was after her time as Chief of that First Nation that she first started weaving.

"A lot of people think these only exist in the museums and they can only see the evidence of them in books. It's good to pass the message that this type of weaving is still done today."

Smith also weaves other dance regalia—aprons and leggings sometimes adorned with beaver fur, abalone and moose and deer toes. The leggings are tied at the back below the knee and when danced in "you can hear the cluttering of the deer toes."

"In olden times," says Smith, "white mountain goat wool was traditionally used and dyed black and yellow," but today she uses merino wool, "the next equal quality." In Chilkat weaving, blue wool is also used.

Smith is best known for her Ravenstail weaving but she also works with the Chilkat style. The Ravenstail weaving uses up to nine variations of the traditional two and three-strand weaving technique, while the Chilkat style uses only three. The Ravenstail weaving, which predated the more well-known Chilkat style, involves working from one corner to the other.

"But with Chilkat," says Smith, "you're dealing a lot with the designs, the crests, the faces and the ovoids and U-forms. You have to weave within those designs. So it'll be one design at a time that you work with." Chilkat robes can take two years to weave.

Smith says she finds the time-consuming art relaxing and peaceful but also creatively demanding. "When I work with the designs, it's challenging for me. Still, I admire the past elders and weavers and the amount of work they've done in the past. And that's what I'm more grateful for—their work," she says.

A lot of Smith's weaving is also in museums, and in private and public collections. One time the first Ravenstail outfit she made came back to her for a few days. It had been bought by the Department of Indian Affairs for the Indian Art Centre Collection in Ottawa/Hull.

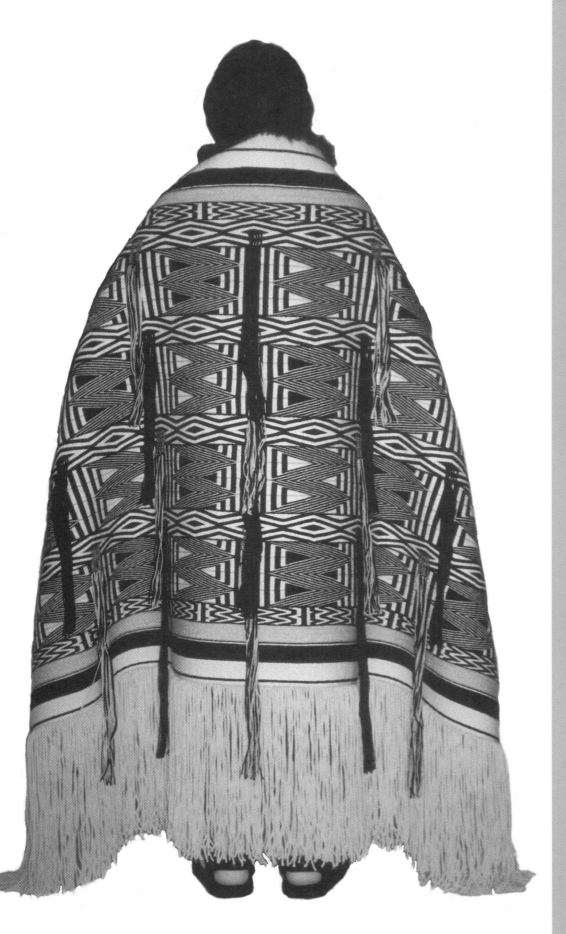

from page 119

There is also a large group of artists who often produce works which are an abstraction from daily life. Artists Janet Moore, Jackie Worrell, Ava Christl and Joanne Seaman might fall into this category. All of these women work in a large format and while there are some similarities between their style (abstraction), each produces entirely unique images dealing with totally different subject matter.

Janet is concerned with the environment and feminist issues which she explores through her acrylic/oil and mixed media canvases. Jackie explores the influence of white society on her First Nations background and culture. She employs materials from nature in her images and often does not stretch the canvas in the conventional manner, showing that she creates in a non-conventional manner.

Ava concentrates on landscape, although what she does is examine that landscape from a perspective with which the viewer is not familiar. Her large canvases may take one tiny aspect of a landscape and transform it into massive shapes and colour.

Joanne deals with societal inequities. Her portrayals are sometimes dark with disturbing ideas and concepts splashed in a chaotic fashion across the paper and words showing the concept of anger or frustration etched on top of the actual images.

There are many artists who create realistic or impressionistic works of art, frequently landscapes. Living in the Yukon it is hard not to be influenced by the massive and inspiring landscapes. Some of these artists include Anne Doyle, Libby Dulac, Cathy Deer and Diana Mae Knobs.

Taking realism and inserting a twist of humour is another approach employed by artist Chris Caldwell. Most know her paintings which show nature playing a joke on people. Then there is John Ogilvy's perspective which can take a pristine wilderness and deposit a piece of completely inappropriate rubbish quietly under a tree or beside a stream. John is also interested in comparisons between people and nature such as city versus bush as seen in the diptych, *Reflections,* on display at Yukon College.

Realism is not the only expression where the Yukon landscape shows its power. A large multimedia work entitled *Northern Lights,* created by Thom Rodger, is hanging in the Andrew Philipsen Law Centre and a similar kinetic sculpture can be viewed in

…continued on page 123

Art

Her husband, Brian Walker, brought the regalia out to Carcross where Smith was teaching a weaving class. "We wanted to take pictures of it so we went up to the mountains there, just before the pass. And it was nice out and here we were on the mountains taking pictures," she says with a smile.

A photo shows Smith with a big smile on her face as she holds the *Box Within a Box* robe with outstretched arms, surrounded by poplar and spruce trees. Thick black tassels hang from the black and white robe. *Knowledge From the Stars* dance apron, decorated with deer toes, is tied around her waist and *Shadows From the Trees* dance leggings are wrapped around her legs below her knees. Tan moccasins peek out above white fringe.

"Just to put on the robe" says Smith, finding words to describe the feeling, "it feels as if you're very protected. It gives you a feeling of pride when you are wearing these robes."

The *Box Within a Box* Ravenstail robe has been to Paris, as part of a display of Canadian First Nations' art works.

Smith laughs; she'd like to travel to Paris with her robe too.

THE BLUE PTARMIGAN HUNT

by Julia Boles

PHOTO: KAREN DIGBY

Art

The northern tundra is an incredible place, a spectacle of seasonal colour spreading out like a great glowing tapestry. The details and wonder of this landscape are often little known, even to residents of the Yukon. Among those who have ventured out for a closer look is a textile artist, Julia Boles, who, for a season in 1993, set up her studio on the tundra. She outfitted a small travel trailer as a silkscreening workshop and towed it with her camperized van. With this get-up she covered most of the accessible Yukon over a six-month period, gathering visual information that would become the theme for her Tundra Textiles exhibition. The resulting series of large, finely detailed wall hangings was exhibited at the Yukon Arts Centre in 1994.

One of the most inspiring areas for Julia has always been the Dempster Highway. Her favourite riverside site in the Tombstone Mountain campground became the base for her mobile studio during September, 1993. From here, she embarked on numerous outings, regardless of weather, and could most often be seen crawling about in the brilliant landscape with her close-up lens glued to her eye. The tourists were always keen to stop by the trailer in the evenings. They could watch Julia sketch the daily gatherings of mosses, lichens, leaves and berries. These drawings were the first step in producing the silkscreen images that would generate the final pieces.

Periodically she would leave the trailer behind for several days, for carefree adventures with her van, camera and journal along the northern reaches of the highway.

As I travel through the rich colour and

texture of the Yukon tundra, I revel in delight at being in the field collecting data, as an artist! For ten years I have been an exploration geologist, wielding a rock hammer and scientific notepad. Camera and sketchbook have now taken over. I am living what has been my dream through the many years that I attended art school during winters and hunted for minerals in the summers.

After several days of delightful, solitary travel through country so wild and open that it seems to grip at some eternity within, I arrived at my far point. This was the pass that marks the Northwest Territories border. It was blowing hard and hoarfrost had formed on all the grasses and weeds. Snow was in the air and it was bitterly cold with the winds that scoured the pass. I put on my down parka and grabbed my macro lens. This harsh environment presented completely new images: crusty white lichens clinging to damp black slate, and twisted willow cowering between the rocky crags.

The light was so low that my photographic exposures were becoming quite a challenge. My parka hood kept falling forward over my head, further reducing the available light. So I detached it at the neck and shoved it in my pocket.

After awhile I had had enough of this frigid activity and decided to return to Tombstone and my trailer in order to document my newest collection of rocks, leaves and lichens. Some kilometres down the highway, stopping for a scenic shot, I discovered that my parka hood was missing. This was a *big deal*! The hood was essential to the function of this expensive garment, and I was not keen on parting with it. I drove back up to the border, scanning the entire area. I retraced my steps up the hillside, straining my eyes to see. The wind had picked up and it was cold, the terrain black and dismal. My search

was fruitless; I gave up and drove south.

Two days later, at Tombstone campground, I was still thinking about the hood. I enquired whether the highways department patrolled that far north and would have a look around, but was not greatly encouraged by the response. My friends at the interpretive centre suggested that I write the hood off, since I didn't have time or gas left in my budget to make the trip again.

However, sitting in my van that night I had a flash of inspiration. I grabbed some paper and started to draw a treasure map. Calling on my resources both as an artist and a geological mapmaker, I indicated the route taken on my sojourn at the pass. I called it "The Blue Ptarmigan Hunt," as the hood was a bright royal, and formulated it as a northern adventure. A reward of a hand printed tundra T-shirt was offered, and I gave a contact location in Whitehorse should a winner materialize.

I myself had to return to Whitehorse at this point, so I made several copies of the map and left them with the campground host. Needless to say, he met the idea with tremendous skepticism, but good-naturedly agreed to hand out the maps to late season tourists travelling up the highway.

Weren't we all surprised a few weeks later when the hood appeared in Whitehorse, in the hands of a very excited American retired couple! They said the hunt had been the highlight of their trip, and wouldn't I please stage another one next year?! They proudly accepted the T-shirt, relating their experience up at the border. When they arrived, they had found two inches of fresh snow on the ground, but had set out over the rocks just the same. The map had led them straight to the mark: just a bit of blue peaking out from its nest on the pass. Funny, this was one colour in the tundra that I had missed!

REINDEER MOSS (SILKSCREEN): JULIA BOLES

by pj johnson
howlin' time
(Indian Drumsong)

This is a song of the spirit. The force behind it is a vision of the northern lights. Native people view the northern lights with a deep sense of spirituality. As they flash across the sky we think of the ancestors who have gone on into the spirit world, as well as the lost ones—people who have lost their earthly existence in a tragic way, perhaps by their own hand (suicide).

when the haunting howl of grey wolf
cuts across the arctic air
and you stand beneath the mountain
and the frost is in your hair
and your soul is bent and bleeding
but there's nothin' you can do
you're awake and yet you're dreaming
all there is is god and you
it's howlin' time
it's howlin' time
when the spirits of the lost ones
come to walk with you again
it's howlin' time
it's howlin' time
when there's only god and you
it's howlin' time

and you are part of everything
and everything is you
yet you walk along forgotten
by a world you never knew
and your life is like a season
when the moon has gone insane
and it shimmers down your shoulder
comes to life and dies again
it's howlin' time

so you wander in the willows
and you cut across your pain
and there's magic in the treetops
and a raven calls your name
and your eyes are bright with sonnets

and you wonder if you're sane
as the spirits of the lost ones
come to walk with you again
it's howlin' time

and you ask about your mother
and the child that never was
as a thousand answers leave you
but the question never does
and you reach out to your father
he's a million miles away
he'll be gone by monday morning
but by god he heard you pray
it's howlin' time

and you know that he is dying
and you know that no one cares
as you stumble up the mountain
and the frost is in your hair
and you hunger for a reason
and you hunger for a clue
and you hunger for a season
but there's only god and you
it's howlin' time
it's howlin' time
when the spirits of the lost ones
come to walk with you again
it's howlin' time
it's howlin' time
when there's only god and you
it's howlin' time

PAINTING: WM. C. SINCLAIR

the main foyer of Yukon College. Glass worker Lise Merchant has produced images that reflect the sun, mountains and lakes, such as *Waves of History* found in the new Tourism Business Centre foyer. Photographer Robin Armour frequently captures the incredible colours of Yukon flowers. Sculptor Alyx Jones creates impossible mosaics constructed of Yukon stone which show a cut of the earth from the core to the surface and include fossils along with a history of the land itself. This is particularly visible in the mosaic on display at Yukon College called *The Land Here*.

Perhaps it is because of the severity of Yukon winters, but there are many weavers who produce a variety of works both utilitarian and non-functional. The Northern Fibres Guild is one of the strongest visual arts groups presently meeting in the Yukon. While they pursue the more traditionally known techniques, they also examine the more unusual procedures of felting and surface design. Tired of purchasing her fabric to create exceptional quilts, Pat White began to produce her own material with their extraordinary designs, using photo transfers and computer assistance. She then fabricated her quilts with the designs on the material as part of her overall images.

from page 121

As well, ancient techniques are re-visited. Ann Smith has learned the almost lost skills of Ravenstail weaving and is now a master of the art. Shiela Alexandrovich uses traditional basketry methods to produce unique abstract non-functional works. Down North, a small business established by one of Whitehorse's local weavers, Wendy Chambers, employs the unusual material of qiviuq (muskox hair) in the production of clothing.

Unusual materials are commonly found in Yukon works of art. Furniture may be made of willow and relief sculpture of moose hair. Bob Atkinson creates tables, chairs, footstools and other unusual items using willow, one of the Yukon's greatest renewable resources. Gladys Lavallee produces incredible flower and animal images using moose hair, a craft which is called moose hair tufting.

Come to think of it, there probably are no lost moose in the Yukon at all. They are all standing around Gladys' backyard, waiting to become famous.

Art

Basic round-based

instructions and illustrations by Shiela Alexandrovich

Gather Yukon willow when the leaves are off, and before the pussywillows start to appear. I prefer springtime as the willows are "freeze-dried" and there is less shrinkage. Roadsides that have been cut will yield a good harvest of straight, un-branched willows the first year after they are cut. Gather larger size for spokes, smaller size for weavers. Try to select a variety, always keeping an eye out for extra long, straight willow.

Weaving green: Bury in the snow to keep them from drying out. Bring into the house what can be used within 48 hours. Thaw well before use.

Drying: Tie into bundles, then dry in a moderate, well-ventilated spot. Season a full year. Before using, soak in a stream, rain barrel, or your bathtub for 7-14 days, depending on the water temperature. When the willow is flexible, wrap it in a wet towel or blanket overnight. Now it is ready to use.

Method

Base: Cut six equal size willows, approximately 6 to 8 inches in length. Sharpen three of them. With a sharp knife, split "F" in the centre, turning the knife blade to open the slot. Slip "A" into the slit, then thread "E" and "D" onto the first sharpened spoke. Slip "B" and "C" on either side of "A." (Figure 1)

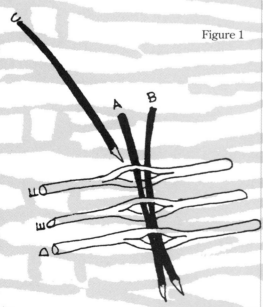

Figure 1

Select two fine weavers and start to twine (over and under) around groups of three spokes at a time. (Figure 2)

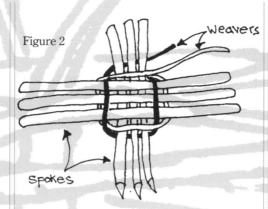

Figure 2

Do two complete rounds, then gently separate and start to twine around each spoke. (Figure 3)

Figure 3

Twining Detail

Use small, fine weavers in this stage, adding new weavers as you run out. Try to keep the butts ending at different times. Fill the spokes to within half an inch of the spoke ends. (Figure 4)

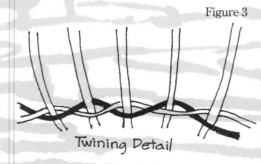

Figure 4

Adding ribs: Find 12 long, strong ribs and bend them around your knees to soften. Make sure that none are brittle. Sharpen the butt ends. Poke each rib alongside a spoke, pushing it as far down as possible towards the centre. After all the ribs are added, continue to twine at least two rows past the end of the spokes.

Sides: Carefully bend up the 12 ribs and tie at the top. (Figure 5)

Continue to twine in the same manner, watching for the over/under pattern. You can release the tie after you are 2 or more inches up the sides. This allows for easier twining. Remember that you can bend and shape the basket at this time.

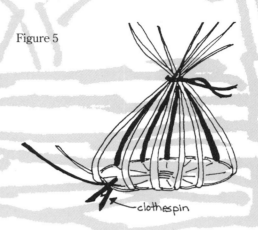

Figure 5

Borders

Scallop: Trim ribs to 6 to 8 inches above the end of the basket sides. Sharpen the ribs. Push a rib beside a rib that is two to the right. Push smoothly and as far down as possible. Continue this pattern until all the ribs have been inserted. (Figure 6)

Figure 6

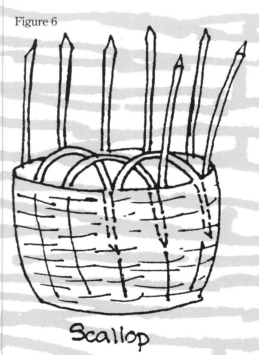

Scallop

basket

Woven: Working towards the right, bend the first rib behind #1, in front of #2 and #3, then behind #4. Continue in this pattern until all the weavers are used up. Trim extra length off on the inside. This is a basic pattern and variations are unlimited. (Figure 7)

Figure 7

Handles: Take two ribs next to each other, then select two opposite ribs to form the other side of the handle. Tie the two sets of ribs together in the centre, wrapping the end around the opposite ribs. Bend the remaining ribs to the right in an over/under pattern until they are all used up. Weave in leftover handle ends wherever there is space. (Figure 8)

Figure 8

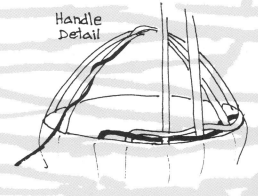

Handle Detail

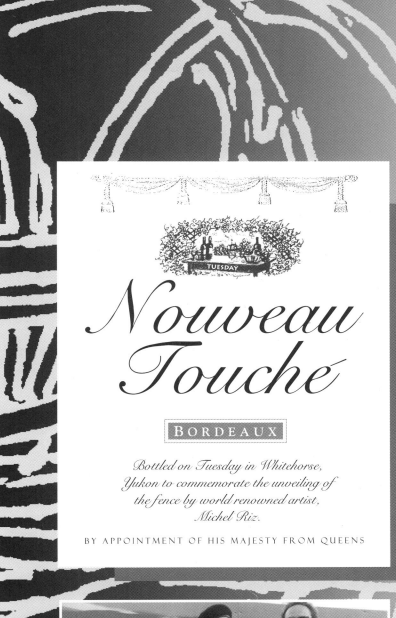

Nouveau Touché

BORDEAUX

Bottled on Tuesday in Whitehorse, Yukon to commemorate the unveiling of the fence by world renowned artist, Michel Riz.

BY APPOINTMENT OF HIS MAJESTY FROM QUEENS

World famous artiste Michel Riz at the unveiling of his latest work - "Le fence autour du yard de Doug et Mary El"

THE muse AT THE end OF THE road

MAUREEN MORRIS
CARVER FROM ATLIN

story and photos by Cathleen Smith

Occasionally one meets a person of great talent, beauty and dignity who is completely down to earth and unpretentious. Maureen Morris, a carver from Atlin, British Columbia, uses the horns shed by moose and caribou in her neighbourhood, and transforms them into elegant bird, fish and humanoid shapes which are achingly beautiful. The sweeping lines can make a tiny bird figure into a monumental sculpture.

The remarkable carvings which Maureen creates in her modest studio in the house at the end of the road, in the town at the end of the road, have "duende." Duende is a quality described by Spanish poet, Garcia Lorca. It refers to a creation that has within itself a strong spirit. It could be the power of a flamingo dancer or a carver. When the essence of feelings come up from the earth through the soles of the feet and through the body of the artist that is duende. Duende causes the onlooker to gasp in wonder and appreciation.

Maureen Morris grew up in Vancouver and attended the Vancouver School of Art when it was down near the old bus depot and the long-gone Alcazar Hotel. She always liked sculpture and as a student she did large fibreglass abstract shapes. In the middle of her four years at art school she took off for a year to travel in England, France and Spain. She became interested in prehistoric carvings and early Greek Cycladic figures as well as Mesopotamian and African sculpture. She has many art books which she pours over. She is drawn to simple shapes.

After she graduated from art school she got a job in North Vancouver in a small workshop which was manufacturing realistic jade carvings of animals. These were for sale in fine gift shops. In that job she became skilled at using water grinding wheels and diamond power saws. Then, in the early '70s, she and her husband headed north, looking for the perfect spot to cultivate their garden. They wanted a place at the end of a road that was also on a lake.

They found Atlin, and for several years Maureen had a carving studio up in the town. There she made small jade things to sell. Eventually, she settled in the place she lives now, a small cottage facing Big Atlin Lake. It is at the end of the road. Surrounding the house is the most beautiful garden imaginable—poppies and columbines galore with sunflowers, sweet peas and pansies in abundance. The greenhouse is filled with fantastic tomatoes, eggplants, and peppers. Every year, Maureen tries out new things and when the short summer comes she spends every morning gardening. There are several whirligigs on the fence and antlers here and there.

Maureen got her first rack of antlers in exchange for a case of beer. She has begun carving sheep horn and she has carved in mastodon and walrus tusk but she finds those materials too precious. Working with caribou and moose antlers gives her more freedom to

Art

126

experiment without worrying. Her first horn carvings were very small and simple. "They were sort of like big cloves of garlic. In fact once someone mistook a garlic clove for one of my birds!"

Maureen feels good about using a local material—the horns are shed annually by the moose and caribou. She was perplexed when a "modern bleeding heart woman" told her down in Vancouver that she felt sorry for the poor moose. Maureen explained that the antlers come off each spring and they are left lying around in the woods. The woman insisted that she still felt sorry for the moose. In fact, Maureen continues to get antlers from hunters and hikers. They usually barter with her. One day when I went to visit Maureen she was gone but her friend Kathy was painting the trim on the house to pay off a carving. There is a huge pile of antlers behind the house and a special shed for the more precious and unusual racks. Some of Maureen's favourite ones are those that have been outdoors for a number of years and have a patina of green or brown.

Every year at Christmas time she makes a dozen or so pendants which are for sale at the historic Atlin courthouse annual holiday sale. Looking back on her several decades of carving, she notes that there have been several series, each of which stretches out for a few years. After the initial small birds there was a period of bird masks—very striking totemic-appearing pieces which are reminiscent of skulls. Skulls and feathers were her next series, culminating in the "Bird Wardrobe," rows of feathers and bird skulls mounted in a wooden box Maureen found in an antique store in Victoria. The small compartments were originally for holding typesetters' letters.

She has also done a series of about 20 pieces inspired by the prehistoric Venus of Willendorf. Perhaps emanating from her love of plants, there has recently been a bulb series of bird forms emerging from bulbs, reeds, and bushes. Many of the sculptures are mounted on the base of an antler, which is naturally ragged. This is a very organic looking way to set off the carving. One of her showings at Yukon Gallery in Whitehorse had another emerging aspect—mounting the figures on clay bases. She intends to further pursue pottery in her new studio just up the hill from her house.

Several local people and groups have assembled sizable collections of Maureen's work over the years. The Yukon government public art collection has three larger pieces which are on display from time to time in government buildings and the library in Whitehorse. These are rotated, simply appearing and then disappearing, from time to time. It is amazing to see in these larger pieces the limits to which Maureen can push the very constrained space which is available in a single antler.

It is very soothing to be in the presence of this woman. Observing Maureen's calm demeanour as she sits in her studio and contemplates the current piece she is working on makes one appreciate the privilege of being in attendance when the deep process of creation is happening.

Her husband, Archie, got her all rigged up with very fine power tools. His companionship in sharing the pleasure of her work, the outings in his boat and skidoo and her exquisite cooking round out her peaceful life. She has two yellow Labs, who are her constant companions at work and on walks in this paradise at the end of the road.

Maureen has a sly sense of humour. She says that sometimes she contemplates taking all the piles of antler dust she sweeps up from her work, bottling it up and selling it as "antlerdisiac"…guaranteed to make things grow!

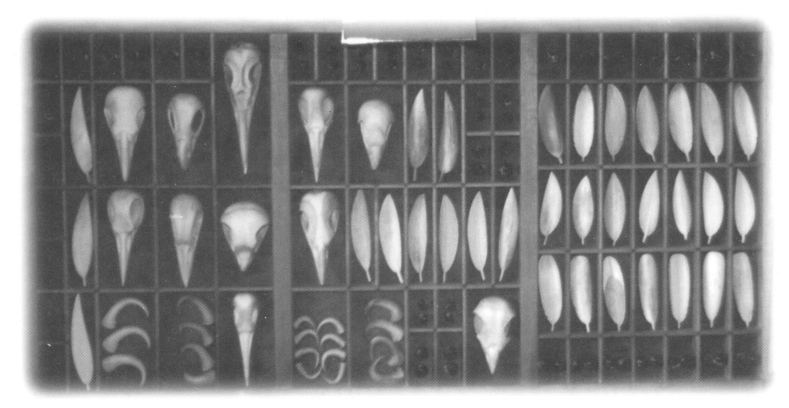

PHOTOVICTIMS

by Alison Reid

The photo: A campfire. On a beach with water and mountains as a backdrop. Dark, the fire lighting the faces of the group of people gathered around. They are talking in a desultory way, or simply gazing reflectively into the flames. Peaceful. Mellow. Northern.

The story behind the photo: Max is yearning for a campfire shot to go into a Yukon photo book. Richard, the photographer, and the others in the small northern publishing company are less excited, but willing to indulge him. The arrangements are made; it is a beautiful September day and this might even be fun!

Ten minutes before heading out the door to the designated spot, the photographer (who has gone ahead to scout things out—obviously he's done this before) phones to say that both the potential idyllic sites are filled with YUKONERS DRINKING BEER. There is some contemplation of calling the cops to turf out the oafs, but in the end we agree to meet in Carcross to look for other options.

The other two vehicles of campfire subjects have already left home, so there is the added anxiety of whether we will be able to flag them down before they get beyond Carcross. Miraculously we do.

Max and Richard find an acceptable site:

on Bennett beach overlooked by a row of Carcross homes. There are the remains of one campfire there, but no other wood, so we haul out everything we've brought and take some from the local campground. As Max indiscreetly points out to our law-abiding six-year-old, we may be breaking at least three laws: taking wood from a campground, having a fire on the Carcross beach, and drinking beer there. Robin reacts strongly to this, saying she doesn't want to break any laws, and furthermore she will never forgive us if we are arrested by the cops.

However, once we are all gathered at the beach, the fire is lit, and our hot dogs and corn are roasting, things begin to feel a little more relaxed. The kids are playing contentedly, the adults chatting and cooking. There's just the minor anxiety of keeping Richard's cocker

spaniel from beating up our much larger dog.

The light begins to dim, and we turn to the creative endeavour at hand. Richard takes a few polaroid shots to get a quick sense of the scene and people placement, and to give us a graphic image of what happens when we move during the shot. So far we're still relaxed.

But as it gets darker, things get more serious. The fire needs to be bigger, we need to get closer to it, and the time we need to stay still lengthens from one to two and finally to five seconds. The heat becomes a real problem. Robin hides her eyes and complains of them burning; during the breaks, Emily and Anna soak their pants to the knees in the cold lake water, and everyone stomps on large embers sparking off the roaring blaze. In between, the coffee pot needs to be rearranged, there are a number of technical difficulties, and it becomes impossible to tell when we're supposed to "freeze" and when we can scratch our nose.

Richard jokes about "torturing the models," and we understand what he means. When some local kids innocently wander by, we find ourselves tensing irritably every time they get close to the photo area. The dogs have given up on us altogether and stay well out of shouting range.

Hours later (or so it seems to us), when we are all quite grumpy and our endurance has been stretched to the limit, Richard tells us he has only 10 shots left. Ah, light at the end of the tunnel! We all make an extra effort, and when Richard shouts "that's it" we are up and cheering. Minutes later, the fire is out, the food and gear packed up, and we are out of there. "Gee," says Max, "I wonder if any of those shots will turn out?" At that moment, I hardly care.

Art

Carol Geddes is best known as director of the 1986 film, *Doctor, Lawyer, Indian Chief*. In 1994, she began filming *Kaash T'la: Tlingit Photographer*. She spoke to Tannis Atkinson in Whitehorse.

Can you tell me how *Doctor, Lawyer, Indian Chief* came about?

That film was a result of the understanding by various federal government departments that the unemployment rate amongst aboriginal women was about 75 percent. They wanted a film to address the issue and so originally they had wanted a very, very practical "how-to" film on how you fill out a resumé, how you find out about training opportunities. But I realized, from my growing up as a First Nations woman in the community of Teslin, that as a young girl I really had very few role models. I had very few opportunities to understand how women could take more charge of their lives and have the opportunity to do the things that they wanted to do. And so, understanding that, I knew that in this film I had to address more or less that issue rather than strictly practical issues of "how-to." It was what underlies that, what kinds of psychological needs do we, as women, need to understand. Particularly as younger women, what kinds of lessons can we take from older women, who have had a wide range of experiences and have overcome negative experiences—stereotypes, racism, lack of opportunities for women, those sorts of things. The whole film was premised on that kind of psychological understanding of what it takes in order for us to prepare ourselves to take charge of our lives.

Was it difficult to narrow down the number of women who were included in the film?

In one way it was difficult and in another way it wasn't. I put in all the qualities that I wanted on a kind of a grid system. I wanted somebody young, I wanted somebody very alternative, I wanted somebody who was older—just to make sure that all those issues were addressed. Once I knew the qualities I wanted, I just had to find people to express those qualities. And we got somebody in her fifties who had done a lot in her life. In terms of First

Nations and women's communities, it's always a mistake just to address things to young people. We have so many people who spend a lot of their younger years in childcare for instance. Very often, we have women who are interested in broadening their experience when they're thirty-five or forty or something like that. This is a very neglected area. It's unfortunate when things are always aimed at younger people and so I wanted some attention to that as well.

When you were commissioned to do that film, what other filmmaking had you done?

I had made only one film—a student film at Concordia in Montreal. But it was really good to make that film because once you have one film you can trot it around and say, "Look, I'm a filmmaker." Even though it's a small, student film, very clumsily made, at least you can still say, "I did that film." I never realized what a good

Focus on
Carol Geddes
Tlingit filmmaker

by Tannis Atkinson

thing that was to do when I took that film course and actually completed the film. Because then it's amazing, it's actually quite incredible, you don't think of it that way but it's true, you are then able to say, "I made a film."

Were you majoring in film at that time?

No, I wasn't, I was majoring in communications. I was very interested in the development of the First Nations community, in development issues. I was doing all sorts of communications and film was just one part of it. I was interested in visual expression, visual communication. But then I became very, very interested in it after I made that one film.

What projects have you done since *Doctor, Lawyer, Indian Chief*?

I've made about twenty-five videos because videos are a lot cheaper to make. One film that I did get a chance to make in those in between years was a film on three Yukon elders. But that film is still in the can. I haven't done anything about editing it.

Now you're working on a film about George Johnston. What are you hoping to do with this film?

I think that a lot of people overlook the fact that in the Yukon at one time the aboriginal people really had the best of both worlds, the best of the Euro-Canadian world which was coming in, as well as an opportunity to live on the land, which was their expertise. George Johnston exemplifies that time of Yukon history, when aboriginal people were just doing incredibly well. They had good health, economic opportunities and opportunities to live in a traditional way on the land.

In my interviews with people, everybody talked about how good life was then. The more research I did on it the more I understood what they meant by that, that they were not economically oppressed, and they had opportunities to express themselves culturally that sustained them in their economic activities. It was admiration of that era that really led me to want to express that somehow in a film. I've said very often that essentially I'm a social worker. I just do that social work through art. Basically, in a certain way, I think it's as prosaic as social work.

There is a photo of Sharon Shorty wearing a bright red jacket with a black polyester skirt. Long underwear peeks out above her mukluks and a red scarf is wrapped around her head.

Shorty is dressed as Grandma Bessie for the Nakai Theatre Ensemble production of *Land(e)scapes*. It is her first acting role and one for which she won the 1995 Aurora Award for outstanding actress.

Shorty was working as assistant director for the play. During rehearsals, she filled in the role of the grandmother and she enjoyed it so much that she kept the role.

Shorty, who is Tlingit and Northern Tutchone, talks about Grandma Bessie's story. "Something happened to her and, for a while, she stopped being in tune with the landscape or connected with the spiritual world. She was impeded by the introduction of European values and education. She was displaced in a way. It became a process for her, as a way to reclaim her power, to help her grandchildren reclaim their power."

The play, written by northern playwright Leslie Hamson, chronicles the rich, complex relationships among three First Nations people and a young white woman. "It's a very intense experience," says Shorty because the play deals with serious issues like mission school, trauma, violence and elders being displaced.

Hamson, whom Shorty refers to as her mentor, actually enlarged the role after seeing Shorty's portrayal. Hamson had modelled the character after some of the elders she's known and one elder very close to Hamson had the same background as Shorty so "everything from the voice to the hand gestures" seemed right.

The play, which emerged out of the 1992 24-Hour Playwriting Competition, focused on the interaction between the land and humans. Hamson says, "Grandma is who we feel it through mostly."

Shorty speaks about the character as a real person. "Grandma Bessie felt she had some responsibility because she hadn't done her roles to prevent where they [her grandchildren] were heading."

And Shorty slipped into the role of playing a traditional elder very well.

"There was a period of time when I was still grandma. It takes a while to come down from it. I don't think I let her go. But it's not a bad thing. To me, she represents all the female elders I know."

"It was very comfortable, too comfortable," Shorty says. "There was a lot of freedom. I can dress comfortably, and you can say whatever you want, there's no censor. There seems to be less boundaries for traditional elders, like they can look at you and say, 'Hey, you're getting fat,'" she says with a smile.

Shorty says she did not want to make fun of elders in any way but she wanted to share the humour, vitality, love, and playfulness of elders with people who don't have access to them.

She describes her own grandma as very funny and frank. "I was very close to her. I could talk to her about anything."

Shorty was the first grandchild to have a baby, "I had a baby late, when I was 27 and she used to say 'What's the matter with you girls? You're not doing it right?'" Shorty laughs. "Because she knew we all had boyfriends."

Shorty's grandmother also influenced her to get involved in the storytelling festival. "Throughout the year I go to school. I retold a lot of stories my grandma told me and I wrote some of my own." As well, she learned to sew traditional regalia and button blankets.

Shorty has also written a play of her own called *Trickster Visits the Old Folks Home*. ("I failed first year university English," says Shorty with a laugh. "Maybe that's good because all those formulas never stuck to me.") The play involves a traditional elder "who moves to an old folks home unwillingly and while she's there she plays tricks." The main grandma character was inspired by Shorty's grandmother who lived in a retirement home.

Trickster Visits the Old Folks Home was produced at the Vancouver Women in View Festival. "I'm thinking about the possibility of getting it produced here and travel it [to other cities]. I feel ready to do that," says Shorty.

"It's odd that I had to come to the Yukon when I was in this cultural mecca of Vancouver," says Shorty about her years in Vancouver attending University of British Columbia and Douglas College. "There is more support for an artist up here."

"When I think back, this is a love I've had for a long time." Shorty, the only girl in a family with four children, says she used to write, act and direct plays in elementary school and hold "full production" puppet shows.

Shorty's own toddler son, Wassnode, is getting early exposure to theatre. He saw his first play when he was 8 weeks old. He didn't attend *Land(e)scapes* though, because both Shorty and the baby's father were in the play; he played her grandson.

In her short acting career, Shorty says she has received something even better than the Aurora Award—"the best compliment I've received ever."

One night, after playing Grandma Bessie, "An elder came up to me and she took my hand," Shorty relates. "She didn't speak and I thought 'Uh oh,' because I was worried about that [how she portrayed an elder]. But then I saw she had a tear running down her face and she said, 'I feel that I saw my grandma tonight.'"

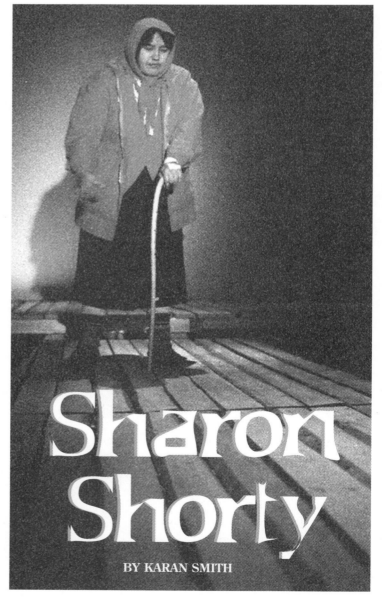

Sharon Shorty

BY KARAN SMITH

GUILD HALL MEMORIES

by Laurel Parry

One of my favourite "nights out" still remains taking in a play at the Guild Hall in Whitehorse. Even with the plethora of artsy things to do in Whitehorse, seeing community theatre has to be the best value for my ticket/babysitter buck. It doesn't seem like that long ago that I was, in some form or another, involved in every single production that the Guild mounted. This was, of course, before all the trappings of being a real grownup came along.

My first effort to get a part in a Guild play was very nearly a disaster. I had just finished a year of theatre training at university and all those months of developing my techniques (involving moaning, breathing and other confusing means of expression) put me in the mood to actually try to perform in front of an audience. I spent a whole eight months in one class developing my monologue of Rose from *Les Belles Soeurs* and was raring to test drive it at an audition.

So I took a night off from my barmaiding job at the KK and showed up at the Guild to audition for *The Effect of Gamma Rays on Man-In-The-Moon Marigolds*. There were three decent parts for women and I was pretty upset seeing the little Guild lobby filling with women all ready to try out for the few roles. My last audition had been at theatre school when I had a huge confidence crisis right in the middle of my Rose monologue and found myself already back in my seat before I had finished the piece so I was a little sensitive about what was ahead.

Thankfully, I was the first to arrive so I got to go in and do my thing first instead of agonizing with the growing number of women who were coming through the door. I won't go into details about the actual au-

dition. Suffice to say, it was humiliating. But I did get the part of Tillie which was the lead so I was over the moon. It was a wonderful experience. We had an unusually long rehearsal period so we got to do a full one-week clown workshop just to get us pumped for our characterizations.

There were a few mishaps. The rabbit, Thumper, borrowed from Whitehorse Elementary School, peed all over me one night. Marjorie, a reformed smoker, had

trouble smoking during the performances and tried to get away without inhaling. We received a very bewildering review from the *Star* reporter that spoke of my Cinderella-like character as "struggling to unleash the evil that lurks within her." The toilets in the Guild went on the blink so we nervous actresses (unlike Thumper) had to make other arrangements for that important pre-show ritual.

Since that first experience in 1982, I have been fortunate enough to be cast in a number of other Guild plays and it became my main form of recreation. There were many hilarious and nail-biting adventures in that "constantly under renovation" building in Porter Creek. I remember the most nerve-racking production of all was *Top Girls*. It had a cast of about fourteen women and we were very spirited. Opening night was the wildest. One volunteer went berserk and spent the whole second act applying makeup and costumes and indicated that she was going to make an entrance on the stage during the performance. Later during the run a woman entered the theatre during a quiet bit, stood on the stage and yelled out, "Is this the Bingo?!"

There was a fire backstage too, started by a bit of burning paper floating out of an ashtray, falling behind the water heater and igniting all the dust mice. I happened to be there—just about to enter with a pitcher of water. I dumped it on the fire and had to mime the filling of water glasses for the scene.

Art

A very wonderful thing happened during that run. Once night Pat and Robin, who were in the booth doing sound and light, noticed that the northern lights were particularly splendid so they called backstage to alert the cast. It was in the quiet bit in the second act when Pam and Sue were doing a scene. The entire cast, crew and all the volunteers dashed outside to admire the other show with quiet whispering exclamations while eighty or so audience members were mesmerized with Sue and Pam's performance. We made it back just in time for curtain.

Another play, *The Rivals*, was an artistic disaster but a social bonanza. The play featured another large cast, this time in really wonderful costumes with a great

ourselves during the performances by drinking hot wine and pacing throughout the building draped in blankets and whispering bits of the dialogue of the play. By the time the third act was in progress some of us were a little tipsy. In fact, we had hilarious post-show parties and spent more money at the bar than the dwindling audience members. There is a legacy from *The Rivals*. All those great felt period costumes that we still see at the Guild were from that play.

The Foreigner production in 1987 was an absolute riot. The play is really well written and we had fun with it. This play was loaded with great characters and we still reminisce about it. One night, while performing my monologue (which perhaps

and I shot out a line to Jack to cover the mistake. Then the drama really began. When I didn't show up for the curtain call, a few doctors made their way backstage just like the cliché. I had to finish the run in a cast.

Since those memorable days at the Guild other priorities have entered my life and I have had to get my theatre fix by taking clown workshops and volunteering for the odd theatresports gig. I did attempt to act in a play in 1990 with a one-year-old to find care for and another one on the way. Somehow, the magic wasn't there. I played Sloth in the production of *Doctor Faustus*. This wasn't even a walk on role; I was wheeled on. My costume was a tight, taupe furry number that stretched over my growing belly and I had one line. During a curtain call one night all

script and a creative set. Just to really gild the lily the director added the mask element. We all had to wear masks and to look totally neutral we had to paint black around our eyes. This was in the winter, the time of dry skin. For two weeks we all had darkened blotches around our eyes. Few people attended this play. We reconciled this to the forty-below weather and the furnace breaking down in the Guild but enough years have passed that I can honestly say it was because it was such a long, boring and indulgent play. We usually outnumbered the audience—a benchmark for failure in the world of theatre.

We tried to plug in heaters but because the show was so overproduced we kept blowing fuses. Instead, we comforted

after all was not the most riveting part of the production) an audience member simply had had enough and walked out of the theatre. In order to do this, he walked across the stage which really put me off. Later, in the second act there was a problem with the trap door. It didn't lock back into place after its use. We all knew it and the actor in charge of things carefully alerted us by not putting the rug back over it. I was having a little difficulty with concentrating that night (I was pretty sensitive about the monologue incident) so I was preoccupied during my exit and planted my foot and all my weight on the broken trap door. I crashed through and ended up doing the splits which was very embarrassing. Roy, who was holding my hand, hoisted me up

forty of us were to take another bow and a mix-up occurred when it ended up being only Sloth and the star, Doctor Faustus, to take that second round of applause.

I always enjoy taking in a Guild play. It is fun to see others experiencing the magic of community theatre. It is also really interesting to see bits of productions I was involved in being recycled on the stage. I did, in fact, participate in a Guild play a few years back. It sure brought back a lot of memories. Trish wore a renovated version of my vest from *The Rivals*, the costume designer handed me a kilt for my character that was originally bought for me to wear for *The Foreigner* and I found myself, once again, experiencing the thrill and risk of community theatre.

Recycling

The Garden Shed Revolution/Evolution

story and photos by Sally Wright

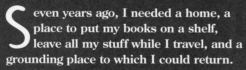
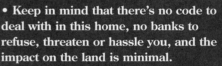

Seven years ago, I needed a home, a place to put my books on a shelf, leave all my stuff while I travel, and a grounding place to which I could return.

Of course, I had very little money and no electricity or running water nearby. So, rather than build a log cabin with a noisy, expensive chainsaw, I decided to buy a Beaver Lumber pre-cut 10 x 16-foot cedar garden shed. I changed a few things with the design. I framed and insulated a 2 x 6 floor instead of using 2 x 4s, insulated the ceiling and used asphalt shingles instead of the cedar shakes that came with the kit. It went up fast because it was all pre-cut. I built it on skids (2 telephone poles) so if need be I could move it.

During the three years I lived in that 160-square-foot space, I built on a greenhouse, a deck, and a woodshed lean-to. Then one day, I spied a steeple from the demolished Anglican church in Haines Junction and knew I had to have it! With frantic manoeuvring and some good luck I managed to retrieve the lovely 5-foot x 5-foot, 10-foot-high structure and now have it as the bedroom on my ever-growing, budding home.

I have a few recommendations for any starter-garden-shed-home-builder.
• Find a consistent and caring landowner who has a little chunk in the back corner to spare.

• Keep in mind that there's no code to deal with in this home, no banks to refuse, threaten or hassle you, and the impact on the land is minimal.
• Try to live in every stage of your home. That way, the next step for building becomes more natural and obvious. I sure appreciate a 320-square-foot home after living in one half the size.
• Live the way YOU want to live.

A CHEAP Bicycle Trailer

story and photos by JP Pinard

The old Bobcat "Bob" was getting rather old for fetching water at the lake. Since we're conscious about spewing oil and exhaust into the atmosphere for the sake of getting water and wood, we wanted an alternative.

Kiddie bike trailers are over $300 these days, which is more than what we paid for Bob. So, I decided to build a bike trailer to do the job.

On my next trip into town, I checked out the landfill and found the material I needed:
- two mountain bike wheels,
- two aluminum folding lawn-chairs for the basket of the trailer,
- one of the stiff galvanized bars that holds cross-ties on telephone poles to hold the wheels and the frame,
- some rubber from an inner tube for attaching the trailer to the bike,
- machine screws from Cambodia Tire for holding the whole thing together, and
- a small piece of plywood for the bottom of the basket.

I took the chairs apart, salvaging four u-shaped tubes. With a hammer, I banged the ends of the tubes so they would fit together.

With the use of a sledgehammer and a boulder with a good V-cut in it, I bent the two ends of the bar into right angles and attached the wheels through the existing holes on the bent ends. I then screwed everything together, liberally using duct tape as a finishing touch.

For the cost of a few hours of my time and fuel to the dump, I made a bike trailer.

Long live the three Rs.

PHOTO: MARTEN BERKMAN

by Mary Armstrong

There is dog fur all over the carpets, couches and the socks on your feet. It's a good sign that your "best friend" needs a brushing. Dog hair, dog hair everywhere! But wait, don't throw that hair in the trash. The soft undercoat that is brushed off can be spun and knit into warm, soft and furry winter wear—hats, scarves, mittens, sweaters and socks. It is the brushed (not clipped) fur that makes the best doggone yarn.

Not only will you have less fur to pick off your socks, but your dog will benefit from the added attention during the shedding season. Go back and get those handfuls of soft fur and place them in a paper bag for future winter wear.

You see, I am a spinner and knitter of any fibres I can get my paws on. I spend many hours spinning the fur that drives many dog owners crazy. Most dog fur is spinnable. I have spun fur from at least twenty breeds of dogs. Some of my favourites include Samoyed, Golden Retriever, Pekinese, Newfie, Malamute, Belgian Shepherd and Husky.

Knitters, weavers, rug-hookers and dog owners can benefit from this unique and wonderful yarn. Not only does it make great winter wear but it becomes a special keepsake and memory from your "best friend."

by Mary Armstrong

Brushed fur sits on my shelf
Like a carefully placed urn of ashes.
Picking the moment, I take this fur
And sit at my wheel.
The smell of your fur
Makes me think,
You are here at my feet.
The colours twist into a continuous strand of life.
With each revolution of the wheel,
Comes the unwinding of my mind's reel.
And the memories of a special dog spun up
Into this never-ending strand.

Recycling

About paper

by Joyce Majiski

An 18th century poet wrote:
RAGS make paper
PAPER makes money
MONEY makes banks
BANKS make loans
LOANS make beggars
BEGGARS make RAGS

Recycling

The paper I make is made from rags. Coloured cotton clothing or fabric scraps, cut into one-inch squares, boiled in water, and then beaten in a machine called a Hollander beater, forms the raw "stuff" or pulp. The pulp needs to be beaten for several hours or more depending on such qualities as the desired fibre length and texture. Each beater load produces approximately two pounds of wet pulp. To make 10 to 15 sheets of paper, 18 inches by 24 inches in size, at least four or five beater loads are required.

Once the pulp is in a suspension in a large vat of water, the sheets are formed by dipping moulds (screens stretched on a wooden frame) into the pulp. The moulds allow the water to drain through, leaving the pulp on the screen surface. The newly formed sheet is transferred, or "couched" onto a drying surface and at this point "pulp painting" can take place.

Sometimes, rather than making plain paper, I create pulp paintings. This refers to the fact that only coloured pulp was used to create the images. Once a base sheet is pulled, colours can be added in layers by a transfer method. Silkscreen silk works well, but can be hard to handle with large sheets. Pulp that has been finely beaten works better for this, because the pulp is often squirted through a tube onto the silk and if the pulp is too coarse, it gets stuck and creates a big lump—not great for fine detail. To create a wash effect, a tub of water with a bit of pulp can be splashed onto the silkscreen. It takes a bit of practice to get an even coating.

The texture of the paper is quite soft, and it makes an excellent surface for etchings, although, due to its absorbency, it is unsuitable for other media such as watercolour painting. It is waterleaf paper, which means that no sizing (a gelatine-like substance which makes the paper stiffer and not as absorbent) has been added.

Making paper

Understandably, most people will never get access to a Hollander beater. Nevertheless, you can still make paper at home. There are now papermaking kits for sale—which makes life even simpler—but if you want to spend a bit of time, you can find everything you need to make paper at home. The materials include a wooden frame to make a mould, a kitchen blender and a tub large enough to hold the mould and pulp, a sponge or two, and a drying board. (Wood is great but you need a couple of coats of floor wax on it or the paper may stick. You can also use foam—similar to what people use in their outhouse.)

By stretching a piece of screen (like mosquito netting) over the wooden frame, and stapling it down all around, you create the mould with which you will be making the actual sheets of paper. The edges should be tucked under and stapled as well. The important thing is to stretch the screen material as taut as possible, so it doesn't sag.

Paper can be made from anything which has cellulose. To make blender paper, you can use recycled paper (the shiny stuff doesn't work very well), apple or pear cartons, cardboard, mattboard scraps, old letters or envelopes. Just experiment. You can also add natural fibres such as leaves, flower petals, grass and vegetables, but most of these need to be cooked first. If the fibres are really long they may NOT be suitable for beating in the blender. Really long fibres will just wrap around the blade and burn out the blender.

To prepare the pulp, soak the paper in water and rip it up into small pieces—about one-half to one inch in size. When filling your blender, use more water than pulp, and if your blender has a "tall" line mark on it then fill with water until it's about two inches from the fill line and add paper till it reaches the mark. You want to keep an eye on how the blender is working once you've added the paper. If it seems like you can add more paper, do so gradually so you don't overload the machine.

When your paper has turned to pulp, it should be suspended throughout the water, and look even. Pour this into your tub, and continue blending the pulp until you have enough pulp/water mixture in the tub to "pull" a sheet. The method of pulling a sheet of paper is quite simple. Hold the screen vertically and put it straight down into the pulp. With a scooping action turn the mould horizontally while in the water, with the top part of the screen facing up, and slowly pull the mould up to the surface. As you do this the pulp will be caught on the screen and the water, when you lift the mould out of the water, will drain out the bottom.

Now you are ready to transfer the paper onto a board to dry. Turn the mould upside-down (the pulp shouldn't fall off if it has drained) and place it on your board or drying surface. Gently push a sponge into the screen to soak up some of the excess water and squeeze into a bucket or back into your tub. When the back side of the screen seems water-free, slowly pull up one edge of the mould. Voila! There is your sheet of paper!

You can add flower petals between layers, or put one colour on top of another—just have fun making your own paper.

"Wow, the van sure is packed full," Yvonne said as we crammed our girls' clothes into one of the last little spaces in our '86 Toyota van. Tomorrow, we would head down the long lonesome highway for what we thought would be an adventurous year at school. But surveying the van, we wondered how we would cram the last of our belongings into this passenger van turned semi. Yvonne, who has an eye for detail, noticed a small platform beside the carrying pod on top of the van.

"David" she said, pointing to the top of the van in that deliberate way of hers, "What do you plan to use that space for?"

I responded in my proudest husky Yukon

or the love of worms

male voice, "That's where my breeding stock of red wiggler worms is going to go!"

And that's where they remained for five days as we drove to Vancouver and then to our final destination, Victoria. I would relive my decision to take worms to the south many times over the next year. Yvonne would often remind me that the decision to bring the worms meant that we had to leave our canoe back in Whitehorse. My wiggly little worms taught me much about relationships.

I n my first winter of raising composting worms, problems were never far away. To raise worms in the Yukon, you must bring them inside before the winter so they won't freeze.

I had a huge bin of worms outside during the summer. To bring them into our basement to overwinter, I used six large brown Rubbermaid containers. Each container had been punctured with holes to provide air circulation. I laid out plastic on the floor to serve as a drop sheet for any moisture that might seep out of their bottoms. Then I placed the containers on top of each of other. Every week to ten days, I would feed them vegetable scraps from our kitchen.

Raising worms seemed simple and straightforward. What could be easier? You provide an aerated container with moistened bedding made of peat moss and paper and then add vegetable and fruit scraps, and poof, you get more worms.

But things don't often go as one plans. During that cold winter, we went on a five-week holiday—two weeks in Hawaii and three weeks in southern B.C. We arranged to have a friend stay in the house. Before we left, I fed and watered my worms. In retrospect, I see now that I over-fed and over-watered them.

While sunning on the tropical beaches of Hawaii, we thought little of wintry Whitehorse or my wiggly friends. When we returned to southern B.C., Marianne, a friend who had recently been to our house, mentioned to us in

a phone conversation that there were thousands of flies in our house. There were so many flies in our house that she wouldn't go into the basement or into the bathrooms. This information was not what Yvonne, nor I, wanted to hear. I, of course, being a Yukon male, shrugged off this information by maintaining that there couldn't be that many flies; Marianne must be exaggerating. Yvonne, though, wasn't convinced. Her disdainful look did not bode well for open communication. And privately, I feared for what we would find when we did get home.

Our holiday over, we looked forward to returning north, but not to the surprise that awaited us. We landed at the airport in Whitehorse and headed directly home to Hillcrest. By this time, Yvonne was not too happy in anticipation of what we would find.

When we got home, I dashed to the basement before Yvonne. It was true. There were little fly bodies all over the basement. The tiny black vinegar flies, which are common with worms, had been thirsty. The little flies had headed for wherever there was water—around windows, around sink drains and around the toilet. As well, there was a horribly pungent smell exuding from the containers which engulfed the laundry room.

Back upstairs, we spent the evening unpacking and settling the children. Having placated my darling upstairs, I dashed to my chores in the basement. It was amazing. In the laundry room, it looked like an insect hatch had taken place. There were flies everywhere. I needed to clean up quickly before the divorce papers could be served. But as quick as I cleaned up the insects, more would appear. The flies were coming from the Rubbermaid containers.

I checked with Yvonne upstairs to see if she needed any help. When she said no, I focused my attention on the containers. Carefully, I opened the top ones. I only found a few flies, and the worms' bedding was slightly moist. It was when I had removed the top containers and opened the three bottom ones that I found where the flies were coming from. And the assaulting smell almost overwhelmed me. By taking the lids off the bottom ones, flies mushroomed out of the containers into my face and the room. They were escaping the slimy smelly mass of ooze that used to be worm bedding. I just hoped that my sweetheart didn't come down those stairs at that moment. If she did, the worms and I would be leaving.

There was no time to delay. The battle had begun. The flies had to be eradicated. I dashed upstairs and brought down my weapon—the vacuum cleaner. I had read that you could vacuum flies. I took off the power

head and started the vacuum. I felt like a general at war with the flies.

It was a battle scene. These little critters massing over the sides of the containers were being slurped up by the vacuum. I picked them out of the air. I sucked them from the windows. Finally, they were gone. I moved the three bottom containers to the minus 35 degrees outdoors to rid the room of the smell and any remaining flies. To prevent any further intrusions from flies or smell, I encased the containers in plastic. My mission now successful, I could again concentrate on my relationship with Yvonne.

T he summer following the eventful fly breeding winter, I moved my worms to a very large outside bin. It was July and the bin needed to be cleaned. With a cup of coffee in hand and an explanation to my partner that I would be out of commission for many hours, I tackled the task of cleaning the bin and separating the worms. It is tedious and time consuming work to hand sort thousands of worms. Put into a northern perspective, the worm bin is like the sluice box on a gold claim. And the worms are the gold. You must separate the worms from their bedding as a gold miner must separate the gold from the dirt. To get worms and gold, you must perform the cleanup.

After the cleanup, I had over a hundred kilograms of rich, dark vermicompost and many pounds of worms. My image of creating a major worm business took over. I envisioned a full-fledged worm farm with worm bins filling my backyard. But two problems stood in my way. Yvonne would not give up her flower beds for worm bins and I had no idea what to do with all those worms and vermicompost.

Before I got too carried away, I needed to get rid of the vermicompost and the worms I had on hand. To market these products, I turned to the open line radio shows. My first sale of worms corresponded to us having a garage sale. I advertised both the garage sale and my products. Lo and behold, one person phoned to reserve 10 pounds of my vermicompost. By the end of the day at our garage sale, I had made over a hundred dollars from my worms. Although I was happy about my business enterprise, Yvonne was ecstatic.

"David, this is the first time one of your ideas has ever made any money," Yvonne exclaimed.

Coming from my personal accountant, this was an incredible compliment. I had learned how to raise worms and, in turn, how to have a relationship. The worms have provided me with a new perspective on life. I am an urban farmer with skills I can apply anywhere. This has boosted my self-confidence which helps me in my relationship. Worms have given me much more than just compost.

by David Greig

Recycling

Rethink, revise, review, react

by David Comchi

Recycling

Someone please pat me on the back because I recycle my newspapers, milk jugs, tin and aluminum cans, plastics, and glass. My friends, neighbours, and co-workers also recycle. In fact, most of us have some notion of recycling and the environmental problems our rampant consumerism has caused. However, few of us realize recycling should be regarded as one of the last steps in waste management. There are a number of things which can be done before recycling is even considered an option. We must begin to focus on two lesser known "R" words: reducing and reusing. These two "precycling" stages will help save time, money, and energy on the road to eliminating the waste problem.

Reducing the amount of waste we throw away should begin as we shop. Learning to recognize our faulty buying habits is the first step. For example, when I moved to Whitehorse, everything I owned fit in my vehicle. One year later, I moved out of my apartment and it took eight trips to get all my "purchases" moved. I couldn't believe I had accumulated that much stuff. How did I end up with so many extras that I felt I needed and haven't touched since? Impulse buying in our disposable product society really puts a burden on our already maxed-out landfills.

Besides buying only what we need, the following are some suggestions on how to reduce the amount of waste we bring home from the store. Buy products with recyclable packaging and avoid those which cannot be recycled. Buy in bulk to reduce the amount of packaging (and save money at the same time). Don't use a bag when picking up one or two items. Bring your own canvas bags to the grocery store. Be creative in your reductions of waste. One of the most innovative means is composting.

Composting is the decomposition of plant remains and other organic materials to make an earthy substance that is excellent for enriching soil. Composting goes on in the natural world all the time and has been practised by agriculturists for thousands of years. Unfortunately, due to our apathy towards alternative solutions, kitchen and yard wastes make up a large part of our landfills. But it is just as easy to dump our grass clippings into a composting bin as it is to pack them into a plastic garbage bag and leave them on the curb. There are plenty of ways to compost; just ask around for ideas and lead your neighbours by example.

The second phase in "precycling" is reusing that which we can. This includes buying products whose containers can be reused once they are empty. Use your own mug instead of disposable cups. Buy products which contain a high level of recycled product. Some polar fleece jackets, for example, are made from old recycled glass. Instead of disposable paper products, use cloth towels, napkins and diapers that can be washed. Environment Canada estimates paper products make up one-third of the materials discarded into Canada's waste stream. We can help each other by reusing each others' unwanted items.

Besides getting rid of things through the classifieds or hosting a yard sale, there are many outlets available where you can buy, sell or donate reusable items. Check the yellow pages under second-hand stores and watch the classifieds for Maryhouse sale dates.

Finally, while the Canadian Council of Ministers of the Environment have agreed to a fifty percent (50%) reduction in waste generation by 2000, the responsibility is firmly on our shoulders to shake the apathy. To stop the indiscriminate abuse of our planet, we must become informed about our situation, re-evaluate our actions, and take on a larger responsibility for society as a whole. Let our actions speak for themselves.

by Dawn at the
Raven Recycling Centre, Whitehorse

• For the world to consume resources at the rate Canada does, three more worlds would be needed.
• Over 11,000 people could stay warm in the fibrefill sleeping bags made from the plastic bottles sent to market by Raven Recycling Centre (RRC) since 1992.
• Over 2,935 standard oil changes could have been done using the refined motor oil made from oil sent to Mohawk Oil by RRC.
• Recycling steel is cheaper than mining ore.
• 44% of waste entering the Whitehorse landfill is compostable material.
• The Canadian paper recycling industry imports 30% of its paper from U.S. markets.
• Each Canadian is throwing away 4% more waste each year.
• It's only recyclable if someone is recycling it. Almost any waste can theoretically be recycled but only if there is a collection and sorting system, a recycling facility in full-scale operation and viable markets established for recycled end-products.
• Potential energy savings from recycling paper, metals, glass and other materials is far greater than the amount of energy recovered from incineration.
• If your cat eats one tin of food per day, and lives to 15 years, you would discard 5,475 cans.
• 6,170 trees were saved by sending printing and writing papers to RRC for recycling.
• In Whitehorse, each person produces one tonne of garbage each year.
• A manufactured product represents an investment. Disposal represents a total loss of that investment.
• Every year in Canada an area the size of Prince Edward Island is logged. 42% of the material we throw into our landfill is wood or wood products.
• "The best way to reduce the amount of rubbish that goes into the domestic bin is not to persuade people to sort unwanted recyclables. It is to persuade them to buy less and buy differently."
The Economist
• RRC diverts 5% of the total waste stream—3% residential, 2% commercial. 31% of Whitehorse's waste stream is potentially recyclable with current programs.
• Communities with recycling programs: Beaver Creek; Burwash Landing; Carcross; Carmacks; Dawson City; Faro; Haines Junction; Mayo; Old Crow, Pelly Crossing; Ross River; Tagish; Teslin; Watson Lake; Whitehorse.

Herb croutons

by Mary El Kerr

These croutons are a great way to use up leftover bread ends and bits. Any type of bread may be used, but I prefer day-old baguettes. The cooled croutons may be stored in tightly sealed plastic bags in the cupboard or, if you prefer, in the freezer. If croutons are removed from the freezer for use in a salad or soup just toast them slightly to remove ice crystals and freshen them.

Preparation time: 20 minutes
Cooking time: 20 minutes
Makes: 6 cups croutons

6 cups cubed bread
2 tablespoons virgin olive oil
6 large cloves garlic crushed
$^1/_4$ teaspoon pepper
$^1/_2$ teaspoon salt
$^1/_2$ cup fresh garden herbs including sage, summer savoury, chervil and sweet basil (If you are using dry herbs, decrease amount of herbs to $^1/_3$ cup and mix in for the whole cooking process.)

Using a serrated knife cut the bread into $^1/_2$–inch cubes. Place on 11 inch x 16 inch cookie sheet. Drizzle with olive oil, add crushed garlic and sprinkle with salt and pepper. Mix well.

Toast for 15 minutes at 180 degrees in a convection oven or 20 minutes in a conventional oven. Five minutes before finished, add and mix fresh herbs into the croutons. Continue to toast.

We Drove The All-Can Highway!

by Carol P. Smith
(a.k.a. phoenix phlyer)

A shopping spree at Maryhouse

Friends tried their best to prepare me for a trip to the rummage sale at Maryhouse. I had often donated clothing and other recyclables, but had never attended a Maryhouse sale (held at 1:00 p.m. on the first Saturday of each month). They told me, "Be sure you take a big green garbage bag with you." "Go early." "Be aggressive." "Women's clothes are downstairs in the building on the right." Good advice, but it did little in actually preparing me for this memorable adventure.

At 12:45 p.m., I drove over to Maryhouse—early by my standards, but obviously not early enough. There were at least 20 people in line ahead of me, all of us standing outside the picket fence, various coloured plastic bags under our arms. Good thing too; those bags doubled as rain gear as we stood in the rain waiting for the gate to open at 1:00 p.m. and not a moment earlier.

Then we were off, stampeding into the yard, up the stairs of the building on the right! I certainly wasn't at the head of the stampede, and within seconds I found myself on the sidelines, watching in amazement as others dashed down the stairs. First wrong move. When I reached the room filled with women's clothes, I um…it, ah…well, I knew I was entering new territory. I stood back and tried to take in what was happening, and how I could possibly fit into this dance.

Two rows of large packing boxes filled with clothing were placed back to back in the middle of the room. Rows of people stood on either side of these boxes emptying them as fast as they could. Clothes were flying everywhere, mostly through the air, from one box to the next. Bodies were dipping down into the boxes, churning the clothes around and around, flinging them up into the air, generally in the direction of the box to the right. After an overwhelming moment or two, I had figured out what I must do, and in I dove. I positioned myself to the right of the last box in the line. Considering the general direction of the flying clothing, I figured everything would end up in front of me sooner or later. But think of all the things I might miss. Better to move

into the fray. I moved closer to the middle of the line and waited. Aha! A six-inch opening. Elbows flapping at my sides, I leaped up to the boxes. Down I dipped, scooping up a sweatshirt…looks too small…and winged it through the air, into the box to my right. Dipping down again, I came up with a pair of shorts…looks about my size…into the green garbage bag. Dip again…a vest…what a find…into the green garbage bag.

I've got it. I know the dance. This is fun. Shuffle to the left…someone moves the clothes from the end of the line back to the beginning and I dip and fling with renewed energy. Now this is shopping! After a few frantic minutes I have about 12 items in my garbage bag. I reluctantly give up my place in the line of dipping bodies and flying clothing and retire to a quiet corner to inspect my potential wardrobe in relative calm. The shirt has a hole in the elbow—into the "no" pile. The vest is perfect, a definite keeper. And on through each item until I have chosen my new wardrobe.

Soon I am sharing this quiet spot with two other women and we are caught up in our own game of sharing and swapping. When we are through, I dump the pile of "no" items back into the boxes so they can become someone else's catch.

With my new summer wardrobe jammed into the green garbage bag, I walk over to the man by the door who will take my money. As I approach, I open the bag to show him what I have found. He grabs the bag around the top and hefts it up and down a couple of times, weighting the contents with a practised lift. I watch. He looks at me and says "A buck." I am speechless. All those "new" clothes for a mere buck? I pay the man quickly, grab my goodies and leave.

Outside, it is sunny again and people fill the yard between the two houses, checking out the toys, record players, typewriters and rubber boots. I hesitate…it looks interesting…maybe I could get those boots for another buck. No, not this time. I'll save the yard items for my next, much-anticipated shopping spree at Maryhouse.

Recycling

by Janne Hicklin

Saving the environment

Recycling

Today, I swung around the corner of the shed to grab what I knew would be the last tin of beer, and it was gone. The only remaining evidence was one of those six-pack hi-cone rings that a bird got its beak stuck in once and died. Now everybody's supposed to cut the damn things up into little pieces before disposing of them. Already disappointed, I sighed and dutifully picked up the scissors.

As I started in on those little plastic bits, I began to feel a bit ridiculous—as I always do standing there snipping away. "Why am I doing this? What difference will it make? I'm not going to save the world doing this, it's just a dumb waste of my precious time!" My mind began to wander…and then something happened. Suddenly, the whole thing started to make sense.

I realized that for just one brief little fragment of a moment, for the few seconds that it took to snip those 14 strips of plastic, I was thinking about the bigger picture, the global environment and my part in protecting it and making it a better place.

I was thinking that clipping a hi-cone really wasn't a very significant contribution, considering all the environmental problems in the world, but that every small thing I do leads me to an interest in doing something else, something more, something that sets an example for other folks and maybe someday will make a difference.

With a flash of clarity, I understood that it doesn't matter whether the task is washing out a used tin can, rinsing out a glass jar for the recycling bin, scraping the carrot tops and garlic skins into the compost bucket, picking up a gum wrapper or a styrofoam cup along a neighbourhood trail, or separating all of the little pieces of wood ends from a construction project into a box for the sauna—every moment I spend doing some little thing gives me time to think about bigger things, and what more I can do to help.

This is part of what sustains my commitment to the environment. It starts in the place we call home and branches out from there into the community and then all over the Yukon and eventually the country and the whole planet. We set the tone in our own backyard and then we can't help it, we just want to do more…and we start paying attention and making decisions based on what we know. This influences other people and inspires them to think differently too.

I realized that I started thinking about litter as a kid. I'd pick up gum wrappers and encourage my friends to stick their garbage into their pockets. Now, most of the decisions I make have an environmental component. I shop for used clothing; I make regular excursions to the local landfill for bicycle parts, lumber, plumbing pieces, old windows and doors and other useful items. Lots of Yukoners are doing the same thing. It's really quite wonderful!

Most of our little greenhouse is made from reused stuff. I know three other people who thought they couldn't afford to build a greenhouse but once they saw what could be done, they started collecting the materials they needed and discovered that it wasn't going to cost much after all. Maybe someday we'll all be producing our own tomatoes instead of enduring the flavourless Californian imports.

Until five or so years ago, only a few people in Whitehorse knew what composting was. Even fewer were actually doing it. Now, largely through the efforts of a non-profit composting group, lots of people are either using compost produced by R.O.T.S. (Recycle Organics Together Society), or composting in their own yards. It took several years of dedicated effort to find out what works in a northern climate, but the group's research and education projects are bringing big rewards!

Think about it—if we all produced home-grown vegetables, there might be fewer trucks coming up the highway, which would save fossil fuel and perhaps protect the calving grounds of the Porcupine caribou herd from oil and gas development forever! We can only hope.

My partner and I are building an energy efficient house. One of our original decisions was to finish the interior, by reusing materials wherever we could. We started collecting old doors and interesting pieces of wood and tile and old sinks and lamps. When I decided to buy good quality taps and faucets for the kitchen, I could justify the cost because of what I saved on the double stainless sink I found at the dump!

Yukoners are addicted to yard sales. It's a weekend ritual for hundreds of people. They spend Friday evenings making lists of addresses and maps to each sale and what time each one starts so they can score the best stuff before someone else gets it. The treasures one can find in somebody else's garage are amazing. But every person who's out at a yard sale buying old stuff is shopping for less new stuff. That helps to keep things out of the landfill, and again, it might even mean we're importing less from outside.

Still, look at the high expectations of our small population—what we bring up the highway and at what cost. It's greedy at best. We have to stay mindful of the resources that we have here and how we can make them last longer and get more use out of them.

There's no way we will ever achieve complete self-sufficiency here in the Yukon. We will always be dependent on the industrialized south to provide us with finished products. This doesn't really matter though, since we're part of a global community anyway and that means global exchange of resources.

So I'm going to keep clipping those damn hi-cones and thinking about endangered species and deforestation and global warming. I'm going to keep setting an example and trying to live as light-impact as I can…and I'm going to listen with my heart and try to touch the lives of others with this inspiration. Something inside me wants to know for sure that we never stop trying to make it better.

Activist builds forest from "green" mail

by Jeff Brown

A pro-development activist recently completed a miniature forest in his backyard—made completely of junk mail from environmentalists. From Sierra Club petitions to Greenpeace stickers, J. Myron Wheedle's stacks of literature resemble a forest of sorts, ranging from a few feet high to "some real old-growth" stacks towering as high as two-hundred feet.

"I sent in a few dollars to stop the clubbing of baby harp seals, and before you could say 'database' I was on the mailing list of hundreds of organizations looking for a handout," Wheedle shouted, knee-deep in a pile of recent literature.

"I'd tape a penny to their postpaid card just to keep on their lists. Look at this 'tree' here, it's less than six months old and already it's over a hundred feet high!"

Not willing to stop there, Wheedle has also collected the Cave of Catalogs, the Bill Billboard, and the Magazine Mountain, all scheduled to open for visitors next summer.

Visit the parklands of Alaska!

Junk cars to move to Mars

by Jeff Brown

City officials, long stymied for a place to tow abandoned vehicles, have teamed up with NASA officials to place them on future space shuttle trips to the red planet.

"They'll be perfect for ballast; they'll help track solar winds; and, perhaps most meaningful to those here, make an interesting abstract viewed from earth," said Don Carol, a spokesperson for the Jet Profusion Laboratory.

Perhaps most unusual will be the newly-designed pick up system. As the shuttle makes its first orbit around the earth, it will drop a long cable which will hook onto a special receiving unit near the Rock Dump, and carry the load (of up to 50 vehicles) off to space and the final destination of the craft.

"Even if they miss and take the Federal Building, it wouldn't be a big loss," according to one city official, Jan Mark, who declined to be named.

With the shuttles going off to space with increasing frequency, the capital city should be able to clear its junked cars within six to eight months. After that, trailers not meeting City Cleanliness Codes might be next in line.

"As long as we've got a pipeline to space, I say, 'The sky's the limit!'" she continued.

THE MAGIC AND THE MESS

by Lewis Rifkind and Joy Snyder

The original Yukoners did not produce garbage. Everything was useful, from moose guts to twigs on the ground. Then euro-centric civilization arrived and with it disposable consumer items. It was exactly then that the Yukon garbage problem started. First, waste was thrown into rivers. When that became unacceptable it was burnt. When that, in turn, became unacceptable, it was buried—at least in Whitehorse. And it is still being buried, right to this very day.

We now realize that garbage is comprised of valuable resources. Within Whitehorse, there exists a composting organization, and most Yukon communities have recycling centres, all devoted to diverting resources from landfills. As noble as the goals of these groups are, there is an inherent flaw in their diversion and recycling philosophy. They are not combating the problem of mass over-consumption that our society encourages. Everything shipped in from outside comes excessively packaged, and even in the north, we feel the pressure to own one of everything our southern neighbours have. It is up to individuals to reduce their own consumption so that there is no garbage to go to the landfill and also, ideally, none going to recycling or composting. Landfills, recycling and composting organizations should, by educating individuals, be trying to put themselves out of business due to lack of waste.

The above idea is neatly summed up in the 3R approach—Reduce, Reuse and Recycle (or compost). The emphasis should be on reducing, but in the Yukon it has been on recycling. That is because it is easy to gain government support and funding for activities that produce concrete products and, theoretically, revenue. This leads to the scenario where consumer guilt is appeased when purchasing an item just because it comes in a recyclable container. But it is no use doubling the amount you recycle if you double the amount you consume. Recycling is an inefficient way to conserve resources.

The first European inhabitants of the Yukon, even though they produced garbage, were a thrifty bunch. Isolated from the outside world for long periods of time, they had to be self-sufficient. Items brought with them had to last, and if they did not they were fixed on the spot as nothing else was available. If an item was no longer needed, it was adapted for use as something else. A simple example is socks ending up as a rug.

However, we post-war children have learned to love our disposable consumer items and the accompanying over-packaging. It is now time to look back to the lifestyle of our thrifty ancestors.

What can you do to reduce and reuse? First, reduce. That does not mean you have to live a life of monastic simplicity—but it would help. Buy, hunt or gather only what you need. Also, buy in bulk. Make sure when buying in bulk you are actually purchasing less packaging. Less packaging means less waste. To help hip and savvy consumers, the Raven Recycling Centre has a Shop Smart program. It educates consumers to choose items that produce less waste.

Then reuse. It doesn't matter if the item's original function is changed in the reusing. A refrigerator can become a raised flower bed or a meat smoker. To encourage reusing, some recycling centres and landfills have "reuse tables" or free stores. In addition, certain Yukon landfills tolerate salvaging. It can be a great place to find stuff, especially construction items. Some locals consider landfill trips like shopping excursions.

Failing reducing or reusing, recycle. Go ahead, feel good about handing in refundables and recyclables. But don't spend the refund money on more popcans or beer bottles. Break the consumption cycle and brew your own beverages in reusable containers. Being hippie and yuppie at the same time is what being a Yukoner is all about.

POSTCARD: JEFF BROWN

PHOTO: ARNOLD HEDSTROM

Recycling

141

Quilted Potholder

instructions and drawings by Barbara Hanulik

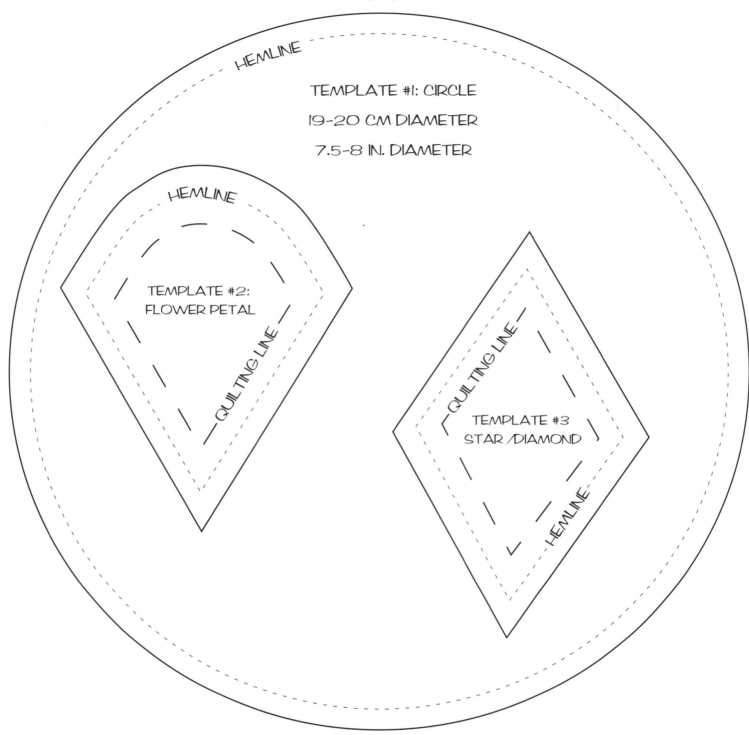

HEMLINE

TEMPLATE #1: CIRCLE

19-20 CM DIAMETER

7.5-8 IN. DIAMETER

HEMLINE

TEMPLATE #2:
FLOWER PETAL

QUILTING LINE

QUILTING LINE

TEMPLATE #3
STAR /DIAMOND

HEMLINE

Recycling

uilting has recently become very popular here in the Yukon. Consequently, there should be enough quilting remnants available in your neighbourhood for you to use in other projects. On cold winter nights, you can whip up some beautiful, useful potholders with the scraps, just like my grandmother did before the turn of the century. This job doesn't require special sewing talents. It's a unisex effort, and all the trappers in your cabin can contribute to the cause.

Besides colourful cottons, you need old towels, sweatshirts, t-shirts and/or underwear for batting and insulation, plus scissors, needles, pins, and thread. You also need to copy the three patterns, or "templates" as they are known in the quilting world, onto heavy paper or cardboard. With them, you'll be able to make either the "flower" potholder consisting of six "petals," or the "star" potholder consisting of six "diamonds."

For each potholder, you need a top round piece (#1), a bottom piece (another #1), assorted batting or insulation pieces (#1), your six petals or diamonds (#2 or #3), and a 70 cm bias strip to go around the edge.

Begin your efforts by cutting template #1, and either #2 or #3, out of several different colours and patterns of material. Along with these, be sure to cut bias (diagonal) strips 2.5 to 3 cm wide along the diagonal of the material

for edging. Short pieces can be connected to make the 70 cm. You also need to cut #1 patterns out of your insulation material. My grandmother used old towels and cotton underwear but today our sweatshirts make great batting, minus all the paint and rubberized decorations. The dark ones can be covered with rounds of white T-shirts to keep them from showing through.

Your first potholder will take a lot of time to put together; the second one only half that amount of time; and if you make a dozen of them you'll quickly get an assembly line operation going that will really produce for you.

And now for the first potholder, the one that you will never give away.

STEP 1

Gather six "petals" (Template #2) in whatever colour combination you choose. Pin two of them, right sides together, inside, and with needle and thread, sew one side from A to B on the straight side along the hemline. Pin a third petal right side down to what will be the centre petal. Sew that seam from A to B. Opened out, you will see half the flower.

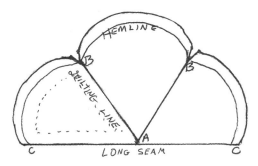

Do the same with the other three petals. Then pin the two right sides together, petal to petal, and sew the long seam (C to C). I do this work by hand allowing 1-cm seams (the continuous line shown as the hemline on the templates), and I press the seams. If template #3 is used, you will finish with a star, good to use with Christmas prints.

STEP 2

Pin the flower, right side up, to the centre of a contrasting colour background round (template #1) that has been backed with one layer of batting of any kind. Turn the raw edges of the flower under at the 1-cm hemline, and pin with as many pins as it takes. You might like to press those edges under. With matching thread, hemstitch the flower to the background, removing the pins as you go. Try to keep these stitches hidden as much as possible, and leave the central pins in place.

STEP 3

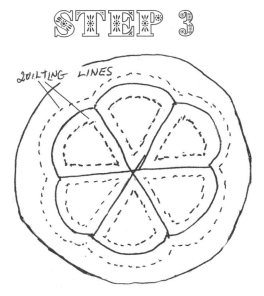

To quilt the petals, use a contrasting colour thread, and run a series of small stitches about 1 cm inside the seams you have made (dotted line on the template), catching the batting layer but not necessarily going through it. Quilt another line of these stitches around the outside edge of the flower.

There are some artistic rules and regulations concerning fancy quilting, and you can contact an expert if you want to learn about them. But for utilitarian potholders, running a contrasting line of small stitches 1 cm from the seams will pass as decent enough quilting.

STEP 4

Before putting the potholder together, the bias strip must be sewed to the quilted top round. Pin the strip, right sides together, about 1 cm from the edge, where the dotted line runs on template #1. When pinned properly it will tend to ruffle toward the centre. With needle and thread, sew the strip on with a basic running stitch, and connect it to itself where it meets on the circle. Trim any excess.

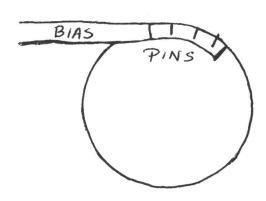

STEP 5

Leave the bias strip unturned until you have pinned the rest of your batting layers, and your choice of back piece (another #1) together. Occasionally you will have to trim the batting circles in order to get everything together.

When all the layers are pinned on, turn over the bias strip and, turning the raw edge under, pin it to the bottom round. It should be hemmed as unobtrusively as possible with matching thread. If all has gone well, this bias strip will form a rim around your potholder holding all the layers together.

You can make a hanger for your potholder by sewing a 1 cm by 12 cm strip of material. Start with a strip 4 cm wide, and turn in the raw edges and hem. Sew one end of this strip beneath the bias on the front, and the other end beneath the bias on the back. It creates a loop on the edge of your potholder with which to hang it up on a kitchen hook.

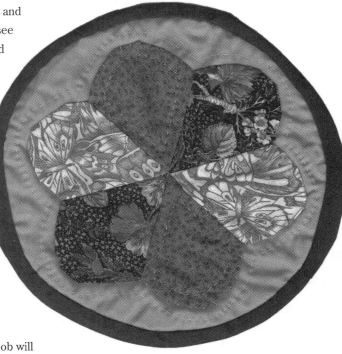

Your family, friends and neighbours will see your colourful quilted potholders (perhaps matching their quilt or your quilt) and demand one or more of their own. The next thing you know, you'll be turning out potholders for everybody you know. The kids can be called upon to help. After that first slow, sweated-over potholder is done, the job will become a fun one around the fire at night.

I have been describing my grandmother's century old design, but I'm sure you artistic ones out there can come up with square designs, log cabin types, and your own special quilting methods. And from here you go directly into matching placemats, table runners, and—aha! But that's another story.

ODE TO THE BUCKET

I n this enlightened era of the three Rs (reduce, reuse, recycle), blessed is the woman, man or child who knows the value of a good bucket. The bucket may one day occupy a special place in the archives of northern history, an artifact of the great northern quest for self-sufficiency.

Recycling buckets has reached uncommon levels of genius and innovation in the far north. Northerners will search far and wide for this coveted treasure. Buckets can be found hidden in the back laneways of town eating establishments, or propped behind chainlink enclosures.

Necessity has been called the mother of invention. In the case of the north, survival may be a more appropriate word, for this is the land of survival under harsh conditions where women and men have pitted themselves against the elements—and seldom have they "pitted" themselves without the handle of a bucket nearby.

Buckets pop from the landscape in a vast array—grey, blue and black petroleum pails, bright white and yellow vessels which once held salad oil and mayonnaise, prized plastic vats once home to pickles and peanut butter, and retired ice cream pails which boasted the exotic contents of Mocha Delight and Almond Swirl. All of these have found their way into many a northerner's backyard, and some have come even closer to the northern soul.

The assorted pails scattered across the backyards of the north are as colourful as the lifestyles they represent. Petro pails once brimming with viscous oils are now overflowing with Kobuk and Field and Farm, for what respectable musher is there anywhere in the north who does not have pails gracing the dogyard? The pail is the workhorse of the northerner's existence and I have seen mushers with shovel and pail in hand, attacking the dogyard with a fierce glint in their eye. Some enterprising Yukoners have recycled an entire fleet of used plastic drums to house their kennel of furry friends. From all accounts, the dogs are quite happy (except for one energetic husky who rolled to the bottom of the dogyard!).

Of course, our northern foremothers and forefathers knew the value of an honest bucket before the days of modern plumbing (the infamous "honey bucket"). Countless buckets have been positioned in unobtrusive corners on howling cold nights which threatened to freeze vital parts if one dared venture out on the wintry trail to the facilities.

The value of the recycled bucket has penetrated deep into the northern psyche. Many northerners have parked their bottoms on the firm base of a dependable bucket to contemplate life and await the bite of an ice-bound trout, afterwards using this same portable stool to carry their catch home. Many have cached their bait or precious rations by hoisting an old reliable pail into the heights of a spruce tree or turned to the same, as to a trusted friend, to bail out the bottom of a leaking canoe. It is a common northern experience to spend an evening gathered around the campfire in amiable conversation, perched on the butt of an overturned pail.

Prizewinning pickles have been soaked in the salty brine at the bottom of a recycled pail and more than one lacy undergarment has been swished delicately around the smooth walls of a household washing bucket. For tougher jobs, the pail and plunger have substituted, depending on the agitated state of the user, for the most modern washing device. In the raging blast of a northern forest fire, it is the savvy bush-dweller who has lined up a bucket brigade in a last ditch effort to save all worldly possessions, and it is the dependable little corner bucket which is rotated from drip to drip in many northern cabins when the deep freeze of winter thaws into the torrent of spring melt-off.

For the northern gardener, the bucket has reached lofty heights—a treasured item in every northern greenhouse whether holding tender young seedlings (many perfect tomatoes and cukes have grown up from the depths of an old peanut butter pail), plunked over young plants as a friendly frost cover or heaped to the brim with prized discards for the compost pile. In testimony to its versatility, the bucket has also found its way to the top of the sauna bench. The Great Northern Sauna would not be complete without a select array of bucketry—one for washing, one for rinsing, one for dirty children, one for dirty feet and one for holding snow to rub into the skin in an invigorating ritual guaranteed to make one glow with new-found health.

Since time immemorial people have harvested the fruit of the land and the utility of the pail is not to be overlooked. It is a proud northerner who heaves a bucket up the mountainside, filling it with red, blue and black berries which shimmer like jewels at the end of a hard day's picking. These same brimming pails have been used as holding vessels to squeeze their precious contents into jams and jellies and wines kissed by the northern sun.

Not to be forgotten is the northern tradition of "wrapping up the moose." When a northerner gathers family and friends to tackle the awesome task of packaging a moose for the winter freezer, a line-up of buckets becomes an efficient assembly line aptly labelled "stew meat," "burger" and "give it to the dogs." The waste of wild meat is equal to the most serious of crimes.

Then there are the haulers of water—those tough Yukon women and men who have strengthened their character by heaving buckets to cabin and bush camp and homestead. The patience and fortitude of many have been tested over the sloshing rim of a bucket about to spill its contents on an icy patch of trail. The very backbone of the north has been moulded in the ongoing relationship between woman, man and bucket. I raise an icy cheer from the depths of a snowpacked pail in tribute to this symbol of northern fortitude and practicality—the sturdy, dependable, reusable, recyclable (though sometimes leaky!) bucket.

Northerner's first law of water conservation: when you must haul your own water, the amount of water used is inversely proportional to the number of buckets which must be carried!

story and photos by Suzette Delmage

Cozy car cover

PHOTO: JENNIFER ELLIS

For those without plug-ins

Jennifer   *Ellis*

The romance of living in a little log cabin in the woods, with the golden glow of kerosene lamps, the radiant heat of the woodstove, the hum of the propane fridge, can be quickly overshadowed as the thermometer dips below minus 25 and the battle to get the car started in the morning looms. Without the convenience of electricity and plug-ins, I learned that keeping the battery inside overnight is a typical tactic used to get a frozen vehicle to turn over the next day. However, after the first winter of wrestling the battery out of the car and into the cabin—without dropping the frozen plastic, acid-filled box or turning the front of my coat into Swiss cheese—I decided to spend the next summer rigging up something a little more efficient for winter number two.

Based on a prototype developed by the previous cabin dweller, I began collecting materials, mostly salvaged, to build a mini-garage: wooden pallets, plywood, a couple of pieces of 2 x 4, chicken wire, fibreglass insulation, tar paper, plastic, a few sections of old stovepipe and some bricks. Oh, yes, and an old bedsheet.

Using the pallets as walls and the plywood as a roof (with chicken wire to hold the insulation in place), I constructed a crude insulated box—with a wind and squirrel barrier—into which I could drive the hood of my car. The bedsheet was used to make curved insulation-filled pillows which filled the spaces above, beside and below the car at the front of the shelter.

The key to making the shelter work in the coldest of winter days was to dig a ditch from the inside of the shelter to a few feet outside and line it with old stovepipe and red bricks. A tiger torch—a large propane-fired torch about two feet long—was the final, and critical, tool. Once lit, the torch could be slipped into the stovepipe allowing the heat, but not the flame, to come up directly under the car. In addition to absorbing some of the heat for the night, the bricks helped to buffer the root-riddled ground when the pipe began to glow red.

I discovered that down to about minus 25, the shelter would keep the car, if driven late the previous day, warm enough to start the next morning without any additional heat. Any colder than that and I was forced to light up the torch and slide the long bar with rumbling blue flame into the stovepipe. With only the heat coming up under the car, I wasn't worried about literally torching my car (a possibility I have heard others have experienced…though that could be just a northern myth). A few minutes at night and another zap in the morning before breakfast, and the car was ready to turn over even at 40 below. Not wanting to leave the torch unattended, I spent the warming time doing jumping jacks to keep my own battery going.

Overall, both my coats and language were much cleaner in the winters that followed. It wasn't exactly necessity, nor was it fully my invention, but the mini-garage served me well. However, for some reason, the next tenant didn't appreciate that the beauty was in the convenience, and many of the construction materials were returned to the landfill whence they came.

Recycle those skis!

Adironski
- western red cedar frame
- stainless steel fasteners included

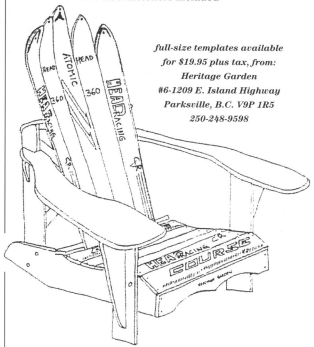

Recycled bird

by Muffy Macdonald

I have a northern flicker in my freezer. Don't get me wrong—I like birds. I fed them year-round until somehow we got cats. (Kids will talk you into anything!) Now it seems a little sadistic to feed the birds, as they in turn feed the cats. (I am patiently waiting for the cats to die.)

But back to the flicker—it has been in my freezer for two years now; it is too beautiful to dispose of. Alas, those pretty picture windows can be lethal to our feathered friends, and that is how the flicker in my freezer met its demise. I ran outside the minute I heard the thud, but this bird had died instantly. It was so beautiful! I wanted my sons to see it when they came home from school, so I packed it in a zip-lock bag and stored it in the freezer. The boys were saddened to learn it had died, but impressed by its colourful markings.

As time went by, I began to wonder what to do with that flicker in my freezer. Since it was in perfect shape (albeit dead), I thought, why not have it stuffed so we can continue to appreciate its beauty? I called a local taxidermist, gasped when I learned how much it would cost, and also discovered I needed a permit to have it stuffed.

Months passed as I mulled over the cost of taxidermy, but finally I called Renewable Resources. To my surprise, they could not issue me a permit because the northern flicker is considered a migratory bird in the Yukon. I would have to write to Delta, B.C. for the permit!

Well, there is no end to this story…yet. Procrastination has left that letter unwritten and the flicker frozen in my freezer.

P.S. A silhouette of a hawk in flight placed in the deadly window seems to work well to prevent the untimely death of our feathered friends.

Recycling

145

PHOTO: MUFFY MACDONALD

R E C Y C L I N G ?

Top 10 Reuses For A Wooden Pallet

(available free at all decent landfills)

by Lewis Rifkind and Joy Snyder

10. Put stuff stored outside on top of one to keep from freezing on the ground.
9. Taste something bland.
8. Very large paperweight.
7. Build a composter.
6. Stack a lot on top of each other for a handy food cache.
5. Rack them side by side, cover with plastic and use as a greenhouse.
4. Lash six together, cover with plywood and raft on down to Dawson.
3. Drive over one and use remnants as weenie roasting sticks.
2. Chuck a couple into the bush and charge tourists lots to see gold rush artifacts.
1. Burn that sucker. Heat your cabin all winter.

Recycling

WHY I GOT MY EARS PIERCED

by ML

The most elegant and classy waitress I ever knew was Jane at the Taku Bar in Whitehorse. She wore her sleek blonde hair long and loose, although it never strayed onto the tray of drinks or dipped over her shoulders as she bent to retrieve empty bottles and glasses. Her smile was as warm and sincere to the high-falutin-dirty-mother-drinking-big-tipping-miners as it was to the down-and-out coffee sippers like myself. She wore homemade but stylish demure clothing that perfectly fit her flawless figure. Simple gold earrings that she wrought herself, and sometimes sold to discerning customers, flashed in the dim bar lighting as she moved gracefully among the tables.

When my dog, Polar, and I tramped the seven miles to town from Croucher Creek across the Yukon River, down the sawmill road, either to cash a U.I.C. cheque or send out for one, we never failed, before making the homeward trip, to stop at the Taku to admire Jane. My not-so-faithful-dog companion would wait outside the side entrance for me until I was either too broke or sufficiently fortified enough to head out for another week. I ate an awful lot of oatmeal and rice that winter on Croucher Creek, especially when a U.I.C. cheque arrived late, but I don't recall ever getting too low on dog food. Polar certainly wasn't used to gnawing on steak bones and eating leftovers, but I treated him well and we tolerated each other's company for lack of something better.

I was feeling about as well fortified as one beer for the road could get me when I noticed Jane was busier than ever at the kitchen window, loading up with tall, thin, sliced beef sandwiches. She could effortlessly deliver six plates at a time. I resolutely shouldered my pack of groceries (more rice and oatmeal) onto my back and as Jane came back for one last call at our table for "happy hour" I politely asked if I could get a few bunwich leftovers for

my dog. Jane looked towards the glass pane door which looked as if it had Polar's thick fur frozen right into it. He fixed his most sorrowful look upon her. "Oh, the poor little thing," she crooned sweetly. "I'll see what we have." I stepped outside to wait with Polar and within minutes she passed out a huge cardboard platter of steamy "leftover" beef. "He looks so hungry, poor little guy," she said as she flashed one of her warmest smiles before disappearing back inside the bar.

I looked at Polar, then at the meat. I began to cram handfuls of hot sliced beef into my mouth. Then the door opened and there stood Jane, so aghast at my blatant thievery from my dog that she nearly dropped the bowl of water she carried. "Just testing to see if it was good enough to eat, Jane," I managed to say with my mouth full and pieces of beef flapping between my teeth. She smiled tightly and shut the door. She took the water with her.

Determined to prove what a person of class I really was, the next U.IC. cheque I received I went to Jane and ordered a pair of gold earrings. I didn't have pierced ears so Jane kindly consented to pierce them for me in her shop.

I never have been able to wear the earrings because those holes have been infected for 15 years.

But the beef was good anyway.

CARTOON: DOUG URQUHART

146

ON THE MOVE

CHILKOOT TRAIL MARATHON

by Sarah Locke

"**S**arah, you're getting ready to head up the Golden Stairs. It's not far to the summit now." We were scrambling up the steepest section of the Chilkoot Pass when Sue's words put a historical fix on our location. More than 30,000 goldrushers had used this route a century earlier. The Chilkoot was billed as the "shortest route to the Klondike," but getting over it was no easy matter in those days.

The most famous historic photograph of the Chilkoot was taken at the Golden Stairs. It shows a line of people, backs bent under heavy loads, struggling up the pass. The photo was taken in April, when the mountain was still smothered in snow. The goldrushers look like pack animals. They look miserable.

Stampeders were required to haul enough goods over the pass to last a year because the Canadian government didn't want them to starve in the goldfields of Dawson City. It took them an average of 20 trips to get their gear over the Chilkoot Pass. Twenty trips up and 20 trips down the Golden Stairs. The people in the photo were probably contemplating a section of trail they already knew far too well.

As we continued towards the summit, I could only wonder at how times have changed. Sue, Leona and I had set out to cover the route in just one day, so we were travelling light. All our gear was crammed into fanny packs around our waists. At the trailhead, we'd agonized over every extra ounce, searching for the perfect combination of high-tech microfibres and polypropylene to take along. Instead of flour and lard, we were packing Power Bars and sport drink.

None of us had done a long mountain run like this before. When I mentioned the idea to Leona, she had a very honest reaction. "Are you crazy?" But it didn't take her long to buy into the idea. Running the Chilkoot in September. What a great way to celebrate the end of summer. One last hurrah before the start of our six-month northern winter.

We knew quite a few people who'd made the same trip. Most importantly, I was quite sure that at least some of them were not masochists. If they could describe it as a worthwhile experience, maybe I could too.

As we reached the summit, I looked for the spot where the Royal Northwest Mounted Police had set up their machine gun. The pass marks the international border, but its location was disputed during the gold rush. The Mounties were charged with defending Canadian sovereignty and ensuring that the goldrushers, who were mainly American, paid their duties.

The view from the summit is stunning. Look back to the south and you see tidewater in the Lynn Canal. Pass through a narrow defile, stepping over decaying burlap and leather mule collars, and classic mountain vistas open up in front of you.

Both Leona and Sue had backpacked this route on several other occasions, and were astounded that we had vistas to look at. On their previous trips the pass had always been shrouded in mist and rain.

The summit also marks the dividing point between the coast and the interior, and is notorious for its stormy weather. But today, here we were, sitting in shorts and t-shirts under clear blue skies.

As we started down the other side of the pass, I had to remind myself that our little adventure was far from over. We'd done the hardest half of the trip, but we still had 28 kilometres to go. We looked forward to the different landmarks to measure our distance.

Somewhere between Crater and Long lakes, I heard Leona call out. I'd been lost in a long distance reverie, and hadn't seen the mountain goats about 10 metres above the trail. We watched four adults and two kids cross the ridge, pausing on the skyline before continuing out of view. Six mountain goats silhouetted against a brilliant blue sky. We'd been too lucky for words.

As we continued along, I lost interest in the trials and tribulations of the sourdoughs. We had our own problems to worry about. We weren't out to set any speed records and would gladly have taken longer rest breaks, but our muscles wouldn't allow it. I'd stop to read an interpretive sign and feel my legs start to stiffen before I'd finished the last sentence. Time to move on.

Lindeman Lake was my personal low point. The goldrushers set up a tent city here and began building boats for their trip down the Yukon River to Dawson. At one point more than 4,000 stampeders were camped here, searching the hillsides for timber.

I could see the site of Lindeman City below us. I knew it would be a fascinating place to visit, full of artifacts, but at that point I wouldn't have walked one extra step to see it. We'd already covered the distance of a marathon, my knees hurt, and the map at the trail junction had confirmed that we had to go five kilometres more than we'd expected.

Eventually I did get a second wind, plus a major pick-me-up when Leona's partner, Carl, met us on the trail. He had real food to offer. Cheese and bread have never tasted so good. Before we knew it, we were at the parking lot at Log Cabin. We'd been on the trail for 12 hours, and we weren't even staggering.

On the drive home to Whitehorse, we were treated to one of the spectacular displays of light and colour which transform the skies here. Streaks of clouds, tinged with red, floated over the mountains. This "Ted Harrison sky" was the perfect finish to an exhilarating day.

Historians say that many goldrushers came north looking for adventure as much as a chance to strike it rich. I wonder whether packing a ton of goods over a high mountain pass fit their definition of adventure. It's not the sort of challenge that would appeal to me. In the late twentieth century, a one-day run over the Chilkoot was enough of a good challenge, especially when it could be followed by a hot bath.

ON THE MOVE

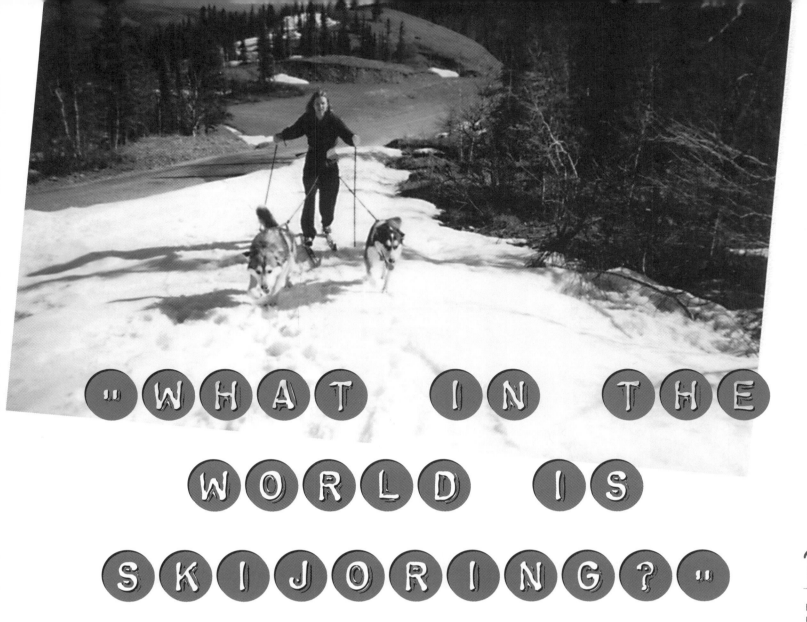

PHOTO: KATE MADDIGAN

"WHAT IN THE WORLD IS SKIJORING?"

Skijoring is a fast growing sport of Scandinavian origin. Basically toned-down dog mushing, it involves using one to three dogs in harness pulling a cross-country skier.

The extra momentum provided by a dog allows for longer trips and more glide to the stride. Climbing hills becomes much easier. A delicious adrenaline element is added.

But perhaps the most satisfying aspect of skijoring is working as a teammate with a healthy and happy animal.

Assuming you have a dog and skis, an investment of about sixty dollars will get you started at skijoring.

If you don't have a dog, there are options available. Perhaps a neighbour's dog is dying to get off the chain. Local shelters are filled with potential work buddies. Be aware, though, a large working dog requires much care, food and year-round exercise.

A quality dog harness that fits your dog properly is of key importance. The end piece (that attaches to the rope) should just reach the end of the back.

Next, a strong line (around two to three metres) is needed to connect skier to canine. Specialized cords include a bungee cord section to ease the strain of quick starts and stops.

Finally, a padded hip-belt with a quick release (very handy) is needed. In a pinch, a decent backpack can be used.

What makes a good pulling dog? Generally speaking, Mexican hairless are out, but any dog over about 30 to 40 pounds can be taught to pull. Besides physique, a keen attitude is very important. Many dogs will be initially shy or sour on the prospect of pulling. It's just a matter of helping them discover their inner wolf.

The ideal age to start training is around six months. First, get the dog used to wearing a harness. Slowly ease it into the idea of pulling (a tire in the summer, a weighted sled in the winter).

It works well to tell the dog to stay and then call it to you. Praise the dog lavishly. When it realizes you're very pleased with pulling, you're on the right track.

The most important command will depend on the beast. For a mellow dog, "let's go." For a hyper critter, "whoa" takes on supreme importance.

Other commands like "easy," "gee" (right) and "haw" (left) can be incorporated gradually.

Consistency is crucial. Praise for good behaviour, discipline for serious transgressions. Dogs live in a black and white world. When you allow them to get away with stuff, a command becomes an option. This may take several truckloads of patience.

Most trainers disagree with beating or striking their animals. A firm shaking, a disapproving voice and a stare-down will almost always do the trick. Remember, it's important that the dog associates the sport with fun.

Some dogs are used for racing, others for longer treks. It seems dogs, like horses or cars, have different gears. For short dog races, fourth gear is best, while third is preferred for exploring the outback.

Some find the commands "pick it up" or "easy" best for modifying velocities.

For both racing and trekking, it's important to keep the dogs hydrated. This can be accomplished by "baiting" their water with such things as meat scraps and fish oil. Save the feast for after the workout.

Having a dog trained for pulling opens up many enticing options. Groceries, gear, or even children can be pulled on sleds. A wide variety of skiing techniques can be used. Skate-skiing and back country with a dog are just a few exciting combinations.

Snowmobile trails, rivers and ski trails are only a few of the avenues open for winter explorations. It is, however, important to be aware of other trail users.

What does the future hold for this amazing sport? A variety of races are being held annually to promote skijoring. Perhaps one day the dog may even replace gas-guzzling machinery! While this seems unlikely, I do hope others will discover the many rewards of hitting the trails with their house pets.

BY CURTIS VOS

story and illustrations by Wendy Bush

Neither rain nor hail nor sleet nor snow

ON THE MOVE

Every year in the Yukon a group of hardy souls gets together to celebrate and commemorate the first mail run from Carcross, Yukon to Atlin, British Columbia. Gear, dogs, food and driving techniques have changed dramatically since those early days.

The comparisons make one marvel at the stamina and dedication of those hearty souls who travelled in all types of weather, from beautiful clear skies to blizzards, and from good trails and hard ice to no trails and open leads.

The cheechako dog mushers of the 1990s toast the mail carriers of years past.

At 56 pawprints a second, on the trail five hours with one hour off for lunch and two rest stops, that means 3,360 pawprints per minute and 201,600 per hour. If I've computed that right, we left about 1,008,000 prints on Lake Laberge that sunny March day in 1993.

We followed the Quest trail across Lake Laberge north for a few days workout before the scheduled Carcross to Atlin mail run. Trying to get the kinks out.

Had a dog kerfuffel at the beginning. None of the leaders cued up on their commands. Thought I was going to have a flip going down the hill to the lake but the plastic runners kept the toboggan on track, or at least that and my fancy footwork. Thought I was going to bust my knee caps on some of those ice hummocks. Thought I was going to die. It's always amusing to note, after the excitement of takeoff, that you're still alive, there's no broken bones and the dogs are generally headed in the direction you were hoping for.

Dinner that night was freeze-dried stew—not the kind of trip food I'm used to. Richard and Diane always pack light; their mail trips are a lot

Vabik   Taiga

tougher than this one. Usually two weeks long, stretching across parts of the Northwest Territories or Alberta. Re-enactments of courage and the old mail-deliverer adage: "Neither rain, nor hail, nor sleet nor snow, can keep the mail from being delivered"…or however that goes.

Diane begged out of this year's mail run—too much going on at home. As a seasoned dogdriver, presently without dogs, I jumped at the chance to drive the Smith's young dogs-in-training and old-dogs-near-retirement on the 1993 Carcross to Atlin mail run.

And make my first trip to the GREAT WHITE NORTH.

Lara   chuche

March 9th, Muncho Lake Café

Alice (my pet name for the waiter) asked if we'd like coffee. Just dinner, no coffee. It took ages to order, my brain's a little groggy from the hours on the road and I'm slightly confused.

Typical dinner in an old time restaurant—good solid food, no new-veau. Mashed potatoes with gravy, a pork chop, peas and carrots, salad on the side. They're smart—they use cabbage. A group of people from Kansas come in. Women sit at one table—men at the other. I ask them if this is because the men's table manners are poor. They deny the allegation and start asking "Dog Questions."

Are you that lady who won that race in Alaska? How many sled dogs do you have? And so forth. The best was, "Are you a 'County Mounty' or a real Mountie?" Watch the waiter take orders around the restaurant, whilst the other buddy serves coffee and tea. I guess the older fellow is the owner, but he's dressed in Junior High Sorel Boots, white rubber bottoms

with fluorescent pink uppers, jeans that sag in the butt and a ledge from his chest to his belly. Taking an order with those saggy pants. Delightful.

March 10th

Sketch the dog boxes and the names of the dogs in order that they come out. Yuri, Lara, Vabik, Sooka, Smoketu, Zoe, Logan, Taiga, Tamarak, Laska, Inok, Zar, Gar and Chuche. Zar still so shy of me, hides under the truck when I try to feed him.

Liard Hot Springs: Walked up the boardwalk through the marsh, three men in the hot pool, just soaking, enjoying the heat. We get in and then the crew from Kansas chuckled in. 'Bout time we washed our smelly dogdriver bodies, and so on. Down the road again and Richard gives me trooper driving lessons, how to set up and bank corners to get the most out of the curve at top speed. Starting to settle into road trip mode.

Finally reach Whitehorse. Stay in log house.

March 11th

Park east of town near the end of road in a snowbank. Zar comes out from under truck to sniff me delicately for kibble. Stretch out the dogs down the rail line towards Carcross. Snow packed and hard. Children squeal, sing Jingle Bells.

March 15th

Walk down to the marge of Lake Laberge to fill the water pot. A family was out camping with their Alaskan huskies and skidoo support. Smooth and fluid as they lope by, they have 40 km to go before they get to town tonight.

March 18th

My inner alarm is set now for 6:45 am, with 10 minutes to think about getting up and going outside to do dogs. Packed gear and ate a leisurely breakfast. While brushing my teeth, I thought about caribou and ran downstairs to ask Steve about a little chunk of meat. He went out to the shed and hauled out the caribou, threw it over the chopping block and hacked a couple of pieces off for our dinner on the mail delivery. I wrapped them in newspaper and put them in my

Logan.   Zoe

Cather's House 03/14/93

Dog personalities

*story and illustration
by Wendy Bush*

Taiga—a good lead dog! When Taiga wants attention or to be let into his box, the "who who" exclamation is soft yet insistent. He shifts his weight from side to side, pointing his nose in the air. Knows that "gee" means "go to the right" but also considers that "haw" means "right" if that's the direction Taiga would rather go.

My buddy Zar! He works so hard! Pull pull pull. And duck under the truck when I come near. Took to carrying kibble in my pocket as bribes so it would be easier to get him out from under the truck without scraping the hair off his back. That worked well and now he's even playing "pat." I slap his paws and he tries to get away but comes back for more if I stop.

Chuche, so cute! She pops her front feet on the tailgate, stretches her body out and twists her head over to entice you to scratch her belly and rub her ears. So cute! A steady puller! Tuff little black Eskimo dog. Much prettier than any of Bill Thompson's. They all look like the giant rats from the fire swamp in the movie "The Princess Bride." She's a bit skinny—I'd like to see more fat on her back end so she doesn't screech when I put her in the dog box.

pack. We jumped in the truck and headed south from Whitehorse.

Carcross is small. The main street seems only two buildings, one pink, the other tones of brown.

Bill Thompson and his wife, Mike, live back north along the Klondike Highway—half an hour, Bill says, legal, but twenty minutes if he's in a hurry from Whitehorse. Bill is a justice of the peace and started raising Eskimo dogs years ago. Some of those Eskimo dogs are sure barrel-chested and ugly of face. Tomorrow, I guess I'll see how they work.

Bill and Mike have some acres backed on crown land, four horses and about 30 dogs. Four new puppies. Two Germans live in their guest cabin, free of charge. In exchange, they feed the sled dogs and clean up in the morning. Peter and Elka. Bill doesn't think they're very good dog drivers. He shook his head with sadness.

Our pre-mail run evening was spent stamping all the postcards and envelopes that would be hauled along with us—stamped, that is, with the "Carried by Dogteam" stamp and then cancelled with the Carcross postal pounder. Fast and furious, that Bill—he just flew at 'er. In no time, with five and a half of us (I was writing and drawing maps on postcards), they were packaged and ready for the morning's mail packet. In Atlin, they'd be stamped again and

hauled by truck into Whitehorse and flown out by air mail to points worldwide.

March 19th

Up and at 'em, dog chores, hot juice, breakfast for ten—busy house. Didn't have much to do as Mike had it all under control; this was the eighteenth mail run she'd participated in!

Got to the parking lot, unloaded. Geared up. Richard takes off right after Bill and the Eskimo dogs. I follow. The descent down to the lake, although it's not particularly steep, has two opposing bumps and I hit one of them broadside. Flipped over. Got dragged. Braced myself, flipped the toboggan back upright. Continued to be dragged. Braced myself then popped up, stood up on the back board, turned and waved to Steve and Murielle who were worrying on the hill behind me. A musher mentioned it later. "Good save," he said.

Hard packed trail, fast going for the first half of the day. Stopped a few times. A ten-minute sketch of Richard, the Mountie and the dogs. The sun on the snow would have been blinding but we all had on sunglasses to cut the glare. The wind would rise when we sledded way out in the open but mostly we kept in the lee of the mountains and the shore.

When we got to Squaw Point I was leading, but that didn't help much. After thirty miles, the dogs really started to lag, what with the oldsters and the pups. Finally pulled into Bill Thompson's Point, the campground they've been staying in for the last 18 years.

Bill had saved us a spot for the dogs and tent. Used my pink climbing rope for the ridge pole and hoisted it up. Stove was soon set and firewood cut.

My inner picture is of bloody fingers cutting the chunks of meat on a small piece of wood beside the tin stove. Put the caribou on to brown, the rice pilaf on to boil and the apple pie to bake. Yup, that's roughing it. Enough writing, time to crawl into a warm sleeping bag. Tomorrow's run to Atlin will come soon enough.

YURI
Hold still!

Time Out

Encounter

by Al Pope

ILLUSTRATION: CATHERINE DEER

With the absolute conviction that he had lost it this time—race, hope, mind, maybe even chance of survival—Danny struggled against the wind, up the line of curled-up dogs.

This was ridiculous, he thought. Fourth time in the Percy de Wolfe Memorial Mail Run Race, fifteen years of mushing experience. I'm supposed to be one of the wily veterans here.

He left Fortymile, halfway from Dawson to Eagle, and one quarter of the way through the race, in good shape. His team had clipped off the fifty miles from Dawson in under five hours despite blowing snow, warm conditions, and a strong crosswind, and he was far enough ahead of the nearest competition that he couldn't see them. The dogs had eaten well, rested in the shade behind the old trading post, and set out looking ready to go. As they swung back onto the Yukon River, first the dogs, and then Danny, were met by a wall of wind that felt like it would blow them back to Dawson.

Danny had considered turning back to Fortymile to sit out the storm. But that would have meant waiting for the other teams to catch up. This was a dog-race, after all, and one of the few chances to earn back some of the money he'd put into this dogteam. He remembered thinking, "Hell, what would Percy have done?" Right now he was thinking the tough old mail-carrier would have known better than to push his dogs out on that river.

It was four o'clock in the afternoon when Danny had left Fortymile, and here he was, maybe thirty miles further along, at ten o'clock at night, chilled to the bone by the constant wind, the dogs and him exhausted, the trail blown in beyond recognition, and his leaders had just quit. The unthinkable moment had come. Izzy and Mike, the two toughest old huskies in his kennel, a couple of five-thousand-mile veterans, were shut down. As long as Danny was able to pick out the reflective trail markers with his headlamp, they trudged from one to another. But the wind had grown even fiercer, and they couldn't see the next marker through the blinding snow. He had tried to coax them to forge ahead, but they were lost, discouraged, dehydrated, tired, and defeated. In the jargon of the trail, his leaders were blown.

Reaching the front of the team, he took Mike by the harness, and lifted him to his feet. "Attaboy," he said, and thumped him encouragingly on the chest. As he reached to do the same for Izzy, Mike slumped back down into the snow. "All right, Iz, it's up to you," said Danny, rubbing her head as she, too, slumped to the ground.

The first thing Danny did when he got back to the sled was to fish out his Thermos and have a cup of tea. It warmed and hydrated him, and reminded him to do the same for the dogs. Out of the sled he pulled a cooler, half-full of warm water. Digging deeper, he came up with two ziploc baggies, one with dry dog food, the other with scraps of fish. Back into the sledbag again for two dog dishes, in which he mixed water and food.

He battled his way back to the leaders, stumbling and spilling a little of the slop. He placed the bowls down carefully in the snow in front of the leaders, and neither dog even lifted its head to sniff. As he went down the line, offering the same two bowls of food to each pair of dogs in turn, he was fighting off panic.

He scanned the near bank with his headlamp. Into the wind he could make out nothing, but looking backward he saw an overhung cliff, probably fifty feet high. It had no breaks and no end within the range of his vision. As he tried to peer through the driving snow, he was estimating what the chances were, should he spy a trail up the steep bank, of getting himself and his dogs to shelter. Could he walk in front, dragging the leaders behind him through the deep snow? Even if the dogs would follow, would he have the strength to break trail? The speculation proved idle. There was nowhere to go but back.

Back. The word sat on his brain like a sack of defeat. Danny had never turned back; he'd made it a matter of pride. If he turned back now, he would not reach shelter until he hit the post office cabin. No doubt there would be teams there, waiting out the storm, dogs and drivers alike getting a good rest for the trail ahead. If he met them there, his dogs exhausted, he would have blown the race by roaring off into the storm like a dumb rookie. Everyone would know it.

Danny was proud, but he was not suicidal. After another cup of hot tea and

a minute's reflection, he struggled back to the leaders again. First, he stooped to rub their heads and speak soft encouragements, and then, taking hold of the neckline between the two leaders, he pulled them roughly to their feet. "Line out!" he snapped, giving the line a yank to emphasize the point. "All right, haw come." This was the infallible command. Exhausted leaders, frustrated by the lack of trail ahead, never seemed to forget that there was broken trail behind. "Haw come" was the command for the leaders to turn back to the left, and return the way they have come. He had seen tired dogs, dragging their tails on the ground, snap into action at these words.

Izzy looked balefully at Danny, and lay down. Mike drooped beside her a moment, and then collapsed to the snow. "You pot lickers. I said, Haw come." Losing his temper now, he cuffed Izzy on the ear with the back of his mitt, and was raising his hand to do the same for a cowering Mike, when a movement behind caught his eye, and he turned to see that he was being passed by a dogteam.

Of the eighteen mushers entered in the race this year, Danny only knew the seven serious Yukon racers, and a couple of the Alaskans. Some of the entries were local bush teams, and this was clearly one of them. Nine dogs running in old-fashioned, single-file harness, pulling a freight toboggan, with handles made from poles and a canvas tarp covering the load. Probably a trapline team. There were still a few who used the old style rigging. That way they didn't have to widen the old trails, and pave the way for new traffic. The driver was wearing a checked woollen jacket, and what looked to be moosehide pants and vest. He had a blue corduroy cap with earflaps pulled down hard, and a woollen scarf over his face. He raised a big wolf fur mitten in salute as he sailed past. A dogteam would almost always follow another team. Danny was trying desperately to coax his dogs to their feet to chase this one, when a dark shape, looming out of the storm ahead, told him that the unknown driver had stopped his team, and come back.

"Looks like you're having some trouble." The man was shouting a bit, to be heard over the storm.

"You got that right. Hey, do you think you could lead them ahead for me for a bit, see if they get the idea to chase you?"

"We can give it a try." The stranger leaned over, petted Izzy and Mike for a moment, and then, taking them by the neckline, pulled them to their feet. The leaders stumbled up and forward, presumably drawn by the unknown scent of the bush person and his dogs. It was only a few steps through the driving snow to where the other team was parked. The musher stood on the back of the toboggan, and still holding the neckline, whistled to his dogs. Danny could just make out the big, hairy rear end of the wheel dog bouncing up, and striding away. Danny's heart sang out with relief as his team followed after the busher's back. Even after the stranger let go of the line, they trotted along quite willingly. The thought crossed his mind that he was likely to lose the race to this ragtag looking outfit, but he didn't care. Let him have the three thousand bucks, the trophy, the reputation of being the best musher in the Yukon, so long as he got Danny and his dogs off this river alive.

Competition didn't seem to be the first thing on this musher's mind, either, as he dragged his foot to hold his team back, always checking behind him to make sure that Danny was keeping up. He had probably entered the race just for the fun of it, with no thought of winning, and was pleasantly surprised that nature had handed his trail-hardened bush dogs the advantage with this dirty weather. His team was unphased by the wind, and his leaders were obviously well used to river travel. They never seemed to doubt that the trail, whether visible or not, lay straight ahead. Danny was looking forward to stopping for a break along the trail, to talk dogs with this guy.

Remarkably, though, that break never came. The busher and his dogs rolled along, hour after hour, slow and easy, till the river took a swing to the west. Suddenly, the intensity of the wind dropped, and a firm trail was visible in the moonlight, under the lee of a long north bank. Turning around, the musher called out to Danny.

"You okay now?" Danny responded with a thumbs up, the other driver gave a wave, whistled twice, and trotted away down the trail. Knowing better than to ask his tired dogs for anything extra at this point, Danny just leaned on his driving bow, and watched the man's back retreating down the river.

It was another hour before Danny reached Eagle, and half an hour more to get to the checkpoint in the old schoolhouse. There was a flurry of activity as people came out to check his gear, to guide him to a good sleeping place for the team, or just to welcome him to Eagle. A woman wearing a headlamp and carrying a clipboard checked her watch, and recorded his time of arrival.

"Congratulations," she said, "you're the first team into Eagle this year."

"What?" Danny said, confused.

"You're in the lead, didn't you know?"

"Well, there was a guy ahead of me, and I never passed him. Big dogs, freight toboggan. He must have got lost or something."

"More likely a local team, out late. Some of these Eagle mushers are pretty crazy guys, you know. I'll get you to show me your mandatory gear now."

"Okay. Here's my snowshoes, there's my axe. Say, that guy really helped me out of a jam. That's my booties there, do you need to count them? If you ever hear who it was, I'd really like to thank him. My leaders were shut down. I might still be sitting out there if he hadn't come along. Yeah, that's my sleeping bag, and here's my lamp, of course. Thanks a lot, I'm going to go feed these guys, and get some rest."

Two more teams pulled up, just as he was parking his dogs, and a third before he was done feeding. One glance at their dogs told Danny he had blown this one. Only fifteen minutes behind him, these teams were fresh-looking, and happy. In four hours' time he had to head these tired dogs back to Dawson, and two big name Alaskans, as well as last year's winner, would be pulling out just behind him, with fresher dogs. The best placing he could hope for was fourth, his worst performance in three years.

The checkpoint, as always, was noisy and full of old, familiar faces. Although he was exhausted, Danny couldn't even think of sleeping. He ate three bowls of stew and drank five cups of coffee while he talked dogs, trail, trapping, hunting, fishing, snowmobiles, politics and religion, and caught up on some news and gossip about old friends and rivals. When his time was up he was wired from the caffeine and lack of sleep, and he headed out into the dawn shivering and depressed.

Before he was even off the Eagle backroad and back on the river, all three of the other teams had caught up and passed him. He seemed to have no trouble keeping up, and settled in to trot out the second hundred miles. Fourth place paid about seven hundred or so, which would cover expenses and give him some spending cash for the banquet. No sense fretting about first place now.

On the river it was clear that the howling winds of last night had died. The stiff breeze was now at their backs, and the four teams had about as easy a time as it was possible to have on the second leg of a two-hundred-mile dog sled race.

For hours they were meeting slower teams, still on their way to Eagle, and no one was close enough behind to be any threat.

After fourteen hours of keeping the top teams in sight, facing no greater difficulty than trying to stay awake through it all, Danny reached Dawson, where he accepted the moderate congratulations due to a fourth place finisher, fed his dogs and put them to bed in his truck. He headed off to the Downtown Hotel, to sleep solidly till the following morning, Saturday.

After two breakfasts with the other top drivers, Danny headed down to the KVA building to see who had come in during the night, and who was still due. Since there was no action in the parking lot, he went through the side door to the checkpoint. Three tired-looking volunteers were drinking coffee at a long table. To the left stood a chalkboard with the results so far. Most of the teams were recorded into Dawson, and all of the rest, it said, had left Fortymile, and were expected back this afternoon. Not bad, considering the conditions.

Turning to speak to the volunteers, he noticed that the race trophies were at the end of the table. Dominating the picture was the massive engraved moose-antler awarded each year to first place. The pang that Danny felt gave way to sudden surprise when he spied a photograph leaning against the side of the trophy. In it was the musher who helped him get his team moving Thursday night. He was dressed for spring. His sled stood behind him, half on snow and half on mud. His hands were stuffed in his pockets, and on his face was the same look of quiet confidence he wore when leading Danny's dogs to their feet.

"Hey, Barrie, who's this guy?" Barrie turned to his partner, and they both laughed.

"Get serious, Danny, that's the Man himself."

"Huh? What man?"

"Haven't you ever seen Percy de Wolfe before?"

"But he's dead. He's been dead for years."

"Ah, that's a photograph, Dan, they had them back then, too, you know. I think you better get some more sleep before the big banquet there, buddy."

The two were still chuckling when Danny went through the door. A small crowd had gathered in the parking lot. Two teams were crossing the ice bridge, battling it out for fifteenth place, the last place in the money. People were cheering, some for one musher, some for the other. No one noticed that Danny walked away, for once uninterested in the race, as he wandered aimlessly past the weird false-fronted buildings of Dawson.

Alaska Highway Memories

The old red Beetle didn't have a lot of room between the driver's face and the window. If there was any trouble at all with the heater, and the defrost system was even a little bit weak, the window could ice over very quickly just from the breath of the people in the front seat.

This lovely day in late winter, the heater had quit working. That's why my wife was scraping like mad to keep the window in front of me clear, why we were limping along at about 70 klicks, and why our feet were slowly turning to blocks of ice somewhere between White River Lodge and Destruction Bay.

It wasn't actually that cold outdoors—maybe -20°C. One of the drawbacks of the Alexander Beetle (we're A.A. Milne fans) was that the floor never really got warm. You had to wear feltpack boots to be at all comfortable in the car, and although nothing that small needed very much heat at all to keep reasonably warm, it did need some.

We hadn't known the heater was going to play games. There were always times when it would weaken and then come back again, but this time it had stayed out for over an hour.

When we lived in Beaver Creek, there were no medical services at all, except for the occasional visit of a nurse, and one of the customs officers who was a bit of a paramedic.

Neither the dentist nor the ophthalmologist was interested in the small commerce such a trip might produce, so the need for anything beyond cough medicine inevitably meant closing the school on Thursday and driving to Whitehorse for a Friday appointment. The drive took a good eight hours in the Bug, and we didn't do it very many times that first year.

Alexander was unnerving for a few other reasons as well. He wasn't very high off the ground, and, in both winter and summer, we had a bit of trouble negotiating the windrows left behind by the road crews. It was a case of waiting until the move became absolutely necessary, finding just the right angle, getting the car up to speed, and then driving onto the windrow, trusting to luck and Newton's laws of motion to coast us over the hump at the moment when all four wheels were off the ground.

It wasn't too bad a coast in the winter, but that fall and the next spring gave us some real scrapes when we had to do the same thing on gravel. Such a noise!

I didn't realize how much of a problem it was until later the same spring when I was driving along to an administrators' meeting in Whitehorse. There was a lot of water on the road and when I stopped in Destruction Bay to pick up the principal there, we discovered that my briefcase, sitting in a pool of water on the floor in the back, was full of soggy papers.

Skimming through some puddles along the way, I had managed to find all the holes in the undercarriage. Must have looked like a bunch of little squirt guns going off all at once.

The other bad thing about the VW was the sense you had that larger vehicles just couldn't see you. Regular half-ton and three-quarter-ton trucks were bad enough, but Alexander hardly came up to the bumper on the big semi-trailers that were so common, and there were several times when we were sure we'd almost been run down. Maybe it was just paranoia, but it left us with a bad feeling about road trips.

You're wondering about the winter trip though, aren't you? We were miserable, but we survived. We stopped at the Talbot Arm in Destruction Bay for something to eat and a chance to get warm again. When we went back out and fired up the engine, everything worked fine. The heater was back to its normal range of tepid to hot, and it stayed that way for the rest of the trip.

I always thought that perhaps the fuel line to the front trunk where the heater was had blocked up, and that it thawed while we were at the restaurant. Whatever it was, we were grateful.

With all those problems, however, not to mention the need for something bigger to fill up with goodies when we went to the big city, it was no wonder that we sold the Beetle that summer and invested in our first truck. It was an enormous (to us) green Ford half-ton which we christened "The Incredible Hulk."

For a while, we used to see Alexander being driven around Whitehorse when we would come to town, and then he dropped out of sight.

by Dan Davidson

ON THE MOVE

Train Song

by Joseph P. Radwanski

It was thirty below when I went for this walk,
Why isn't it funny how we couldn't talk ?
Tell me when did it all start to go wrong ?
I could sure use a good old Train Song.

Around the next corner a cold engine stalls,
and on a lone street lamp an old Raven calls.
It's the time of the year for movin' on.
I could sure use a good old Train Song.

I could sure use a good old Train Song
— something my heart could help sing along
— something so sad and mournfully strong,
like a good old Hank William's Train Song.

There's no chance of hearing that lone whistle blow,
the White Pass stopped runnin' a long time ago.
Everything good is going or gone.
I could sure use a good old Train Song.

I guess that I'll go see good old Hank Karr,
he's a country picker down at the bar,
and while I'm there I might tie one on.
I could sure use a good old Train Song.

I'm usually quite stiff in the morning. The time I get up depends on when my wheelchair, Bessie, has recharged. I can still get myself dressed and get my breakfast. Although I can still do these things by myself it takes me much longer to do this year than last year. Whether I have to go downtown or just can hang around home and the neighbourhood depends on how I have to plan my day. Because I rely on the Handybus for my transportation I also plan one week, and even two weeks, in advance.

I will tell you about Monday, one of the days I spend downtown. The Handybus comes to get me at 9:30 in the morning and my return trip is at 2:00 in the afternoon. I usually have breakfast at the Gold Rush Inn restaurant as they're fully wheelchair accessible and I can use their washroom without any assistance. The waitress also cuts up my food and caters to my needs as they know me well. After breakfast I usually stop by Audrey McLaughlin's office to visit with her staff. I'm off to the Yukon NDP office to visit with my friend Sid for a few minutes. Then, I'm off on my errands for the day. I visit either the Women's Centre or the Aids Yukon Alliance, depending on the time and if Bessie can go that far—she has broken down several times. I get quite angry when I cannot go to restaurants of my choice; there are very few that I can get into without assistance. I like to eat healthy food just like able-bodied people. Anyway, at the end of my time out, if I've told the Handybus driver to pick me up at Shoppers on Main Street, I whiz back.

It is a more tiring day for me than for able-bodied people. They don't have to deal with sidewalks with inadequate curbs, and businesses, stores, government buildings, agencies and politicians' offices which claim to be wheelchair accessible. This is more aggravating, since I'm hyped up to go and see someone, only to be disappointed. When I get there, I cannot get into the building, or if I do it takes great manoeuvrability on my part.

Today, Whitehorse still isn't wheelchair accessible! We are past the stage of encouraging; we should be in the stage of enforcing physical accessibility and that includes getting rid of the "suicide" ramps. I realize that money is the issue but to me it looks like every time people cut, they first cut off services to people with disabilities. Quite ironic isn't it? We're taxpayers as well. We want to see our money spent on accessibility.

Phone calls are something in themselves. I use a TDD/TTY (Telecommunication device for the deaf). I communicate through my keyboard, rather than my voice. I call the Relay Service in Calgary for assistance since most of my hearing friends don't own a TDD/TTY. The relay operator is my voice to the hearing people. A fifteen-minute call is about a thirty to forty-five minute conversation on TDD/TTY. I also watch TV with a close caption decoder which shows the typed interpretation of the TV program. So I literally "see words" all day!

I usually have a three-hour nap, so my afternoons are taken care of! Then I have supper, watch TV for the evening or make phone calls. I also do many hours of volunteer work at home. I'm involved with many organizations, committees, boards and groups.

I do know that I have more abilities than disabilities, so please let your friends with disabilities use their abilities alongside you.

A day in the life
by Judi Johnny

PHOTO: LINDA HILTON

like to think of myself as a meditator of Bhakti yoga, but actually come from the premise that I'm just an old-fashioned neurotic, a-doin' her thing (and darndest!)…singing and listening to her muses and "hymns to-and-of the Silence." The Universal Pulse, the Divine Orchestration and Intervention! The Cosmic play of like minds and kindred spirits.

For me, it's a grand thank you and salutation to the ol' friends from other lifetimes, who I acknowledge 'a la Julio Iglesia (instead of, "to all the girls I've loved before"…who opened every door," 'tis, "To all the souls I've encountered before," the "doors" symbolically referring to the doors of perception and consciousness, and…of course, the doors of their vehicles).

I've been hitchhiking for many-a-year (probably over seven). The exact date of the initial thrust into the "pot-luck-potpourri," eludes me. My aspiration is to be fully present, in the flow…and to recognize the "no such thing as coincidences syndrome"…the synchronicity of Carl Jung and the "music of the spheres!" The interplay, the weaving of common threads and bonds. To be in the right place at the right time, which is a given (given one is in the so-called integrated right place in their heart). It's an art and a discipline, which I find fascinating. A huge love affair with the "powers that be!" It's a terrific mirror and Buddhist practice for me to watch my monkey mind, my Achilles heel, and all the polarities and kindness in the equation of "N!"

And over and above all my spiritual aspirations, simply put, I just love meeting and unravelling the magical formula of serendipity, the amazing and amusing "whys" of our pulling together! I play with the theme, "If you meet the Buddha on the Road what do you do and say?" notion. I find that the Higher Self of others speaks to me… so there's so much to discover and learn. The "soul purpose" (in a synopsis) is to actually experience and embody the "state of grace"… and to have yet another opportunity to sing my praises! The right people, coming into my life at opportune times. For example, when I was writing in Nelson and Vancouver, I'd have rides with publishers and writers looking for illustrators. When I was working for the Waldorf School in Nelson, my clustering mind would attract fellow-focused folk into my arena. Wherever and whatever my mind is dwelling on, the Universe provides an exciting and healing gift and experience. I evoke the position of no-position, and allow the unfolding… rising into the blissful state of dancing receptivity and joyful turned-on/output! The "radiating yin and yang dynamic"…

Metaphysically speaking, that's my thrill! Now…on a more grounded reality, it's purely to get from A to B. And yet, keeping mindful of the journey, and not so much the destination—to keep that delicate balance of structure and fluidity. The "creative spirit in play," performing in as graceful and enjoyable manner as possible!

I enjoy our Divine Human comedy, with all its paradoxes; the sublime and the ridiculous… and because I do thrive on writing and illustrating, I draw on my experiences as inspiration for songs, stories and plays. The day I jumped at the opportunity to hitch a ride to church, and the driver and companion yelled to "hop into the back of the pickup" I did; it was full of manure! Well! What can ye say?! Experiences with Mac truck truckers, kibbitzing and joking one to the other on walky-talkies, gravel trucks (so far from the ground!), children bursting with excitement, news and the desire to connect!

My experiences have only been more than wonderful, and although some worry for my seeming naivety and disconcern for the "realities of violence," my launching into this lifestyle has proven time and again the "power of One." It's perhaps daring to the dubious, but Helen Keller's maxim of "Life is a daring adventure or nothing" are my sentiments also! (Except that, I might add… "AND" nothing!) Comments, such as from a priest one day: "Thank you for choosing me," set my soul-a-soaring!…He knew what I was about!

I "hitch my wagon to a star" (as thus spake Emerson) and "shift gears at a moment's notice," intuition being the guide. The sheer and shared delight of self-expression and spontaneous, improvised fun…in BEING! I could rhapsodize forever, re: this gypsy mode of "hobo-hobnobbing," but really! All I need to say is… (like the commercial), "Try it, you'll like it!" A challenging and rewarding adventure of trust, faith and reaffirming belief in the Human spirit, and the magic of the inter-connectedness, "behind our ken." I'll keep doing it, and hopefully, one day, write a homage to the beauty of it all!

BY HETTY WILLEUMIER

MY FUN IN "HITCHHIKING"

PHOTO: PETER BECKER

Impressions from an ultralight journey to the Yukon

by Peter Becker

wings to russia

story and illustration
by Blake W. Smith

The exciting and often heroic exploits of our early pioneering bush pilots are well chronicled for their efforts in "opening up" the Yukon and Alaska. Less known and equally interesting and deserving of recognition are the exploits of a small group of American military flyers belonging to the 7th Ferrying Group of Air Transport Command, USAAF. Their mission was simple—deliver lend-lease warplanes, by way of Alaska, to our World War II ally, Russia.

The ALSIB route (contraction of the words ALaska-SIBeria) stretched from Great Falls, Montana, through northwestern Canada to Fairbanks, Alaska—a distance of some 2,000 miles. Russian pilots continued the marathon relay race from Fairbanks, across the Bering Strait and Siberia to the battlefield. The hazards of this sub-Arctic, wilderness route were plentiful —winter weather, poor weather reporting, incomplete navigational facilities and the vastness of the uninhabited land they were overflying. Though the mission of the group was simple, by definition the cost in wrecked planes and lost lives was high. But the urgency of the times demanded the sacrifice.

In all, nearly 8,000 "red-starred" warplanes made their way north through Yukon skies between August 1942 and the termination of hostilities in August 1945. At that time, the 7th Ferrying Group was disbanded. The defeat of Nazi Germany and the survival of the Soviet Union were at least partially accomplished by the availability of lend-lease airplanes delivered through the Yukon (about 10% of all Soviet warplanes were lend-lease). During this period, the airways through northwestern Canada evolved from the primitive domain of the bush pilot to today's modern, safe, efficient services.

① July 29, 1995, 8 a.m., grassfield St. Paul, Alberta with a job: ferry plane to Whitehorse. Finger on Edmonton sheet, to my left a pile of four more VFR charts, total track length 271 x $^3/_4$ inch (6 mile) increments.

② Chinook aircraft:

430	pounds empty
205	pounds pilot
150	pounds fuel
4	pounds sleeping roll, tent
4	pounds oats
40	pounds tools, clothes, misc.
833	pounds gross weight

③ Sky is muffled with thunderstorms here and there roiling up to ignite a fork of lightning, scooting on little wings over the prairie broken up with lakes and bushes, a mosquito buzzing towards the sunny patches illuminated in full fall-like colours. Lesser Slave Lake, aiming for High Prairie, through the horizon slot.

④ Short of Fort St. John, sky turns black right across, landing in a hay field, farmer's response; never a dull moment. Rain slows down, tiptoeing out of the woods comes a doe and her fawn to inspect the strange red bird resting momentarily on their field.

⑤ Clouds are low in the morning. Plan: breakfast in Shell gas station, Charlie Lake. The experience is between the landscape and me. Lonely but not lonesome. I can see dogs and cow cakes sneakily hugging the Fort St. John control zone radius. Peace Valley points the way, crossing it.

⑥ Made Fort Nelson in one long flight leg, only rain drops fell. Alaska Highway from above, peak summer traffic dilutes into the occasional vehicle, surplus room for emergencies.

⑦ Ground fog over Liard Hotsprings. A 360 degree closed rainbow circle on ground with airplane shade centred shows a spot for highway landings with rest area, big eyes in motor homes, boredom and romance.

⑧ Picking weather windows, 30 hours flying stretched into a week, punching through rain curtain between narrow cloud gap at northern end of Teslin; happy trails from Johnsons Crossing to mile eight air field Whitehorse, last landing roll, last pedal shuffle: Hi Lenn, Hi Ken.

⑨ Hey, if you need a barnstormer, there is a whole bunch around.

PHOTOS: LOIS MOORCROFT, (INSET) ROB MATHEWSON

ON THE MOVE

MOE'S AIR SERVICE: FIFTEEN REASONS TO FLY WITH MOE

1. WE GET YOU CLOSE MOST OF THE TIME.
2. TERRORISTS ARE AFRAID TO FLY WITH US.
3. WE NEVER MAKE THE SAME MISTAKE THREE TIMES.
4. REAL PILOTS LAND WHERE THEY WANT TO.
5. SO THAT'S WHAT THOSE BUTTONS DO.
6. WEAR YOUR BATHING SUIT WHEN WE FLY OVER WATER.
7. JOIN OUR FREQUENT NEAR-MISS PROGRAM.
8. ASK ABOUT OUR OUT-OF-COURT SETTLEMENTS.
9. NOISY ENGINE? WE'LL SHUT IT OFF.
10. COMPLIMENTARY CHAMPAGNE DURING FREE FALL.
11. ENJOY THE FREE IN-FLIGHT MOVIE ON THE PLANE NEXT TO YOU.
12. THE KIDS LOVE OUR INFLATABLE SLIDES.
13. OUR PILOTS ARE BANKRUPT AND HAVE NOTHING TO LOSE.
14. WE COULD BE LANDING ON YOUR STREET NEXT.
15. IF YOU THINK IT'S SO EASY, GET YOUR OWN PLANE.

BY MOE GRANT

BALLOONS IN THE YUKON

Yellows, blues, reds and greens floating over the Yukon landscape with only the wind to guide them. Whimsy, fantasy, history, technology and meteorology all combined to fill our February winter skies with hot-air balloons

for a week-long festival during Whitehorse's Rendezvous week.

But why February? The balloonists need our lakes frozen for takeoff and landing. After all, it's a lot easier to pull in a 300-400 kg balloon and wicker basket off a lake than it is to pull it off a mountain.

But February? Isn't it freezing in February? Well, yes, but the winds over the territory are lighter in February than any other time of year. But if the balloons are guided by wind speed only, wouldn't the balloonists want a good stiff wind to push them along? Not if the wind is over 15 kilometres per hour. They want to drift—not rocket over the landscape.

So how did these guys end up here anyway? The Yukon's not really a hotbed of ballooning activity, is it?

The balloonists were all from Germany and they wanted to fly here because of our spectacular scenery, the remoteness and just for the fun of it. Alaska was an option, but with three airforce bases and two international airports, there was too much controlled airspace restricting balloon traffic. In total, five balloons and 22 people attended the festival. Of the eight days they were here, only one day of flying was cancelled due to bad weather. Another day the balloonists booked off so they could have a chance to be tourists and take in some of the sights around Whitehorse. Six flying days in eight is better success than they usually have at home. Sometimes the weather is so bad they can only get in four flights a month. By the time the festival was over, they were glad they could quit flying for a little while.

We drove about 2,000 kilometres in and around the Whitehorse area, to takeoff and retrieval sites. A large area was used to catch the best wind direction so the balloonists could estimate from the ground where they would land in relation to the winds. We had weather-readers stationed at Shallow Bay on Lake Laberge, the Tagish bridge and on Marsh Lake. Our weather reports varied greatly.

Tuesday, February 21. Marsh Lake: -21°C, no wind, high cloud moving southeast to north; Shallow Bay: -12°C, strong winds from the south; Tagish bridge: -18°C, slow wind. The balloonist who was coordinating weather reports for the others couldn't believe the information. How can the wind vary so much in a 80-kilometre radius around Whitehorse? How can the temperature rise and fall like that? We obviously don't know how to read the weather!

With our highly suspect weather information, and reports from the Yukon weather office at the airport, the balloonists decided to head out toward the Tagish bridge. Though we had a late start, by 3 p.m. they were setting up by the side of the road. A busload of school children returning home for the day pulled over to watch. The thirty excited kids leaning out the windows were quite an audience.

Gusty winds delayed some of the takeoffs but by 4 p.m. all the balloons were airborne. The sun beamed down and the wind buoyed the balloons aloft. Gently bobbing through the air, who could have known there was a summer-style hailstorm on the Yukon River bridge at the opposite end of Marsh Lake. Once over the mountain ridge separating the Tagish Road from Marsh Lake, the balloons were whisked along at 30 kilometres per hour—twice the preferred speed of travel.

Three balloons made pinpoint landings in front of the Marsh Lake Marina. The Holsten Pilsener team was dragged 200 metres through the snowmobile race track oval on their landing. Once the basket touched down and tipped over on its side the wind was still pulling the inflated balloon and rigging along the ground—passengers and all. When we pulled up to load the gear in the back of the rental pickup, I asked, about all the snow piled up there. Nonchalantly, the balloon team said, "Oh,

we had to dig our way out when we landed. That was all in our basket." No joking! The pile was three metres high. We glanced up to see two balloons heading for the black clouds at the north end of the lake. Luckily, the hailstorm skirted the west side of the lake and disappeared behind the mountains, leaving us unscathed.

Every first-time balloon passenger has to be inducted into the aristocracy of balloon travellers. This stems from the first balloon flight in France where the inventors, brothers Montgolfier, sent up a dog, a rooster and a sheep in a basket—the first flight into space was way too dangerous for a living human. On the landing, which was pretty bumpy, the dog stepped on the rooster and broke the rooster's leg. That fixed it! Broken bones meant this was too risky for regular (noble) people. So the King of France decided only peasants or convicts would make the flights until this new transport form was perfected. But the other nobility didn't really want their hired help, farm hands and vassals floating around "above" the nobility, the bosses. So anyone who flew in a balloon, aside from being crazy, would be inducted into the nobility, and have the honour of owning the land under their flight path. This involved some fire and water ceremony including tattooing and baptising.

Today, for ballooning purposes, this has been changed to setting a lock of hair on fire and dousing it with champagne, in our case Yukon champagne—a beer. A highly skilled operation—especially when the inductee is someone like my husband who has a quarter inch of hair all the way round. And passengers own the view, not the property of their flight path.

My baronial title is Baroness-Jessica-of-the-gently-fluttering-maple-leaf-over-the-Takhini-River-to-Lake-Laberge. Any balloonist can test you at any time on your name. Failure to correctly repeat the name means you buy the next round.

Wednesday, February 22. Beautiful weather made for a magnificent flight from the gravel pit on the north Alaska Highway by the dog sled track, to the Lake Laberge campground. We were airborne for one hour fifteen minutes. The co-pilot was piloting the first-ever hot-air balloon flight in the Yukon by an East German. We saw four deer foraging in the bush behind the mountains I usually only see from the ground. The wildlife were completely undisturbed by our presence. They didn't hear us or smell us. When we had to open the propane flame for more lift the noise of the burner startled them and then they scattered lightly, but not before we got a

by Jessica Simon

ON THE MOVE

PHOTOS: AXEL KAISER

—IT'S SO UPLIFTING

good look. On subsequent days, the balloonists saw moose and caribou in other areas.

Wednesday night a Night Glow static display was scheduled on the riverfront in Whitehorse. The event was to start at 7 p.m. Spectators started arriving at 6 p.m. I had arranged for the snowshoe can can dancers, the Kapital Kickers and the regular can can dancers to entertain. One of the balloonists told me this was rather unusual. Normally, the idea of the hot-air balloons lit up by the propane flames of their burners, glowing like giant candles in the night sky, was enough excitement for an audience. They didn't need stuff like dancers, too. I figured we'd give it a try. At least the balloonists would have a good seat to see the dancing—an event they definitely don't get to experience in Germany.

As it turned out it was a good thing the entertainment was scheduled with the Night Glow event. Since the audience arrived so early, they were entertained by the snowshoe dancers who performed while the balloons were set up. Then the Kapital Kickers were scheduled. It looked like the whole event was going to work out fine, in spite of the strong gusts blowing down the valley along the river. But, just as we were announcing the sponsors and thanking the balloonists, I heard my husband say, "We'd like to thank the balloonists, who have— COULD YOU PLEASE CLEAR THE AREA—THE BALLOONS ARE COMING DOWN!" Right on top of the Kapital Kickers! People scattered everywhere to avoid being trapped under the balloon cloth. Half-dressed miners in red long johns were yanking up their jeans and hobbling along trying to get dressed on the run. Everyone agreed that if the balloon had to come down in the middle of the show it was best it came down on the Kickers. They seemed to have a good sense of humour. Though most of the crowd dispersed after this, the can can dancers stayed to entertain the remaining spectators and the balloonists as they packed their equipment.

Thursday, February 23/Friday, February 24. These days were very calm flying days compared to the previous days. Hopping along on Lake Laberge was more for the balloonists' fun. The weather was slightly inclement though it brightened up in the late afternoon. The balloonists had a chance to fool around on the snowmachines too. I think they liked snowmobiling as much as they enjoyed ballooning. Friday, they flew from the sawmill at the Yukon River bridge on the north end of Marsh Lake to the marina. They especially liked the jagged coastal mountains in this area.

Saturday, February 25. This was the day when we got a lesson on what nature is really like. It was another perfect flying day. The temperature was -30°C. The balloonists were prepared with warm gear. We launched from the roadside 10 kilometres north of Rat Lake on the Carcross Road. A Highways crew came by and put up "SLOW CONSTRUCTION AHEAD" signs at either end of our area and then watched until we were airborne and they could retrieve their signs. The flight path was directly over the coastal mountains between Rat Lake and Tagish Lake at a height of 9,000 metres. The sky was a clear, dazzling blue and the balloonists caught a glimpse of the ocean at Skagway about 80 kilometres to the southwest.

Then the balloons started their descents—in three different locations. One came down right on the road. Stuck in traffic, the travellers on Tagish Road that day got to see a hot-air balloon whether they liked it or not. It couldn't be missed since the balloon covered the whole road. At 9,000 metres, one of the other balloons had difficulty with the propane burner system. Puttering along with the backup burner, they battled low-level winds and came down a short distance into the trees on the left side of Tagish Road. The hand-held radio had given up. The cold sapped the batteries.

One of the team members from the downed balloon walked out of the bush to the road and met up with the chase crew. The only problem was the landing area was in a swamp. Driving the snowmachine back in to pull out the balloon and basket was a real chore. Duke Connelly took this on. He plowed through the area four times. Each time he was either bogged down in the slushy unfrozen swamp or he ran a path that ended in a wall of deadfall trees. Eventually, he made a one kilometre loop to reach the balloon 150 metres in the trees. The crew were bundled up in their sleeping bags. When they got back three hours later, they were really glad to see a road, with people, traffic and hot coffee,.

The third balloon was on Tagish Lake, "right at the end of the road where we took off from on Monday," they said. Not quite. It was at the end of a road three kilometres to the left of where we were on Monday. In

the winter all dirt roads look the same—especially if you've only seen it once before. We got them out and back to the highway at about the same time as the second balloon came back out to the road.

These balloonists now truly believe all that stuff about being prepared for bad weather, even when it looks beautiful outside, and how the wind can play tricks on you at any moment, around any mountain or along any valley. After the day's events, I said to one of the balloonists, "It really is God's work, eh?" "No, no, Jessica," he said, "It's God's fun."

Sunday, February 26. -30°C. Calm winds 9 kilometres per hour, expected to cloud over in the afternoon. The balloonists went to Haines Junction for a test flight and a change of scenery. The experience they had on this day would decide for them if they would have flights over this area in 1996. They were very impressed by the area and the flying they had on Dezadeash Lake.

It was a round-trip day. The winds at low levels took the balloons northward toward Haines Junction. A couple of hundred metres higher and the winds brought them back, close to the launch point—the Dezadeash Lake lookout on the Haines Road. Round trips are a rarity in ballooning. More likely is guaranteed one-way transportation to a destination to be named later. This reinforced the balloonists understanding of how the wind can blow

in two different directions within 80 kilometres of each other and how the temperature can change in the same area. Our weather-readers weren't crazy, they were just in different locations.

The balloonists were teary-eyed on the day they departed for home. But, they'll return for more ballooning adventures over our clear wintry landscape.

Getting the jump on summer or "How did a nice guy like me get into a dive like this?"

by Steven Smyth

The little aircraft's engine roared into life as four of us huddled in the back of a tiny Cessna stripped of its passenger seats and door. The plane taxied down the gravel strip, turned, and sped back up the runway into takeoff. The cold wind poured through the open door and I timidly peeked out the window at the diminishing trees below. I was not confident on the ascent to my first parachute jump.

The day was glorious, with the sun reflecting off nearby lakes. But somehow it was hard to appreciate the splendour of the Yukon's Carcross valley. I waited tensely as we climbed to 2,800 feet, repeating the jump procedures over and over again in my mind.

The jump master, Ken Kroocmo, motioning to the pilot to turn, pulled out a small flag to use as a wind drift indicator. He peered down at the ground awhile, then suddenly flung the indicator out the doorway. The plane banked sharply so that we could watch the flag fall slowly earthward; where it landed would assist in determining where we should exit. The pilot circled again until we were back on course. The jump master looked at me, reached for my static line, and clipped it to a ring on the floor. "Get ready!" he shouted.

I crawled forward nervously to execute the rather intricate process of "getting ready." My hands grasped the wing strut like vices....right foot stepped to the doorway...left foot swung past the right to balance on the tiny rubber aircraft tire...right foot swung out into space...a pause. I looked back at the instructor..."Go!"

Almost without hesitation, I pushed away from the strut and gave a tiny hop off the tire... then...blind panic! Everything went white as I realized what I had done. My feeble attempt at the necessary arch position, required for a stabilized fall, disintegrated into a frantic waving of arms and legs. My counting, which was supposed to reach "six thousand," did not make it past "two thousand."

Suddenly, there was a gentle tug at my shoulders, and I was floating gently earthwards. Relief swept over me as I gazed about, appreciating only then the beauty and serenity of the scenery around me, though not for long. I would soon be down, and I had to adjust the direction I was drifting. I grasped the parachute toggles above me and pulled on one to experiment. I turned slowly and saw the ground control crew pointing out the direction I was to face. The arrow they were holding moved, and pulling the toggles again, I spun to face the direction it pointed.

The ground was getting closer now, and I prepared for landing by turning into the wind, feet together, and knees slightly bent. The next instant I was flat on my back, without even a chance to do the landing roll I had practised so diligently during the jump course. There wasn't time to worry about that, however. The wind tugged at my parachute and began dragging me slowly across the desert. I reached up and grasped a parachute line and pulled on it to collapse the chute. On the other side of the desert I saw a figure being dragged up and over a sand dune, and out of sight. The jump was over for me, but someone else was getting an additional ride!

I went on to complete three more jumps that summer, and with each jump, progressed a little in technique. Each jump requires preparation, safety checks, and several procedures which must be executed properly: exit, body arch, and count. Additional movements must be counted and executed when doing TRCPs (training rip-cord pulls) and free falls. After the canopy opens, it must be visibly checked to ensure there are no line-overs (a line over the canopy, which can cause a tear). The AOD (automatic opening device, attached to the reserve parachute) must be disengaged. Then, considering wind drift, you must concentrate on steering your descent toward the target on the ground. Proper landing position is important as broken limbs can easily result if you land unprepared.

It is difficult to describe the multitude of feelings associated with skydiving. There are long, tense minutes of anticipation during jump preparation; the exquisite thrill of the exit and fall; the gratifying relief of the tug of the opened canopy; the serenity of floating through the sky as if descending on a cloud; the disappointment of realizing, as you prepare to land, that your "ride" will quickly end; and finally, what can only be described as the "afterglow" of a successful jump. It is not difficult to see how some people have become addicted to this sport.

A further bonus to skydiving in the Yukon is the opportunity to jump in the most beautiful of surroundings, the Carcross valley. High mountains on either side of the valley retain their snow into the summer months, and the dark green forests are offset by the brilliant emerald and fluorescent greens of nearby Spirit, Crag, Nares, and Bennett lakes. The target is the fine, white sand of the Carcross desert, an irregular series of dunes which cushion landings like a huge mattress. That is, providing you are on target. Occasionally, novices will let themselves drift a little too far and end up in nearby trees! Fortunately, this is the exception, rather than the rule.

Skydivers are now a regular feature of events like the Sourdough Rendezvous, held in Whitehorse every February. Skydiving was included as one of the sporting events in the first territory-wide Yukon Games, held in 1981. It is a thrilling sport which few Canadians enjoy. With a small investment of time and money, anyone in good health can participate. This may be the sport for you—dive in!

ON THE MOVE

PHOTOS: KEN KROOCMO

160

paragliding

story and photo by Steven Kurth

I have a passion. Merely one among many, yet great among them all. Throughout the ages it has been one of people's highest aspirations and has inspired poet to pen and singer to song. I share this passion with so many others around the world, yet so very few here at home. This passion is pure. This passion is simple. This passion is flight.

Its precise flavour bears a humble name—paragliding. It is a sport born in the mid-1980s, an offshoot of skydiving, and has evolved into a sport unto itself. Hang gliding is now a closer cousin than sky diving. Although a paraglider still strongly resembles a parachute in appearance, a parachute it is not. It is a wing, and is governed by and must obey the same laws of physics that all wings must, be they sparrow or Boeing 747.

I have made my way to the summit of this hill, known locally as the Dome. All around, the Klondike hills roll away in full summer splendour, while the Klondike and Yukon rivers meander through to meet in the valley below. There, nestled along the banks of these two rivers, and flanked by the Dome, lies my home, Dawson City.

I am surveying the conditions. The day looks promising. The secrets whispered by the wind, the sun, the birds and the clouds all excite me. In my modest backpack is that which will carry me there, my paraglider. The colourful nylon spills from the bag and I spread it open on the ground. Already the wind is tugging at it, teasing it, begging it to come and play. Hurriedly, I don my flight suit and helmet, slip into my harness and attach myself to my wing. I pause for a moment to sniff the wind before I proceed.

I tauten the lines and the glider awakens, expanding, pressurized by the force of the wind rushing into it. So awakened it leaps off the ground, rising into the air above me in a splendid arc. Skilfully I restrain its eagerness to fly until I am ready. The glider hovers impatiently above me in the wind. I turn, step, and gracefully slip the bonds of gravity.

Immediately I pass over a small depression in the hillside that affords a small gaggle of picnickers a lovely spot, hidden from the summit, in which they are eating and taking in the view. They are startled by my sudden, swooping appearance above them. Their surprise turns to awe and makes me smile broadly. The hillside falls steeply and steadily away as I head south towards open air. I find a weak thermal updraught and I play in it for a while. To the north, above Moosehide Slide, I notice the ravens are soaring playfully. I watch enviously as they dive and swoop, climb and roll expertly in the wind. I cannot resist the temptation to join them so I exit this rather weak thermal and easily glide over to them.

I am flying just above treetop level now, hugging the contour of the bowl-shaped landslide, the wind against the hillside keeping me aloft. The ravens keep a cautious distance, accustomed to but distrustful of my presence. I skim happily back and forth along the ridgeline, occasionally tapping the crown of a tree as I pass over.

My reverie is interrupted by a sudden and powerful yank on my outside wingtip. I know what it is. It is another thermal but it feels like a strong one. On my next pass I edge out away from the ridge to the safety of open air. I encounter strong turbulence signaling the imminence of the thermal. Very suddenly I hit its edge. My glider pitches back as it hits what amounts to a wall of rapidly rising air. The wing then surges forward seeking to recover from the hit. I must be quick to control it.

I am in the thermal now and I begin to circle. This thermal is very tight, very well defined and very, very strong. I am not turning tightly enough though, and my wingtip passes outside the boundary of the thermal. Instantly the wingtip collapses and folds underneath the rest of the glider. I am now flying with only 60 percent of my glider inflated. I take corrective action, turn deeper into the thermal to escape its edge. I hear encouraging sounds from my wing and I look up to see the tip reinflating. I am pleased with the designers for making such a well-behaved glider. I continue to circle.

I am rising rapidly now. I quickly glance at my variometer to gauge the rate of climb. It is off-scale, pegged at its maximum. I am thrilled and concerned at the same time. I am totally impressed with the speed at which the ground below my dangling feet appears to be dropping. As I climb higher and higher, the lift gets smoother and stronger and the thermal gets larger. A second glance at my vario indicates that I am about 4,000 feet above Dawson City while my rate of climb is still pegged out. I continue to circle.

I look up to see how my glider is doing but also to see where I am being rocketed to. I see the cloud being formed by and fed by this thermal and to which I am being served on my nylon platter. Clouds are deceptive in their size. They appear quite pretty when viewed from the ground but they can be quite intimidating when you're directly underneath one, hanging from a bunch of nylon.

I am about 8,000 feet above Dawson City now. The air is cold and noticeably thin. I am only hundreds of feet below this behemoth of a cloud. I can see its flat belly churning and swirling and I've no desire to enter its domain. I turn to make for the edge of the thermal. My proximity to cloudbase is becoming uncomfortable and I start to worry that I will be sucked up into the cloud before I reach the thermal's edge. I slam on full speed-bar, lean back and tuck in my arms. My glider is flying for all it is worth now. Already, thin wisps of cloud are streaking by me. I am nervous as the seconds tick slowly by.

I am getting near now to where the edge of the thermal must be. I release the speed-bar and retake the control toggles in anticipation of a rough exit from this powerful thermal. Nine thousand, one hundred feet below, the edge was very sharp and abrupt—such an edge is always turbulent. I have every reason to believe that here the edge will be just as forceful.

Suddenly, I am at the edge. It seems as if the thermal has taken an intense dislike to the flavour of flesh and nylon and forcefully expectorates the offending tidbit. My glider surges violently in front of me as I exit and begins to twist. I yard on the brakes to prevent the glider surging all the way underneath me and at the same time correct for the twist. I see my glider directly, horizontally, in front of me. It is an interesting view of my glider and more than a little unnerving. After one or two wild, swinging pendulums, my glider stabilizes above me once again and I find myself calmly floating thousands of feet above my troubles.

The air is smooth now, and cold. The rush of air in my face refreshes me while it hums a soothing tune through the lines. I look back at the cloud from under which I've just emerged. It looks much more benign now then it did just a few moments ago. I break out in laughter at my angst and start to whoop with glee. I look down past my boots to see my home. I can only distinguish blocks and streets, not individual houses. I reflect on how good life can be as I meanderingly descend from the clouds.

I am getting low now. It is time to prepare for landing. My primary landing zone is the green belt along the dike, adjacent the Yukon River. From many parts of town I see children scurrying, like little cockroaches, by foot and by pedal, all converging on that grass strip where they know I will be landing.

I am on final approach now, one hundred feet above the ground. Most everyone on Front Street pauses to watch me land. The wind is moderate and crossing from the left, but the landing should be smooth. Fifty feet, twenty feet, ten feet, three feet, apply brakes! My glider slows and I extend my feet to lightly touch down as soft as if I were Peter Pan. I turn and deflate my glider and it falls harmless to the ground. I take a deep breath and revel in a feeling of immense satisfaction.

I have a passion. Merely one among many. Perhaps, greatest of them all.

Medevac
A northern story

story and illustration by Gail Cyr

The sound of the telephone eventually reached through my subconscious, cutting short the unremarkable videotape of my life's accomplishments. My dream's freefall towards Ground Zero dissolved in a violent start. What time is it? I always look for the time before I answer the phone, so I can feel justifiably annoyed. Having flown a seven-hour flight the night before, my body felt like I had actually hit the ground.

It's 0400 hours. It's dispatch calling to tell me of a medevac. The patient is in the early stages of labour in Deline. I'm fully awake, my dream no longer part of memory. Twenty years…first baby…seven weeks early…two centimetres dilated…Charter from North of 60 Air. I hang up and phone the nursing station for more details. "How long ago did contractions start?"…"Any known cause for early labour?" "A fever—from what?…The flu? What's the temperature?"…"Bleeding—how long and how much?"…"Blood type?"…I.V. started…I indicate the meds to slow the process of labour…

While most babies are born in the communities, first deliveries usually come to a hospital prior to the expected due date. Because of early labour, the fever and bleeding, air medevac has been contacted to bring the mother to Yellowknife. An obstetric call involves two medevac personnel, one for the mother, one for the baby if it decides to be born in the skies over the Arctic shield. By the way, dispatch said, "It's forty below." O Joy! I hang up to wake up another flight nurse, Sheila. Then I phone the hospital to requisition a blood supply, give our flight plan and relate our medical protocol for this situation.

The pilots will be waiting for us with the coffee. They're a good bunch. As I gather my clothes, I think how firefighters jump out of bed into coveralls and boots. Just swing your feet out, jump in and pull up. I'll have to try it sometime.

We cab to the hospital and the hanger. There's a ghostliness about the empty streets with the greenish lights wafting through the icefog and chimney smoke. The streets are empty, as if a giant hand had plucked away all the people, and we—a true representation of humanity, two medevac nurses and a cab driver—are the only survivors. Our driver comments how we "girls" pack a lot of gear, referring to the four hundred pounds of medevac equipment, the stretcher, isolette,

boxes of medical supplies, Arctic survival gear for ourselves and our patients. Humm. Sexism survives the new world order.

Forty minutes later, we're airborne in a Twin Otter. It will take just over two hours to fly to Deline. There, we'll be another forty minutes on the ground before we'll be airborne again. We have to get to the nursing station, examine the patient, debrief with the nurse in charge, and prepare Gina for the flight. While we have extensive training and experience, we have to be ready for anything and everything.

Inside the nursing station, family members wait while Gina's husband, Frank, is with her in the patient room, holding her hand. As we come in, he smiles in relief and shakes our hands. I've always been impressed by the friendliness of the community people, even during stressful situations. It is evident Frank is frightened for his wife and baby. Gina manages a smile through her discomfort. The flu has heightened all her aches and pains. Frank takes his leave as we examine his wife and ready her for travel. The police Suburban that picked us up doubles as an ambulance.

We set up in the plane and prepare for takeoff when the pilot advises we are in for a change in weather. A warm front from the west is heading our way, likely to push back the cold towards the Arctic coast. We are to expect turbulence. We make our preparations and say our prayers.

Aviation medicine is different from that

practised on the ground. The body undergoes changes to compensate for the lack of air pressure and lower oxygen levels it is normally used to. Labour progresses faster. Blood loss occurs easier and faster. Intestinal gases cause more discomfort and push on the baby. Oxygen counteracts some of these changes. Mag Sulphate, a drug used to delay Gina's labour, has kicked in nicely. The bleeding has slowed and we do not need the extra blood for now. For the time being, Gina's discomfort is more emotional. The delivery of a baby is an event more blessed with family nearby; instead, she is on an emergency medevac. In spite of her fears, she maintains a quiet dignity. When we hit our first air pocket, Gina's hold on my hand turns into a vice grip. The pilot motions he will gain altitude.

It is one of the more memorable flights. The warm and cold front fight and push each other for mastery of the skies and possession of the small aircraft caught in its path. The pilots fight back and the plane alternates between thrust and stall. As professionals, we must have a calm attitude. Our facial expression cannot betray any fears we have for the patient's or our own well-being. It's easier for me to mask my feelings than it is for Sheila. I attribute my superior masking skills to my family history where it was dangerous to show emotion. I am glad to put this skill to good purpose. A medevac nurse once told me I look as if I held the secret to our survival. Gina, bless her heart, goes into labour again. This time, the babe is determined not to be put off. We have three quarters of an hour's flight left. If this had been a second baby, there is every chance the babe would have been born over the tundra. It is a frightening thought. For all the experience I gained through hundreds of medevacs, premature babes are scary because they need the final weeks to grow stronger, with the final touches on their cardiac, respiratory and digestive systems.

Contractions are more frequent and longer duration. Dilation size has increased to five centimetres. A sudden onset of bleeding is our main concern. Bleeding can mean the placenta has a blood clot or it will deliver first, depriving the baby of oxygenated blood and nourishment. An event like this can cause the death of the babe and the mother. The bleeding is nominal and indications are we won't have a failure of the placenta.

Thousands of medevac hours have honed my ability to close out environmental sounds so that despite the noise of the plane, the rattling of medical and aeronautical equipment, and Gina's discomfort, I can hear the baby's heart beat. It is not in distress. "Hold on, Kiddo!" I say. Twenty minutes to

go. The turbulence decreases. Sheila goes to the pilot to give orders for an ambulance and makes contact with the hospital detailing Gina's progress.

Our pilot gets priority landing status. The city is now covered in cloud and has that deep winter grey tone of a young morning. I can see the ambulance lights flashing. As we move Gina from the plane to the ambulance, I thank our pilot for pulling us through such a dreadful flight. He indicates he wasn't about to let anything wrong happen on "his" flight or he might have taken it personally. People involved in emergency services extend themselves to the saving of the sick and injured, and in the case of newborns, to their growth and development. I believe his projections progressed to the first fishing trip. He will be a good father one day, l tell him. I hope life's sideswipes never overtake him.

The ambulance doors close and Sheila and I encourage Gina to resist the urge to push. We stay with her until she is taken into the delivery room.

While I'm completing my charts, the telephone rings to tell me Gina had a healthy boy. Both mother and son are fine and will stay in town for a few days. Her husband is

on his way to Yellowknife.

I am going for a long sleep. I've been at this job for three years, longer than most medevac personnel—both men and women. The combination of extensive flight hours combined with the stress of providing critical care eventually takes its toll. Medevac professionals sometimes develop a fear of flying so intensive they have to leave the job. It can happen to the best of personnel. We don't have the luxury of picking and choosing the flights or the weather conditions. What starts as healthy concern develops into apprehension as if each hour in the air is taunting the gods.

As to a significant other, relationships are hard to cultivate for time and talk are necessary for its survival. Long absences and exhaustion have caused the break-up of more than one relationship. I have thought of leaving, but I love my job. There is a little three-year-old in Fort Simpson who is my namesake, I being her mother's medevac nurse in circumstances not dissimilar to Gina's. Like Scarlett in the movie *Gone With the Wind*, "I won't think about this today, I'll think about it tomorrow." I've learned never to make major decisions when I'm exhausted.

Let that lonesome whistle blow…

Relationship

by S.D. Picot

She told him she wanted their relationship to be like the train in Skagway. There was no room in her life for the archaic concept of running flat out for a train and then, once caught, to sit passively for the journey. She'd heard that the best way to experience the ride was to be standing on the very back platform, to feel the mist of the Bridal Veil Falls, the ricketiness of the tressles, the ragged raw beauty all around, and the cold nipping at her backside.

PHOTO: PETER LONG

Skagway Harbour Horror

by Marie Carr

Sometimes your non-diving friends all want to know whether you're crazed enough to dive under ice. I used to shiver just thinking about it because, in my experience as a wet suit diver, even in lakes that were straight liquid, I'd often emerged feeling quite cube-like. (When you find yourself empathizing with that stiff lump of Christmas turkey in your deep freeze, take it from me, your days as a wet suit diver are drawing to a close.) Graham and I were once tough enough to manage three to four dives a day for days on end in salt water temperatures of less than 50°F (and we weren't wearing those sissy titanium jobs either), but at some point I realized that at the rate we were eating to keep up with the calories this required, we would probably require a substantial bank loan just to pay our grocery bill. So we

came to a crossroads in our diving careers: which would it be—truckloads of Ding-Dongs and Mars Bars, vats of animal fats, and huge sacks of sugar or…a dry suit? Graham, it goes without saying, required convincing, but eventually we made the plunge. That's how we found ourselves standing in the bone-chilling wind on the shores of Skagway one April, caked in baby powder and apprehensively eyeing the waves around the ore dock for our first dry suit experience. Sadly, we had an audience.

Now, these dry suits were quite special to us. We had them custom fitted and had chosen our colours with great care from the sample batches. Never mind that from the moment Graham donned his, he became known as the "Green Hornet" and everyone thought he only needed antennae on his hood to complete the look — we felt quite sophisticated and wouldn't have been the least surprised if someone from *Diver Magazine* had wanted our photos for ads. That's why, when cameras started snapping around us, we just acted very casual and ended

up with shots of my bum, Graham appearing about to vomit, and profiles of our huge sagging bellies. (Take it from me, if you see a camera anywhere in your vicinity, the best strategy is to suck in your stomach and turn so you're always facing it with a toothy grin.)

Anyway, back to the dive proper. As the initiated will quickly tell you if you express any interest at all, a dry suit is "another piece of equipment." That's putting it mildly. You have two new valves to contend with, besides the ones on your BCD (buoyancy compensator device), and believe me, it takes some practice to realize that they don't operate quite the way you may have expected. You have an extra hose to hook up, and rest assured, you will forget to hook it up at least once—ask Graham (alias Tube Steak) Henderson how that feels at two extra atmospheres of pressure. And by the way, your feet are no longer the sleek little ballet slippers that once made your mother so proud. You've graduated from the rubber socks set to diving in skidoo boots now. My

feet felt so clunky in the dry suit that I was absolutely convinced I would need extra large fins to fit over them. I ordered those too, along with shotgun type mitts to really enhance my normally "B-grade" manual dexterity. Oh yes, and I haven't mentioned the extra weight required yet, have I?

As they say, the more you wear under the suit, the more weight you'll need on top of the suit. Well, I figured no problem…I was wearing a long-sleeved turtleneck under two pairs of wool Stanfield combinations with two pairs of socks, the outside pair being thigh-high wool cross-country ski socks, not to mention the usual other stuff in the underwear department. I toyed with adding my Woods parka, but figured there'd be a problem with the fur trim breaking my mask seal so I reluctantly dropped that idea. It's kind of like packing a suitcase, I guess. What's the rule? Pack everything you think you'll need, then take half out and leave it

behind. Anyway, for weight I was wearing thirty pounds total including my ankle weights—that was nine pounds more than I was used to—and guess what, it wasn't enough.

Or at least I thought it wasn't enough. You see, there was a small problem with my extra large fins. As soon as I got down to ten feet, the dry suit boots compressed and pop went the fins. Anyone who has just cleaned out their bank account to buy dive gear will appreciate my horror at this development. The visibility was six feet tops due to the dredging going on in the harbour, so faster than you could say "Jacques Cousteau" those brand new blades were out of sight. Several times I managed to retrieve them by simply jackknifing down and blindly grabbing at them, but then it would be "boink, surprise!" I was up at the surface again being pummelled about in the waves—this in full view of all the spectators on shore, you understand. (What's the hand signal for "MY #@*! FINS KEEP FALLING OFF! and "NO, I HAVE NOT ADDED ANY AIR TO MY SUIT!") Somehow, I couldn't make my buddies understand the dilemma; if I did add air to the suit to keep my fins from popping off, then I couldn't get down. Within minutes, I was experiencing the novel sensation of sweating like a pig in 43°F water. Finally, Larry, the person with the unhappy task of overseeing this fiasco, yelled "abort the dive!" and we clambered up onto the rocks on all fours, over-weighted, exhausted, pissed off, and much photographed. I thought to myself "it doesn't get much worse." Then we tried a second dive.

This dive involved only three of us; Larry, our trusty mentor, Graham and myself. Just to be safe, I'd strapped on my old fins which were a size smaller, and I'd borrowed an extra three pounds and stuffed it loose into the pocket of my BCD. The water was calm. The day was drawing to a close. We geared up and picked our way through driftwood to the water's edge, where we walked in off the shore, dropping slowly to a depth of fifty feet or so. I figured I was doing pretty well, because whenever I started to feel the least bit chilly, I'd just slap my chest like Tarzan and add a few more hits of air. Bingo, I'd feel toasty warm again. It was the first time I'd ever dove in the ocean up here that I was actually comfortable and it gave me a sense of euphoria I'd never experienced before except maybe diving in Hawaii.

Well, about fifteen minutes into the dive, while we were eyeballing some neat shells on the bottom, I was struck by a sudden sensation of fullness in my legs. It dawned on me then that when you put air into a dry suit, it doesn't just spread all around in there like pink insulation. In fact, a dry suit is like that little window in a carpenter's level and the air in it is the bubble that never stays still. My bubble by this time was rather larger than anyone else's because from the moment we'd submerged I'd been giving myself a couple of shots of air every thirty seconds or so. Now, inverted as I was to examine life forms on the bottom, I had unintentionally pushed the bubble up into my feet, which had then bloated up like fish bladders. Later, when we were reconstructing the incident, we

decided that it was at this moment the extra three-pounder in my pocket dropped out.

I grabbed a rock, then another one, then I grabbed Graham, then Larry grabbed me and we all sailed up to the surface like balloonists hanging from a blimp shaped like moon boots. I broke the surface feet first bouncing out of the water almost to my hips before I fell over sideways and air began ignominiously farting out my neck. The good news was my fins had stayed on. The bad news was my dry suit boots had actually blown off my feet and my feet were now trapped above the fin straps in the legs of the dry suit. Try to fix that one when you're bloated up like the Michelin person and can't bend at the waist even if your life depended on it. Larry struggled to push my feet back in, and finally he managed to do it. By this time, though, we were rather weary, and we snorkelled in. "My feet did not blow off," my super supportive buddy kept saying to all and sundry for the rest of the trip.

The next day, undaunted (after all, when you've just sunk as much dough as we had into this new piece of gear, you really have no choice but to be undaunted), we tried again. This time, Graham and I went out alone. "I've taught you all you need to know; now you just have to practise," said Larry, with a genial smile, his ear drums still ringing from yesterday's rapid ascent. This time I was wearing 33 pounds of weight which, make no mistake about it, was strapped on securely.

"Feet low, feet low, feet low," I kept chanting to myself like a kind of mantra. We descended to about fifty feet. Visibility was so poor we had to hold hands to stay in buddy contact. We had our dive lights though, so we were able to surprise a number of hapless crabs and shrimp. We even found a few neat shells to bring back. (If you stay at one level for awhile and you can finally resist playing all those valves like a piano, it's amazing what you can do with your free hands.) I kept sneaking a little air into my suit, but very cautiously. As it was, we were down for over half an hour, and when we started coming up and I pressed the valve on my upper arm to let the air out, guess what I discovered? You don't dump air from a suit like you do a BCD. You can press a hole through your arm, but if the air isn't under the valve ("arm high, arm high, arm high") or if the valve isn't adjusted to flow quickly, the air comes out at about the rate of one bubble every two minutes or so. At least I bounced out of the surface head up this time.

So a dry suit is definitely "another piece of equipment" and let's face it, there have been times when it seemed like more hassle and expense than it's worth. On the other hand, when you're wallowing about in a glacial stream to wash the salt off your suit after a dive and you're still feeling warmer than the bystanders shivering in their parkas, you kind of forget about any problems the thing might have given you. Hey, just ask T.S. Henderson.

Surfing The Trans-Alaska Pipeline

Of Frozen Canoes

by Don Wilkinson

It was on a Friday in December when Geoff and I decided that boredom had set in. We hadn't done any four-by-fouring in some time, hunting season was over and Christmas was still too far away (3 days). We desperately needed something to do.

We started thinking about where in the Yukon we could canoe in mid-December. The only rivers open were the Yukon River, which is incredibly boring, and the Takhini River from Kusawa Lake, which is much too fast and dangerous in the summer, let alone the winter. We, of course, chose the Takhini.

We travelled fifty miles north of Whitehorse and came to the turnoff to Kusawa Lake, our dropout point. No one had been down that road since the first snowfall back in September and it was totally impassable. Down we went. After numerous shovelling sessions we remembered the winch mounted on the front and proceeded to use it for the final 23 miles to the lake. This went without a hitch and we got there within four hours.

The point where we planned to set in was about 175 feet down a near vertical cliff. Covered in snow. And ice. We figured that carrying our gear plus the canoe all the way down the hill would be difficult, if not impossible. Normal people would therefore look for a better place. Not Geoff—no one could, or ever has, accused him of being normal. We loaded all the gear into the canoe and pushed it over the edge. It looked great. I was beginning to think that maybe we should have gotten in as well for what would surely prove to be an exciting ride, when the canoe disappeared over a small vertical cliff face. A few minutes later, we heard it hit bottom and shortly after we could see our canoe and gear appear way down below. Unfortunately, it wasn't together. There wasn't a piece of camping gear, food supply or canoe within 50 yards of one another.

We scrambled down the cliff and gathered up the equipment and loaded it back into the canoe. There didn't seem to be any damage, but with that canoe you really couldn't tell what was new damage and what was old.

I explained to Geoff that since his canoeing skills were so much better than mine, it would be much better if he sat up front where his superiority could safely get us through the rapids. Geoff is rather gullible where his ego is concerned. I had been through those rapids before and knew how the waves would wash up over the bow soaking whoever was in front. My loyalty suffers a bit when it comes to comfort.

I coaxed my dog, Nahanni, into the canoe and off we went. The first mile was fast but smooth—until we hit the first set of rapids. I had recently read a book on sailing and knew the technical terms needed for steering. I maybe should have told them to Geoff as well. As we headed into the set of standing waves, I could see a line of rocks dead ahead that we had to steer through. I yelled "port" and after bouncing off the first rock I explained what port meant. Unfortunately, the next rock had to be missed by going right. I yelled, "sherry" which really confused Geoff as his girlfriend was named Sherry at the time. It still is, actually, though she's no longer his girlfriend. Geoff turned around and asked, "Where?" just as we careened off the rock and crashed down the other side. I tried to explain to him that port meant to turn left and sherry meant turn right. I wasn't quite sure about the sherry part but I knew it was an "S" word. I actually heard a lot of "S" words on that trip. Every time a wave came aboard and soaked him.

We continued down the rapids, safely navigating through some of them and finally came out in a nice quiet section where we pulled over to dry off and warm up around a fire.

The next section of the river was peaceful and calm and we were starting to enjoy ourselves. Bad mistake. Around the next corner was the most impressive set of rapids I have ever seen. They looked like Niagara Falls laid on its side. Well, that's the way I remember them. There didn't appear to be any rocks in this set so we just laid down our paddles and enjoyed the ride through the rapids. Actually, we dropped our paddles in shear unadulterated fear and panic and

cowered in the bottom of the canoe and prayed. We were in the correct position for praying anyway. With the canoe flexing crazily and us praying prayerfully, we somehow made it safely through. When we finally looked up, we were proceeding down the river peacefully. And backwards.

Pulling into shore again, we emptied the water out of the canoe, started a roaring fire and dried out once more.

We had a hard time coaxing the dog back into the canoe. She wanted no part of this trip anymore. We finally got her in with a bit of prodding and Geoff's chocolate bar that he had been hoarding. He didn't know until later what it was I used. The river calmed down somewhat, shortly before our hearts did, and we started to enjoy the trip. Then we came across an ice bridge extending from shore to shore and about 30 feet wide. We tested it and realized that it was too strong to break with our paddles and too weak to support us walking across. We backed the canoe upstream about fifty feet and paddling like mad, we hit the edge of the ice, bounced up onto it and slid across to open water on the other side. I think this should be an Olympic event. It was great fun except where the canoe tipped the dog out onto the ice.

It was late afternoon when we came across the largest ice bridge yet. We dug in our paddles from way upstream and hit the ice doing 40. As we lifted off I just knew that we weren't going to make it. Sure enough, we didn't. We crashed back onto the ice about 20 feet later, still 30 feet from the other edge. And there we stopped. Well, Geoff and I stopped. The dog, who wasn't holding on as well as we told her to, was launched out of the canoe, hit the ice 10 feet away, slid across the remaining distance and disappeared out of sight into the river.

She came up about 30 feet downstream and headed for shore as fast as she could. Geoff and I were having a heck of a time trying to push the canoe across the ice with our paddles but we did finally manage it. As we stepped out onto the ice just before climbing the bank, we fell through and got soaked up over our knees. Normally, this wouldn't have been a problem, but the temperature was down around -20°C and dropping with the onset of night.

The dog finally caught up to us, carrying a suit of armour in the form of a coating of ice. We cracked it off with the axe, only to find that the water had frozen for the depth of an inch into her fur and the rest of her was bone dry. Not so Geoff and I. We were frozen solid from the knees down. I don't know about Geoff, but my legs don't have near the amount of fur as the dog does.

We decided that this was where we were going to spend the night. We got a fire roaring, set up the tent, changed our clothes and warmed up. The wolves were howling on the hills around us as we fell asleep that night. I love the sound and slept well. Geoff and Nahanni hate wolves so they didn't get a lot of sleep. Geoff stayed up all night feeding the fire, which is probably why I was so comfortable. During the night, the temperature dropped to what we later found out was -43°C.

When we got up the next morning we looked out at the river. As far as we could see upstream and down, it was frozen solid. We knew that we had a 15-mile walk out to the highway, so we abandoned everything after breakfast and headed out. When we eventually got to the highway, we walked for several hours before someone came along and picked us up. After explaining to the driver what we were doing way out in the middle of nowhere in those temperatures we decided that we'd rather walk than endure that kind of laughter again.

After he let us off at the turnoff to the lake we were picked up by a snowmobiler. We had a totally uninteresting trip to the truck, which made me decide never to buy one. Boring. We managed to get the landcruiser going after the judicious placement of some minor woodfires, and drove back to town.

The following weekend, we retrieved the gear. We left the canoe. It is still probably right where we left it. After all, no one in their right mind would ever again attempt to float that thing, let alone go down the Takhini River in it.

ON THE MOVE

After 20 years of calling the Yukon home, I have come to realize the importance of travelling for my survival. I accept the trip outside each year as an imperative part of Yukon life.

In past travels I have been fortunate to taste a wide range of cuisines, including European, North African, Caribbean, Mexican, Costa Rican and ethnic Canadian. Those flavours have influenced my cooking, and have contributed to my survival in the Yukon. Each trip outside is an experience in collecting the tastes of the world.

Having had professional training in cooking, and having worked for most of my time in the Yukon in this field, I return north after each trip and incorporate new tastes into my repertoire of food ideas. Being at home for the past two years has allowed me the opportunity to work my craft in a very different way. I am transforming these foreign food ideas into recipes for a cookbook. Using past travel experiences, I have re-visited each destination by preparing food from that area. Once the recipe is perfected, a mere taste can transport me to other continents and other times.

As Yukoners, being a well-travelled people, we have developed tastes for ethnic cuisines. Our local retailers are aware of this and now provide us with a great choice of food products. We can find all the ingredients we need to prepare dishes from any cuisine from Sushi to Babaganooj. Fresh organic fruits, vegetables and herbs are easily found, and new exotic veggies we have never heard of are often available.

Being winter bound in the Yukon provides us with the opportunity to go "taste tripping" and I have some very favourite taste trips I like to take. One place I love to go is Paris. When preparing a batch of fresh sourdough baguettes, I re-visit a Parisienne bakery by filling my home with the steamy, heady aroma of sourdough rising and baking. A good starter is all that's required.

In the Yukon, many of us think of a "good starter" as the gizmo which will make our cars start at -40. A good starter, to me, is an essential flavouring agent and a delicious cure for the northern winter doldrums. I live just a five minute walk from one of the north's best

Taste Tripping

by Mary El Kerr

bakeries and therefore need not bake a whole-wheat sourdough bread at home. I do, however, enjoy the aroma of sourdough, and use my grape musk sourdough starter at least once a week in baguettes, pancakes, waffles, crepes, scones, focaccia and for special occasions, panetonne.

For another olfactory trip which can also be done at -40, simply bundle up in winter gear for a brisk walk to the neighbourhood health food store to purchase what I believe is the most underrated food product available in Whitehorse: Italian parsley. To keep it safe from the cold on the return trip, I stow the precious

bundle inside my parka. Just bringing home a taste of spring adds a little to my step.

While the taste experience from adding this little bunch of fresh green organic parsley to an ordinary meal justifies the effort, the health benefits are also considerable. Fresh parsley has a very high vitamin C and A content. One tablespoon of each provides a healthy daily requirement. Fresh parsley is also a purifying agent and a mild diuretic. A basic salsa verde can be made easily by blending the parsley with freshly squeezed lemon juice, a bit of garlic and capers to serve on fresh seafood or with smoked salmon. Topping freshly cooked vegetables, potatoes, egg dishes or salads with a bit of chopped fresh Italian parsley can add the summer fresh flavour of our greatly missed Yukon herb garden. For the taste tripper, an Italian spring garden.

Taste tripping to tropical climates can be easier than getting through to an agent at Canadian Airlines. Fresh jalepeño peppers are available most of the year. On a warm winter day of -25, I barbecue the jalepeño with mesquite wood chips tossed onto the barbecue coals. The pungent aroma of mesquite burning can take me to a favourite restaurant in Mexico where everything is cooked on open grills over mesquite fires. The jalepeño are blackened during the process but, once cooked, the tough outer black skin may be peeled and discarded. Adding fresh cilantro, which is also available throughout the year, along with the mesquite smoked jalepeño, to a salsa fresca, bean dip, burritos or mesquite barbecued fish or chicken can easily transport the taste tripper to the tropics.

Seasonal taste tripping is also on my itinerary. By having wild Yukon cranberry chutney with any meal or using frozen wild cranberries, I time travel to autumn days of gathering the precious harvest.

The necessity of getting "out" is satisfied through re-visiting exotic destinations by creating ethnic recipes with Yukon food. I love to create food which people relish as new flavours or recognize as a taste from their travel memories. My favourite dishes are a combination of this foreign fare with wild Yukon twists and flavours added.

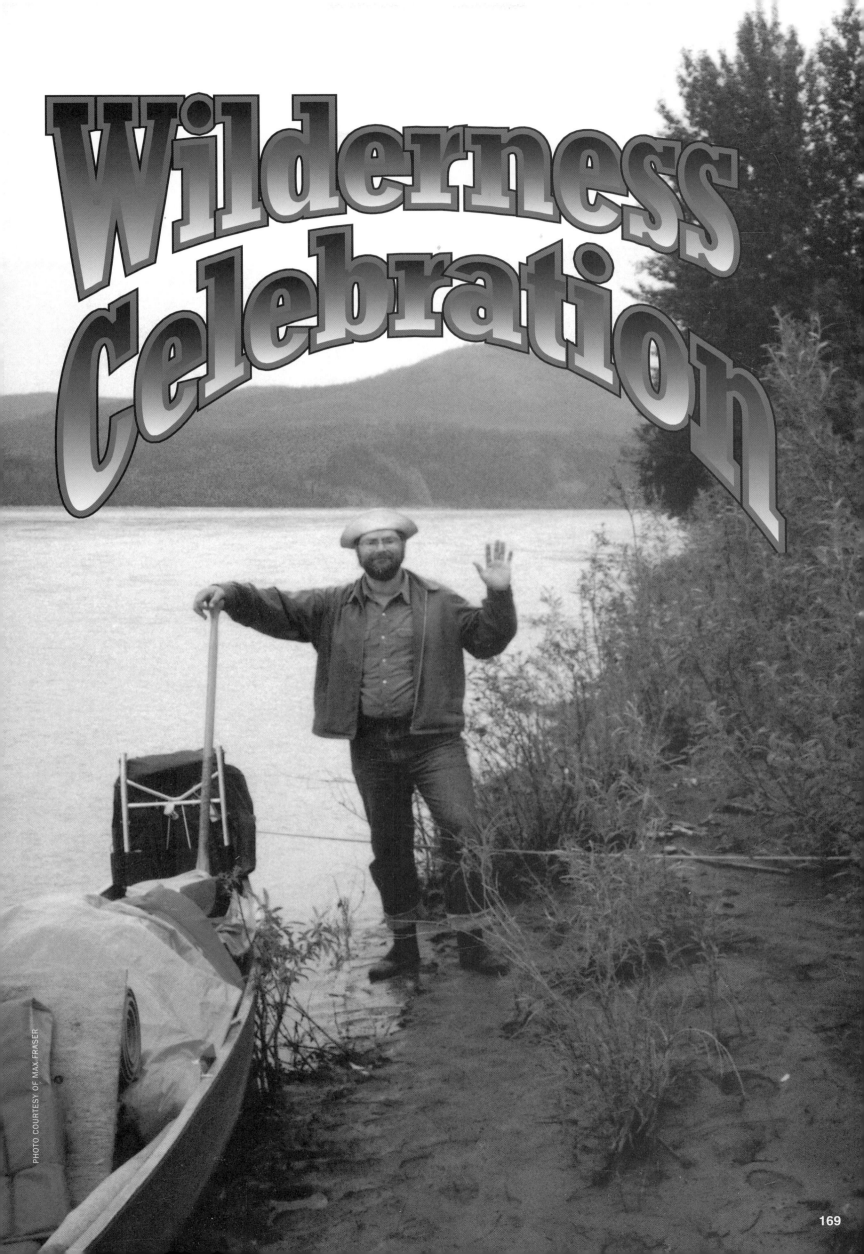

Wilderness Celebration

Teslin River Sketch

by Anne D. Wolf

Our canoe trip seemed cursed from the start. Our faithful VW bus had transported us 150 kilometres, from Atlin, B.C., to the start of the Teslin River, with five people, one dog and all the gear inside; the roof rack was laden with three 16-foot canoes.

Then, on the way to deliver our bus to the take-out point, it began to cough and sputter. Within five minutes, the transmission had died a quick death.

My husband, Chris, and I had to take the bus to Johnsons Crossing and relay the news to our canoeing party—Jochen, Henning and Frank. The problem now was how we would transport our gear back to Atlin from the take-out at Carmacks, a distance of almost 500 kilometres.

We decided to leave that question to chance. In the late afternoon, we set off on the Teslin River in heavy rain, under a grey sky. That first day, we travelled a total of three kilometres. Then we pulled our canoes on-shore and made camp on a bank that earlier in the year would have been covered by the river.

The low water in late July made paddling easy, and easy was what we needed with three greenhorns and a dog who wasn't quite sure if she liked sitting in the bow of the canoe.

The Teslin is known as a slow and picturesque river, good for canoeists who just want to kick up their feet and let the river take them to Carmacks or beyond. It is one of the gold rush rivers and the remains of settlements and cabins are scattered along the shores. In recent years, some travellers have taken to repairing old cabins, like Chris and Ulrike, who fixed up one in '93. They repaired the windows and the roof, leaving a pair of large rectangular Swiss cow bells hanging on the door. The bells jingle each time the wooden door opens to new arrivals.

Three straight days of rain. Our group was wet and miserable. Besides the innumerable bald-headed eagles, wildlife was keeping itself at a great distance from us. Not exactly what our friends from Germany were expecting. I had to explain to them that with such a vast amount of wilderness, moose and bear aren't exactly hanging out on the shores of the river with their best sides facing out for photos.

Finally, the rain stopped. The river became a slow-flowing, dark blue ribbon of silk. We floated down, splitting up for the occasional riffle or rock protruding in the middle of the river.

The shores of the river alternate from low sandy banks to high cliffs where a hoodoo facade is crowned by black spruce forests. The swallows swoop and dive from the river to the cliffs for most of the trip and when we didn't see swallows, kingfishers took their place.

After four days our conversations have slipped into the basics of life: bowel movements. It didn't seem to matter what we had been discussing—astronomical charts, wind direction, river speed—the conversation always drifted back to shitting. How to shit, where to shit, who shits how and who can't shit. The most difficult problem for the city slickers was the actual act of shitting in the great outdoors. Even before we set out, Chris and I had explained in explicit detail how to shit in the woods without making a mess all over one's self.

The elusive wildlife was finally seen, in all its majestic glory. Lying in the reeds was the largest bull moose I have ever seen. It was the first bull moose that Frank had ever laid eyes on. He squealed like a little kid and yelled, "Pass me my camera! Pass me my camera!" His cries were loud enough to rout the bull from his resting place and with a few graceful steps, long knobby legs carried the barrel-like body into the woods and he disappeared into the thick boreal forest.

Where the Teslin River joins the Yukon, the riverway widens. On that day, we found more canoeists than we'd seen on the Teslin, and they were all Germans.

We made the mandatory overnight stop

just before the confluence of the Big Salmon and Yukon rivers. On the opposite side of the river, the forest and hills beyond had been burned earlier in the year by fire; the whole riverside was woven in rusty reds and charcoal black, like some giant oriental carpet covering the expansive landscape.

I experienced one of those legendary northern sunsets and immediately penned the following poem:

> She's diving between the clouds
> all golden, tawny and mild
> slipping, slinking
> every beam, long elegant ray
> She's melting into the horizon
> as the river rolls past
> laughing softly I hear her whisper:
> "This is your present, not your past."
> She dives with fury and passion
> teasing colours of fuchsia and gold
> I know there will be no lover
> like the one in my arms I hold
> There will be no other love
> like the one in my dreams I behold.

The next morning, we canoed to Big Salmon village which was alive with four parties of canoeists. I can imagine how the village looked in its heyday during the gold rush: vibrant with commerce and conversation; everyone looking to claim their own part of the Klondike.

The cabins are in various stages of disrepair, though good enough to spend a dry night in. At the village, we met two Germans, Flipper (as in the dolphin)—dreadlocked and leatherclad, and Paul—relatively normal looking. We later nicknamed them Rasta Man and Power Man because they paddled so hard that you would think they had an engine propelling their canoe. (Three days later, when we camped with them in Carmacks, they told us that at first they thought we were government officials sent to inspect Big Salmon village and collect fees for overnighting. It must have been the army fatigues that Henning, Jochen and Frank were wearing: drab olive green from head to toe, complete with combat boots. German travelling attire.)

Six days into the trip and the troupe was getting cranky. No meat left, so it was chilli without carne and when two out five don't eat beans…well. Frank and Henning were paired up in one canoe and Henning was complaining that every time Frank adjusted his position in the bow he nearly tipped the canoe. This happened each time he rolled a cigarette, and that was just about every half hour. The smokers were running out of tobacco. Frank and Henning kept comparing how much each of them had left, wondering if they would make it to Carmacks, two days away.

The seventh day proved to be as difficult as that number can be in years. We had agreed to do 40 kilometres and then camp. At 30 kilometres the wind picked up. Jochen, alone in his canoe, could barely paddle against the stiff breeze, which was whipping up waves and sending them crashing over his bow. We couldn't find a good place to stop. There was no campsite marked on the map and it was clear that if we decided to keep paddling, it would be a hard-fought battle with this force of nature.

Not far ahead I could see where a stream ran into the river. It opened to a sandy beach, where a short bluff sheltered it from the relentless wind, just on the edge of the burn area. We put up our tents and spent the night listening to the wind toy with our tarps and the sound of burnt trees falling hard with loud crashes.

The wind was a ruse; the storm we expected never materialised and the next morning was as calm as the days before.

We were not far from Carmacks. We could see cars driving on the Campbell Highway and the telephone cable running next to the road. The end of the trip meant civilization; it meant cars and motorboats.

All that remained was to paddle, and paddle we did. The one thought that went through our heads was Carmacks. Frank, Henning and Jochen were pushing each other on with shouts of, "Beer! Beer!"

During the eight days that we had been on the river, we never paddled that hard. The end was near and with a bum flattened by a canoe seat, land was needed desperately.

We passed Eagle's Nest mountain, a large rock formation resembling a science fiction creature that might come to life and, with one massive paw, sweep helpless canoeists into its cavernous mouth.

Then there were 15 kilometres, five, three and finally, the bridge lay ahead, announcing the end of our canoe trip.

How did we get back? For a fee, a canoe rental company carried our canoes to Whitehorse, and for nothing, a guy working at the Carmacks Hotel took us to Whitehorse in his hippie van.

We had a great time on the river and met a lot of people, all of whom dropped by our cabin in Atlin for a visit before heading off on other travels. It was fun, it was an experience and next year we're going to try another river.

As for curses, there really weren't any, only the wonders of the Yukon.

NINE DAYS OF EATING

on the Teslin and Yukon rivers

story and photo by Shelley Gerber

When you are wilderness travelling there are two things to keep in mind: eating well ensures the trip is a success, and appetites sharpened by fresh air, sun, wind and rain are appreciative of almost any meal if it is tasty and abundant. The following menu was taste-tested by four hungry canoeists and passed with flying colours. We had a great paddle and float down the Teslin and Yukon rivers, putting in at Johnsons Crossing and taking out nine days later at Carmacks. We enjoyed excellent weather (for the most part), (almost) no bugs, great companionship, and delicious food. We could have taken more beverages.

Planning the menu

If you are considering a long trip you want to be sure to take the right amount of food—not too much and definitely not too little. To do this, develop a detailed menu, including ingredients and estimated amounts of each item. Keep items separated—have two packages of pre-mixed bannock instead of one. A couple of times during the trip, review your supplies to make sure you have enough to finish the trip. You may decide to reorganize meals, paddle more and float less or invite someone you meet on the river over for supper.

Food storage, wilderness etiquette

Ziploc bags are an excellent way to carry food. They are strong, easily reused and keep the river out. Wash out food containers thoroughly to eliminate odours and pack out all garbage. Cook on a campstove or on a fire located on gravel bars. Make sure you leave no trace of your ever having been there.

A word about the end result. It is common for folks to get bunged up when on extended canoe trips. Be sure to keep lots of fruit in the diet and get out for a walk everyday. Six rolls of toilet paper for four people over nine days was just enough. Remember to pack out or burn all used toilet paper.

DAY 1
Breakfast: at 11 Redwood
Lunch: cinnamon buns at Johnsons Crossing
Supper: steak, potatoes, onions, carrots, apples

DAY 2
Breakfast: bacon, eggs, toast
Lunch: sandwich of cucumber, mayo, cheese, onion
Supper: pork chops, rice, broccoli, oranges

DAY 3
Breakfast: pancakes, granola
Lunch: wasa, cheese, sausage, fruit
Supper: chilli (made in town and frozen), bannock

DAY 4
Breakfast: oatmeal
Lunch: crackers, nuts, cheese, peanut butter
Supper: rehydrated dehydrated potatoes, canned creamed corn, canned corned beef, fruit

DAY 5
Breakfast: canned bacon, granola, raisins
Lunch: canned ham, wasa, fruit, dehydrated soup
Supper: whole canned chicken with noodles, canned peaches

DAY 6
Breakfast: bannock, canned bacon, cream of wheat
Lunch: smoked oysters, crackers, cheese, apricots
Supper: pasta, prepared sauce livened up with garlic, onions, dried peppers and tomatoes, dried fruit

DAY 7
Breakfast: oatmeal, granola bars
Lunch: cherry surprise (kraft dinner with tuna and kernel corn)
Supper: pasta salad (made from dried and canned ingredients) and canned ham

DAY 8
Breakfast: oatmeal, granola bars
Lunch: bannock, cheese
Supper: leftover pasta salad, pantry steaks

DAY 9
Breakfast: pancakes, granola
Lunch: noodles, peanut sauce, crackers, fruit
Supper: canned sausage, pasta, spaghetti sauce with enliveners

Grub box staples

salt, pepper, peanut butter, oil, butter, powdered milk, jam, lemon juice, graham wafers, marshmallows, popcorn, hot chocolate, candy, coffee, tea, brandy, schnapps, toothpicks, garbage bags, ziploc bags, matches, lighters in a jar, duct tape, first-aid kit, toilet paper, dog food (only if you are taking a dog), foil, sugar, brown sugar, chocolate bars, flour, juice crystals (a nice change from smoky tasting (boiled) purified water), sun dried tomatoes, onions, garlic, assorted dried spices, river grits (a.k.a. gorp)

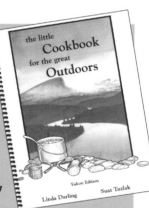

The Little Cookbook for the Great Outdoors
by Suat Tuzlak and Linda Darling Blueberry Creek Press, Whitehorse ISBN 0-9697186-0-8 $11.95 plus shipping and handling

This Yukon-published cookbook, founded on the idea that food should be nutritious for the great outdoors, also points out, "having a tasty meal after a long, tiring day…enhances the total enjoyment."

In addition to simple and practical recipes, there are tips for planning food on your outdoor adventure, pointers on nutritional needs that should be met in your plan, lists of things you'll need to prepare meals and cooking tips for higher altitudes.

BEEF TETRAZZINI

1 handful of spaghetti
125 ml (½ cup) dried corn
250 ml (1 cup) cooked beef cubes or dried beef
1 package of cream of mushroom soup mix
125 ml (½ cup) cheddar cheese, grated

Add spaghetti and dried corn to about 750 ml (3 cups) boiling water. Simmer until tender, then drain off all but one cup of water. Stir in soup mix, beef, and cheese. Heat through.

by C.J. Pettigrew

A bird's-eye view of spring in Kluane

Summer packs her bags early on the Duke Meadows, stripping the colour from the landscape, sending life into migration or early stasis. The ice age that created this place sweeps down again from its temporary retreat behind the St. Elias Mountains, silencing the Duke and Kluane rivers and freezing Kluane Lake to gemlike hardness in a single night. Winter magnifies the emptiness; the Ruby Range curls like a backbone around the landscape, breathing with only the ceaseless wind for eight long months.

But even as the Duke Meadows lies sleeping in winter's shawl, it is remembered as a dream in the genetic coding of thousands of migratory birds. As the season turns on a planetary axis, the flocks prepare to launch themselves through the Shakwak valley to Alaska and their Arctic nesting grounds. On the heel of winter, on the first full moon, I also return to open up my summer home in Kluane country.

By the end of April on the Duke Meadows, snowbanks still lurk in the poplar groves and in the hollows facing north, but anemones spring from the few inches of thawed ground. Viewed distantly, they are a faint blue haze, seeming more a fragrance than something visual. Huddled in furry clumps of six or more, they sometimes mature and wither before there is enough warmth for their petals to open fully. Despite the lingering cold and snow flurries that still sweep daily across the sky, the long hours of daylight draw them cruelly upwards.

Day and night, squadrons of sandhill cranes pass overhead, arrowing northward. Although the ice on Kluane Lake will not break up until the end of June, the meltwater along its edges is already teeming with flocks of Canada geese and swans. A few lesser Canadas loiter in our field at the north end of the lake, searching the stubble for loose oats. They wing back to the lake every evening, honking urgently, as though to remind each other that this is only a whistle stop, that the greater journey still lies ahead.

Then one morning, great flocks of Lapland longspurs sweep through the skies in short, curved flights of eyeblinding speed. They fly with a synchronisity that is breathtaking. Following the Shakwak valley trench northwards, they swarm along the Alaska Highway, feeding on the cleared right of way until my truck flushes them. For a moment they race alongside, and then veer across the road. The highway is littered with victims of miscalculation—small bundles of feathers stuck to the asphalt. Each flock moves as a single huge creature in flight, but as they merge on the Meadows, they spend longer periods on the ground. At first, they appear as some kind of moving ground cover. But close observation reveals each bird an individual again. Feeding very close together, jostling and sparring frequently when space becomes crowded, they search with beak and eye for the very last of winter's gleanings. A great twittering and fluttering accompanies their discovery of the oatfield. They swarm over the fences like a biblical plague and settle with a rustling sigh onto the stubble.

To my eye, there is little to be excited about here. The crop was cut and removed for greenfeed last September and the horses have grazed the stubble all winter. The wild geese have sifted the chaff once in the fall and eaten their fill again in the early spring. Ground squirrels, chipmunks, mice and voles have filled their larders. What is left for the longspurs must be the smallest of miracles. But feeding on this meagre ground, each bird is silent and intent on the calories that are desperately needed for its energetic flight. Brown speckled backs teem across the ground, each bird a spark in the flame of the flock.

As far as the eye can see, the longspur flocks flicker over the landscape like wildfire. Never grounded long, they leap into the air every few minutes, sweeping in arcs up and over like wind-tossed flames, each bird perfectly tuned to what seems like swift and random motion. They whirl over the trees like small brown tornados and swoop down into the yard. Herds of birds. Veritable blizzards of feathers and appetites. I pour out the birdseed—five pounds is consumed in a few hours. The clamour and motion breaks the sombre stillness with a frenzy of passionate life.

Science alone cannot explain the reason for the longspurs' swift erratic flight. Perhaps a poet, or one with the ancestral memory of 50,000 springtimes in this land, will know this flight for what it is—the fiery and impassioned enjoining of earth and heaven, the ancient elemental ritual of returning life. The first brilliant notes of blackbird's song in spring, the first glimpse of bluebird blue in the willows cannot match in intensity, the ardent descent of the longspur flocks to Kluane.

Today, while pouring out more seed, still more feed, I find the small corpse of one small longspur out in the open yard. There is no sign of violence, or any obvious reason for its death. I imagine its heart simply gave out, too avid for life and motion. It landed here with the flock, and expired among its comrades, who fed all around it, unconcerned with the stillness that had come upon one of their number. So, when the flock swept into air again, there was one left behind. I cradle it in my palm. It is so weightless I must confirm with my eye that I am holding something more than a spirit of the air.

Normally, the great American golden plover flocks follow the coastal route in their northern

continued…

migration, but something, whether the mysteries of the earth's magnetism, or the vagaries of the jetstream, something has brought them here this spring. In 12 years of observing the spring cycle on the Duke Meadows, I have never seen these great flocks pass by here. Perhaps they are a reminder that we have only begun to understand the complexities of nature's cycles in the north.

The American golden plover could easily form huge flocks of their own, they are so numerous, but they prefer to fly and forage among the longspurs. Stalking along the ground on their stilted legs, they look like herders or shepherds of the smaller birds, though I suspect it is the longspurs who keep the lookout. The plovers slice the air with their crescent wings and scurry over the ground in their landings. Their golden mottled backs blend so well into the bleached grasses that only movement betrays their presence. Their black bellies and heads are marked with an S-shaped white patch that echoes the curve of their graceful necks.

The plovers must find the Duke Meadows a welcome surprise; a small piece of familiar terrain, a reasonable facsimile for the Argentinian Pampas. They rest as much as possible, having winged across two continents. They poke about, searching in the winter debris for edibles—step-step-stab-step-step. The number of steps that follow a successful stab are fewer than when the bird finds nothing: a dance both expressive and practical.

Though the plovers seem to prefer resting on the ground, they are swept up frequently by the nervous flights of the longspurs. This, however, offers little protection from the aerial hunters that had been attracted by the activity. Raptors both great and small congregate in the air above them. There, close to the tips of the meadowgrass, is the tilting glide of the marsh hawk; further up, the powerful, short-tailed spirals of the rough-legged hawk; and higher yet, the floating silhouette of the resident goshawk who has abandoned its secretive ways and ventured out to investigate the commotion.

And finally, above them all, a pair of golden eagles display the sole phenomena beyond the comprehension of Solomon—the way of the eagle in the air.

The prey is so abundant, the hawks abandon their territorial imperatives. They circle within plain sight of each other and pluck the plovers out of the air carelessly, even leisurely. Most have even dispensed with the wild cry that would normally accompany the kill. At the edge of the spruce grove by the river, several birds mantle fiercely over their feathered meals. Though the plovers frequently leap into the air and wheel about briefly before landing again, they seem not too concerned with the predators in their midst.

Walking back to the ranch at the edge of the Kluane River, I see the bluebirds have returned to the birdhouse on the clothesline pole. The male escorts the female around the yard as she collects nesting material, belting out his song like a small boombox. What heart could fail to lift at the first spring sighting of a Rocky Mountain bluebird? It is the quintessential spring bird, as John Burroughs noted, possessing a back of blue for fairweather skies and a breast of red brown to remember the earth.

For years, the same pair of bluebirds nested in a cutout bleach bottle attached to the clothesline, originally hung there to shelter the clothespins. They nested there quite undisturbed while I strung a temporary clothesline between two poplars. But recently, I reclaimed the clothesline and provided them with a finely-crafted birdhouse, hung on the endpole. Now they must battle the swallows for possession every spring. Despite their plump, soft appearance, they are aggressive in defence of their nest, and they never fail to win the birdhouse war every spring.

The swallows, on the other hand, think they can occupy the house by sheer force of numbers. Taking advantage of a momentary absence by the bluebirds, five or six swallows at a time crowd inside the house, while others

hang in the trees or bask with wings spread on the little roof of the house until they are scattered by the returning charge of the indignant male bluebird. Swallows, admittedly, are beautiful birds—trim iridescent coats over neat white shirt fronts—and their aerial displays are unmatched in these skies. Watching them, I am reminded of the tragic story of tongue-cut Procne who was transformed into a swallow by the gods to save her from the wrath of her husband. But nevertheless, I confess that there is something repellent in the way they cling to the willow and cover the birdhouse like bats, or huge sluggish house flies.

The mouth of the Kluane river rings with the cries of waterbirds and today there is a small flock of merganzers feeding along the shore. They are extremely cautious, and once they have spotted me, they are gone.

While watching the ducks, I am discovered by my old friends, the kingfishers, who chastise me thoroughly for approaching their nest. Their dry rattle fairly shakes the banks of the river with echoes. They dart from tree to tree around me, their feathers ruffed with rage and alarm.

Chased away from the river, I wander along the edge of the field, and through the air floats the husky mellow sound of a blackbird. At first, I cannot spot the bird, but I recall the sound from my childhood on the Peace River prairie. I look around, and sure enough, there in the stubble is Brewer's blackbird, looking at me with its yellow eye. It hops about on the ground, gobbling up grain and singing simultaneously as if there wasn't time to do one thing at a time. And perhaps there isn't. Already, in the wet warm furrows of the field, living things have begun to green.

The long winter has taught a long patience here on the Duke Meadows, but the land has now been awakened from its winter meditations by the impetuous and ecstatic return of spring. The bird migrations have quickened the landscape and as surely as sap rises to the warmth of the sun, the greenness of this place rises in response to their precipitate passing.

Inviting beauty of St. Elias invokes awe

story and photo by Sheila Serup

With delight and relief, we freed our blistered toes from heavy ski boots and gingerly walked on the dry prickly grass. The scent of sage filled our sunburnt nostrils.

We stretched, shed clothes and marvelled at this small oasis between rivers of ice. After seven days of ski touring over glaciers, the feeling of bare feet on this earth was wonderful.

In mid-May, six of us flew into the St. Elias mountains for a two-week ski trip. It was a privilege to join Yukon wilderness guide Hector Mackenzie on one of his numerous adventures. The first day was spent acclimatizing in our large tent on the Eclipse snowfield at 3,000 metres, while low clouds and wind tore across the stark landscape and down the Donjek glacier. We shared stories, compared books, drank tea, simulated crevasse rescues and practised our knots within the roomy tent. As the wind quietened and the light faded, we began reading aloud *Touching the Void* by Joe Simpson. Every evening we took to reading chapters. We felt its powerful impact later on.

As it crested the mountain ridges, the bright sun lured us from our tents, tousled and excited. From this morning on, brilliant spring sunshine reigned. Clouds passed over but never diminished our joy at being in this magnificent world of sun and snow, wind and ice, rock and sky.

Feeling quite mellow yet euphoric in the high altitude, we packed our sleds and skied to the edge of the snowfield. Roped up, we began the descent to the immense Hubbard Glacier, curving around gaping crevasses, while the hot sun shimmered on the icy seracs and jagged bergschrunds lining the valley.

In the ensuing days, we never ceased to be awed by the spectacular beauty of the St. Elias mountains. The changing light, sweeping low clouds, and glistening peaks sharpened our senses.

It seemed that words could not convey the immensity of these mountains, glaciers and avalanches. Our rest stops, as we skied along the Hubbard, up and around the Kaskawulsh, and onto the Lowell, were often spent in quiet contemplation of this splendid mountainscape. Life in these mountains seemed simple, stripped to its bare essence, influenced by weather and terrain. We easily adapted to our nomadic lifestyle.

As a cohesive team, we set up camp each day—building a semicircular windbreak of snow blocks, erecting our two tents, boiling water for tea and setting up the radio—then packed up each morning and skied on. On the day prior to reaching this grassy knoll, we had skied in flat light across an endless expanse of snow. We had mistakenly taken a wrong turn down the Kaskawulsh, bewitched by the gradual slope. Skiing through the soppy snow at 1,500 metres, we arrived at this point—a pleasant change from the glaciers.

After lunch, we began to explore the hill which divides the middle arm of the Kaskawulsh. To our amazement we saw two Dall rams feeding on the new grass. They were equally surprised to see us in this world of ice and rock, and bounded up the mountainside. While we found spring flowers blooming, curious ground squirrels nibbled Lis' ski pole straps and Craig's gloves, left among our ski equipment where snow and earth met.

Here we set up camp. Hector bustled about in his bare feet reorganizing food and equipment. Craig followed the sheep up the rocky slope until it got too steep. And the rest of us found an icy spring gushing from a snowfield in which to wash. Our scalps ached from the icy coldness but our bodies felt fresh and new.

The next morning, we awoke and tuned into our daily 8 a.m. radio contact with Andy Williams, pilot and manager of the Arctic Institute of North America at Kluane Lake. We heard one of the three Germans on Mount Logan relay the news of the terrible avalanche which poured down on them while they were climbing in the middle of the night. We initially felt some hope that the missing climber would be found alive, perhaps stumbling in the thick fog or, worse, badly injured and waiting to be rescued. As the morning dragged on, with each passing hour and radio contact, the outcome for the missing climber seemed grim. Andy became the constant, reassuringly standing by the radio, waiting for the weather to clear. At midmorning, he flew over to see if he could land but was turned back.

Skiing up towards Lowell Pass that day, we wondered and hoped for a miracle. We had just finished reading *Touching the Void*, and we felt the fear and the loss. During the evening radio contact, we did not hear of the outcome, but Andy's compassion to the two surviving climbers confirmed the worst. We hoped the body of the missing climber would not be found. Perhaps he would have preferred to be buried in the mountains which he loved, on the slope of Canada's most enticing goddess. We hoped the two Germans would feel the warmth of all the groups in the St. Elias, and the unwavering support of Andy, who flew these challenging airways.

The death of a climber was humbling and sobering. It did not lessen the inviting beauty of the St. Elias mountains, but only reinforced the power of a world spun by wind, snow and sun. This environment commanded respect, and gained it.

It seemed so soon when we reached our destination, the South Arm of the Kaskawulsh Glacier, after a strenuous traverse up a 630-metre pass from the Lowell glacier. Within these two weeks, we had skied 170 kilometres across a very small portion of the St. Elias. Low clouds moved in on the last day, delaying our departure, but we just snuggled into our sleeping bags, read and munched on gorp.

The sound of Andy's plane droning closer snapped us into mad packing. While the first group flew out, I made one last trip up the slope above our camp and relished those last curving runs down. Within minutes, we were transported from the serenity of the mountains into the tumultuous world of cars, houses, noises and people. However, any despondency and desolation I felt was soon tempered by spring, young and green on the earth, and the call of a Yukon summer to experience.

PROTECTING THE
wild heart
OF THE YUKON

by Juri Peepre

I could hear the muffled drone of a distant highway—an unmistakable sound that swirled around me like fog, filling every available space. It seemed out of place up here on Wind Ridge in the Rocky Mountains of Alberta. As I neared the crest and looked a thousand metres down on the Bow Valley, the din grew louder. There it was, the four-lane Trans-Canada Highway, gobbling up the valley bottom, consuming grassy meadows, aspen parkland, grizzly bears and wolves—anything in its path. Then the whistle and rumble of the CPR train reminded me that this was a legendary spot. I was standing at the edge of Canadian history where the pioneer engineers and dreamers knitted this wild country together with steel, and later, pavement.

Growing up, I too dreamed of crossing the Canadian Rockies, and that ribbon of pavement promised a grand adventure in the mountain wilderness. Now, as I looked down on the choked and noisy valley at the entrance to Banff National Park, I asked myself how anything wild could still live in this place. Two hundred years ago, what a sight the Bow Valley must have been—elk, bears and wolves moving freely along the riverbanks and out onto the great plains amongst the vast herds of bison. Wild animals still travel startling distances. Biologists say a radio-collared wolf from Montana travelled up the Canadian Rockies all the way to Dawson Creek, B.C., at Mile 0 of the Alaska Highway—a distance of some 1,000 km—only to be shot at the roadside.

As I turned around and began the descent from Wind Ridge, the imagery of the Canadian Rockies as a refuge for wild nature seemed a

little pale. The north, our north, will be the symbol of Canadian wildlands as we pass into the next millennium. Here in the Yukon, we are living as it was more than a century ago in the Bow Valley, 2,000 km to the south. What choices will we make for wild nature in the Yukon? Will our story use the same language and end the same way as in the south?

Preserving the wild heart of North America along the mountain chain from Yellowstone to the Yukon is part of the continental Wildlands Project. This is a grassroots coalition of concerned citizens and conservation biologists working together to stop the disappearance of wildlife and the wild places they depend upon.

At the southern end of this vast ecosystem Yellowstone National Park is already an island of wild nature, with large carnivores cut off from protected lands to the north. A respected bear biologist says that the grizzly bear population along the northern border of the United States depends on the survival of bears in Canada. The conclusion from this evidence is clear: large carnivores can't be saved without protecting large wilderness. Parks are important, but on their own they won't help the carnivores at the top end of the food chain. Even the famous four mountain parks of Banff, Jasper, Yoho and Kootenay are not big enough to save grizzly bears. We have to think about the health of whole ecosystems. We must ensure that wildlife can move freely between protected areas to allow for genetic exchange between species populations.

Here in the Yukon, we have a different challenge ahead. To the south, people are attempting to protect remnant habitats and restore what were once viable ecosystems. In the north, we don't have to imagine the wild—much of it is still relatively intact. But the recent pace of development, the decline of wildlife such as caribou and mountain sheep, and the eagerness with which industrial interests wish to convert the Yukon into a spaghetti network of roads for resource extraction is daunting. Our challenge here is to slow down, question and re-direct this headlong rush. What do we need to do to sustain our way of life and protect wild nature as it is now? Which choices will lead to enduring communities and a place for my child?

The Yukon Wildlands Project is part of the Yellowstone to Yukon vision—anchored in

PHOTOS: (LEFT) WORLD WILDLIFE FUND, (RIGHT) JURI PEEPRE, (TOP) KEN MADSEN

the north by the Wind, the Snake and the Bonnet Plume watersheds. One recent summer, the cool mist lifted as I lay and watched the Dall sheep grazing high above the Snake River valley. In an instant, a herd of ten woodland caribou along with calves appeared behind the sheep. The animals shuffled, observed each other, sensed no danger and lowered their heads again to feed on the lush alpine herbs and lichens. On the river the next day I could see red on a distant bank. A young caribou had tried to swim the river before it was pulled down by a grizzly bear. The struggle had ended on the gravel bar a short time before and we knew that the bear might still be nearby, waiting to finish its partly eaten cache.

It is unthinkable—the prospect of building new roads, powerlines, towns, river diversions and huge open pit mines in these wild river basins, BEFORE we stake out claims for wilderness and the life it supports. How would we explain the Bonnet Plume ghost bears and the lengthening shadows of the Snake River wilds to a generation not yet born?

Far to the south, the headwaters of the Coal River rise in the rugged Logan Mountains along the Northwest Territories border. Beavers have crafted the tiny stream into a series of deep canals before releasing it down a boulder-strewn waterslide to the main stem of the river. A hundred kilometres downstream, pristine forests of spruce and larch shelter a variety of resident and migrating songbirds.

PHOTOS: (BOTTOM LEFT) JURI PEEPRE, (RIGHT) KEN MADSEN, MAP: YUKON WILDLANDS PROJECT

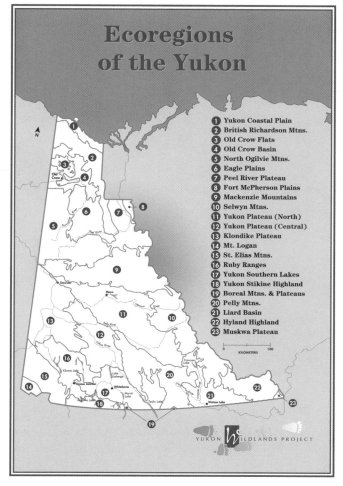

Ecoregions of the Yukon

1 Yukon Coastal Plain
2 British Richardson Mtns.
3 Old Crow Flats
4 Old Crow Basin
5 North Ogilvie Mtns.
6 Eagle Plains
7 Peel River Plateau
8 Fort McPherson Plains
9 Mackenzie Mountains
10 Selwyn Mtns.
11 Yukon Plateau (North)
12 Yukon Plateau (Central)
13 Klondike Plateau
14 Mt. Logan
15 St. Elias Mtns.
16 Ruby Ranges
17 Yukon Southern Lakes
18 Yukon Stikine Highland
19 Boreal Mtns. & Plateaus
20 Pelly Mtns.
21 Liard Basin
22 Hyland Highland
23 Muskwa Plateau

YUKON WILDLANDS PROJECT

When you first see the layered tufa steps and deep green and blue pools of the Coal River springs, a sense of quiet wonder envelopes the mind. This rare valley forms part of the ecological link to the boreal forests of British Columbia. Along this same border of the Yukon a timber and road-building rush is on. Our past habits hint that these ecosystems are destined to be dismembered quickly, with pieces sold for export in distant lands.

It's a long way from the Coal to the Bonnet Plume, and we know so little about the ecosystems that lie between. The Yukon Wildlands Project's work on these two parts of the Yellowstone to Yukon strategy is just a scratch at the surface of a complex wild landscape. Yet, in both the Bonnet Plume and lower Coal River watersheds, we are already nearing a critical choice: what room will we leave for nature and the species it supports?

A map of Canada reminds me of what's different here and what's at stake. In the Yukon, 23 distinct natural regions define our northern home— from the icy expanses of the St. Elias Mountains to the spruce forests of the Liard Basin, and the arctic tundra at the edge of the polar sea. In six of these magnificent landscapes we have protected at least some of what is needed to ensure the survival of wild species and the healthy ecosystems they depend upon. That's less than a third of the natural variety inherent in the Yukon—17 ecoregions have little or no protection yet.

The Yukon Wildlands Project and the Endangered Spaces Campaign aim to complete the protected areas network in the Yukon. Our wetlands, river valleys, critical wildlife habitat and representative examples of each of the 23 ecoregions will form the heart and arteries of what we need to protect. We want to ensure that in 100 years the variety of wild species that now inhabit the north will still be here.

Campfires
and cognac

by Lorrina Mitchell

Planning an overnight camping trip is not much of a challenge, but I do allow that there were a few extenuating circumstances. The weather forecast was hardly encouraging. Cloudy with showers, 80 percent chance of precipitation, snow at higher elevations—fairly normal for September in Whitehorse.

Our group consisted of five women, none of us "girls." By name and occupation, they were: Wendy the x-ray technician, Jan the school teacher, Cheryl the lounge hostess and Lauraine the recreation and park attendant. I bill myself as a horse trainer and outdoor adventurer, so I was co-ordinator for this little jaunt.

Jan would be driving 180 km to overnight with a friend, Lauraine would come 40 km in the early morning and Wendy would ride her horse to the stable on Friday night. Five women, five horses and a four-horse trailer means two trips with a bit over an hour turnaround to factor in.

Friday evening arrives, as does Wendy, her mount and the rain. Wendy has been packed for over a week. "7:00 a.m.?" she asks hopefully. I confirm. The phone rings and it's Jan. She's already in town and the rain is incredible. I assure her that coffee will be on as planned, rain or shine. Cheryl calls from work. She's on shift until 2:00 a.m. and are we really still leaving at 7:00 a.m.?

Actually, some of us are up at 5:45 to make sure the horses get a hearty breakfast. The stars are faintly visible in the still-dark sky. Wendy arrives first, as expected, followed by Jan. I toss her a saddle pack with permission to take anything that will fit in it. Cheryl is next, trailing tarp and sleeping bag and we quickly go through bedroll class #101. Lauraine rushes in, anxious that she's late and uncertain if she's left the water running to her trough at home. I assign her to the second trailer shift and send her on tour to check that faucet.

Our departure point is 30 km distant, the last bit in four-wheel drive. It is 10:30 before we are finally all on horseback and underway —in the most glorious autumn day I can recall in years.

Perhaps a lot of today's stress is caused by unreliable weather forecasts, but we're not about to complain. The footing is good, the horses are fresh and with a few minor adjustments, the loads are secure. We make good mileage to our first creek crossing and break for lunch on the far side. After securing the horses well off the trail, we check out the wares. Wendy has porkchops, Cheryl has pumpernickel with salami and cheese and Jan has potato salad! I'm wolfing down salami on rye and pork cutlets but Lauraine's homemade cookies are the most popular of all.

Underway once more, we jog along,

startling a spruce grouse out of its cranberry-gobbling reverie. Jan marks its landing like a hunting dog. I dismount with the .22 calibre rifle, sole proprietor of a hunting license in our group. I aim for a neck shot, hoping not to damage the choice breast meat. At the report of the rifle, the dozing horses spring to and the grouse flushes deeper into cover, minus a bit of downy feather. Slightly embarrassed, I stalk my quarry, bringing it down with an off-hand shot at 30 metres.

I return with the bird to an appreciative audience so my pride is somewhat mollified. I dress the grouse and stash it in Jan's saddlebag as her mount has packhorse on its resume and is not troubled by blood and such. Midday is not prime grouse hunting time but we soon spot and bag another berry-satiated bird. Jan and her horse put up with endless "bear-bait" remarks.

Afternoon break involves tying up horses and laying around on the moss drinking hot beverages and eating snacks. Cheryl indulges in a catnap while the rest of us coerce Wendy into sharing that oversize chocolate bar. Jan has her own secret vice and is seen to dispatch her second O'Henry bar of the day.

The late afternoon sun is shining on a south-facing slope in the foreground and we start sizing it up for a campsite. It is on the far side of the creek, 100 metres from water. Gentle benches rise 15 metres, levelling out in

ILLUSTRATION: WYATT TREMBLAY

a stand of big old spruce trees. We scout the location briefly, decide on a layout, then begin limbing trees to secure the horses. Everyone helps and soon all the limbs and nearby deadfall are neatly stacked by our scraped fire site. The horses are tied and stripped and a tarp is strung up. Ground sheets and bedrolls appear like mushrooms and Wendy is lighting a fire. Jan and Cheryl return from the creek with water and rocks for a fire ring. Lauraine takes her saddlebags to help out.

As we wait for the water to boil, we check out various freeze-dried and boil-in-a-bag entrees. Jan has brought pita bread and hummus and I scavenge a quick meal of cutlets, fruit and sandwiches while planning a walkabout. Lauraine offers to come with me and we hike, hunt and pick, returning to camp at sunset with some cranberries and another unwary grouse. We join the rest of our party in letting our horses graze on their leadropes. Although we are carrying hobbles, some of the younger horses are not very experienced in dealing with the uneven footing in the buckbrush and meadow grass. After grazing and watering, we feed the horses their meal of pellets and secure them for the night.

Sitting around the campfire with our coffee and cognac, we admire the stars and postpone the inevitable—climbing into a cold sleeping bag! There is much chatter and giggling as we all attempt to shed our clothes and gain our covers without a chill. As the bedrolls warm up, the conversation dies down.

I awake to deep silence and my nerves feel startled. I hear a small but distinct snap just north of camp and then another. Flashlight in hand, I scan the area. No movement, no more sounds and the horses seem unconcerned. I am puzzled until Wendy appears out of the darkness, apologetic for waking me and thankful that no one is trigger happy.

Daybreak arrives at 6:30 a.m. and has a grey look to it. There is a lack of activity and I have almost resigned myself to morning fire duty. Wendy breaks camp first, though, and I settle back for a few more winks as the fire begins to crackle and pop.

Wendy's voice interrupts the morning stillness. "I think we've got about an hour, ladies, before it rains." The resulting scene of activity is impressive. In minutes, we are all dressed, beds rolled and packed. Breakfast is mystical as the first dry, downy snowflakes of the year begin to fall. Jan is quite ecstatic about the snow and no one takes offence.

We make sure our fire is out, saddle up and head back down the trail. The horses are pretty fizzy. A good night's rest, another meal of pellets and frost in the air. We dance, prance and two-step down the trail for the first half an hour. They soon settle down to their work and strike a ground-covering walk. Snow continues to fall lightly and we descend into an overcast, chilly day. We break shortly and have hot beverages. Thoughts of berry picking are

abandoned and we proceed afoot to regain circulation in our legs and arms. Remounting, the horses are now mannerly and we jog along until lunch, reusing our site of the previous day.

The air is much warmer and so are we as we share thermos contents and trade edibles. Jan magnanimously donates her apple to the horses, carefully slicing it in equal portions. In its stead, she devours her fourth O'Henry of the trip. By now we are harassing her about her Jeckyl and Hyde eating habits!

As we continue on the homeward leg of our journey, our sandy footing gives way to hard, slippery clay and we slow our pace once more. I feel my mount startle beneath me and peer ahead, seeking a moose or a black bear. There is only the same large grey log that she had spooked at on the previous day and I undertake to allay her fears. We ride wide and return at a less threatening angle and my mare walks right up to the log. I loosen the rein to permit her to inspect the terror and she impertinently reaches over it and grabs a mouthful of brush. I am not impressed by her cheekiness and lean ahead to remove the food before she chews it in with the bit.

In retrospect, I am certain that it was my sudden reach forward that startled her. She flings up her head, stiffens when she sees the log once again and her braced and shod hind feet slip forward, leaving us unsupported. My friends watch in horror as my horse comes over backwards and I am lost to their view. Things aren't great from my perspective either, and I kick out of my stirrups and lean right as I feel my horse pulling left. Her head connects with my helmet and nose and then I lose contact with the horizon as we strike the ground. The bedroll and saddlebags absorb some of our impact and I am successful in getting my spine

out of alignment with hers. Most of the weight falls on my right thigh and is quickly removed as my horse regains her feet. I assume a sitting position, my nose streaming blood. I know my spine is okay and I'm not leaving my head on the ground among 20 hooves.

I am aware of Wendy's voice telling me not to move and the others attending her horse and mine. Time goes by in a surreal manner as we both assess my health, objectively and personally. I pass the verbal quiz and the pupil dilation test. All my parts move appropriately, my nose has quit bleeding and I want my face wiped clean, please. I confess to being a lousy patient, but I am glad that Wendy and the others are there. They are all very capable and had my situation been serious, they would have done the necessary, efficiently.

I am the first to hear vehicles approaching and I instruct everyone to move the horses off the track. The moment of grim reality yields and we are once more an organized group with a mission. Remounting in the wake of ATVs, we set out with Cheryl and Lauraine riding point. Wendy keeps a watchful eye beside me, leaving Jan to ride drag. Before long we are back at the truck, unsaddled and loaded. Some creative organizing allows me to shoehorn all five very cooperative horses into our stock-type trailer. Wendy gives me a second pupil dilation test and decides that it is okay to let me drive the horses and humans home, especially since no one else has any experience in hauling. We see Jan off on her homeward trip, then the rest of us head on back to the ranch.

Within the hour, the horses are turned out, tack has been put up and the truck is unloaded. Nursing tea and cognac, we are scrutinizing a table covered in maps and planning our next adventure.

Second Gift

The colours of Autumn
splash across Nares Mountain
like bursts of light,
a song for the eyes
in radiant tones
& brilliant verse,
a second gift of summer
singing its joy & warmth
in the whisper of the season

R.J.L. '95 Nares Lake, Yukon

Some would say we lead the ideal lifestyle. As wilderness guides and owners of Sila Sojourns and Ecosummer Yukon Expeditions, we spend the summers traipsing through some of the most gorgeous wildlands in the Yukon. And we devote the winters to world travel, exploration and creative endeavours. Well, it is pretty ideal. However, nothing is ever as perfect as it seems. So why don't you hop into our soggy boots and we'll give you an inside look at some of our "real-life" experiences in the guiding business.

Scenario 1

You've been up all night packing food, making last minute tent repairs (that you swore you'd do last season), and tending to that never-ending errand list. Rendezvous-with-the-group time is fast approaching. You just have time to zoom into town, screech to a halt outside the corner store and rummage through the shelves for that oh-so-essential can of diced pineapple (without which day five dinner would surely be a disaster), grab a latté-on-the-run, and have a last second chat with a long lost friend! You spy the group and give them a quick "once-over" to suss out who'll get to carry the pots, fuel, ten-pound radio, jars of PB and jam (although we often end up with the bulk of it). The trick is to decide what they can do without in order to cram that extra ten to twenty pounds of food plus part of a tent into those already-jammed packs. They just don't make packs big enough anymore.

And off we go, onto Day 1.

Scenario 2

You are nimbly negotiating the tundra tussocks with 60 pounds on your back. Over lunch, while you sit with your shorts and t-shirt, a hail stone hits your cheek. It is the 14th of July, which is supposedly summer, and the hail turns into a full-fledged snowstorm. Everyone looks to you with disbelief, you look back with a shrug and say "anything can happen in the Yukon."

Scenario 3

You're camped beside the biggest and gnarliest rapid in the river. The anticipation of running it fills you with dread, but the roar lulls you to sleep, a sleep racked by nightmares. The day dawns steely grey and foreboding and it will surely rain. The water will surely rise and the rapids will rise a notch on the "foreboding" scale. This is not something to look forward to. As you push off from shore, your heart racing wildly, you mutter to yourself "what am I doing here??!!" all the while maintaining that external calm and a smile on your face.

Scenario 4

It is 2:00 a.m. and you've had a 15-hour day on the river, including a long dragging session to get the raft out of the shallow channels to the Beaufort coast. You can finally sleep. At 7:00 a.m., mother nature calls, and as you stumble out of the tent, eyes still glued shut, and are about to drop your drawers, something tells you that the white lump 15 feet away is not an iceberg but a polar bear!

So, what ARE we doing here? Is it because we're too stubborn to get a REAL job or that we can't live without the divine pleasure of munching our muscles on a regular basis? Or is it because our memories are selective and we only remember the good times?

Well, it's a little of the above, but most of all, we do it because we LOVE it! We meet the most diverse collection of people in the most inspiring places. We don't have a pension plan but we do have flexibility. The recovery time for aching joints DOES seem to get longer each year, but so far we have avoided the midlife bulges.

The intriguing thing is that we are at natures' whim—her wildly fluctuating moods, her exquisite beauty, the inhabitants of the wild places—and we really have to adapt to each situation as it presents itself.

What else need we say? This lifestyle truly does feed our souls. It energizes us, motivates us, and inspires us. It hones our bodies and triggers our creative minds, and despite the hard times, it saves us from the 9 to 5.

Footloose and on the move

story and illustration by
Joyce Majiski and
Jill Pangman

We were away for our fill of short, primitive adventure. As we rounded the final turn, I realized no one knew our destination. How could they? Until we left the yard, we hadn't decided exactly where to try our luck for lake trout and grouse. Even my best friend was ignorant of where we would camp. Mistake number one.

As we arrived at our destination, the late October light was dimming. Still, we figured

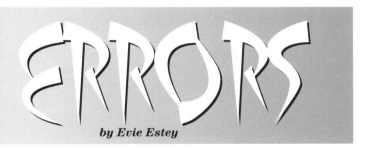

ERRORS

by Evie Estey

we could squeeze an hour of time on the lake before it would be too dangerous to be out on the water. So we launched the boat and gaily zoomed off to explore and drag a line for fish. Mistake number two.

We did catch a fish. Its bloody gills splattered red over the bottom of the aluminum craft where it flopped its death dance before I clobbered it to silence. As its blood pooled at my feet, I looked up to notice in surprise that someone had "turned out the lights!" It was dark! Suddenly, and unexpectedly, we had been enveloped in obscurity. The shore was no longer visible; we were bobbing in an unfamiliar part of the lake with no landmarks in sight. Mistake number three.

Panic. We began to argue over where we were. I was certain we had drifted close to the mouth of the river which empties the lake. He was just as certain that I was wrong; we could not have come that far in the little time we had been afloat. I was sure that I could hear the rush of water. Oh, dear God, we were going to die! I had neglected to bring emergency gear. Here we were in the ideal situation for the survival package, and where was it? In the truck! Mistake number four.

I started to cry. I would never see my daughter again! How could we survive this? He took command of the situation and slowly, very slowly and cautiously, idled the boat along as I perched over the bow to scout for submerged objects. My night vision is excellent, but I trembled in fear of ramming a log or rock. I lifted my gaze from the water's surface and saw a faint outline of beach. God willing, we could at least get off the lake and make a fire. He smoked cigarettes; he had a lighter. I had read somewhere that the main use of a fire was to give you something to do while you took stock of your situation. Well, it seemed to me this was a fine situation which needed some stock-taking.

We beached the boat on coarse gravel strewn with dry wood, and soon had a small fire lit. We rolled the boat over, intending to

use it as cover from the elements. It quickly became apparent that the metal behaved like a refrigerator and we were more cold under the boat than in the open air.

Time to take inventory. We wore sturdy hiking boots, jeans and long underwear, flannel shirts and down-filled jackets. Our pockets held one beer, a packet of peanuts, a book of matches, and a length of toilet paper. No hats, no gloves. I thought about the emergency pack and how welcome the space blanket, billy can, tea and soup mix would be.

It was a long, cold, black night. So cold, in fact, that to keep warm we heated small stones by the fire then placed them inside our shirt sleeves and pant legs for warmth. Fourteen hours of darkness, of sitting close to the fire doing "the rotisserie" to warm all parts

equally. Fourteen hours of trying to figure out exactly where on the lake we were. Fourteen hours of listening to the sounds of the night, trying not to mistake every little snap as the footfall of a grizzly coming to eat us. Fourteen long, cold, miserable hours of an October night never to be forgotten. Fourteen hours that passed agonizingly slowly.

Yet, they did pass, and the darkness gave way to grey pre-dawn, then, finally, to the pinkish hint of sunrise. By our wits we had survived the abyss of the full Yukon night and now were free to return, as if we had been banished by some ogre in a fairy tale. We had expected to find the rime of frost over the boat, but we were not prepared to see the 15 feet of ice that had formed at the water's edge overnight. How cold had it been? So cold that we each wore paths of burned flesh from the hot little rocks we had slipped inside our clothing.

We launched the boat through an incision in the frozen shore ice. By some miracle, the usually lethargic motor caught on the first pull. We were free from exile! One good look around showed that we were indeed at the far end of the lake near the river that rushed the water away. We could hardly believe we had travelled so far in our brief time the night before, a distance that took three hours to retrace. I was very, very thankful to whomever-it-is-that-looks-after-fools for doing the job so well.

I have learned valuable lessons from my follies, and realize that people have perished in similar circumstances. We were lucky, the fates were kind; they did not exact the ultimate cost for the errors of our ways. The experience has instilled a greater respect for "the bush." I have never repeated my mistakes, and now tend to err on the side of caution. The bush will always be there to enjoy, and I want to be around to enjoy it for a long time. Older and wiser, one might say.

Montana

WILDERNESS CELEBRATION

If you have been to the Mountain... If you have been to the Mountain and have seen the Other Side... If you have struggled through the first feeble innocence of your ability, and then through strength and wisdom... If you have looked over the Other Side into the cardiovascular abyss which is neither strength nor wisdom, but more like the abiding eternal will of a blade of grass pushing its way up through the concrete... If you have passed through these initiations, then the ride up Montana Mountain beckons. It also offers some amazing high views of the lakes and mountains surrounding the Carcross area.

You arrive in Carcross at the base of a thickly-treed slope rising up, up to the peaks that are just visible beyond the high plateau. The perspective induces the feeling that we are mortal specks—perhaps more than a blade of grass, but perhaps not as competent, milling around at the bottom of an enormous power. Parking one's car in the convenient lot adjacent to the Carcross Information Centre, amid the buzz of buses and secure vacationers, can help to alleviate this daunting sense. From here you ride your mountain bike a few hundred metres back to the highway and turn right. Continue across the road bridge and take the first right a couple hundred metres past it. The next few hundred metres are the last level ground you will enjoy for a while. The road forks at the end of this short gravel stretch. To the right, it dips lightly into the village alongside the short "river" connecting Lake Bennett to Nares Lake. The river flows in a relaxed way, and, similarly, so do the people there. Everything looks green and easy, and this also beckons the initiated. However, to the left—and these things are always to the left—the gravel road turns up steeply. Everything looks dryer and harder; this really beckons, and the choice is made.

This first incline, a moderate indication of what lies ahead, levels out onto an open area soon enough, and you feel pretty good, in touch with yourself. Lake Bennett glinting between and beyond the treetops gives you an encouraging sense of the elevation you have already gained. A sign informs you at the end of this short mild grade that you are on a mining road. It also advises you to "have a nice day" and to not sue anyone for your mishaps on the road. The irony of that doesn't strike too deeply. And neither does the irony that roads like this one, leading to big iron buckets tearing up the high ground for money, also provide access to some sublime views of nature: iron buckets of irony that do not usually strike too deep.

Beyond this sign, the road is walled in by thick growth, and the visible sense of elevation gain is lost. That doesn't matter because now you are concentrating on the loose gravel and rocks directly under your wheels. There is lots of that to occupy your attention, and you're glad you're using the knarliest knobbies you have for this ride. The sense of elevation gain now resides completely within your body because it doesn't feel this way doing anything else. A few more steeper sections, and soon your breath, saturated with the spores of growth around you, is claiming your attention as much as the rocks. Eventually, your breath feels heavier than the rocks. Eventually, your thoughts become indistinguishable from breath and rocks. Eventually, you wonder when these steep, rocky, breath-ridden sections will end and return your thoughts back to you. Eventually they do end, and the level ground is yours to enjoy again, enjoyed maybe even more than your own thoughts.

At the end of this short sweet stretch, the wall of thick growth opens up onto a clearing which provides another view of elevation gain. The great red bowl of the rock slide which can be seen from the highway driving south toward Carcross is now almost at eye level, and it looms large. Between that and what seems to be an abandoned mining operation directly to the right—those things are always to the right—you can see farther into the mountains of the Lake Bennett corridor. The road turns left and begins a long easy grade which is visible for some distance traversing the steep slope below the Montana plateau. Trees are giving way to shrubs, and the right side of the road sweeps down into the valley and drainage at the base of the rock slide bowl.

It is fortunate that the longest, straightest section of this traverse, which is also visible from the highway, offers some of the easiest cycling and best views of the ride. Now that your mind is no longer preoccupied by your breath and rocks, you can cast easy glances back towards the immense valley connecting Carcross to Whitehorse, or down into sections of Lake Bennett, Millhaven Bay, and the steep mountain walls that lock in West Arm. And if that's not good enough, you can easily talk to your friends about things that may or may not matter as you cycle. And if that's not good enough you can entertain your own thoughts which won't matter at all soon after the next turn.

The turn at the end of this long stretch leaves those vistas behind as it approaches what is often a washed out area of the road. This several-metre section is rideable, though not always driveable. The terrain has changed with the turn. The steep embankment on the left falls into a deep gorge on the right—always the left and the right. Snowmelt from small saddles and gullies rushes from mountain shoulders into the gorge. A few small firs are clustered here and there between open stretches of tundra. And beyond this, it is high and austere.

There is a strange circular structure a little distance ahead, incongruously perched off the side of the road, overlooking all of this terrible beauty. It is, naturally enough, the remains of

ILLUSTRATION: MARCELLA NOWATZKI

A ride not for the uninitiated

a Buddhist temple. It was built sometime in the '70s by a Tibetan Lama who had come to this place by some direction prosaic or profound, and felt it to be one of our planet's points of energy. That may be very likely because the quality of your ride will change dramatically now, and for no apparent reason.

Although the distance from the turn to the temple doesn't appear very steep and long, it is very steep and long. Of course, you're tired by now and have begun to breath rocks and ride over your thoughts while trying to keep some traction in your mind as your wheels slip over your breath. You're very grateful when you come alongside the temple because it's a good excuse to put your bike down and go have a look. Like any good temple should, it still induces rest along the way, even though it's in ruins. Up close, there are signs warning about stealing and prosecution—why not Crime and Punishment—and the irony here strikes a little deeper than the earlier ironies because we're just made that way. After you feel you've absorbed enough cultural interest, and drained enough lactate acid out of your legs, you'll go back to your bike, encouraged to finish the rest of the ride without too much sacrifice.

But once you've got your bike moving again you suddenly realize that something's happening here and you don't exactly know what it is. Once abreast of the tattered prayer flags you realize you can barely keep those prayer wheels under your tattered legs from coming to a dead stop. Once past those tattered prayer flags everything weighs a ton, and you can't make some unwanted, tattered thoughts of yours come to a dead stop. You think about the keys you may have locked in the car back at the parking lot. You think about the argument with your boss. You think about the lover you hurt, and the one that hurt you. You think about this expensive lightweight mountain bike that now weighs more than the

world. But somehow, breathing rocks and thoughts in tattered traction get you to the level turn after this incline to hallucination.

After this turn something else is happening here and you really don't know exactly what it is. There probably is a good explanation, and there probably isn't one; maybe it's just that the mind/matter of the mountain has changed. Whatever it is, you're coasting uphill. It's true, you are, but for just a little way, until the next turn.

After this turn you know you're going up again, but nothing weighs so much anymore. Your unwanted thoughts have left, your strength has left, and whatever you once considered as wisdom has left. Nothing is left but the movement up the horizonless curve. And somewhere infinitely in between the beginning and the end of it, and another push on the pedal, you can see a small figure walking down the road towards you. The figure appears stunted, maybe it's the old keeper of the temple. Another push on the pedal, and you see it is a child. Another push on the pedal, and you see the child is you, standing there looking up expectantly at you. The sudden urge to pass on some life-long advice about checking the car keys, about arguing with the boss, about happy and unhappy love, and about bicycles, disappears with another push on the pedal; after all, was it all really so important? Another push on the pedal, you take a quick look back, and where the child had stood you now see a blade of grass moving gently in the high rarefied breezes.

Somewhere infinitely in between the beginning and the end of it, and another push on the pedal, you reach the end. You stand there like a blade of grass, a few thousand feet closer to the sun, blood rushing through your veins like the melting snow through the gullies and gorges, breathing deeply like the swelling breezes between the mountain lungs, and your mind is as clear and endless as the dome of the sky surrounding your head. But

all that doesn't last longer than a trillionth of a second: long enough to create a universe, but not long enough to keep ourselves amused. And that's just as well because the winds are cold up there, and it's time to put on extra layers of clothes to keep the chills away. It's also time to eat something for those worn and tattered limbs. It's also time to check the panniers for the car keys.

The road continues left or right—it always goes one way or the other—lower into a kind of rolling valley between the saddle on which you now stand, and the ridge leading up to the actual peak of Montana Mountain. The road to the right continues out of the valley to a small pass with a great view of a large gorge draining into Lake Bennett. The road left continues down and around the other side of Montana Mountain towards Windy Arm. But at this point you will agree that these roads are better explored after you have driven most of the way up by truck. However, it is reasonable to ride the road to the right a little way until it branches off toward the cirque of Montana Mountain. Soon the rocks are too big to ride over and it is necessary to walk the rest of the way to the cirque. This little effort is rewarded by a visit to a cool and peaceful tarn within the cirque.

Good brakes are mandatory for the descent. Except for the short section where you will have to pedal downhill (the same place where you coasted uphill) it is necessary to use your brakes almost all the way down. And if a blade of grass offers you a set of keys on the way down, don't bother to stop; you're in control now, going down fast, full of accomplishment. And down in the parking lot, while trying to figure how to get into your car, should a very old and strangely familiar face walk up and toss you the keys, saying it has been the wait of a lifetime since you dropped them in the dirt on your way out, check your watch and insist that the entire ride didn't take more than 4 to 6 hours. You're in control again.

by Lance Scoville

story and photos by Mary Whitley

SEA KAYAKING: A SEAL'S EYE VIEW

Dip. Push. Dip. Push. The rhythm was hypnotic. The rocking of the kayak felt gentle and restful. The sea was calm and it wasn't raining! What a perfect way to begin a sea kayak trip.

This was my first experience sea kayaking. I'll admit I had many reservations—about wind, tides, currents, weather. Everything seems so much bigger when you say "ocean." The initiation trip my husband and I had planned took us from Bartlett Cove, the centre of activity at Glacier Bay, into a complex of islands called the Beardslees. They were protected from the wind and waves of the main arm of Glacier Bay. They had bird and seal colonies. They had everything we were looking for, without the problems.

The extent of our pre-trip instruction had been brief, mostly designed to protect our kayaks from our bumbling attempts at landing and embarking. We were very careful to ensure that the kayak was afloat before getting in. This is harder than it sounds. The tide is always rising or falling. If the former, then the kayak, after it is carried to the water's edge for loading must be moved up the beach every five minutes or you risk losing it completely while your back is turned. If the tide is falling, the opposite problem occurs. The craft must be moved seaward every five minutes or so, or the loaded, and very heavy, kayak will be high and dry when you are ready to set off.

Rubber boots are essential to this entry and exit. They should have firm soles and come almost up to the knees.

Loading the beast. What a chore that was! Yet it really didn't take long. Just dealing with all the little packages and standing on your head to stow them in the available space was a nuisance. Kayaks have lots of room, we discovered. But the space is in small increments. A plastic bag of clothes here, a bag of shoes there, another with reading material.

The rudder of the two-person kayak was easy to handle as long as it was trimmed each time we started out. This meant the stern paddler didn't need to adjust the rudder except when we were changing course, or in wind, waves or currents.

The paddling motion is quite easy to learn. The hardest part for me was remembering to push the paddle with the upper hand rather than pulling with the lower hand. After a long stretch of paddling, my fingers tingled, which, I was assured by seasoned paddlers, meant I was doing it right. Sea kayaking is ideal for people who aren't as interested in getting somewhere as in going. The pace is relaxed and even if you aren't moving quickly, it is still quite peaceful and comfortable being in a boat.

This activity would lend itself well to a single parent and child team, as long as the child is strong enough to lift the kayak and carry it a short distance, as it must be moved well above the high tide line every night. One lesson that is quickly learned is to paddle with the tides. It is better to wait on shore and watch the activity around than to try yourself against the force of the sea. For example, on the day we were dropped off in the upper bay, with a rising tide we travelled 12 miles in just over four hours. An average day is said to be ten miles and that might entail over six hours of paddling.

One day, near the end of our trip, we found ourselves in wind and waves. The kayak handled well, even with the waves rolling over the stern. It was stable and steady when we weren't. It got us a seal's eye view of the surface of the sea, and many times of a seal. It taught us respect for the forces of the sea and patience for its rhythms.

Mount Bostock re-visited

story and photo by KH Poulsen

Following a submission to the Yukon geographical names board by C.H. Smith, on October 6, 1994, a summit in the Yukon was officially named Mount Bostock. The peak, with co-ordinates 63°46'N and 136°43'W, is located approximately 45 km west northwest of the town of Mayo. At an elevation of 5,882 feet (1,793 metres) above sea level it is a relatively inconspicuous, small plateau atop a broader mountainous area, the East Ridge, which rises more than one kilometre above the McQuesten River valley.

The site is one that H.S. Bostock personally approved of, having made special reference to it in his 1979 memoirs, *Pack Horse Tracks* recalling a traverse made in August 1947:

"About three miles from the south end of the East Ridge and almost overlooking the deep McQuesten valley is a summit of 5882 feet a.s.l. From here the view in all directions is amazing for so inconspicuous a top. Standing on this eminence and looking northwesterly one sees a broad open hollow in the upland sloping gently away to the main South Klondike River valley beyond which rises the Ogilvie Mountains.... Looking now in the opposite direction one views another wide hollow sloping southeastward across the McQuesten valley to the Stewart River valley while away to the left or east the heads of Johnson and Seattle creeks flow northeastward as though to join some master stream draining in that general direction.... From here, in the heart of the McQuesten area, I could see much of the Carmacks area to the south, the Ogilvie area on the west and the Mayo area on the east embracing close to 17,300 square miles. Their study had been my interest during the last 15 years. This point, though not conspicuous is indeed a remarkable lookout."

My Chilkoot trip

This is a story of my hike over the Chilkoot Trail with my father, who works for Parks Canada. On the first day we took the train to Bennett where Christine, the trail interpreter, gave us a tour. After the tour, I made tomato noodle soup with the trail crew in Bennett. Then we hiked down the track where we met a German hiker on the way to the cut-off trail. At Lindeman, Dad gave a tour of the historic site. I learned how to play cribbage with Mike. He was a good teacher—he lost all the games.

The next day, we hiked to the summit. On the way we stopped to take pictures. There was a metal boat frame beside Deep Lake from the gold rush. We hiked over a ridge and stopped so I could play in the snow there. From the top of the ridge we could see a grave from 1897. We walked through a river canyon, then stopped at Happy Camp for lunch with a group of ten people. They were kids from Whitehorse. Near Morrow Lake there was a waterfall. Here, I could smell the spruce and feel on my face the strong, cold wind from the summit of the pass. My feet were sore and my pack was getting heavy on my back. The water rushed over the rocks with

story and photos by
Erin Neufeld

a tinkling sound like a bell. The sun was warm and up ahead I could see the summit of the pass.

We got to the summit in the afternoon. We had seafood for supper and then my dad and I went for a walk down to Crater Lake. We saw the bones of a gold rush horse. Then Lise and Donna came to visit us. They were looking for an old cable engine and an old blacksmith's forge.

In the morning, there was so much fog, you could hardly see the pond in front of our tent. Just before the fog broke up we caught sight of a mother and some baby ptarmigan. They were hard to see because they were so well camouflaged.

That day we picked three-quarters of a litre of blueberries so we could make a blueberry pie. At Sheep Camp it was really green, because it was in the middle of the enchanted forest.

The next day, we left early so we could walk 21 kilometres. The last hour and a half was a little harsh, but we got by. We had supper in Skagway. When we got home it was late at night and I went straight to bed. The next morning I had to go to school.

The Lynx

by Glen Bunbury

It was bitterly cold. Frost hung heavily as it clung to hair and clothing. My uncle Norman and I mounted our skidoos—he on a little 240 Elan, and myself on a 340 Polaris Longtrack. Four or five pulls later the skidoos fired up, shattering the frozen morning quiet. Down the winding snowtrail we went. The traps had to be run.

I remember that day clearly. It was a good day for trapping and we had done well with a total of four lynx. This was good because lynx were about $300 for a medium-size lynx pelt.

We were trapping around the Fox Lake area where my grandfather had a trapline. It was on the south side of Fox Lake, five or six miles off the Klondike Highway. At this time I was young (around 15), but I really enjoyed the work. To me, it felt like one big adventure. On this particular day I was feeling rather speedy and managed to slide off the packed snowtrail several times within a short period. This was not fun because once that big old Longtrack got bogged down, we had a heck of a time getting it out. It usually took both of us to put it back on the trail.

The second and third trap we came to had lynxes. I was just catching up to my uncle who was at the fourth trap. As I got off the Polaris I noticed his agitation. He seemed rather pissed off and there was a look of deep consternation on his face. He was actively cussing away. "What's the matter?" I asked him. "A lynx got away with the trap," he replied. "It dragged the trap and the toggle out onto the main trail. It could be miles away by now."

As my uncle busied himself lamenting the loss of both the lynx and the trap, I got busy sizing up the situation. I followed the trail the cat had left, over the skidoo tracks and back toward the way we had just come. I walked back a short distance and stopped. Looking up I could just make out the pale ghostly form of the lynx crouching among the spruce trees. I guess as it was making its escape it must have heard us coming up the trail. It then tried to take off into the bushes.

This caused the toggle to get tangled up in the trees and deadfall, holding it there. "It's over here!" I shouted to my uncle. He was greatly relieved and ran down the trail towards me. "Where!" he asked urgently. "Over there!" I pointed. It took him a little while to make out the cat, as lynx are superbly camouflaged in snowy conditions. There was quite a bit of deadfall and the snow was pretty deep.

My uncle began to walk towards it. He was very close. He put one foot down into the deep snow. It met with deadfall. Suddenly, he slipped. Everything seemed to happen at once, in a blur of motion. My uncle slipped and his foot came out from under him. The lynx lunged and bit viciously down on his boot. He pulled it quickly away. In the excitement of the moment, I shouted "Holy shit!" or something to that effect. My uncle turned and glared angrily at me.

"Fuck you! Fuck you! Don't you laugh!" he shouted. "I wasn't laughing," I protested meekly. I didn't press the matter as I could see he was fairly shaken up over the whole thing.

We made the trip home, each of us packing two lynx. Later that evening, as we

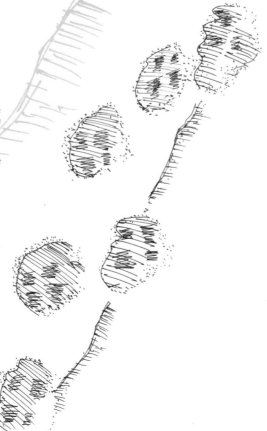

were sitting around in my grandfather's nice warm house, we went over the day's events as we sipped tea around a cozy fire. I related the story to my grandfather and he listened quietly, nodding once in a while. My uncle then showed me one of his snowpacks, the one that the lynx had bitten into. There were four puncture marks where the lynx had bitten deeply into the vulcanized rubber of the boot.

It was then that the enormity of the situation began to dawn on me. We were lucky. If my uncle had been wearing moccasins or the lynx had bitten further up on the leg, that could have meant real trouble for us. We were miles from the highway and it was extremely cold. As far as a first-aid kit went we did not have so much as a bandaid. It would have been a heck of a thing to have to haul a wounded man out of the wilderness under those harsh conditions. It was a good thing that this wasn't necessary.

After this happened, whenever my uncle went out on the trapline, he always travelled prepared for any eventuality. He started to faithfully carry a .22 calibre rifle so that he would not have to get too close to any trapped animal.

It's always a good idea to trap in pairs and to carry a good sleeping bag with you in case you find yourself staying out in the cold for any prolonged period of time. A first-aid kit is essential to have along.

I learned a lot from my uncle that season and he impressed me with his skill and knowledge of the land. He knew a great deal about the animals and their habitat, and he was always willing to share that knowledge with me.

It's been quite a few years since this happened, and since then, neither of us has been trapping much. Once in a while I may go down to the trapline to harvest a beaver and the odd muskrat, but the fur prices don't really warrant any large-scale trapping venture.

All in all, I would say it was a really good experience, and that if I had it to do over again, I most certainly would.

ILLUSTRATIONS: WENDY BUSH

Coal River provides
waterfall
of memories

by Kirsten Madsen

We didn't want to run the rapid, but we had to take the toad through. It was the fourth and final day of our journey down the Coal River. We'd stopped above what would be the final whitewater section, and I looked down at the frothy white with both excitement and fear. Then my eyes caught a small toad who was stuck in the eddy, kicking frantically. Doris leaned over to grab it, seconds before the shadow of a large fish surfaced and broke the water, mouth agape. The tired toad was placed in a plastic container to be rafted to safety.

We would have run the drop anyway, but it was a funny excuse. It was my second trip down the Coal. I'd canoed it four years before, but remembering my fears at each rapid—really, 17 is too young to die—I'd eagerly agreed to take the raft this time. Sue J. and my father, Ken, would kayak.

We flew in from Watson Lake. Polly grabbed my hand and jerked it hard towards her as the Otter plane dipped and rose. It made tighter and tighter circles down towards the tiny lake, and then a splash, which frightened a moose as we landed. Strangely, it leaped towards us, into the water.

We tugged the raft upstream to reach the Coal River springs that first night. The tufa formations, oddly white in that atmosphere of mushy green, were lacy and tiered like rice fields. Some were pooled with water so deep it gave me shivers, peering nervously into the greenish depths. We wandered around, carefully skirting the fragile tufa crust, each of us with camera in hand. Polly and Doris posed for each other near the forest line. Jocylyn pointed her lens at a floating water plant and my father carefully set up his tripod to snap a tiny waterfall. I wandered around, but found myself mostly photographing everyone's faces, expressions of wonder clearly evident. I realized that no one was taking the same picture. What appealed to each of us differed in small but important ways. It occurred to me that in this way we are all artists, because the wild area offered us each a different vista to appreciate and capture on film, to sketch and to write about.

That evening, we watched a cow and calf moose cross the river near our campsite. Their ears were shaped like candle flames, their bodies, awkward and graceful at the same time, were the colour that defines brown. The young moose shook swiftly, like a dog, as it stepped from the water.

Jocylyn slept each night under a circus-tent-like shelter with the high-tech name "mega-mid." However, she could never quite remember the name and it soon became known as the Mega Digs. One night she awoke to a rustling sound and discerned a fist-sized lump peering at her. The frog hopped out again with only a little prodding.

The days of flat water made me wish for a canoe. The raft was saggy and sluggish, and our bums sunk lower by the minute. Polly and Doris amused themselves rescuing dragonflies trapped on the sticky surface of the water, scooping them onto the raft with their paddle blades. The dragonflies, blue and gold with huge glittering eyes, stretched their long bodies and gratefully perched on Doris' shoulder as their wings dried.

The river had changed since I had canoed it four years before. The water level was higher, the sandy banks reformed by

high water. A small beach lining a canyon wall was tilted rakishly. We had camped there before with room to spare, but now were forced to slap the sand flat with our paddles, hollowing out narrow spaces for seven bodies. A beaver had moved in, slapping the water angrily every 15 minutes as we heated water, unrolled sleeping bags, and shook out tents.

On the fourth day, we reached The Grand Canyon of the Coal—capital letters added by me—and mowed through the whitewater, the raft buckling in the hollow of each wave. Like true rafters, we shouted loudly at each bounce, squealed at each splash, yelled loudly at the end of each rapid. All this was much to the disgust, I'm sure, of Sue J. and my father, who, like all kayakers, are strong and silent, in control, enjoying themselves without obnoxiousness ...yeah, right.

The Coal's canyon is made of striped, opposing layers of grey and tan rock, running at strange tilting angles towards the water as though drunk. The water is clear and runs over ledges and through a few narrow chutes which I had decided not to canoe on our last trip. This time, bolstered perhaps by a combination of age, experience, and the paddling of the unsinkable raft, I steered us down all of them. The others called me "Raft Master," but with infinitely more sarcasm than confidence.

My second journey down the Coal River gave me new memories to add to the others—Polly and Darren shivering with an attempt at enthusiasm under a dashing waterfall, a beaver that swam right underneath our raft, the gummybear cheesecake we made for my father's birthday, and the final rapid which I will always think of as "toad drop" from now on.

I'm not quite sure if there should be some sort of message or lesson in this article, or even if one arose out of our trip. To me, it was a bunch of feelings and experiences like the ones above. I wanted to try and write about the river, just as Jocylyn wanted to sketch it and my father to photograph it.

If there's one feeling that is predominant as I write, it is thankfulness. I was very lucky to be able to take time off from work to do that trip, to have a father with a strange kayaking obsession, and to be in the Yukon, where rivers like the Coal are still wild. I'm looking forward to a third trip already.

WILDERNESS CELEBRATION

SNOWBOARDING IN JULY

by Anna Pugh

As I ran out of the office, I couldn't help but smile in anticipation of the night to come. It was a hot July day, and any normal person would have been looking forward to a nice cold glass of beer and a lawn chair in the shade. But I had my mind set on something a little colder. I was going to drive up Montana Mountain near Carcross, and go for a snowboard under the midnight sun.

Not so long ago, I was among the many people who would look upon this sort of plan as quite insane. After all, we already have snow for about eight months of the year. What kind of freak goes seeking it out on the hottest day of the summer? I guess the answer to that is, "freaks like me." I began snowboarding several years ago, and like most people who tried it, I was hooked after the first few runs.

However, my love of snowboarding did not happen without considerable personal sacrifice. I learned the hard way, in -20°C temperatures on the hills behind the Whitehorse hospital. My method of learning

was to strap on the board and point it down the hill. This meant a lot of speed and basically no control. Turning, or carving, was not an option, and to wipe out meant spending several minutes lying still, groaning and trying to gather my senses.

But the threat of pain is good incentive to gain control, and after only a few painful experiences, I began to be able to complete a few shaky turns before the bottom of the run. After that, things like jumps and carving began to fall into place.

Snowboarding has a very fast learning curve, one of the reasons it has become so popular. There are not very many sports in which you are unable to stay upright one day, and are cruising down the hills in style on the next. By the time Mt. Sima ski hill opened, I was a reasonably competent snowboarder. The ski lift was a bit harder to get under control (getting off a chair and down an embankment while facing sideways is not an easy thing), but these days, I don't totally disgrace the snowboarding community with

my loading and off-loading abilities.

On this particular day, I wasn't going to have to worry about lifts. I was off to the mountains to ride the open slopes.

Backcountry boarding is a totally different game from lift-served boarding. There are drawbacks to each, but both are great experiences. I have to admit I am a lazy boarder, and I really do not enjoy hiking up a mountain in order to board back down, only seconds later. Part of this is due to the fact that my boarding companions are taller, faster, and generally, fitter, men. Another reason I do not like hiking is that it puts pressure on you to have a good run, since you only have a limited amount of time in a day, and you spend such a long time hiking, you don't want to waste it.

On the other hand, though, there is nothing like the feeling of carving sweeping turns into a long slope of untouched powder snow. It is a freedom that you don't find at ski hills, where everything is tracked or groomed long before you make it up the lift.

But ski hills are great places to learn and improve. You can do a lot of runs in a day, and help is nearby if you have problems. In the backcountry, there is always the threat of an avalanche, or of injuring yourself a long way from a hospital or first-aid station.

I still haven't resolved whether backcountry or lift-served boarding is better, but they are both exhilarating and I enjoy both for different reasons. The way to get the best of both worlds is to get a snowmachine and a willing driver. This will give you unlimited runs and untracked powder, which is what makes a great day of boarding.

If, like myself, you can't afford a snowmobile, there are two other options for relatively painless and fun backcountry boarding. One is to make friends with a snowmobiler who wants nothing more in life than to drive you up and down a mountain. The other is to go in July, when the road runs to the base of the snow, and the patch of snow that you are boarding on is so small that it only takes a short time to hike up. I have tried to find that elusive snowmobiler/chauffeur, but without any luck so far. So I found myself loading up my car, with boots, board, mittens and Gortex, while wearing a summer dress and Birkenstocks. I received a few strange looks from the neighbours, but I felt less conspicuous once I met up with my friends, who looked equally out of place. We bounced our way up the mountain and then began the hike up the scree to the snow. It was pretty icy, but where the sun was beaming onto the snow, it was heavy and slushy—ideal boarding conditions. After a few runs, there were smiles all around.

As the sun began to dip lower in the sky, long shadows spread out below us, across Bennett Lake and the Wheaton valley. We took our last run as the sun disappeared. I drove back to town, satisfied with my quick fix in the summer sun, and content to put the board away until the snow flies. As this is the Yukon, it may be only a short wait.

When the temperature starts to creep up after a long northern winter, rational people hit the outdoors in search of adventure. Imbeciles go ice fishing. There were five of us and Elsa, my dog, a pea-brained Dawson City mongrel. We were a jaunty crew, happy to be breathing fresh air on a bright spring afternoon. Innocents all. Not so our guide.

He was a local teacher, a gnarly Albertan who liked to stuff his front lip with strands of the black weed. He possessed a near joyous love of the wilds, especially hooking big lake trout.

Whether he did this while drifting on a mirror-smooth lake in shirtsleeves or through a hole in the ice didn't matter. Outsmarting brainless lunkers with a flashy spoon was a lifelong passion, the payoff roasting its succulent flesh over a fire, cheeks and all. Besides, he said, ice fishing is a great excuse to sit in the warm spring sun, drink beer and roast wieners. So we signed on.

The plan was to drive to a lake near Carcross and traverse its windswept ice to the far shore. There, following a short hike through the bush, we'd find a second lake. Actually, it's little more than a frozen puddle, the Albertan confessed. But it's thick with trout. Massive fish, the size of small dogs, and all of them a bit gnarly after the long winter. They'll be fighting over your lures, he said. "It'll be great."

He didn't tell us ice fishing never goes according to plan. The road ended abruptly, kilometres from the shore of the first lake. So, our guide, his eight-month-pregnant wife, and another pregnant woman, her spouse and I plowed down the road's waist-deep snow to our starting point. "Who's got the maggots?" I asked. True icers pack the squirming Rice Krispee-like larvae between their gums and cheek, to keep their succulent juices from freezing. Or so I'd read somewhere. The guide, however, scoffed at the age-old bait. After all, this is the age of polar fleece and Gortex. Besides, his lip was filled with tobacco. No, there were no maggots for us. We were packing Power Bait, biodegradable plastercine-like gunk in neon colours. And that wasn't all we carried.

ICE FISHING

The expectant mothers packed the babies, the rest of us hauled packs stuffed with fishing gear, lawn chairs, food, beer and cameras. Now, in more populous areas, people drive four-by-fours onto lakes. Sometimes they drag a wooden hut resembling an outhouse, for protection from the wind and snow. Others bring nylon ice fishing tents. From inside these tiny cabins and tents, the adult equivalent of a child's cardboard-box fort, they jig maggots in the hope of coaxing a fish onto the line. When they tire of jigging the line, a hopelessly idiotic task, they play cards, drink beer, admire each other's lures and swap tales. We, of course, had no cabin. Just the lawn chairs, a pack of matches and a blunt folding saw to hack down dead trees for a fire.

Exhausted by the hike to our "starting point," we abandoned the trip to the fish-filled puddle and set up a makeshift camp on the first lake. As if on cue, storm clouds blew over the surrounding mountains, snuffing out the sun and obliterating the horizon behind a dense wall of grey. And the wind shifted, turning our protected bay into a wind tunnel. Stinging rain blew into our faces. The guide and I started drilling the hole.

This is another ice fishing ritual, the most tasking chore the fisher is expected to perform.

story and photo
by Richard Mostyn

Between swigs of Kokanee, brawny fishers drill a dinner-plate-sized hole in the ice with an auger—a glorified corkscrew. They're almost always as dull as a wooden spoon, so the cutting takes a long time, involves a lot of sweat and many Kokanees. There's a bright side to everything.

Once the auger hits open water, fishers scoop Slurpee-like slush from the hole with a skimmer, a serving spoon with holes punched in it. After about 30 minutes of this, a true fisher will heave the skimmer to the middle of the lake and use both hands. Then they get down to business, sticking bright marbles of Power Bait on the hooks and jigging. In our case, this lasted about five minutes.

Once the fire was going, we stuck our poles in the snow, cracked open more beer, hauled out wieners and frozen peanut butter cups and huddled around the sputtering flame, turning our backs to the rain. The guide, not willing to be outsmarted by any trout, kept jigging his line, stopping only momentarily to eat a hot dog. I took the blunt saw and went hunting for firewood. Elsa followed, destined to prove she was as dumb as the rest of us. Not content to chase kindling, she leapt into the only finger of open water in 50 kilometres. And the mongrel couldn't haul herself back onto the ice. Alerted by her whimpers, I considered letting the saphead drown. (It was only a passing thought.) On my belly, I had to crawl up to the edge of the water and haul the dripping wet hound back onto firm ice. She was traumatized by the whole adventure. While master sat wheezing from the adrenaline rush, she shook herself dry, rolled in the snow and pounced on a stick, bringing it over for a fresh throw. I glared at the mutt, picked up the deadfall I'd cut and splooshed back to camp to dry myself before the candle-sized fire. We sat there for four hours, occasionally jigging our lines, just for the heck of it, until the guide told us we'd put in a decent effort. Then, empty-handed, soaking wet and cold, we reeled in the lines and slogged off the ice, just as the sun broke through the clouds. The lunkers outsmarted us. But we'd avoided the mosquitoes.

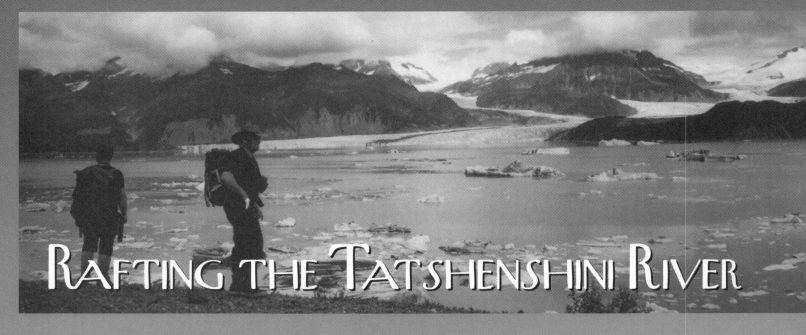

RAFTING THE TATSHENSHINI RIVER

The shallow river flows past the stern of the rafts, two grey, one tomato red. The water is clear. It riffles over the rocky bed of the stream and rounds to the right, its route hidden by the forest. Above the trees the rugged mountains of the coastal range rise into the grey skies. These folded and fractured heaps of rock, driven upwards by the collision of continent-sized tectonic plates against the shores of ancient North America, are made of the tortured bottom of a million-year-old sea. Then the river, twisting through faults and weaving a channel as it reaches for the sea, cuts a valley through the chronological layers of alluvium. The exposed faces of the rock, the load of grey silt fed into the river by glaciers and side streams with names like Sediments, Melt and Silver, the water boiling over boulders and rock shelves, the eddy fences where the water rejoins after an obstacle and the deep holes and splashes behind snags and sweepers show the work continues. This is the Tatshenshini.

A strong upstream wind lifts fine silt from the stony flats of the river. The bright sunshine picks out highlights on the forested mountain sides. It is cooler on the river, just enough to heighten the sense of difference between hiking and floating.

Gord rowed until lunch. I took the afternoon shift. It seemed straightforward, following the other two rafts, varying our position in the river channel as they did, watching ahead for sweepers or holes. Towards the end of the day we could see the hill slopes come closer to the river, a canyon! Fast water, rocks and tight corners.

The tension rises as the river narrows. The raft accelerates. The bow is angled towards potential dangers to allow quick movements back and forth across the stream, except when there are big waves which we must hit bow on. Suddenly, immediately before us, the water is smooth, glassy—it drops into a hole as big as the raft. Spin the bow in and pull on the outside oar; the raft pivots on its bow. Gord and Elise get a close look into the hole before we're spat into the next set of four-foot standing waves.

The rest of the day, I search out the quiet side of the river. The mountains fade back from the river and the huge valley of the Tatshenshini-Alsek confluence opens before us. The wind is stronger, colder and there is a new smell—the sea? The river triples, quadruples in width—there are channels all over, every one of them full of rolling waves of grey, icy water. To our left, the Fairweather Range of jagged peaks and shining glaciers rise against the blue sky. Behind us, dark clouds have closed off the light from the interior. There is no turning back.

With wind and sun in our faces and boiling channels of water in several directions, we don't row much, but the tension of watching, monitoring the river and feeling the tug on the oars, is tiring. At last, we scramble onto a stony beach on river left, just behind the other rafts. Helpful hands grab the bow and sidelines before the current can snatch us back into the river. A quick inspection of the site and we're busy setting up camp—some hauling equipment, others setting up tents. Later, supper is cooking and we all work over the Saskatoon berry bushes surrounding the tents. Except Tom, who settles into his camp chair with a book and a beer to share with me.

Trying to classify the rafting experience is difficult—three people sit together for four to six hours per day in a confined, though extraordinarily open space. Conversation carries on all day, usually just observations of passing scenery and the character of the river, or the quality of the boat-handling. Being on, travelling on the river on a raft, is an interesting experience. Perhaps the most important characteristic is the speed. Travelling about eight to ten kilometres per hour, there is lots of time to observe the surroundings and talk about them. Unlike the intimate solitude of hiking, rafting is very much a communal experience. Unlike car travel, the speed is slow and the river uneven enough to demand a direct connection to the landscape. Auto or rail travel has an imposed and unbearable right of way negating or denying the landscape and choices. Rafting, with its relaxed speed and watery spray, makes demands on the observer to read the river and assess the ongoing

navigational choices over the whole course of the river. It demands and creates an intimate connection with place. The river is the landscape.

While the river is open, the edges of the valley are walled in with thick, impenetrable forests of alder and cottonwood. Approaching the line of bush you look for a gap or an opening to enter the woods. But there is nothing, except branches, trunks and leaves. Entry doesn't seem possible. However, there are spots which were home to First Nations families. Noqwaik, an abandoned Tlingit village site, sits on a long rounded ridge overlooking an eddy on the river. Probably an excellent fishing spot, the ridge is flanked by a creek and a rich beaver flat on one side and a pair of small swampy lakes and prime moose habitat on the other. Southern Tutchone have trapped on the site in more recent times; the remains of an old camp rest on the fading trail down the ridge. Only a few years ago, Ron Chambers brought out a group of Champagne and Aishihik First Nations kids to visit the camp. Mary Ann Porter, an elder and U.S. National Parks Service interpreter from Yakutat, finds a rich supply of medicine plants here as well, sages and juniper, "a good place."

A day further downstream we land in a snug little harbour on a small rocky island. Trudging up the hill topped with huge cottonwoods (the large canoes of the old stories are obviously still possible), we struggle through fireweed towering over our heads, the air cloudy with downy seed. The rainforest is lush and it is only with some difficulty that we find our way back to the rafts and float to the other side of the island. The north of the island is dramatically different. Open rock outcrops, juniper and short pine and spruce trees show an interior influence. From here we look north up the Alsek River valley. Over time, the Lowell Glacier far to the north has surged, blocking off this river's flow. We try to imagine the dramatic wall of water that must have swept down the valley when pent-up Lake Alsek last broached such a blockage about 150 years ago.

Rick retells stories as we drift down the river. There is the tale of Lenny, the middle-aged Chicago shoe seller, whose first overnight camping trip became an eight-day epic of

story and photos by David Neufeld

survival—the naming of Bear Bite Creek; the array of First Nations stories about respect, duty and stewardship. Less happy stories of accidents, drownings and failures remind us of the continuing human relationship with the river.

And amongst our group we have stories as well. Mary Ann, who was born in Kotzebue, married a Tlingit man and has lived and raised her family in Yakutat. She spoke of the mixed blessings of being at home for her children—she enjoyed a rich family life. But now, with her children grown, she thought out loud, "I always stayed in camp and got the fire going so it's nice and warm when everybody comes back." As we hiked through a lovely wood of colouring aspen she added, "I really like it out here. I'm not staying in camp anymore."

One afternoon, we stopped for lunch on a small beach. Pebbles lay scattered along the waterline. One, however, appeared to bounce from one rock to another. Looking like a small fuzzy ping-pong ball, the strange creature scuttled continually in a random zig-zag up the beach line, eating whatever it could find. It was a pygmy shrew, looking just like a cartoon character, bouncing along the surface on impossibly thin legs. Although we crowded around to follow its antics it ignored us completely, even to the point of looking under Julie's boot for something to eat.

In the evenings, we set up comfortable camps on exposed gravel bars, dried up stream beds and moraines of retreating glaciers. Spectacular evening views of snow-draped mountains were the backdrop to Gord's spicy Italian sausage stew or Jim's curried chicken. Around a small fire of driftwood we conversed on a wide range of topics—river rescues, mountain rescues, bush rescues (a lot of wardens and rangers here!), experiences in past jobs, challenges of present ones and a sunset reading of outdoor stories.

One night, a large number of river rocks were placed in the fire. Oars and the canary yellow tarp were lashed up and in the darkness the first bucket of hot rocks was carried into our makeshift sauna. Clouds of steam rose from the rocks and we crowded into the now tepid space.

A second load of rocks was added and soon we all sat hunched over in the low space, clouds of hot steam drawing the sweat and sand from our pores. By the time the third load of rocks was dowsed with water the interior of the sauna looked like a Fellini movie. Lit only by the feeble rays of a pocket flashlight hanging from the roof peak, the steam filled the space like water and occasional glimpses of rosy flesh, a head of hair, or a sweaty limb contrasted sharply with the darkness around us.

In the middle of night I get up for a pee. It is dark, dark, dark. Stumbling through the night in only my underwear and rubber boots, I imagine bears are everywhere—invisible in their dark fur, while I, in white skin and blazing white underwear must look like a candlelit dinner. Slowly, I see the beauty of the clear moonless night and the stars; two faint bands of northern lights waver in the distance, replacing fear with wonder.

In the morning, the sounds of the camp build one upon another. The clatter of dishes being washed, the bubble of the coffee percolating and the crackle of the fire accompany the chatter of voices discussing unemployment insurance for Newfoundland fishers, the comments of rafters at Dry Bay and the passage of a wolf just behind the camp last night. Above us, the thin roar of a high flying jet links us back to the major cities we call home.

However, just beyond the confines of our kitchen, a sandpiper chirps irregularly. The gentle rush and gurgle of the river, and the occasional rattle of a rock tumbling down the fractured talus opposite, add unfamiliar notes to the soundscape. Beyond the sand spit, the rumble of the glacier calving sounds like thunder or the roll of distant artillery echoing between the mountains. Penetrating all of these layers is the persistent howl of a wolf on the folded mountainside across the river.

The disputed moose

by Sharren Breen

I could see the other cabins through tiny patches of window not covered in frost. They all leaned and some had swaybacked roofs that pushed closer to the ground with each snowfall. Before the big strike on Bonanza Creek, thousands of dreamers and schemers had lived in the village of Forty Mile. Now all that remained were a few old cabins that had been abandoned, along with many miners' dreams.

I was living in the old store. The faded Swanson's Store sign lay discarded in the willows beside the cabin. The cabin stood on the edge of the river and offered a panoramic view of the Ogilvie Mountains. To the left was a two-room log building that had lost half its roof and all the doors and windows. When viewed from the front, the cabin reminded me of the empty face of a drunk. Past this building were the remains of an old church and a telegraph station. Beside the station was a two-storey log building that had housed the NWMP (North-West Mounted Police) detachment. It was in use again, though now it housed our fall moose which hung in quarters from the upstairs ridgepole. The doors and windows were simply gaps but the structure was sound and the upstairs floor intact.

Each morning, I would venture out of my cabin, swede-saw in gloved hand, to cut the steaks or other chunks around which our meals revolved. One morning, I had finished sawing the meat and was starting down the dark stairs when something sprang from the gap between the ceiling of the first floor and the floorboards of the second floor. Fur brushed against my nose as it dropped in front of me, hit the stairs and dashed away. I was so startled that I screamed and threw myself back up the stairs. From the top, I aimed my headlamp downstairs and just caught a glimpse of a marten climbing out one of the windows on the ground floor. Ezra, my partner, came running up with his old Winchester rifle in hand ready to defend me (or was it the moose meat?) from whatever threatened. Ezra was not amused to have been summoned from a warm cabin over "A !!=*\? MARTEN!"

The next morning, I had collected the meat and was heading back downstairs when I heard a growl coming from beneath the stairwell. I was not about to let a marten get the better of me again! Arriving on the main floor, I put the saw and meat down and strode boldly up to a black hole underneath the stairwell. There was an old wooden packing crate at the very back and I thrust my face forward to get a better look. Suddenly, an enormous furred face was not a foot from mine. I thought it was a bear! In the split second before I threw myself backwards I could have sworn that I saw myself reflected in the droplets of saliva hanging from large fangs. I wound up on the floor with my headlamp around my neck, reflecting only my booted feet. I screamed, jumped up and sprinted out of the building. I was standing outside trembling when I heard the squeaking of snowpacks on 30 below snow. Ezra was standing beside me. "Another marten?" he asked. He didn't even bring his gun with him this time!

"It's huge and has fangs and it's under the stairs!!!" I squealed. That sent Ezra back to the cabin for the rifle. I stood alone in the darkness, loudly belting out old Blues standards while attempting to appear nonchalant. Ezra returned halfway through "God bless the moose, oops, child."

Now armed, we returned to the room which contained "it." Shining our headlamps into the hole, at first we saw nothing. Then a wolverine head popped up out of the crate. We found a long pole and tried to prod "Teeth" into vacating the premises but it was not in the mood to be left without a fixed address. We stood back and silently waited, hoping it would wander off into the night. Then we tried yelling, stomping, swearing and pleading—but still no movement. Finally, we were forced to shoot the wolverine.

Ezra skinned the critter and then stuffed it with newspapers and put Whinny, as our silent pet became known, on the coffee table in a hunched-over, upright position. In our one-room cabin, this table was very visible to anyone who walked in the front door. We derived a certain amount of entertainment watching the faces of the occasional trapper who opened the door looking for a friendly face and a cup of coffee.

When I'm wading through snow drifts with my trusty shovel I often wish I had a "I'd rather be diving" bumper sticker sewn to my toque.

But, hey, before we get too misty-eyed about those summer days gone by, let's recall that there's a little more to skin-diving than just getting wet and breathing from a hose. There's that whole part we seldom include in our fond recollections…you know, that interval between the truck and the water when in your mind you're thinking, "Gee, I don't know why we're doing this, but I guess if he wants to." Of course, these are thoughts seldom voiced because no one wants to be considered a wuss. But looking back on it, I'm inclined to believe that if Graham and I were little cartoon characters with readable thought balloons, we might have done one or two fewer dives over the last season. Not that we ever took dangerous risks, or were reckless in the least, but…well, maybe an excerpt from the old log books will best explain what I mean.

October 2nd, Fox Lake, Advanced Course Dive #5, objective: dive deep. Now I don't know about you, but all my friends who don't dive always ask the same question, "How deep do you go?" I was really looking forward to this dive because finally I'd be able to answer them with a triple digit. How macho, eh? Of course, we'd been warned that we would feel the effects of nitrogen narcosis down there and that was the point of the exercise, so the main thing was to be relaxed and deliberate in all your movements and descend and ascend slowly. We'd talked about this between ourselves the day before, and we figured we were well prepared.

The first thing we observed as we drove down to the Fox Lake campground was that even though it was a Saturday afternoon the beach was deserted. When we turned into the wind to park, the truck started to lug. We saw the water…a kind of churning grey swirl of two-foot white caps the texture of liquid metal…you know, the texture lakes up here get when they're thickening into ice?

"Maybe you'd better turn the heater on full blast now," I said.

"Right," Graham said.

Anyone brave enough to have tried fishing at this spot earlier was probably plastered up against a road sign somewhere around Mayo by now. Not daunted, we noticed there was a kitchen shelter over in the trees—a good place to change—and in fact Larry and Richard were already there, sitting in the cab of a truck waiting for us. Well, if they can, I can, I told myself.

I had cleverly changed into my wet suit at home, so I could only smile smugly—I mean sympathize—while Graham searched about for cover to dress up in his. The kitchen shelter was staked out already by a group of

Fox Lake in October

by Marie Carr

campers in parkas huddled around the cookstove. Since squeezing your torso into damp neoprene is not physically possible in the cab of a half ton, Graham was stuck with the tried and true method we learned way back at Certification in June: lay a tarp on the ground with all your gear on it, nice and clean, and once you get your booties on, "GET OFF IT!"

I can still hear Ota Halley's voice ringing in my ears every time I perform that little exercise. When we learned this method, there wasn't a 30 mile-an-hour wind blowing off the biggest subpolar ice cap in the world. Picture me, scurrying around like a little black ant in my wet suit, getting rocks to pin down the flapping tarp while Graham, stripped to his diving schniks, hops on one leg and squashes his reluctant form into the shape it was meant to be several hundred tortilla chips ago. This isn't a silent movie I'm describing. There's a pro-active audience of kids from the kitchen shelter and the wind isn't the only thing shrieking.

So much for being "relaxed and deliberate in all our actions." By the time we were actually ready for the water, it felt like we'd run the four-forty at Olympic speed. "Don't worry," said Larry, smiling out of the toasty warmth of his drysuit, "once we get below twenty or thirty feet, it will be calm."

Try to imagine the act of faith it takes to wade out into waves of silty opaque water you can barely stand up in, in weather you should have stayed in bed for, when the water temperature in the low forties Fahrenheit

seems warm compared to the air, and when you know that just ahead is a steep hundred foot drop at the bottom of which your regulator will probably freeze and you will mercifully die. (Pure exaggeration…we don't use equipment that would ever do that. I'm only quoting my thought balloons here).

Larry was right, however. Once we dropped down through the blinding swirl it became clear and dark and calm. The math question we had to solve at 110 feet was simple, so simple in fact that when Richard handed me the slate I did both questions on it, not realizing until he took it from me and handed it to Graham, that I'd done Graham's too. But nitrogen narcosis? Naw, I didn't feel a thing.

The total dive time was about 26 minutes. Then came the interval from the water to the truck. Foolishly, we came out of the water and stood around to babble a bit about the experience, only deciding to change when we realized it was a bit nippier than we liked. As I stripped off my suit, it occurred to me that I couldn't actually remember ever having been this cold before. My hands were like flippers. The fingers wouldn't bend but I could still operate a zipper by kind of pawing it down. Sadly, that let in the wind. I remember shivering so much I was actually gagging, and as for any semblance of modesty, I threw that to the breeze, as it were. Graham says he recalls a fair bit of profanity about purple appendages and gawking onlookers, but I plead temporary insanity and I think I should be excused. I'm a diver, after all.

Wintering in a teepee in the north

story and illustrations by Stephen Badhwar

The teepee was folded, packed and roped to the roof of the cab of our '75 Dodge half-ton. The truck carried most of what Fiona and I owned, plus 450 pounds of rice, beans, and flour. We were moving up north to live in the bush and become hunter/gatherers. We were Yukon-bound or bust.

We bought the truck for $200 and put $800 into it. Our mechanic, who incidentally sold us the truck, laughed knowingly when I told him I wished to drive it all the way to the Yukon from Omemee, Ontario. The good thing about having a teepee strapped to the roof of your truck is that if the truck breaks down you have your home right there. I figured we could just set up camp, find a job and generate some money to pay for the repairs and then continue on our journey. Three weeks, and $7.82 for a caliper retention clip later, we reached Jake's Corner and hung a left.

Two days later, we found ourselves on an abandoned gold rush homestead. We walked into the meadow and there was a set of teepee poles nestled together, leaning into the crotch of a tree. In days gone by, it used to be common practice in this land to leave one's teepee or wall tent poles behind at a good campsite so that others could benefit from their use. We made camp.

The previous two years, we had spent living in our teepee in Ontario. But the northern winter still daunted us. Our fears were allayed by our neighbours, Dorothy and Mike, who lived in their teepee for five years and even homeschooled young Naomi. A mile down the road, our other neighbours, Cathy and Jim, assured us that we

would have no problem. They had lived in their teepee five miles past the end of the road for seven years and thought nothing of it.

For Fiona and I, the summer was pure, utter bliss. The leaves began to flutter and fall and I started digging. I was digging an oblong pit eight

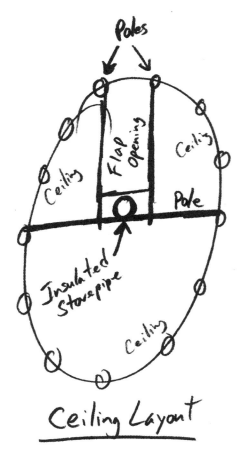

Ceiling Layout

feet across by 18 inches deep over which the teepee would sit. Into the pit I backfilled rocks and pebbles from the lakeshore; this would be our heat-sink. Cathy loaned us their compact-cookstove, which they had used in their teepee days. We set the stove upon this pad and sank the short legs into the pebbles so that we could cook kneeling and sitting. One of the novel things about teepee life is that it brings you closer to the earth, quite literally. I find it humbling to seat my posterior flat to the ground that gives us life. Even today, I find that, when visiting people who live in houses with furniture, I often choose to sit on the floor with my back leaning against the couch. Conversely, I find that people who live in rectilinear dwellings with furnishings, invariably walk into my teepee and remain standing, gaping up at the smoke hole. Sit down please. Grab a blanket. Make yourself at home. Love the earth.

Beside the cookstove we recessed a large apple box into the pebbles to use as our wood box. In advance of the cookstove we had our hearth lined with round rocks. On either side of the hearth we recessed two food caches into the ground. These little root cellars were old wooden concrete forms, approximately 18 inches by 18 inches, used to make cement pads. We built insulated wooden lids for them and then just lay wool blankets over top to conceal them. They worked great for keeping our perishables from freezing overnight or even when we were gone for a day or so.

Rather than send the stovepipe all the way up through the smokeflaps as most people do these days, we installed only two three-foot sections of pipe. This brought the pipe to just above our canvas ceiling which sealed the teepee at the seven-foot height. Above the ceiling the smoke would billow in this "attic" chamber before finding its way out the smokehole. Our ceiling was tied around its circumference to the rope which the teepee liner hangs from. The ceiling was supported in the centre by a pole that ran across the diameter of the teepee just behind the stovepipe. This pole became the place to hang everything that needed to be hung: pots, pans, ladles, flippers, wet gloves, cold boots.

The second section of stovepipe was an insulated piece so we were able to wire the pipe to the pole, to secure them both. Perpendicular to this pole, we ran two smaller poles towards the front of the teepee and tied them off to the teepee poles on either side of the door. These two smaller poles supported the ceiling in the front half of the teepee and accommodated a flap opening between them to allow the smoke from the open fire to exit when we had a hearth fire. This flap was also our little window to the sky. We used it to let in daylight and to regulate temperature. The use of such a flap in a canvas ceiling allows one to have either an open fire or a stove fire or both. Heat is retained, or at least detained, by the ceiling, making the teepee a snug and cozy place to dwell.

Just as important as what is over you is what is under you. We first laid down fir boughs, one foot thick. Over this we laid cardboard, then canvas, then buffalo hides, then wool blankets. Comfy.

Our bed was laid upon the wool blankets. First ThermaRests, then cotton sheets, then flannel sheets, then warm naked bodies, then a flannel-covered Queen-sized goose down quilt, then a light wool blanket, then a heavy wool blanket, then hope you don't have to get up to go pee. Going to bed is made easier by tossing in hot rocks wrapped in leather, or a Mason jar full of hot water. We would let the cookstove fire die out as we went to sleep and within a few hours the teepee would be down to just a few degrees above the outside temperature.

We picked straws to see who would be the one to jump out of bed in the morning to light the fire. The fire-tender would get dressed in bed, under the blankets, where clothing had been kept warm. They would stuff the firebox and ash drawer full of newspaper, grass, dried fir boughs, kindling and fuelwood, put a match to it and then dive back under the covers, emerging once the place warmed up—fifteen minutes later.

For a cookstove, a quick-burning, hot fire can be had with pine, spruce or fir. For a lasting, even heat, willow is the best in the northern boreal forest.

In the hearth, willow is the choice in this neck of the woods—easy to cut and buck by bow-saw, found standing (leaning) dead in great quantity and producing a mild smoke and good coals. Use the entire limb from base to twig tips. The tips can be broken into a manageable size by hand and will keep the fire burning hot and bright, an extremely important condition to maintain so as to keep the fire burning relatively smokeless. Split any wood that is thicker than

your arm and discard any rotten or punky wood—there is no excuse for a smoky fire in a teepee.

Poplar is second choice for an open fire north of 60, as it has a pleasant light smoke and burns fiercely, dry or green. Green poplar needs to be split and added to an already hot fire, or it won't take. Poplar will give you plenty of powdery ash suitable for the outhouse or for traction on slippery snow.

Spruce, pine and fir rank last, in that order. All of these conifers are resinous and will give plenty of sparks. Wool coverblankets and wool tunics will protect your bed and your clothing from sparks. Use a spark blotter of leather for stamping out live embers. Avoid pine, as its smoke is toxic and darkens canvas quickly. Avoid fir, except as kindling, as it is the most resinous and spark-prone.

The fire is the essence of the teepee. It gives light, it gives heat, it gives focus. The fire invites us all together and draws the circle. The circle defines the social. With the walls being white, we only required three candles to light the teepee interior, with the additional use of a propane lamp to illuminate activities such as cooking and craftwork. The flickering light of candles gave a cozy warm glow to our home, and further drew us closer around the source of light.

The snow fell that winter of '91-92 and kept on falling all winter long. It accumulated on our teepee and slid down until it hit the bank, piling higher and higher. By late winter, the snowbank around the teepee was six feet high and up to four feet thick at the bottom—insulation from the sky. We rigged up a vestibule over the doorway to keep the snow out and to provide a double door to prevent the wind from blowing in when we entered. The vestibule consisted of a pair of

crossed poles set as a bipod four feet in advance of the door. A ridgepole rested in the crotch and ran to the teepee where it was tied to a lacing pin. A set of army shelter-half tarps were draped over the ridgepole to form the roof and doors of the vestibule. A wreath topped off the whole affair, hung from a lacing pin on the teepee above the vestibule. Let it snow, let it snow, let it snow.

It is vitally important for the fire and cookstove to have a source of oxygen to burn, or you may find yourself with a poorly-burning fire and lack of oxygen for breathing. When building the hearth, we laid two pipes into the ground, on either side of the door, leading from outside the teepee into the ring of rocks in the hearth. This provided a direct line for air to reach the fire and an indirect line to reach the stove. This arrangement lessened the amount of cold air that was drawn by the burning fire from the doorway and thus created a less drafty living space.

Living in a teepee, one learns a few things. Humility is learned as one bows one's head to enter the oval doorway—perhaps a symbolic return to the womb. Inside, one sits on the floor, in deference to the earth. Equality is attained by sitting in a circle around the fire, where women, men, children and dogs look each other in the eye as they all sit at the same level. I sorely miss the communion with my dog; it just isn't the same in a cabin where he always seems to be underfoot.

Human meekness is realized when the temperature plummets and you haven't cut enough wood or you run out of candles or propane or your rechargeable batteries fade so you can no longer receive CBC radio and then you're really standing out in the dark, cold silence. It is then that people turn to each other and the warmth of that sanctuary—the bed.

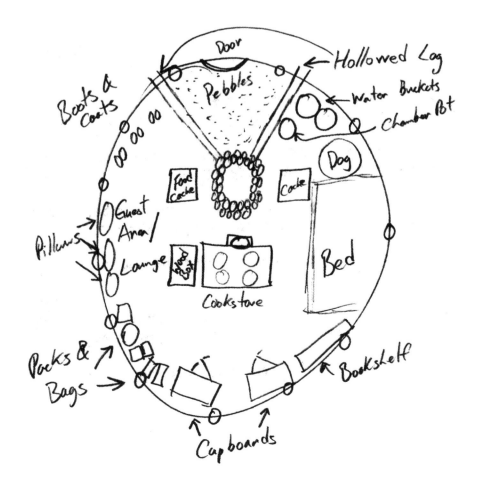

STAYING HEALTHY IN THE GREAT OUTDOORS

The ins and outs of beaver fever

by Laura Spicer

Giardia (Gee-are-dee-ah) is an intestinal parasite which causes giardiasis (gee-are-dieah-sis), commonly referred to as "beaver fever," which is alive and well in the Yukon. There were 28 reported cases in 1994 and 437 cases in 1995. Giardia has been around for a long time, but greater concentrations of people and animals and better diagnoses have made us more aware of giardia.

Giardia is a single cell parasite which lives in the intestinal tract in the first stage of its life and then gets expelled as a cyst in faeces. The cyst can live for up to two months in cold water. The next person or animal to drink the contaminated water may get giardiasis. Giardia is also spread through the fecal/oral route. This means people preparing food after changing an infected infant's diaper are at risk, making daycare centres a great place to spread giardia. Many people have no symptoms of giardiasis so they may spread the disease without realizing it. People can cause the infection of animals who may later return the compliment.

The term beaver fever is used because

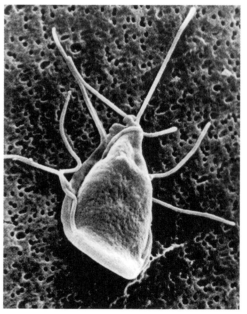

beavers are often blamed for spreading the parasite. Although beavers are very effective in contaminating water supplies (since they defecate in the water), no one knows whether giardia originated in humans or animals.

The symptoms of giardiasis include diarrhoea, abdominal cramps, bloating, fatigue and weight loss. Since the symptoms are similar for many gastro-intestinal diseases, giardiasis is often mis-diagnosed. A positive diagnosis can only be made through examination of a stool sample under a microscope. Most healthy people in North America will be rid of the symptoms in two weeks. Sometimes your body has actually rid itself of the giardia; other times it is just in remission. Taking antibiotics should kill the parasite for sure.

There are several options to prevent exposure to giardia: use groundwater, filter surface water, or bring it to a boil. Any filter that traps particles smaller than five microns is safe. Normal levels of municipal chlorination do not kill all giardia. Wash your hands well after using the toilet and before handling food. Don't contaminate the public water supply (i.e., the Schwatka Lake area in Whitehorse should not be used as a toilet).

When away from a toilet and your bowels call, bury your stool (if possible) and avoid using areas near surface water sources.

ILLUSTRATION: JELEA BINKLEY; PHOTO COURTESY OF LAURA SPICER

Solitude

by Dorothy LeBel

*S*omeone was once recounting to me his participation in a wilderness survival program. I asked him what he found the most challenging about it. He answered that it was spending three days alone in the bush. He had previously never spent that much time alone. The aloneness of the experience was something he found very difficult to deal with.

How strange this sounded to me!

Solitude has always been my natural inclination. I've arranged my life so that I can spend a good deal of time alone in natural surroundings. The bush trips I've done were not only to enjoy the beauty of the wilderness, but also a strong spiritual experience. It's about meeting your self and feeling the true nature of your connections to this world. There's a lot of strengths and insights to be acquired from this. Perhaps this is what the traditional vision quests of native people were about.

Solitary quests have not been actively encouraged in western culture, where the emphasis is on structure and productivity. This is reflected in our educational institutions, starting at kindergarten level. Aloneness has a negative connotation, something to be avoided. Very few, if any, teachings are provided for dealing with our inner life. This could explain why many people who unexpectedly find themselves alone for a period of time experience such a sense of emptiness, anxiety, even panic. As traditional native cultures have shown us, a good way to deal with these problems is to explore our spiritual dimension and the active search for one's inner voice.

Making whipped cream
YUKON · STYLE

story and photo by Mike Wanner

One Sunday, our family was visiting my cousin Kevin Dukart and his partner Kim Outridge
at their property in Robinson, just south of Whitehorse.
The barbecue was going great until it came time for the dessert.
We needed whipped cream, but Kevin and Kim didn't have electricity,
much less the mixer to whip the cream with.
So Kevin took one of those wire whisks and stuck it to the end of a cordless drill.
Voila! Instant power eggbeater.
By the way, the whipped cream turned out great.

MY LITTLE CABIN

by Mike Camp

My modest little wilderness cabin,
With vertical log walls and a canvas roof,
A dusty gravel floor and a round steel stove,
Two hundred twenty nearly square feet,
Of private peace in the bush.

On the scale of wealth,
It's low, I know,
And the luxuries are few,
The conveniences are too.

But...but...but,
The setting and view,
A rich man couldn't buy,
The water, it be crystal clear.
The neighbours are the best,
You could ever get:
Twenty miles away, like the beer.

The hunting is good,
And the fishing is too,
When I'm here, best of all,
No one is ever around,
To dare tell me what I should do.

Peace and quiet here are abundant and free,
To think, to read, to write some poetry.
(My bannock is ready to turn!)
To snowshoe, or make an igloo,
Or prepare yet another gourmet meal;
Moose and rice sounds really nice for a change,
Let's see, we've only had it about 20 times this month.

Lonely? Why sure, at times, I guess,
But it never seems to last for very long.
You see, there's always so much to do:
Like water to haul, wood to cut,
Or a grouse to shoot for the stew.
A fish to catch, a dog to pet,
Or new country to wander through.

So when the time comes, to move along,
To another part of this bush,
No money will be made,
On this real estate.
You see, I was paid,
With interest, all along.

And the only thing left, after a while,
Of my humble home in the woods,
Will be wonderful, wonderful memories —
The best investment of all.

Hot tips for ski trips

story and photo by Bonnie Burns

Well, actually, it's just one hot tip. It's
called the hot-face-cloth-treatment.
There's nothing quite so wonderful as a spring
ski trip, gliding under blue clear skies over
glistening white snow. The hardest thing about
ski trips though, is rousting your warm drowsy
body out of the cozy sleeping bag and
emerging into the bracing cold of morning.
And the first brave soul must start the fire and
get the snow melting for coffee and breakfast.
Well, hang an extra billy can of snow on the
dingle stick. Once the melted snow has
become piping hot water, dip a face cloth into
it. Gently squeeze some of the excess water
out of the face cloth, then place said face cloth
upon your upturned face. Ahhhhhhhhhh! Not
only is it an invigorating way to start your day,
you also get a clean face in the bargain. Try it
next time you are on a ski trip!

Inside Out, Outside In

Friendly's Kiss

by Lillian Seapy

Martha's dog, Friendly, has no smart bump on her head. That's why, says Martha, the dog has been in nine fights with porcupines (all losing) in the eight months I've lived here. If she had a smart bump, maybe she wouldn't be so…

Nervous. Friendly is full nervous husky. My parents call her Wolf Dog because of the way she paces and stares. Martha says most village dogs from up north have some wolf in them. Martha got Friendly from up north.

One night's run-in was worse than usual. Friendly emerged from the woods, her face looking like a sea urchin. Time to pull out the pliers. There's no money for another vet appointment and anaesthetics. I pull together the poor person's anaesthetic: beer. I added milk to make it more palatable (It was my first time getting a dog drunk.) From the dog's perspective, each quill has tiny barbs on the end, smaller versions of the things on the end of fish hooks. Pulling a quill out feels similar to a bee sting. Friendly, the dog with no smart bump, has experienced this feeling before. She knows what happens when the pliers come out.

At this point, Friendly was now rapidly pacing through the house, jumping over furniture, 60 small white arrows sticking out of her face and mouth. We tried getting her to drink the beer and milk mixture, but the quills under her tongue made it too painful for her to wilfully swallow. Jim, my other roommate, said, "This isn't working. Do we have something to force feed her with— something like a turkey baster?"

Pause.

Martha, "Yes, but I used it for something else."

Jim, "That's fine, just wash it out."

Pause.

Martha, "I used it to douche with."

Pause.

Jim, "We'll need it."

Martha, "I'll clean it really good."

Jim held Friendly, one arm at her neck, the other underneath her chest to keep her from jumping up and down. I held her face to keep it from moving side to side. Martha had the douche/baster. The first squeeze she rejected, shaking her head and showering us with the mixture of beer, milk, and dog slobber.

After a few basterfuls, things changed. Jim held her in his lap, like you would a baby sitting up with its back against you. She was smiling, and, with the quills in her face, she looked like a scruffy bearded man, drunk, smiling and leaning against a wall. Now she gulped the stuff down.

Once her motor functions were good and hindered, we assumed the previous position, only with pliers in hand instead of the baster. Although inhibited by alcohol, the dog would rear back with each pull, almost throwing all three of us off. These quills were worse than usual—smaller, harder to grasp. Some bled.

We got what we could out of her face, leaving two in her chin. The pliers kept slipping—we'd have to come back for those. Moving on to her mouth, Jim had to hold both of her jaws separate, like they do in cartoons when the strong man separates the jaws of an alligator. The ones in her gums and under her tongue were the worst. She really shook then.

We pinched and pulled. Finally, all were out except the two in her chin. They were in too deep for us to quickly yank them out before she would shake her head and we'd lose our grip. Between the blood, slobber, and struggles, we coaxed, "Good girl, Friendly. It's okay. Just a few more." Thinking only, "Dumb dog, Friendly."

Failure after failure of fingers slipping on slick quills. Suddenly, without any words or warning, Martha looked as if she was going to give Friendly a kiss. Pulling her head back quickly, she rose with the last two quills in her teeth.

We dropped to the floor, laughing and sticky. Friendly jumped over us, around us, and through the house much as she has the other eight times her quills have come out.

(Wedding) Bell(e)s Along the Yukon

by Steven Smyth

One obtains an appreciation for the diversity of life in the Yukon by being a justice of the peace. This is particularly true when I am called upon to perform weddings for northern residents and visitors.

The diversity of ceremonies, locations and personalities is truly amazing. From backyards to boats, mountaintops to mezzanines, government offices to gardens, hotel bars to gravel bars—each ceremony is special and unique, often reflecting the personalities of the couple being married.

Occasionally, the ceremony poses some unique challenges, such as when the bride or groom (or both) are unable to speak English, and a competent translator must be found. The cosmopolitan nature of the Yukon becomes evident, yet often unnoticed by the casual observer, by virtue of the range of nationalities that are resident here. One couple—Bulgarian Muslims who were recent immigrants to Canada—required a Turkish translator. I was somewhat concerned when the bride was a little later than usual in making her appearance (two hours, to be exact), and the translator had departed an hour earlier! Fortunately, he was only a phone call away, and the wedding proceeded quickly after he returned.

On another occasion a couple requested that I conduct their ceremony in English and French so that the bride's parents, visiting from Quebec, could follow along. Unfortunately, my French was so rusty the bride and groom could barely keep from bursting out laughing when some of things I said in French could hardy be understood at all.

On still another occasion, I was approached to perform a ceremony for a Chinese couple who could speak no English whatsoever. Fortunately, the young lady I was dating at the time was a Malaysian Chinese, and was able to provide translation for the event, which, incidentally, was held in a local restaurant.

Visitors to the Yukon often provide some interesting challenges and opportunities. Many arrive without knowing anyone in town, or having any location in mind for a ceremony. In such circumstances, I have been known to call upon friends, family and co-workers to serve as witnesses for the ceremonies, which have been held in locations as diverse as offices, my living room and backyard, and a local hotel room. However, one adventuresome couple from New York had their hearts set on a mountaintop wedding. They chartered a helicopter to take us to the top of Golden Horn mountain, near Whitehorse, late one evening in July. It was so cold at that elevation, even without any wind, that I could almost see the bride, in her long gown, and the groom in his tux, turn blue!

Another couple, from Juneau, Alaska, wanted a remote wilderness wedding in northern B.C. After explaining that my appointment did not extend beyond the borders of the territory, they settled for a ceremony on Bennett Lake—in March. Fortunately, it was a sunny day and only -2°C instead of -20°C. After a half hour ski from Carcross we were able to doff our jackets and enjoy a glass of champagne "on ice" after the ceremony.

Most weddings are private affairs involving only family and friends. Once in a while, however, they are recorded for public enjoyment as well. Brenda and "Yukon fiddler" Joe Loutchan's wedding in the '98 Hotel in Whitehorse was one such public celebration, recorded by Northern Native Broadcasting as part of a documentary on this celebrated Yukon musician. And the wedding of Michael and Jessica Simon at Kusawa Lake was recounted by Jessica in *Another Whole Lost Moose Catalogue*.

Occasionally, there are the "theme" weddings, such as biker weddings, where black leather vests and motorcycle regalia are obligatory, and western weddings, where cowboy hats and boots are the order of the day. And although I have prepared for the eventuality by taking lessons and doing a bit of practising (see page 160), I have yet to be asked to perform a ceremony while leaping from an aircraft over the Carcross desert. Perhaps it is best left that way—even "falling in love" has its limits.

A HOT LAP

by Bruce Barrett

Some years ago, while I was driving along the Robert Campbell Highway just east of Carmacks, I passed through a freshly burned area. A forest fire had jumped the road at that spot a few weeks previously and the smell of scorched organic material filled the truck. I noticed that dwarf fireweed were flowering profusely in the charred ground. There are two reasons for the ground-hugging size of these plants. First, because it was August, the fireweed had to make up for lost time by blooming very quickly. Second, being the first plants to re-colonize the burn, they didn't need to invest energy growing tall to beat competing plants to the sun.

The contrast between the sooty earth and the brilliant fireweed, caught in the slanting rays of the afternoon sun, called out to the photographer in me. In a moment, I had pulled over, jumped out of the truck and crossed the ditch in search of the perfect natural floral arrangement. Not too far off I could see a large cluster of fireweed glowing against a matte black background, and I set off, camera ready, to get a better look. As I neared my goal, I didn't notice that the patch of ground between me and the flowers was streaked grey with ash. My first footstep onto that streak revealed a shocking lack of substance. I dropped like a stone into a gully that had filled with ash barely cooled from the blaze. In that instant I paused, mentally, to wonder how far down I was going. The answer came quickly—nearly up to my neck. I didn't wait around to find out just how hot that ash was. Taking advantage of a big dose of adrenaline, I hauled myself out of what was starting to feel like one of the gates of hell.

Every inch of my body, hair and clothing was permeated with the ash, which right away started to feel pretty miserable. I stripped down on the spot and shook all my clothes as hard as I could. I wondered what this might look like to passers-by, but, fortunately, there wasn't much traffic that day. I got my pictures and carried on, looking a bit like a tourist from beyond the grave.

Amazingly, since I got the camera cleaned, it hasn't missed a beat. As for me, I sometimes stop and thank my lucky stars that that gully wasn't a foot deeper. Now I always look before I leap!

Inside Out, Outside In

This place

by Darryl James

The place I am going to tell you about is called Carcross. It is also my home town. Before the name was changed it was called Caribou Crossing; that was in the old days. This was long before my time. The reason it was called Caribou Crossing was because a long time ago, the people say, that's where the caribou used to cross the river. Long ago, I believe, Carcross was used as a trading place for the gold miners, who were travelling from Skagway to Dawson during the gold rush.

I remember when I was younger, I didn't want to stay, or spend too much time there. Now that I am older and look at things a lot differently, I see Carcross as a place of calmness and serenity. The people that live in Carcross are very pleasant and good natured. The overall

beauty and delightful scenes that the lakes and mountains provide, are somewhat breathtaking at times. I spent my childhood years in Carcross and then left during my adolescence. Upon returning, I noticed the changes in the people and the land; or is it maybe just the times are changing and our people are trying to keep up to the ever-changing times.

Snow-covered land

by Patricia Old

A white sheet falls on the land. It is winter once again. Thoughts of snow make you huddle around the stove, hoping this winter won't be that cold.

It's a joke in the Yukon to not bother with the wood 'til the first snowfall. Summer's not all that long. Everyone hopes the summer will last forever, but here we are once again, cutting wood in the cold brisk wind, wishing we were in our warm cabins.

Just look at the children's smiling faces as they rush out to play. Yes, it's easy to see they love this snow-covered land. They go down the hill on their favourite sleds. They crouch real low to see how far they can go. They get together and make a funny snow figure. They play in the snow as you worry about their hands getting cold. They race down the rink to show you how much talent they now have. They reflect our childhood and how many moons ago we loved this snow-covered land.

Inside Out, Outside In

THE TRAPPER

by Ailsa Hebert

The man could wait no longer
For the call was loud—God knows
He'd been a long time in the mountains,
Or so the story goes.

He'd spent a long cold winter
Snowed in and all alone
But now the weather'd cleared right up
And he could feel it in his bones.

And so he packed his knapsack
With some bannock and some beans,
Matches, a bedroll,
And an extra pair of jeans.

To help him on his journey
For the call was loud and clear
When springtime hits those mountains
He just had to have a beer.

THE INVITATION

by Serena Lee Mis.Ta-Nash

It was a beautiful winter night. The sky was clear, stars slung so low it seemed they were a blanket. Close tinges of green northern lights built into castles and cathedrals high overhead.

Although the cabin was cold when I got home from work, Miss Piggy, the stove, chomped wood wildly as she warmed the spaces. My partner, a trucker away on a road trip into the nether reaches of the Yukon, had left the porch full of wood. Miss Piggy had lots of fuel.

Before long, the cabin was warm and glowing with the yellow light of kerosene lamps. A whole evening to myself. I'd looked forward to this and curled up in my favourite chair by the big picture window. A new book, a cup of tea, peace and quiet. My palace on the hill. I loved this place where I felt so connected to the earth and the other beings whose space I was invading. There's a pine forest with a squirrel midden. The small pond, where the ducks raise their young in the short northern summers, is backed by rock cliffs and covered with crocuses each spring. The Hudson's Bay tea, picked last summer, was relaxing. The pages of the book quit turning as I slipped into the other-world space deep within.

Far away, from up the mountain, sound drifted down and gradually penetrated my consciousness. The book dropped from my hand with a thud and I jerked out of my dream-state. Yip, yip, hoohoo, over and over, growing louder and clearer as the coyotes moved down into the valley for a night of rabbit hunting.

I listened intently as the wolves joined the chorus, followed by neighbourhood dogs. My dog, Red, lay on his rug by Miss Piggy, the end of his tail twitching slightly. He was obviously deep in his own dreamworld. Well, whatever was going on out there, even if the wild ones came into the yard, I was safe in here and quite enjoying the music of the forest creatures.

Back to my book, the sounds faded again. This was a good story about Australia and the Aboriginal people there. It all seemed so pleasant, singing your way happily around the country. The songs told you where you were and I wondered if the songs of my four-legged friends were like that too.

The crunch of snow on the step caused me to stop reading and listen closely. Only one thud. It sounded like someone coming, but now stopped. I waited a moment then walked to the door to listen again. No more sound. I opened the door and looked out. No sign of anyone or anything, just the bright night sky and the crackle of green dancing light.

Back to my chair and book, I took note of the yipping and howling. It sounded like they were still on the other side of the pond. They usually didn't come into the yard. Red slept on. I skimmed the next pages quickly, staying aware of my surroundings, not really absorbing the contents of the story.

There it was again, that crunch sound, two of them. Must be someone here this time. Starting to feel nervous I glanced at Red. He was still sleeping, paws going rabbit chase speed. Must be okay, he's a good dog and lets us know when people are coming. Convinced there was no problem, I opened the door to check. Nothing, same sky, same green crackle, and same castles.

I filled my teacup, and Miss Piggy, and got settled down with the song-lines again. This time it took longer to read each page, more alert for strange sounds than before.

Suddenly, there it was, that crunch, only this time the thuds continued all the way up the steps and across the outside porch. The hair on the back of my neck rose and I felt a cold sweat break out. I moved slightly, and Red woke up, ears perked.

I waited for whoever was there to knock. Silence, no knock, no retreating footsteps. Shakily, I got to my feet and crept towards the door, taking slow baby steps. As I passed Red I signalled for him to come and together we silently approached the only door in the place. I was sure the being on the other side of the door could hear my every breath, which sounded like thunder in my ears. No movement, not a whisper from out there. I reached for the wooden handle deciding just to fling it open and confront whatever was there.

My hand closed tightly on the familiar worn wood and my brain willed my arm to make the motion. At last I could feel my arm move and just as the door opened a crack Red broke into a blood curdling yowl. The door seemed to finish opening on its own. I screamed and Red howled louder. The wolves and coyotes answered until I was surrounded by their collective voices.

I froze for what felt like hours, then looked out and around. There wasn't anything there. Slowly, I caught my breath.

I still don't know if anything was out there that very cold winter night, but when I returned to my senses I put on my outdoor winter garb, took the flashlight and went into the yard. Red came along, and we watched the green castles and touched the stars.

Thank you, Great Spirit, for the Invitation.

Inside Out, Outside In

Reflections, how-to's, and a few warnings:

A GUIDE TO THE DAWSON CITY MUSIC FESTIVAL

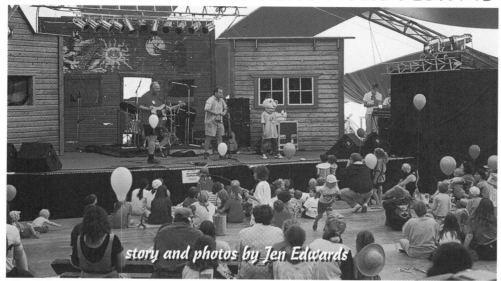

story and photos by Jen Edwards

The Dawson City Music Festival first happened in 1979. In 1998, it will celebrate its 20th anniversary, in conjunction with the centennial of the Klondike gold rush.

As the dogged board has already begun planning for a music festival to end all music festivals, we cannot help but reflect on what has become a raucous, but treasured, tradition.

Every summer for many years, Yukoners look forward to that one weekend in late July when Dawson City hosts its summertime musical extravaganza. Not only does it give people the opportunity to hear wonderful music, but it also provides people from all over the territory with the chance to reunite, carouse and shake and shimmy until the wee hours of the morning.

In order to enjoy, you've got to get here, which can prove to be an interesting feat. Chances are if you're a Yukon resident from anywhere but Dawson, you'll arrange to leave work no later than 5:01 p.m. on Musicfest Friday. If you're a Whitehorse musician, you'll likely have to wait to finish your gig at the bar on Friday night and then bolt out the door and drive furiously to Dawson in order to make your sound check Saturday morning.

If you're a musician from outside the Yukon, you'll board a DC-3 in Whitehorse and land, an hour later, in Dawson, looking a little green, wondering where the hell you are and how you ended up here.

If you're a Dawsonite, however, physically getting there doesn't pose much of a problem. It's getting there mentally that can prove to be a little tricky. If you're not busy baking, you're probably cleaning your house in anticipation of billets or despairing over that last-minute forgotten item. (What do you mean we forgot to order beer cups?!) Only those rare souls who aren't overrun and overwrought with stuff to do are lucky enough to walk down to Minto Park on Thursday night to see the progress the bullgang has made. It is a momentous and almost sacred occasion when they finally hoist up the big striped tent—mouths agape, eyes wide, a beautiful sight which tells of the joyous weekend to come.

Now, as a festival-goer, the only struggle you're likely to have during the weekend is trying to be everywhere at once. At night, you might find yourself asking the following: do I mingle in the beer garden, dance in the tent, get some munchies, attend the church concert, or do I make a run for the washrooms before my favourite band comes on? Where will the line-up be shorter, at the washrooms in the concession stand or the port-a-potties?

During the day, you can generally catch the children's concert without worry, but then there are all those workshops to choose from. You can do like some and sit calmly, enjoying a workshop in its entirety, or you can do like others and frantically bike, run or speedwalk from St. Paul's Church to the DCF Church to the Palace Grand to the gazebo and back to the park, only to arrive just in time to pass out on the grass before the night-time concert begins and think of the next day, when you'll have to make these decisions all over again. Maybe the Musicfest should look into offering some time management counselling as well.

If you are new to town and to the festival, you'll probably make the acquaintance of some of the festival's core organizers. If you're really lucky, you might hear lore of the golden years of the DCMF. You may hear about the first music festival and the barbecue they held, during which the salmon was lovingly cut into steaks using a bandsaw lubricated with Mazola Oil. Or the time when one of the acts mysteriously disappeared off the face of the earth. You might also hear about the wild bus trips that the musicians used to make between Whitehorse and Dawson. Or more recently, how the rental car got filled with diesel instead of gasoline by one of the board members just before two musicians were supposed to embark on the long journey home.

It doesn't take long to realize that the festival has remained an intimate one, groomed and carried on by friends. Decisions often get made late at night and involve a few frantic phone calls to each of the board members. Meetings, believe it or not, are actually enjoyable, and most of the people involved in the festival have known each other for so long that any personal differences have been smoothed out.

The committee heads, on the other hand, may not know what they are getting into when they're given the reins of responsibility, but they somehow always manage to pull it off. The particularly gullible ones may even offer to do it again next year.

Then there are the workers. I doubt you could find a group with much more stamina. Whether they've just finished a day of waiting tables, housekeeping, scooping ice cream, cooking or giving tours around town, they always make it down to the park to report for duty and often work well into the night.

The hospitality Dawsonites offer continues to astound me. To understand why a warm welcome and continuous fussing over is so important, all you have to do is ask yourself: how else are we going to get the musicians to come all the way up here? Word of mouth is the key. One of the best tactics we've come up with is to get to their hearts through their stomachs. If you serve it, they will come.

Where else can you get heaping-full plates of sushi, baklava and burritos, all within the space of a weekend? The endless hospitality can backfire, especially on the Monday when the transportation crew is desperately trying to round everyone up, toss them into the van and send them on the plane that will carry them home. There are always a few that either simply want to be left behind or who wind up downing too many beers at the party the night before to be able to make it to the ten o'clock meeting time.

They can hardly be blamed. Take the 1994 Sunday night wrap-up party, for example. Improvised jazz inside, whimsical campfire tunes outside and if you can picture it, an ensemble of power drills, shovels, buckets and tools make orchestral waves from inside the garage.

There in front of us lay a moment of pure, musical, impromptu perfection, definitely not the right recipe to get everyone tucked into bed and up early for the next morning's wake-up call.

Monday morning comes with a thud. Although you may be left with an aching heart after you send off the plane and watch the bullgang tearing down the tent, you snap out of it, especially when you realize that chances are you couldn't survive another night with only three hours of sleep. Thus begins the cleaning, the packing and the putting away of another successful festival.

Keno City

story and photos by Dave White

At the end of the road, I found a little museum with a locked door. Luckily, a guy named Mike had the key. I had been on the Dempster Highway for a week, a week spent in the rust browns and bright reds of late summer. We returned to Dawson City, only to be overwhelmed by the last of the summer hordes. So wanting to go somewhere else, we chose Keno City.

Statistics show that, at that time, about 30 people called Keno City home. I didn't know what most of them did, because Mike seemed to do everything. He had the key to the firetruck (and the brand-new, government-built firehall), the watertruck, the museum, and probably every other locked door in Keno.

When we first arrived, we parked our car and wandered empty streets, stuck our faces up against the glass of the Keno City Hotel and peered into the hotel lounge, getting a first-hand look at bar life in the 1950s. We looked into empty cabins, probably untouched for years, and got a glimpse into the thirties, maybe forties. And of course, we checked out the house made of beer bottles (good insulation, someone insisted), maybe a look into the future.

After about 15 minutes of exploring, a stocky guy approached us. "Hi, I'm Mike. Someone saw you guys trying the door of the museum."

"Yeah, but it's locked."

"Well, I have the key."

So we spent an hour in one of the coolest tourist attractions in the Yukon. Mike gave us the story of the building, and of the community's efforts to refurbish it and keep it open, of their quest for funding. He explained the exhibits, where and how they were found, what they meant to the town's history.

Then we started talking to Mike, about why he lives in a place that's practically a ghost town, a pleasant, but lonely collection of buildings. Keno is a 30-minute drive down a dirt road from the abandoned company town of Elsa, and another 30 minutes from Mayo. Dawson is the closest major community. Getting anywhere from Keno is a big deal. Getting anywhere in the winter is practically out of the question.

Mike said he'd lived in Keno City for years. His seemingly endless community jobs kept him busy and employed, his work with the museum society kept him fulfilled. Mike had obviously put the worries of the Big City World—even if

that city is Whitehorse —behind him, traded it in for a life smack-dab in the middle of the living history of Keno City. He knew more than the town's residents, he knew more than the stories. He was living in them. For him, history was more than a book or an old, cracked and faded newspaper in the archives. History was in Keno's twisty streets and sometimes crumbling, sometimes immaculate, buildings. Mike was doing more than anyone else to preserve the history of what had been, for a brief while, a booming mining town at the end of a road hardly anyone travelled.

After that day, I found a few reasons to phone Mike in Keno City and find out what was going on. One summer, three years after the first trip, I went back to Keno City for an afternoon. The museum was expanded, the exhibits new and improved, and the town itself had undergone a few changes. I didn't find Mike, but I suspect he still carried most of the keys to Keno.

Mike's love for Keno City, and his love of living there, was honest and practical. It made me think of living the same way, of how important it would be. It made me wonder if I'd ever feel the same way about a dusty little town, or any place.

TOYOTAS don't float

by Don Wilkinson

©1996 PETERSEN

Toyota pickups do not float! Even the four-by-four versions do not float. My friends and I have discovered this to be a serious shortcoming of an otherwise excellent vehicle. There have been several occasions when a floating Toyota would have been of great benefit to us, but never more so than during a hunting trip in the Ruby Range of the Yukon a few years ago.

For years in the fall, my friend, Geoff, and I made a point of going moose hunting on as many weekends as possible. We called it hunting; my wife called it camping. I won't tell you what some of our friends called it. We never did bother shooting anything. It always seemed to be too much work.

This particular weekend we took along another friend who didn't like hunting either. Lenny was a short little guy with a substantial pot belly. (This factors into the story later on.)

Our favourite non-hunting spot was Gladstone Creek, about 45 miles up the east side of Kluane Lake. Why it's called a creek at all is beyond me because the entire Canadian submarine fleet could very easily navigate its full length with room to spare. The reason we liked this area for not hunting was because it no longer had any moose in it. It used to have lots of moose so one year we were obliged to shoot one. It ruined the entire weekend for us, and it didn't do much for the moose's weekend either. (It also had lots of Dall sheep, but since we didn't have a license to hunt sheep we didn't have to worry about them.)

After several bone-shaking hours of hard four-

by-fouring we finally descended the cliff that leads down into the Gladstone valley and proceeded towards our campsite on the other side of the river. As we approached the river we could see that the ford where we usually crossed was no longer where it was supposed to be. In fact, it was no longer anywhere. Geoff and I got out of the truck and went looking for it, but it was not to be found. We could see where it used to be by the old tire tracks on the other side leading up out of the water. In fact, it looked like someone else had recently been across. We got back into the vehicle and sat there looking at the river and trying to decide if we should attempt the crossing despite the ford not being there anymore. The river did look a bit deeper and faster than normal. Geoff looked at me and I spoke the fateful words, "Let's go for it."

Now, by themselves and taken at face value, these four little words seem harmless. However, they have gotten Geoff and I into more trouble than everything else that we have ever said in our lifetimes. Geoff is not too bright sometimes. Like when he listens to me.

Geoff leaned over, put the shift lever into four low and drove down the bank into the river. So far, so good. Then we were about fifteen feet out into the river, with the waves lapping only half-way up the door on the downriver side. No problem, we've been in worse trouble before (Neither of us can recall just when, though.) It was then that the front of the truck dropped out of sight underwater and I noticed the entire river pouring in through my window. We began to think maybe this wasn't such a good idea after all. As the river swung us sideways

and washed us downstream, we became convinced of it.

As we gently floated downstream, pushed by the 30 knot current, Geoff and I quietly and calmly panicked. We climbed out the side windows and swam onto the roof of the truck. Lenny, who was sitting in the middle, didn't have much of a window to crawl out of. The only available way out for him was the sliding rear window of the cab.

These windows, when fully opened, are only about one foot square. A cross-section of Lenny is approximately two and a half feet square. It seemed that there was no way Lenny could fit through that opening, but he did!

There we were. Soaking wet, perched on the roof of a truck determined to float down the river, and for all we knew, eventually to the Arctic Ocean. As the river made a sharp turn past an enormous pile of deadfall and trees trapped in the bend, the truck ground to a halt, with a large tree trunk rammed through its side. We could tell that we probably wouldn't be able to drive the truck out of there without some help, and seeing that the hood and most of the cab was already under water, we thought that it might be a good idea to abandon ship (or truck).

Lenny jumped onto the pile of driftwood and then to shore. Geoff and I started to throw all our gear at Lenny as the truck settled slowly under the water. We got all of it and ourselves safely onto shore just as the truck slipped under. It was about this time that I realized that my wallet and camera were still in the cab, along with a pair of binoculars, one rifle, all our money and every rifle shell we had. "Please, Lord, keep the bears away." As we took stock of our situation we could still make out the headlights of the truck shining brightly about eight feet under water. They stayed lit all the rest of the time we were there. About two hours.

We also noticed we were on the wrong side of the river, 45 miles from the nearest road, with no vehicle to get us there. Actually, we noticed that one almost right away. Another thing we noticed was that it was getting dark, we were cold and wet and getting hungry. We decided that the most important thing to do was have a pot of coffee each. By then, somehow, things might have miraculously improved.

We had the coffee, but things didn't improve at all. The only thing we noticed was that we were peeing a lot more.

Geoff and Lenny decided that we might as well start walking out to the highway, 45 miles away. Like I said before, Geoff sometimes isn't too bright and Lenny's no better. I figured that if we walked to the lake, we might be able to attract some attention on the highway 12 miles across it. That seemed a much better idea than walking 45 miles, so, after crossing the river on a series of logs, we started off. Geoff and I weren't worried about the numerous grizzlies in the area, in spite of not having any bullets for our rifles that we didn't have anyway. We knew that we couldn't outrun a mad grizzly, or even a slightly ticked-off one, but we wouldn't have had to. All we would have to do is outrun Lenny, which wouldn't be too difficult.

By the time we reached the lake, it was fully dark. The three of us gathered up all the driftwood we could find into three great huge piles spaced along the shore. We lit the fires, made some more coffee and sat back, waiting to be rescued. What we didn't know was that from the other side, our fires lined up behind each other and looked like a single fire, not a distress signal.

Four hours later we were still waiting, with considerably less hope. We gave up finally and went to bed. Wouldn't you know it? Just as we fell asleep, Gary Van Der Veen, who operates the Talbot Arm Motel in Destruction Bay across the lake, came to see what all the fuss was about. He had seen our fires shortly after we lit them, but being a practical man, he waited until the bar closed for the night before coming to get us.

Even though all of our money was sitting in the truck at the bottom of the river, Gary gave us a room for the night, fed us the next day and let us watch TV in the lounge for six hours until a friend could drive the 180 miles from Whitehorse to get us. For Gary's generosity to the three of us, we will be eternally grateful.

Postscript: The next weekend, Dan and his party located a pair of dupes in Whitehorse and borrowed a four-by-four truck to return to the scene of the crime and remove the soggy Toyota. They managed to wreck two more vehicles and drink an estimated 19 gallons of coffee before limping back into Whitehorse.

As Dan reports, "Geoff cleaned up the Toyota and sold it to a very gullible individual after settling with an even more gullible insurance company. Lenny and Dennis (the dupe) never went camping with Geoff and I again. Lisa left Geoff shortly after they moved to Victoria and I quietly spend my time destroying vehicles on my own. I am still convinced that everything would have turned out better if only Toyota made vehicles that float."

Baseball, Dawson and Herschel

by Dave White

If you're gonna live in the Yukon, you'd better be prepared to do just about anything to have a little fun. You'd better be prepared to try some new things, you'd better throw out a few old prejudices, and you'd better be willing to break some new ground in the name of keeping busy.

Yukoners have been doing that for hundreds of years, but sporting types didn't always have the lighted ski trails, fancy curling rinks and modern facilities the north boasts these days.

Long before they built the first indoor baseball stadium in Texas, Dawsonites had taken the game indoors. And even though whalers/baseball fanatics on Herschel Island didn't have the Arctic Brotherhood Hall to play in, they played the game anyway. A look around the modern-day territory will confirm Yukoners are mad about their ball. Whitehorse has one of the nicest community diamond complexes in Canada, and it's just not summer in this neck of the woods until you hold a ball tournament.

The sport has roots, buddy, roots deeper than any other sport in the Yukon.

One hundred years ago, Herschel Island was a booming whaling community. Ships left San Francisco with their often press-ganged crews early in the summer, racing down the Pacific coast to make it into Herschel Island's Pauline Cove before freeze-up. After a winter of being stuck fast in the Arctic ice, the whalers would spent the brief summer hunting bowheads before leaving for the south, just ahead of the winter, with their holds filled with the valuable cargo.

The whalers, mostly down-and-out southerners, poor bastards who missed out on one gold rush or another, lived on their ships from October until the end of June. Seven ships spent the winter of 1893-94 in Pauline Cove, 15 called it home the following year and 13 more were stuck in 1895-96.

These whalers were sportin' men. They laid out a soccer pitch in the snow, staged boxing matches on the icy decks of their boats and skied across the ice. But the most popular, and perhaps unusual, sporting concern was the Herschel Island Baseball League.

The games must have started promptly at noon, because that's just about the only time the sun would crack the horizon. According to John R. Bockstoce's *Whales, Ice & Men: The History of Whaling in the Western Arctic*, the games on the diamond were pitched battles, and on one occasion even deadly.

The league consisted of the Herschels, the Arctics, the Northern Lights and the Pick-Ups. The diamond was laid out on the ice using ash from cabin stoves. Game details were often included in the ship's logs. Three years after the first game, the ball players staged the most memorable game in the league's short history. The details of the March 7, 1897 contest even became the subject of an article in *Sports Illustrated* magazine.

The temperature bottomed out at around 20 degrees Fahrenheit, wrote Bockstoce, unseasonably warm for that time of year. The game was in its second inning when a dark cloud suddenly dropped over the island.

"Within minutes it was blowing the worst gale some of the men could remember.... Almost at once they would see only a few feet and the temperature plunged towards minus 20. The players scattered, scrambling for ships and buildings. Most made it to safety, but three whalers and two natives were soon reported missing."

"About 4 p.m. on Sunday someone was heard banging on the storm door of the *Wanderer*," wrote Arthur James Allen in his book, *A Whaler and Trader in the Arctic*.

"It was opened, and into the shelter staggered one of the missing men. He was a big, young, strong Norwegian and he was well-clothed. When they brought him into the bull room they had to knock 15 lbs of ice from the hood of his parka where the moisture from his mouth had frozen, nearly closing the opening."

The Norwegian survived, but several body parts had to be amputated. The frozen corpses of the missing four players were found when the storm died down the next day.

The deaths were the only fatalities during the history of the Herschel Island Baseball League, three more than have died playing baseball in the major leagues.

Residents of Dawson liked their baseball, too, and they also saw it as a winter diversion. But Dawsonites opted to play their games indoors, under the high ceiling at the Arctic Brotherhood Hall. The game was modified, only two bases were used, hits into the spectators section on the stage were called "gallery hits" and treated like homeruns, and the huge chandelier hanging from the ceiling was in play.

One of the best players in the Dawson City Indoor Baseball League was Albert Forrest, who made his mark as a goaltender when he played for the Dawson City Seven in their ill-fated challenge for hockey's Stanley Cup in 1905.

The Dawson City Indoor Baseball League was a big deal, too. The regular schedule was covered faithfully by the Klondike's newspapers. Things haven't really changed all that much in the last 100 years. Yukoners still like to speed up the pace of the long winters by taking part in sports, and they still play ball.

At least no one loses their outfield in a snowstorm.

Inside Out, Outside In

Mirror in blue plastic

Mirror in blue plastic

story and photos by Serena Lee Mis.Ta-Nash

Sakhalin Island lies north of Japan, close to the coast of the Russian Far East. I went to this island in the fall of 1992 to tell stories

at an Indigenous Peoples Festival in Poronaysk, a community of about 25,000 half-way up the island. Our group of seven performers were the first Canadians to visit the area in recent memory, at least since before the 1917 Russian Revolution.

We were greeted like long-lost friends. The Rythmes of the North Festival was wonderful—we sang, we danced and we feasted. We learned their games and taught them ours. We spent happy hours listening to the stories of the elders.

All too soon the festival was over and we were on the train travelling south to Yuhzno-Sakalinsk, the capital city of the island, where we would meet the governor and perform at a hospital.

Parting from our new friends in Poronaysk was painful. We had grown to love these warm, caring people. Many came to the train station to say desvadanya—goodbye. They brought gifts—food and drinks, juice made from birch trees, dried and smoked salmon, hard-boiled eggs, cheese, and chi—tea with heaps of sugar mixed in. All this bounty from people who had so little.

On this leg of the journey we were six—three fellow Canadian performers, our Russian host Sasha and our translator, Nicolai—all packed into one small compartment. The train would take many hours to reach our destination. After all the excitement of the festival—ten days of performing, playing and the sadness of parting—we were tired. As the hours passed, we grew quiet. Some slept, while others enjoyed the seashore scenery sliding past the window.

I needed to stretch my legs and slipped out of our compartment into the hallway. Down at the other end, looking out the window, was a small girl and her babushka (grandmother). What a beautiful sight they were. I imagined the babushka's words to the child, as she pointed out the window, "Look, there's the best place to gather sea cucumber and over there is where I found a big piece of amber."

I had taken many rolls of pictures because I wanted to take Russia and the warm faces of these new friends home with me. So I ducked back into our compartment and fished out my camera. I moved down the hallway and tapped Babushka on the shoulder. Showing her the camera, I pointed to her and the child and pretended to take a picture. "I Canada," I said. "Canada," she answered, grinning broadly, and nodded yes. I snapped three

or four times. "Spasybo—thank you," I said and gave each of them a Canadian pin.

A while later, I again walked down the hallway. This time, the grandmother and child were sitting in their compartment, still looking out the window, Babushka still pointing and talking. The silhouette caught my fancy and I reached for the camera hanging around my neck. They hadn't noticed me so I just quickly snapped and walked away.

In my compartment, the whole crowd was awake and I returned to the sound of Nicolai playing his guitar and

singing "Michelle, My Belle," voices blending on the parts each knew. The last chords were abruptly interrupted by an angry man filling the entire doorway. His face was beet red and he was hollering in Russian. He had steel grey hair, covered with a navy blue wool tam. His clear blue eyes looked straight at me and I felt them pierce to my middle. "Oh, no," I thought, "he saw me take that picture without permission."

I moved a bit closer to Michelle and she took my hand as the stranger continued to holler. Nicolai answered quietly, pointing at each of us in turn. The only word I understood was the man's name, Ivan. Sasha, our Russian host, said nothing. As they talked the stranger became calmer.

At last, he left and Nicolai explained. Ivan was upset because the babushka, whose picture I'd taken, was angry with him. He and his son were drinking Vodka and she said they were too loud. She told him he shouldn't be like that in front of children and that he was a bad man. He had overheard us talking English and was afraid we would form the wrong opinion to take back to Canada.

At the end of Nicolai's explanation I hesitated but a moment before taking a pin and heading for Ivan's compartment. I paused at the door and held out my hand to him. "Canada," I said, pointing to myself. "Friends," I continued, handing him the pin and quickly returning to our compartment.

Within a moment he appeared in our doorway again. This time a big smile lit his face. Nicolai translated. Ivan wanted to talk to me, so we squeezed together and made room for Ivan and his son. Ivan started by thanking me over and over for the gift from Canada. He told me about joining the Russian Army as a young man and being sent to Germany during the war. I told him that my own grandfather had fought for Canada in Germany at the same time. Ivan said that Canada and Russia

were friends then and remain friends now. He had never actually met a Canadian while in Germany but one time, he had seen two Canadian nurses in a car from a distance. He said those women were beautiful.

"I'm not a bad man," he repeated. One time during that terrible war, when he was an 18-year-old private, his commanding officer had sent him out in the woods with a German prisoner. "I was told to shoot this young man," he explained, "but I couldn't do it. I let the young man go, told him to run far and fast. When I returned to my officer I lied and said I had killed the prisoner."

Tears steamed down Ivan's face as he went on. "I've kept this secret in my heart all the long years since. To reveal the truth could have led to my own death." By this time, tears were streaming down my face too.

I gave him a tissue and, as he wiped his eyes, he continued to talk. He removed his tam and unscrewed a war medal which he pressed into my hand. This medal was the highest honour a Russian soldier could be given and he wanted me to take it back to Canada, to show our friendship and seal it forever.

With shaking hands I took the gift, took back the tissue and wrapped the medal with Ivan's tears of friendship. As the train pulled into the village station where Ivan and his son lived, I pulled out my camera to take pictures of Ivan, his son, the medal and me. The smiles were huge. We hugged and I kissed Ivan on the cheek as we said goodbye.

The train was slowly pulling away when, through the window, I saw Ivan running toward me. He rushed to the compartment and held his hand out to me. A small package gaily wrapped with Christmas paper and decorated with a small red bow lay there. Ivan told me it was for the most beautiful woman he had ever met. He said to remember our friendship and his love whenever I used this gift. Then he left. As the train picked up speed, I opened his gift. It was a small purse-sized mirror, in a blue plastic case.

I carry this precious gift with me. Whenever I look in the mirror, I see the face of Ivan, his bright blue eyes and wide smile. I remember his story and his kindness. Mostly, though, I remember how lucky I am to have a friend in Russia called Ivan.

Inside Out, Outside In

Letter

wonder what everyone's up to, where they actually care what's going on in the lives of the people they share their roads, sidewalks and barstools with.

You know, it's a pretty great place to live. I walk to work everyday and wave to about 15 people, all wrapped up in their coats and scarves in the winter. (You dare not say hi for fear of insulting a good friend, even if you don't recognize the parka.) Summer's different. Everyone's in a good mood, running around in shorts and sandals, wondering what you're up to this weekend.

Yeah, I guess it does sound a bit like home, everybody smiling on their way to work. I walk past this little apartment building everyday, once on the way to work and once on the way home. All last summer, at least every sunny day, this same guy sat in a cheap plastic lawnchair on the tiny lawn of the building, relaxing in the shade. This old fella

reasons I'm waiting for summer. Maybe I'll rate a beer this year. I know I'd like to hear his stories, and I know he has some. Everyone around here does.

Last winter, when I was following the Yukon Quest—that's the dogsled race I told you about—we flew out of Dawson on this absolutely perfect day. It was about 35 below, not a trace of cloud. I could see forever from the co-pilot seat of our Piper Navajo—snow-white hills, grey mountains, blue sky.

We followed the trail along the river for a while, dropping down to twist along with the ice. We passed a couple of cabins tucked into the wilderness, smoke drifting up, someone living out there, surviving, probably thriving.

We then flew over the two lead teams, low enough to make out the dogs stretching out the gangline. If you looked down, you could see the mushers and their teams, about half a kilometre apart,

Y eah, hi Ma, it's me. Today? Oh, I guess it'd be about minus 30. No, it's not too bad. You can't ski or anything, and the car hasn't started for a week, but it's really beautiful, you should see it. The air is so still, woodsmoke rises in columns 30 feet over the roofs. It's so quiet the only sound you hear is the snow crunching under your boots. Yeah, I guess it is cold. Funny thing is, you really don't notice it after a couple of days. You get good at coping.

So, how's everyone? Good, good. No, I don't think I'll be home this winter, too expensive. Besides, there's some talk of doing a ski trip into Kluane. It won't be too bad. We've got all the winter gear, and a few guys have done the trip before.

I don't know when I'll be home next. I know it's been six years now, and yes, I know I said I'd be coming up here for one year. I don't know what happened, but the same thing happened to a lot of people around here.

It's kind of hard to explain. I mean, I didn't really like this place when I first came here. You remember, it was the fall, cold and grey and raining, like home but a lot colder. I met some people quickly, but I was still homesick. This place was a lot of things, but it just wasn't home. It's hard to say when I stopped missing home; there wasn't really one thing. It may have been the first week when I realized I recognized a face almost everywhere I went. Maybe it was the time it took me an hour to walk two blocks and get my groceries because I ran into so many people. Maybe it was after the music festival, when it seemed to be the only thing anyone was talking about.

Maybe it was just the realization that this is a true community, a place where people

was always sipping from cans of beer, pulled out of a sack kept under his chair.

He always wore long pants, and leaned back in his chair so you could see his worn cowboy boots hanging out underneath the cuffs. He always wore a once-colourful western shirt, and an old straw cowboy hat on his head.

After a week or two, he started nodding to me as I went by. Then he'd raise his beer, maybe lift up the brim of his hat. Soon, we had little conversations, usually about the weather. I hated rainy days for a lot of reasons, a big one being the rain drove the cowboy indoors.

He doesn't sit out there now, of course. It's way too cold for a thin snap-button shirt and a too-short pair of polyester pants. His chair is still there, covered in snow. Seeing this old guy everyday again is one of the

pushing along near the west bank of the river. If you looked up, you could see the hundred kilometres of beauty and challenge that lay between them and the town of Eagle, Alaska. It literally took my breath away, and I've been thankful ever since for the chance to have seen it.

Starting to sound like this place is becoming home, eh? You know, I did plan to come home. Last fall, practically quit the job and everything to move back to be closer to you guys, but something stopped me. I don't know, Ma, I just decided to stay. I mean, I was feeling a little homesick again, I guess, and I just wanted to be back home. But I decided to stay, again, and I don't know, things have been going great since then.

There's just something about this place, Ma, it just takes hold. Then it gets tough to even think about living somewhere else. Must be something in that 30 below air.

Take care.

Above town

by Evie Estey

A tube of wooden slats
Bound by wire
Protrudes from the hillside
Under the ancient dirt road
Hard packed now by much traffic.
I discover this relic
As my dog sniffs its orifice.
A coursing waterway in the spring,
A hiding place of small animals.
Summer flowers create a colourful garden
For some fairy
Or pygmy
To dance in the pungent fragrance
Of sweet wild sage
During moonless northern nights of
everlasting daylight.
A miniature valley of erosion
Is testimony to the existence of a trickle
Of water to nourish the wild growth
Which nourishes the small creatures
Who scamper in the shadows.
An old wooden culvert.
In the fading snow on the high hills
Are the melting skidoo tracks
And broken glass from a midwinter collision
At the distant end of the wooden tube.
It will cost a fortune to repair,
So it will not be mended, just left.
Fifty years ago
This was a town of
Harried and prosperous people
Seeing life through tear-stained eyes
Which dried
Without leaving stains.
Not like that trickle from the wooden tube,
Where the little erosion valley
Must seem like a mountain to a mole
Caught in the crevice;
Lucky if an iceberg floats down
from the breaking snow
To provide a vehicle of escape
For deliverance from a muddy demise.
My reverie is interrupted
By a scolding black raven.
Leaving the timid world
at the base of the hill
And I call my dog to my side.
We continue
Above Town.

gone/now

by Stuart Mueller

gone: sitting at the arborite top kitchen table across from my grandfather. a radio (toaster?) is on a small shelf level with my chin to the right. next to it a small door which hides the fold-down ironing board. my grandmother is moving around the kitchen—opening the cupboard, pulling on the green glass knob—putting something away on the top shelf, next to the biscuit tin, next to the leftover ration coupons. my grandfather goes off to the spare room, thump, thump, comes back with something, starts telling a story. now: walking on a dirt road in Dawson, holding Isaac's hand. he's splashing in the puddles, I am looking at the hills, the buildings, stories clanking around my head.

Returning home
by SharonAnne LaDue

I left the Yukon resolved never to return. I did not want to return. There was nothing here except people who did not accept or respect me. How could I live and lead a happy life if no one cared?

Adios Yukon! I'm outta here! I wandered across Canada from city to city, leaving mysterious remarks about my past. My prairie friends were convinced I grew up in the bush with no modern amenities. After leading an anonymous life, I heard the faint echoing of a call. A call I had never heard before. It was calling directly to my soul, telling me it was time to go home.

Home? That was a strange idea. Home, a place to feel comfortable, welcome and happy. I let the call lead me to my home. I wasn't sure where it would take me. After 72 hours on the bus, I was home. I was in the Yukon, surrounded by mountains, fresh air, blue rivers, and people who were my family.

When the bus entered the Yukon, I knew I was home. I didn't have to see an "Entering the Yukon" sign. The aura surrounding all told me when I had entered the home zone. Coming down the last stretch of the highway, I knew I was home. My spirit felt light and airy. My soul was at peace.

I have seen other parts of Canada but my soul will only call the Yukon home. This is home because my people have been here for too many generations to count. If ever I feel down or lost, I look up and see the purple grey mountains and cornflower blue sky. The beauty takes away my blues. Only then can I smile and laugh at life's little jokes and mysteries.

Silent song

by "Lousetown" Carole Legace

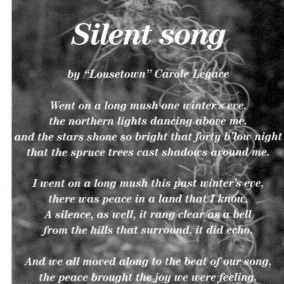

Went on a long mush one winter's eve,
the northern lights dancing above me.
and the stars shone so bright that forty b'low night
that the spruce trees cast shadows around me.

I went on a long mush this past winter's eve,
there was peace in a land that I know.
A silence, as well, it rang clear as a bell
from the hills that surround, it did echo.

And we all moved along to the beat of our song,
the peace brought the joy we were feeling.
In a land that is ruled by a mother so cruel,
why at forty below am I beaming?

The payoff

by Bob McCauley

Probably every teacher wonders if they have made any kind of an impact on their students. As a 20-year-plus veteran of the profession in the Yukon, I had often fantasized about my contribution to the development of our youth. The results of my efforts were made apparent to me in a recent encounter.

One Saturday, I was jogging down a usually isolated trail near town when I heard the sounds of a traditional Yukon bush party in progress directly ahead of me. I hesitated, but then decided to carry on. As I proceeded, several hulking, surly, and definitely intimidating figures emerged from the brush cover and blocked my progress. I became very uneasy, since among the group, I recognized an ex-student of mine from several years past. I recalled that he had "graduated early to avoid the rush" and we had terminated our pedagogic relationship on a confrontational note.

I was met on the trail with stares that I took to be questioning, at best, and (without trying), hostile, at second best, from the now silent group. My eyes met theirs and passed from member to member until I met his impassive gaze. A flash of recognition passed over his face and, surprisingly, a friendly smile slowly formed on his face. He called out to me, and then everyone came over. He put his arm around my shoulder and introduced me around to the group in a loud voice. "Hey this is Mr. McCauley. He used to be one of my teachers."

This brought out some definitely hostile looks and grumbles. "No ! No! He was the best teacher I ever had. He taught me how to play table tennis really good, and every time I go to jail I always win all the cigarettes!"

Scowls turned to smiles all around, grumbles turned to friendly banter, and amid great camaraderie and jocularity, we exchanged a few more amicable remarks and I carried on my way. Thinking back on this encounter, you can imagine how thankful I was that I had had such a positive influence on his life, not only socially and academically, but also in the category of development that could be classified as "life skills."

A little rain must fall

by Jolie Lewis

I live in Alaska. And it is winter. Therefore, my igloo is buried in snowdrifts, the temperature is plummeting toward forty degrees below zero, the wind chill factor is lower than I can count backward, and I haven't seen sunlight for weeks. I even have a pet penguin, right?

Not a chance.

Though our curio shops do a convincing business selling figurines of the comical birds, penguins live only in the southern hemisphere. And weather-wise, all that really falls here in Ketchikan is rain, day after day after day.

Take today's forecast: a 100 percent chance of the sopping stuff. On a regular basis with stereotype-defying accuracy, our local weather people actually call for an "absolute chance of precipitation."

Average yearly rainfall in Ketchikan totals 155 inches—more than twelve feet! Compare that to Seattle, the so-called City of Rain, where a mere thirty inches is likely to drip out of the sky.

In Ketchikan, winter is the wettest. The rain starts in September, ends in May—if it ends at all. At about thirty-five degrees Fahrenheit, it's just warm enough not to snow. The sun sets around 3:15 p.m., meaning that the sky has shifted from a cloud-covered noontime grey to pitch black by four o'clock. And it rains nearly everyday.

Ketchikan, with its 8,000 inhabitants, is the southernmost city on the southeast Alaskan panhandle. Superimposed on a map of the lower 48, Alaska's borders stretch from Georgia to North Dakota to New Mexico. In terms of weather, it's not surprising that our island has little in common with an icebox like Barrow, about 1,400 miles away. There, the mercury drops and stays in the negative thirties and the sun doesn't come up for sixty-seven days.

But we southern Alaskans still suffer from a similar strain of December's psychological flu as our northern neighbours. When a company based near Anchorage took out a classified ad in a local tabloid promoting their "Northern Lights bright light therapy box—helps with Seasonal Affective Disorder, winter depression, fatigue, and weight gain the drug-free way," it got seven calls from Ketchikan within hours. For some $300, the company sells sunshine in a box—presumably made from concentrate and shipped from Florida.

I could have used some sun, boxed or otherwise, in October. Dark, dreary, and drenching, it rained every day through the first three and a half weeks. I found myself perversely wishing it would keep pouring. If nothing else, we could at least set a new record for "number of consecutive days with measurable rainfall."

A few days into November, I was flabbergasted to hear a reporter and editor at my newspaper discussing what a lovely month October had been. As keeper of the weather statistics, I hit them with the facts: twenty-seven days and twenty inches of rain.

"Oh, sure," the ten-year veterans of Ketchikan-living said, "but it wasn't raining *side*ways like it usually does in October." The lesson: the difference between a drab and a fine day here is the angle of the rain—not its presence or absence.

I'm sure you can't help wondering, if the weather's that miserable, why have I spent the last eighteen months in the isolated First City of the Last Frontier?

The truth is, this area is so fantastically beautiful, the people so friendly, and the fresh halibut so tasty that we Ketchikanites like to say: if it weren't for the deterrent rain, everybody would want to live here. And we couldn't have that.

Inside Out, Outside In

The visitor from Outside

by Adam Killick

Since moving to the Yukon in 1994, I have found the unique vocabulary of its residents to be a fascinating study, particularly in the way Yukoners characterize themselves as separate and distinct from, well, just about everyone and everywhere else. Leading the way in our peculiar lexicon is the term "Outside," used as a proper noun, with a capital "O." I could never understand how "Outside" could be used as a generic home for everyone who doesn't live here. Until last summer, that is. That was when Edward, a former professor of mine, came for a visit.

Edward had taught me the nuances of late Victorian literature a number of years ago, while I was at university in eastern Ontario, and since then we had intermittently kept in touch via the Internet. He has lived alone all his adult life, mostly in downtown Toronto, and very rarely has he left the city. His proposed trip to the Yukon for 10 days, then, was an unusual venture. "Don't worry," he said, as he invited himself in an e-mail message. "I'm an easy guest. I'll just rent a car and explore things on my own." Nothing, I soon found, could have been further from the truth.

"I have my routines," he said, as we drove from the Whitehorse Airport to my home in the Golden Horn subdivision, "but I'm here for something completely different. I'm here to get away from my inner sanctum of computers, dusty books, and British television serials. I want to get outside and explore the Yukon and your wonderful capital, Yellowknife. And I've always wanted to do the Chilkoot Trail."

After some discussion, it turned out that about the closest to "wilderness" Edward had ever come was in trying to negotiate his way among the various skinheads, dreads, grunge and drag queens that inhabit Toronto's trendy Queen Street West district at midnight on a Saturday. That was okay though, I thought, many of his urban skills were probably transferable.

The first thing we had to do was set up his sleeping arrangements. My partner and I lived in a reasonably small house, and, given our age and circumstances, purchasing furniture had never been much of a priority. In fact, the only piece of furniture we had ever bought was our second-hand futon. The rest of our "furnishings" were either donated or built from scavenged materials. We did not have a second bed. I had asked Edward to bring a sleeping bag (which he had done—a brand new bag rated to -20) but he didn't realize he would have to use it inside, on the floor. So, after some effort, behind the hot water tank we found an old piece of thick foam to use as a mattress (a ThermaRest was deemed to be insufficient). Then we found him a pillow, although he insisted we put a new pillowcase on it, despite the fact that the one already on the pillow had recently been washed.

Next I started to cook dinner.

I have always prided myself on my made-from-scratch Caesar salad dressing. I learned it while working at a restaurant which prepared meals at the customer's table. I passed Edward his plate of lovingly hand-crafted salad, looking for the approval of a former mentor. He sniffed it, sneered, and walked out to the kitchen to pour salt all over it—not from the salt shaker, but from the bulk container.

"Oh," I said, trying to sound sympathetic, "is it a bit bland for you?"

He looked up with his mouth full and told me that it might not have been if I had used enough Parmesan.

"I'm sorry, Edward. Both my parents suffered from hypertension, so I was raised on a virtually salt-free diet."

"Yes, well," he glared, "you should keep in mind that I wasn't."

Edward had arrived on a Thursday. The next day, I left work at noon to spend the afternoon giving him a tour of Whitehorse. Or, rather, I had planned to, but he insisted on giving the tour himself. Edward's tour began by going into the tourist centre in downtown Whitehorse and asking questions like:

"What, and where, is the MacBride Museum?"

"Where can I hike around Whitehorse?"

"What is the population here?"

Such questions, one might assume, are logical for the uninitiated tourist to ask. He had already asked me, however, the same questions the night before. And I thought I had answered them, having been a resident of the Yukon for some time. I had even given him a copy of the brand new book detailing all the hikes around Whitehorse. But I guess my undergraduate opinions weren't good enough. So I spent my Friday afternoon following Edward around,

standing silently in the background looking, and feeling, like a tourist. And as anyone who lives in Whitehorse knows, we will go to almost any length to avoid looking like a tourist, though I must admit I learned a few things. I even took advantage of the opportunity to visit the "Klingon gas station" Visitor Reception Centre (something I had never done before for fear of looking like a tourist).

The next day we took Edward to Haines Junction for a music festival (where he single-handedly managed to insult the intelligence of all my friends with his self-absorbed didactic meandering) and to allow him the pleasure of sleeping in a tent. ("I was a Boy Scout, you know, when I was 13, so I've done this before," he said. Edward was now 46.) This time he was upset because he didn't have a ThermaRest (we had offered him the traditional blue foamie) so my partner gave him hers. When we awoke the next morning at around 10:00 a.m. Edward was pacing around fuming because he couldn't sleep and had been up since seven. He had wanted coffee, but couldn't work the camp stove. When we climbed out of our (separate) tent, he gruffly mumbled something about his impatience with us and stormed off.

After a reconciliatory breakfast at the campsite and two espressos at the bakery, we left Haines Junction and drove to Sheep Mountain for a hike. Edward wanted to see some wildlife (which, in his estimation, did not include anything airborne or smaller than a coyote), so I figured Sheep Mountain would be a reasonably sure bet—or it would have been, if we hadn't stopped after twenty minutes because Edward was too tired to continue up the slope.

As we climbed back into the truck I asked him if we should reconsider our attack on the Chilkoot, scheduled for later that week. In a momentary flash of reason, he agreed with me.

SKAGWAY—HOME OF THE NORTH WIND

POSTCARD: JEFF BROWN

Inside Out, Outside In

I had to work during the week, so, as he had promised, Edward rented a car and set out to try some of the day hikes detailed in the hiking guide. He returned in the evenings to harass my partner and I, add salt to our cooking, and brag about his adventures of that day. He would describe his hikes as though he were a wily old trapper. "I thought I heard a grizzly by Miles Canyon. If it had attacked me I might have lain there for days before I was found," and implied that I should try it—hiking, that is—some time.

He decided on Wednesday that, despite all his accumulated experience, he would probably have to forgo the Chilkoot, and, besides, he said, it would "probably be too much for your partner anyway."

Friday night, he took us out for dinner, to thank us for our hospitality—which was very nice, and we appreciated it—except that he asked us to pay for dessert. But the gesture of buying the main course was nice, and certainly unexpected. And Edward raved about his strawberry-rhubarb pie. He enjoyed it so much, in fact, that he ordered a second piece.

I took Edward out on a day hike the following morning, up the side of White Mountain. It took us a while, but we eventually made it to the summit plateau, and, despite the constant complaining going up and coming down ("When I get back home—if I make it back home—I swear I'm never leaving my sofa again!"), I think he appreciated the view. A solitary mountain goat allowed us observation privileges from a car's length away. I even watched Edward take a brief moment to savour the scenery for its intrinsic value, instead of launching into some tired diatribe about Roman culture or Ontario politics or his dental hygiene. The Yukon can have strange effects on people.

All in all, I think Edward did have a good time during his visit to the Yukon, for all his posturing. He escaped his routine (I don't own a TV, he simply sneered at my books, and didn't go near my computer), and I believe that from time to time, when he's stuck in downtown Toronto traffic, or looking out his eleventh floor window at the grime and sweat of reptile modernity, he will remember, fondly, the view of Little Atlin Lake from atop White Mountain. And, although I found his visit stressful, it was no worse than being stuck behind an RV going up the South Access road. And besides, both Edward and I got something tangible out of the experience. I was acutely reminded of why I left Toronto when I did, and Edward now knows where he can get the best fruit pie in North America.

Moreover, I learned something further, something subtle, but very relevant: I now know, exactly, where Outside is. And I'm glad I'm not there.

story and photos by Herb Cohen

The Jews of the Yukon Territory

With the Klondike gold rush of 1898, fine strands of Jewish history came to be woven into the fabric of Yukon life. The Canadian census of 1901 counted 163 Jews in the territory and a 1903 business directory survey recorded over 60 Jewish names in Dawson.

Most were Americans, though some were from distant lands. Five from England wrote to the Jewish Chronicle of London that they were "the only Jews up on the trail" and thought it significant to add that "up to now [they had] met with civility and courtesy." They also passed on the contradictory news of "a Jew on the trail who had come all the way from Jerusalem with an outfit."

Few made their living prospecting and mining. Some were restauranteurs or dry goods merchants; others sold real estate, taught school or worked as musicians.

A menorah (brass candelabrum) in a back room of Dawson's museum, and the tiny Jewish cemetery bear silent witness to the adherence of the Jews of the Yukon to some of their ancient customs and laws and their separate identity.

I first visited the cemetery one November night in 1982, with Mike Johnston, Dawson's doctor, and Wilburt Wiggins, the custodian of Father Judge Memorial Hospital. Armed with a flashlight and ink sketch, drawn for me on a napkin by Mel Orecklin, a Whitehorse friend, we began to climb the Dome Road. We emerged from Wilbert's four-by-four, beside the RCMP graveside, into a pelting snowfall which covered the tombstones, obliterated the footpaths and reduced Dawson below to smudges of lamp post light.

Relying on Wilburt's hunches, we followed the edge of the Yukon Order of Pioneers' cemetery which led us to Solomon Packer's solitary headstone. Engraved on it were his Hebrew names in the ancient script and the dates of his birth and death according to the Jewish calendar.

The cemetery is enclosed by a picket fence, mostly leaning or down, of spruce, weathered grey, and naked but for vestiges of white paint applied decades before by the First Dawson Girl Guides, who attempted to restore it. At the perimeter stands the simple arched gateway with the Hebrew words "Beit Chaim" ("House of Life") carved into the wood.

Summer visits reveal the forest's relentless encroachment. The earth is overgrown with cranberry bushes, cinquefoil, yarrow, delphiniums and wild roses, and poplar and spruce saplings. Still, it is possible to make out, in a single row aside the headstone of Samuel Packer, four burial mounds, only one of which retains a faded wooden marker.

THE MOOSE AND I ARE NOT LOST

story and photo by Elizabeth Hewlett

The moose aren't really lost, folks. Very sensible these moose. They are exactly where the great one intended them to be—in the north. Where the wilderness and habitat of animals is foremost. What is changing, I'm told, is that people are forgetting to leave. Or, in "dropping out from it all" they are finding their way up north, where the moose are. This describes me, a single, 37-year-old woman, born and raised on the prairies.

Having narrowly escaped a Toronto career track, I've chosen instead life in a northern British Columbia tidewater paradise.

It's been over a year since I've seen my family and friends, and, yes, I miss them a lot. But it's been a year of new wonders, in this land where the biggest spruce trees on earth line the mystical fjords and coastline. Coming home from the theatre last night we saw a fox and a deer skipping through town. I've seen many bears — including a mother with twin cubs on the path where my ever-faithful Brittany spaniel companion, Tara, and I used to walk. I've burned a quick u-turn in a golf cart when a bear crossing the green decided to come closer for a look. I've had my golf balls stolen by red fox cubs who live on the 15th hole. I've seen moose in muskeg swamps contentedly "chewing their cud" and bald eagles soaring above my house. And so far, I haven't even spent much time out of town.

Oh, how the tides turn. It was 1979 that I ventured into the wilderness of Takhini (outside of Whitehorse) to see the crazy guy who held my heart captive as he worked a seasonal job at the hot springs. The scenery, people, wildlife, history—everything fascinated me. Today, he is

lost somewhere in Toronto and I am maintaining my own heart, at 54 degrees north. I live in Kitimat, British Columbia. The native translation means "people of the snow."

I marvel at how this came about. The exposure in 1979 to Whitehorse, Takhini, Kluane National Park, Skagway, Haines and Haines Junction, as well as the *Lost Whole Moose Catalogue* (purchased for my father) held great delight and left long-term impressions. In 1994, I found *Another Lost Whole Moose Catalogue* while visiting my aunt's bookstore in Uxbridge, Ontario. It brought back a flood of memories, a longing for the beauty and magnitude of the north and set into motion a plan to change the course of my life. The transition was relatively short. I spent from October to February in Dawson Creek and then across northern B.C. to Kitimat.

The abolishment of my department head

position in Calgary and rejection of the subsequent transfer seems so easy now. My better idea came when I saw the posting of my current job on the northwest coast of B.C. Another beloved pursuit could be at hand— SAILING. Sailing on the eternally uncrowded, clear blue waters of coastal fjords, exploring rugged coastline, thousands of islands, encountering pods of Orca whales that have not been "catalogued" into family groups.

I traded in my penthouse apartment for a conservative job with the municipality and a "modular" home. People from the south use the "T" word—"trailer" to describe my choice of housing. I imagine some friends, due to embarrassment, omit from conversation all reference to the degradation I must be suffering in my chosen lifestyle. However, what they do not realize is that my small, comfortable home features fresh mountain air, clear water, pristine wilderness access, views of Claque Mountain to the west, Mount Elizabeth to the east, and from an eagle's-eye view, the magnificent Douglas Channel to the southeast. Very acceptable to a gal who, somehow, was able to shape her own destiny in order to get here.

Funny how things work out when you take a risk, isn't it? It looks like my dream could start to come true soon. I'm negotiating the lease of a 30-foot Catalan sailboat from an absentee owner, off making his fortune in Saudi Arabia. Rather than his boat growing six-foot weeds at the local marina, I've suggested mutual benefits.

Myself and my friend, both certified sailing skippers with six years under our belts, are

Inside Out, Outside In

Spin
by Tanya Handley

itching to experience the treasures found in the channels between here and the 90-nautical-mile trek to open sea. Our ultimate goals include circumnavigating the Queen Charlotte Islands, gunkholing the wonders of beautiful, quiet, undisturbed bays and inlets between here and the Alaska Panhandle, and perhaps a once-in-a-lifetime retirement voyage to the Mexican Baja, Hawaii and back home again to Kitimat.

For now, my dreams give way to reality. It is Thanksgiving weekend. Rising at 6:30 this morning to stuff my turkey, amid the pitch blackness of a cloudy rainy day (the same type of day for the past month), I have begun the quest of a great meal. Joining me will be two other Kitimat "orphans"—single women here for the work. Today was a little difficult; I am missing my family a great deal. With a quick "Tell me how to cook a turkey again?" call last night to my mom and older sister, we prearranged a family call this morning allowing the chance to talk to five of my six siblings and their families. In many ways, I told them, the reality that I am very far away has just set in. Driving to be with loved ones during holidays and celebrations is no longer an option. Flying out of here from now until next April is "iffy." I'm told our airport will land only one in three flights during this time frame due to the ever-present low cloud, fog and snow of the winter season.

The locals say it will rain from now until the snow comes, and then snow until the spring rains begin in April. The snow will be like I've never seen before, I'm told. These locals are to be believed, more due to the Kitimat namesake—People of the Snow—than for integrity. I have heard stories of 10-foot snowfalls in one night. Snow gets piled so high along driveways and streets that houses disappear, and everyone knows you have to shovel your roof to keep the snow load to bearable amounts. I purchased my first snow shovel last week. The locals have a lottery going at the office. Five dollars to enter your guess as to the date of the first snowfall that stays on the sidewalk of the town's public works building. I'm told the $70 pot will grow to upwards of $200 and the majority of the bets predict snow in the next couple of weeks. Just to be different, I may lay my fiver on November 11. I'll deem it my "remember-what-sunshine-looks-like" bet. But my snowshoes, and cross-country skis are ready. I've added more indoor lighting to combat SAD—seasonal affected disorder. My sailor friend is coming from Dawson Creek for Christmas and is looking for work here. Life is good.

If you live in the Yukon, chances are that you're a bit odd. Maybe you didn't quite fit in down south or maybe you are just irresistibly drawn to long, cold, dark winters. One of the great things about the Yukon, though, is that if you weren't odd in the first place, prolonged exposure to the territory will definitely fix that! Life here changes your perspective on a surprising number of things. And because it's happening to everyone, it's rather hard to notice. Trips outside or visitors from down south are perfect for pointing out these idiosyncrasies.

For example, the last time I undertook the long drive to the prairies, road conditions didn't really enter my mind until I got to Alberta. The roads there were suddenly so wide and smooth that for a moment I thought that I'd been beamed onto an airport runway. It was as if the steering wheel had suddenly been made into just a place to rest my hands. The opposing traffic was too far away to even notice and there were no potholes or yawning crevasses to avoid or leap over! I kept having to resist the urge to start reading a book and just let the truck handle the driving.

When we were in Belize, we'd meet other tourists who, after finishing with the "whew!-it-sure-is-hot-here-isn't-it?" conversation would attempt to launch into either "aren't-the-roads-just-awful?" or "can-you-believe-the-bugs?" We couldn't really go on about these topics as they were no worse than back home, so we'd end up steering the conversation back to the "whew!-it-sure-is-hot- here" and "did-you-notice-the-great-fruit-selection?"

Life in the Yukon also changes your views on basic living conditions. My mom came up for a visit and kept referring to my friends' house as "that beautiful cabin." "That beautiful cabin" is actually one of the nicest homes in Whitehorse and considered by many of us to be the ultimate lap of luxury. The other night, a bunch of us were sitting around watching a video. One of the main characters lived out in the woods in a cabin with no electricity, no running water and no phone. All the other characters were appalled at these "primitive" living conditions and much of the story wound about trying to "save" her from them. It took a deliberate suspension of belief for us to get on with the story. We thought the cabin looked beautiful. It had quite a number of different rooms, big windows, and even a second storey. We would have considered ourselves lucky to live in such a home and couldn't help bursting out in laughter each time one of the characters remarked disparagingly about it!

Another noticeable thing about Yukoners is their obsession with dogs, a topic that comes up almost instantly at any gathering of Yukoners. Dogs are an integral part of most Yukon households.

I once attended a big Thanksgiving gathering and at one point I noticed the rather bemused look on a visiting mother's face. I realized that 14 grown people had just spent much of the last half hour talking about their dogs, like they were furry people with peculiar breath. People often recognize each other's dogs before they recognize each other (of course this is more understandable during winter as the dogs usually wear less clothing).

Yukoners have pictures of their dogs in their wallets and the confusion with children does not end there. I have one set of friends who, having given their dog their favourite name, are left with having to christen their first-born Fluffy.

The progressive process of Yukonization leads me to suspect that my ability to recognize these types of Yukon idiosyncrasies will not last much longer. I've been here for three years now and, with each passing year, find it more and more difficult to establish just where a Yukon spin has been put on a perspective. This is fine by me though, because there's nothing like a spinning perspective to keep you from getting stuck in a rut!

PHOTO: ROB MATHEWSON

Outside

by Donna Pendziwol-MacMillan

Outside

Flowers bloom in March

Outside

Lakes are free of ice before May

Outside

Vehicles are newer and cleaner

Outside

There are overpasses to my children's delight

Outside

The sun sets in summer

Outside

There are a lot more people

Outside

You can travel for miles and not see an open space

Outside

It is more difficult to listen to the sounds of silence

Outside

The cost of living is less

Outside

Is a nice place to visit

But I am glad I pay the price

To live Inside the Yukon

Inside Out, Outside In

216

BACK PAGES

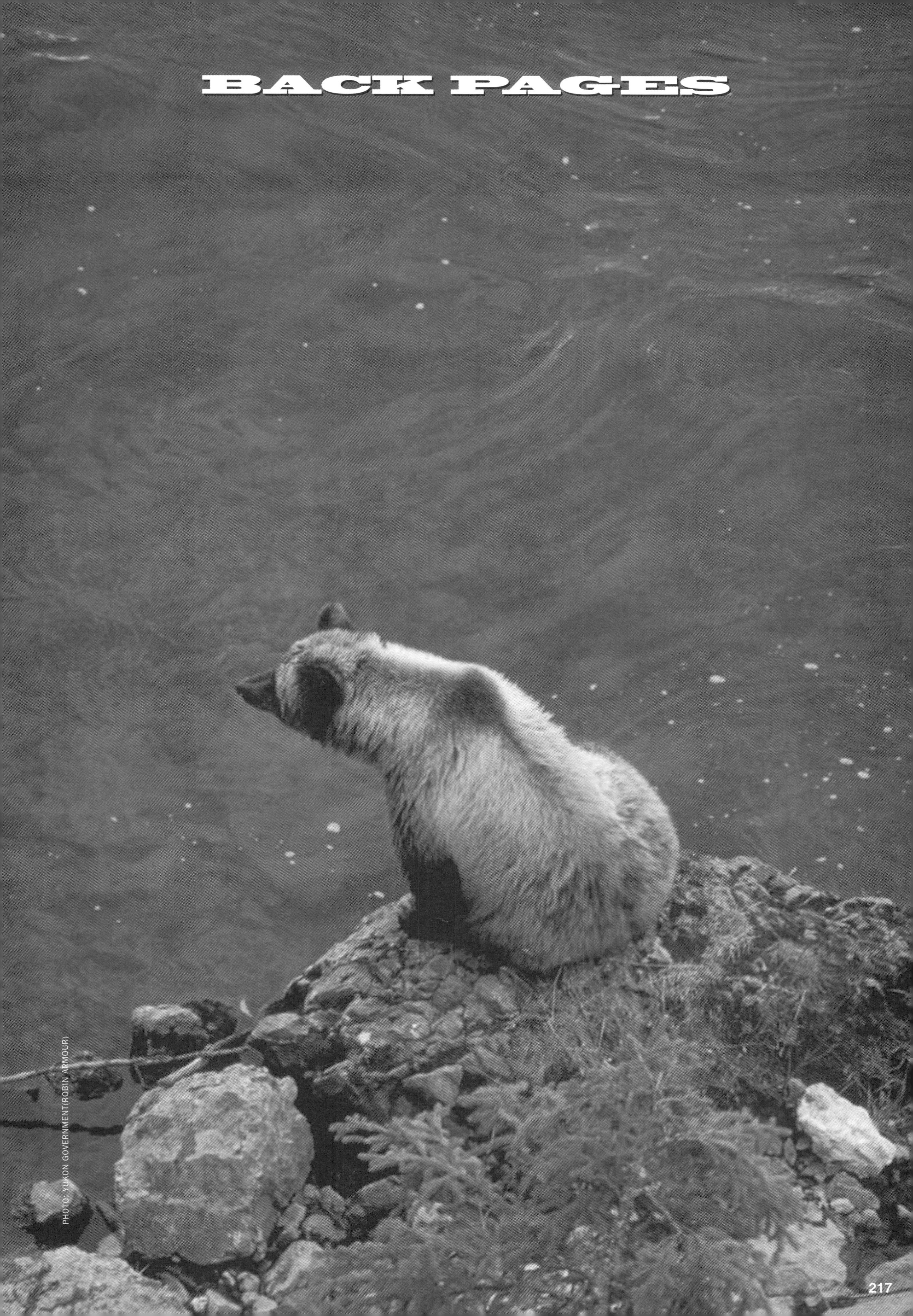

PHOTO: YUKON GOVERNMENT(ROBIN ARMOUR)

Design
Mike Rice

Project co-ordination
Wynne Krangle
Peter Long
Alison Reid

Section heads
Lay of the Land: Max Fraser
Animals: Sarah Locke
Self-sufficiency: Al Pope
Growing Kids: Lynda Ehrlich
Art: Alison Reid
Recycling: Muffy Macdonald
  and Alison Reid
On the Move: Alison Reid
Wilderness Celebration:
  Max Fraser
Inside Out, Outside In: Arnold
  Hedstrom and Dave White

Special thanks go to the
  following people who
  helped us put this book
  together:
Robin Armour
Bruce Barrett (Heritage
  Branch, Tourism)
Jeff Brady
Canadian Parks and
  Wilderness Society
Lorraine Cardin
Peter Carr
Claire Desmarais
Marcelle Dubé
Isabelle Dumont
Patty Ann Finlay
Marco-André Fiola
Patricia Halladay
Peter Harms
Jane Haydock-Lane
Wendy Jickling
Anna Krangle-Long
Emily Krangle-Long
Mary Jane Lawson
Deborah McNevin
Ben Moise
Dennis Murray
Frank Norris
Juri Peepre
JP Pinard
Gayle Roodman
Lois Rudd
Denis Senger (Renewable
  Resources)
Kitty Sperling
Mark Stephens
Karen-Jane Stevens
Lucy Van Oldenbarneveld
Whitehorse Correctional
  Centre
World Wildlife Fund

Contributors
Sally Wright
Alexandrovich, Bea 77
Alexandrovich, Shiela 60, 61,
  79, 86, 87, 124, 125
Alton, Heather 108
Andison, Gloria 89
Armour, Robin 26, 63, 217
Armstrong, Eliza 92
Armstrong, Mary 135
Atkinson, Tannis 129
Badhwar, Stephen 194, 195
Barnhart, David 93
Barrett, Bruce 65, 201
Beattie, Mary 48
Beattie, Pete 48

Becker, Peter 157
Berdahl, Scott 2
Bergmann, Barb 85
Berkman, Marten 100, 101,
  135, 174, 224
Binger, Alan 104
Binkley, Jelea 196
Boles, Julia 115, 122
Boss, Robyn 109
Bourque, Marlynn 22, 23, 24,
  85, 86, 87, 98, 99
Branch, Dan 19, 33, 46, 47, 119
Brault, Naomi 109
Breen, Sharren 192
Brewster, Cameron 188
Brown, Jeff 24, 35, 48, 102, 103,
  139, 141, 165, 212
Brown, Kevin 211
Buerge, Kate 81
Bunbury, Glen 79, 186
Bunbury, Hazel 111
Burns, Bonnie 198
Bush, Wendy 40, 41, 68, 69, 71,
  124, 125, 150, 151, 186
Buzga, Heinrich 72
Caley, Margaret 54
Camp, Mike 198
Campagna, France 73
Carr, Marie 23, 148, 164, 165,
  193
Catlin, Karen 24
Charlebois, Rick 13, 14, 21
Chatterton, Sharron 22, 23
Cherian, Jay 83
Christl, Ava 116
Church, Ev 80
Cohen, Herb 213
Collins, Jovian 89
Comchi, David 30, 138
Copland, Ginna Sue 41
Corbeirer, Orein 117
Corriveau, Suzanne 104
Crawshay, Aven 101
Cuthbertson, Jenny 107
Cyr, Gail 162, 163
Dabbs, Bhreagh 108
Darling, Linda 172
Davidson, Dan 21, 25, 31, 154
Deer, Catherine 41, 53, 83, 152,
  153, 198
Delmage, Suzette 72, 144
Dept. of Indian Affairs 31
Digby, Karen 69, 122
Dobrowolsky, Helene 70
Doyle, Anne 197
Dubé, Marcelle 49, 91
Dufort, Julian 59
Eamer, Claire 71
Edmunds, Lindsey 109
Edwards, Jen 204
Ehrlich, Lynda 74, 107, 109
Ellis, Jennifer 145
Erkiletian, Jim 50, 51
Estey, Evie 24, 28, 181, 210
Evers, Carl 148
Fink, Bob 82
Forrest, Judy 65, 81
Francis, Chad 92
Fraser, Jayne 54, 55
Fraser, Max 0, 7, 26, 27, 88,
  169
Geophysical Institute,
  University of Alaska
  Fairbanks 29, 45, 52, 67
Gerber, Shelley 32, 170, 171,
  172
Girard, Cécile 90, 91, 97
Glassby, Pam 106
Gonda, David 104

Grant, Moe 157
Greig, David 137
Grump, Ima 12
Haist, Yvonne 30
Handley, Tanya 2, 3, 6, 215
Hanulik, Barbara 10, 142, 143
Hargrave, Anne 64, 65
Harms, Jodi 100
Harms, Peter 51, 53, 76, 110
Harrigan, Fiona 194
Harris, Yvonne 15
Hartmier, Richard 118, 128
Hayden, Joyce 63, 96, 97
Haydock-Lane, Jane 109
Hebert, Ailsa 203
Hedstrom, Arnold Three
  Moose page, 52, 77, 80, 81,
  102, 106, 141, 201, 202, 210
Heritage Garden 145
Hewlett, Elizabeth 214, 215
Hicklin, Janne 23, 140
Hilton, Linda 155
Hobbs, Lona 62
Hodgson, Mike 38, 82
Hubley, Blair 111
Humphries, Jackson 80, 81
Hutchins, Chris 72
Ingram, Pixie 111
Ingram, Rob 19, 28, 137
Istchenko, Victor 203
James, Darryl 9, 202
Janssen, Manfred 85
Jobin, Jessica 110, 111
Johnny, Judi 155
Johnson, Joanne Jackson 116
johnson, pj 123
Johnston, Sandy 39
Kaiser, Axel 158, 159
Kassi, Norma 88
Kennedy, Catherine 218
Kerr, Mary El 79, 139, 168
Killick, Adam 212, 213
Kirkwood, Vera 80, 81
Knight, Leslie 106
Krangle, Wynne 105, 139
Krangle-Long, Anna 108, 109
Krangle-Long, Emily 12, 48,
  85, 92, 105
Kroocmo, Ken 160
Kuiack, Marguerite 48
Kurth, Steven 161
Kwanlin Dun First Nation 15
Lacoste, Jude 86
Lacoste, Levon 86, 87
LaDue, SharonAnne 20, 89, 96,
  98, 99, 210
Lane, Angela 104, 109
Layman, John 179
LeBel, Dorothy 197
Legace, Carole 210
Lewis, Jolie 211
Lindsay, Scott 38
Locke, Sarah 39, 148
Long, Peter 2, 3, 21, 85, 163,
  216
Lybrand, Karen 33
Macdonald, Muffy 125, 145,
  146

MacMillan, Leigh 87
Maddigan, Kate 149
Madsen, Ken 15, 43, 58, 78,
  108, 138, 176, 177, 187, 225
Madsen, Kirsten 187
Majiski, Joyce 4, 36, 46, 47, 78,
  136, 180, 214
Marion, Heidi 1, 71, 156
Mathewson, Rob 6, 66, 140,
  157, 171, 199, 202, 215
McCauley, Bob 211
McClelland, Brenda 78
McCullough, T. Ruth 22, 24,
  117, 119, 121, 123
McDiarmid, Denise 97
McFarlane, Arlin 15
McGrath, John 25
McIntyre, Norman 84
Meister, Brianne 95
Mervin, Roy 89
Mis.Ta-Nash, Serena Lee 20,
  203, 208
Mitchell, Lorrina 178, 179
Moorcroft, Caitlin 88
Moorcroft, Lois 85, 154, 157
Moore, Janet cover, 96, 132
Moore, Pat 16, 17
Mossop, David 44
Mostyn, Richard 189
Mueller, Stuart 210
Neilson, Pete 69
Nelson, Sarah R. 93
Nesgaard, Tyler 104
Neufeld, David 8, 9, 190, 191
Neufeld, Erin 185
Nixon, Wendy 107
Northern Gifts Ltd. 34
Nowatzki, Marcella 181, 182,
  183
O'Connor, Helen 29, 61, 64, 65,
  67
Old, Patricia 202
Osland, Len 130
Overbo, Jason 99, 101, 103,
  105, 107, 109
Pangman, Jill 82, 180, 219
Papequash, Christian 51
Parhizgar, Frank 2
Parry, Laurel 131, 132
Pasquali, Paula 106
Peepre, Juri copyright page,
  table of contents page, 176,
  177, 226, 227
Pendziwol-MacMillan, Donna
  29, 105, 216
Person, Dick 42, 66
Peters, Akira 104
Peters, Echo 89
Petersen, Albert 206
Pettigrew, C.J. 173, 174
Picot, S.D. 23, 31, 163
Pinard, JP 135
Pope, Al 68, 69, 152, 153, 228
Pope, Angus 93
Porter, Marie 108
Porter, Michael 43
Poulsen, KH 184
Price, Scott 20, 129, 218
Profeit-Leblanc, Louise 14, 62
Pruner, Jacqueline 85, 94, 95,
  112, 113, 114
Pugh, Anna 188
Pugh, Lee 80
Purdy, Irwin 50
Pyke, Laura 23
Quinlan, Judith 7, 18
Quinsey, Kira 104
Quock, Tyler 104
Radwanski, Joseph P. 154, 224

Recycling Centre 138
Reid, Alison 14, 67, 85, 124,
  128, 138
Reid-Fraser, Robin 14, 88
Rice, Mike 70, 85, 131, 201
Rifkind, Lewis 141, 146
Rodger, Thom 49
Ross, David 5
Rozell, Ned 29, 52, 67
Scherbarth, Chris 22, 81, 85,
  88, 96, 105
Schmidt, Jerimy 108
Scoville, Lance 182, 183
Seapy, Lillian 11, 200
Sellars, Kellie 101
Serup, Sheila 44, 45, 175
Shepherd, Steve 11, 27
Shiell, Mary 62, 83, 168
Sidhu, Mandeep 102
Simon, Jessica 147, 158, 159
Sinclair, Lindsay 110, 111
Sinclair, Pam 58
Sinclair, Wm. C. 123
Smith, Blake W. 157
Smith, Carol P. 139
Smith, Cathleen 126, 127
Smith, Ian 92
Smith, Karan 56, 117, 118, 120,
  121, 130
Smith, Lisa 82
Smith, Marilyn 74, 75
Smith, Merran 104
Smyth, Steven 160, 201
Snyder, Joy 141, 146
Speyers, Judith A. 56, 57
Spicer, Laura 196
Staniforth, Jennifer 2, 3, 34,
  110, 111, 173
Stewart, Dylan 104
Stewart, Kirk 48
Steins, John inside covers, title
  page
Strachan, Amy 92
Swerhun, Ernie 92
Thomas, Mike 75
Tremblay, Wyatt 14, 25, 31,
  178, 200
Tuzlak, Suat 172
Urquhart, Doug 37, 52, 62, 83,
  146
Verheyen, Stephanie 9
Vos, Curtis 149
Waldman, Marty 32
Walker, Brian 120, 121
Wanner, Mike 61, 198
Watt, Donald C. 5
Wheelock, Angela 17
White, Dave 205, 207, 209
Whitley, Mary 184
Wilkinson, Don 166, 167, 206,
  207
Willeumier, Hetty 156
Williams, Bruce 164, 193
Wohlfarth, Ilse 80
Wolf, Anne D. 170, 171
Woods, Chris 29
World Wildlife Fund 2, 176
Wright, Sally 41, 133, 134, 167
Wright, Skeeter 4, 35
Yakimow, Gord 5
Yukon Archives 192
Yukon Government 18, 34, 41,
  44, 45, 46, 47, 49, 53, 76, 88,
  118, 217
Yukon Wildlands Project 5, 82,
  177
Zimmer, Rodene 71

PHOTO: CATHERINE KENNEDY. ILLUSTRATION: SCOTT PRICE

INDEX

PHOTO: JILL PANGMAN

Back Pages

Another Lost Whole Moose Catalogue

A Yukon Way of Knowledge

by the Lost Moose Collective

$19.95 • 1991• ISBN 0-9694612-0-8
• 156 pages, B&W photos and graphics

Editor's choice--a welcome tonic in tough times.

The Globe and Mail

Good browsing for cold winter nights.
The Anchorage Times

Visitors who would like to become better aware of our northern lifestyle should study this book.

Arctic Circle

This northern bestseller is a popular gift item and a "must have" for every cabin in the north! It's all about the traditional Yukon bush lifestyle, by people who live here. More than 200 Yukoners contributed photos, stories and how-to articles about surviving in this unique part of the world. Part sourcebook, part almanac, part guidebook and part storybook—this book, which has sold over 22,000 copies, is about life today.

Lost Whole Moose perfect for throne room.

Don Sawatsky, *The Yukon News*

All you need to know about the Yukon.
Julia Elliott, *The Ottawa Citizen*

Moose Catalogue is about being Canadian.
Arthur Black, *Northern Living*

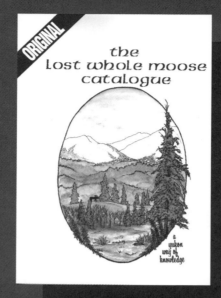

The ORIGINAL Lost Whole Moose Catalogue

A Yukon Way of Knowledge

by the Rock and Roll Moose Meat Collective

$14.95 • 1979 • ISBN 0-9694612-1-6
• 112 pages, B&W photos and graphics

Back by popular demand! This reprint of the original 1979 *Lost Whole Moose Catalogue* is a perennial favourite. It's the classic '70s statement about preserving a unique northern bush lifestyle.

From the title page…"Don't let your children read this book. As a matter of fact, you shouldn't read this book. Just put it down and run out of the store, screaming."

With over 13,000 copies sold, it looks like not everyone took our advice!

Wild Rivers, Wild Lands

by Ken Madsen

$29.95 •1996• ISBN 1-896758-01-0 •
120 pages, 75 colour photos with maps

The "Spell of the Yukon" that Robert Service found in the North is wilderness. Ken Madsen tells us how it is threatened and why it is so important.

Dave Foreman, The Wildlands Project; author, *Confessions of an Eco-Warrior*

Ken Madsen's description of the excitement of running the "Everests" of rivers in the Yukon and northern B.C. is nicely balanced with the "Shangrila" of the Peel watershed. Great reading for those who have been, and for those who want to go.

Pat Morrow, photographer & adventurer

…single, heartfelt message to the reader.
Explore

Adventurer Ken Madsen makes the case for preserving northern wilderness through heart-stopping stories and dramatic colour photos of wild rivers of the Yukon, British Columbia and Alaska. The book profiles three watersheds (Alsek-Tatshenshini, Peel and Stikine) where it is still possible to protect the natural ecosystems needed by wildlife whose range in North America is shrinking rapidly.

The author has canoed or kayaked the rivers featured in the book, and his writing and photography will enchant anyone who reads this book.

Ken works to protect North America's fast disappearing wilderness heritage. He was instrumental in the campaign that resulted in the establishment of the Tatshenshini-Alsek Wilderness Park. A portion of the royalties from *Wild Rivers, Wild Lands* will go to the Yukon Wildlands Project.

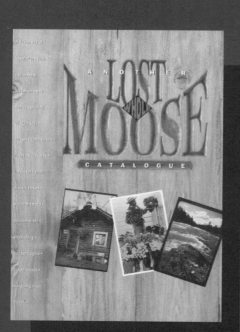

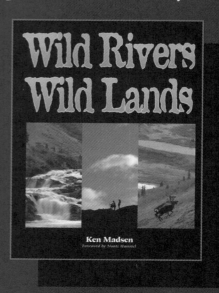

Back Pages

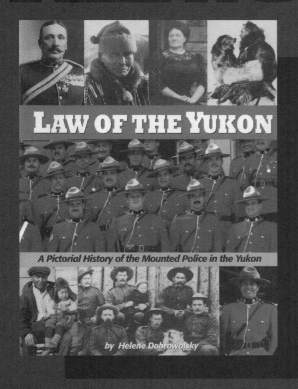

Law of the Yukon

A Pictorial History of the Mounted Police in the Yukon

by Helene Dobrowolsky

$29.95 • 1995 • ISBN 0-9694612-8-3 • 192 pages, B&W, colour photos, illustrations, index, bibliography, references, honour roll

This book is sure to leave its mark in the reader's imagination. Seldom does a book of this quality and insight into an important part of Canadian history come along.

Morley Lymburner, *Blue Line Magazine*

This book, written for the centennial celebrations of the arrival of the force in the Yukon, is an excellent coffee table book…. It would be a great gift for history buffs and, of course anyone interested in the RCMP.

Hazel Jardine, *The Leader-Post*, Regina

A bright and colourful presentation…will appeal to readers interested in the Yukon, its history and its police.

The Northern Review

*L*aw of the Yukon presents the fascinating history of the Royal Canadian Mounted Police in the Yukon in a thoroughly entertaining and informative book. A northern author looks at the challenges faced by the Mounted Police in Canada's Yukon Territory over the last 100 years, since their arrival on the eve of the world-famous Klondike gold rush.

There is no other part of Canada where the Mounties have made such a deeply entrenched impression. Here, police history is inseparable from Yukon history and the author skillfully blends both. Interspersed with stories of the various detachments are numerous biographical sketches of members, both rank and file and officers, their wives and the First Nations special constables. They show both the life of a constable in small remote communities, and how the force evolved into the modern-day RCMP.

Through vivid photos, careful research and use of personal diaries and correspondence, Helene Dobrowolsky shows the reality of Mountie history to be even more intriguing than the fiction of Hollywood's Sergeant Preston. And then there are dog stories, lots of them, some hilarious, some tragic.

Chilkoot Trail

Heritage Route to the Klondike

by David Neufeld and Frank Norris

$24.95 • 1996 • ISBN 0-9694612-9-1 • 192 pages, more than 250 B&W photos, maps, illustrations, index, references

… recipients of a Canadian Historical Association Certificate of Merit in Regional History. …Chilkoot Trail is judged to have made the most significant contribution to an understanding of the Canadian past.

Canadian Historical Association

Practically every page takes the reader back a century to one of the most fascinating periods of United States and Canadian history….A must read.

Jim Forst, *Northwest Travel*

This lively book is a bi-national collaboration between two government historians… Both men have been involved professionally with the trail for years, and it shows in their familiarity with the terrain and their commitment to the subject.

D. Francis, *Canadian Geographic*

*C*o-authored by Parks Canada historian David Neufeld and United States National Park Service historian Frank Norris, this book is a comprehensive, popular history shedding new light on the use of the trail made popular during the world-famous Klondike gold rush of 1897-98.

The Chilkoot Trail connects the Alaska coast with the uplands of the Yukon River headwaters. Through the 19th century, the coastal Tlingit controlled the trail as a fur trade route and later for packing to the Yukon interior. During the gold rush, the trail posed daunting challenges to thousands of gold-hungry stampeders.

Chilkoot Trail describes this history, as well as the continuing traditional First Nations activities in the Chilkoot region, rising tourist interest in the trail, and the work undertaken by two national park services to commemorate the trail as the world's first international historic site.

This fully-illustrated history will help foster greater awareness and understanding of the trail, and is sure to be popular with the hiking crowd and anyone interested in the north or the Klondike gold rush.

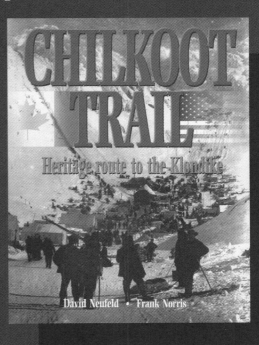

Whitehorse & Area Hikes & Bikes

by the Yukon Conservation Society
$18.95 •1995 • ISBN 0-9694612-5-9
• 144 pages

An excellent current example [of a guidebook]...this slim volume is exactly what an outdoor guidebook should be: well written and organized; full of clear two-colour maps and drawings; comprehensively indexed; and fun to read.

Alec Ross, *Quill & Quire*

One of the principle charms of Hikes and Bikes...is the sense that it has been prepared by a community of enthusiastic practitioners for the convenience and pleasure of fellow enthusiasts.

Eve D'Aeth, *Northern Review*

This one-and-only guide to trails for walking, hiking and mountain biking in the Whitehorse area is a necessary item for every household and visitor to our great outdoors. It contains detailed maps and descriptions of 35 trails plus options, and slips easily into a knapsack!

Whitehorse & Area Hikes & Bikes is for those who want to enjoy our outdoors and are looking for anything from an easy walk along the Yukon River near town, to a mountain bike adventure in the forest or alpine. Trails cover four regions around Whitehorse and all can be done in a day.

Trail descriptions include the degree of difficulty, length of time to complete, elevation gain and access points. For example, the Fish Lake hike, at 7.5 kilometres, is moderately difficult, takes three hours to complete and features a 1,100-foot elevation gain.

"Although a little boggy in places, the trail quickly takes you above the treeline and onto a flat-topped ridge..."

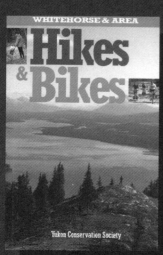

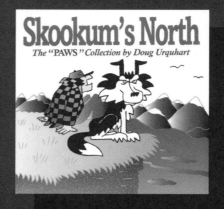

Skookum's North

The "PAWS" Collection

by Doug Urquhart
$14.95 • 1994 •ISBN 0-9694612-3-2
• 165 pages

...captures the atmosphere of the Yukon tradition with subtle and sometimes not-so-subtle mockery

Doug Bell, Publisher, *The Yukon News*

...offers a refreshingly humorous look at the lifestyles of the great North land. It's a favourite with our readers

Loretta Nistler, Editor, *Delta Wind*

A dog's-eye view of life in the north. Nearly 500 "PAWS" comic strips—the complete 10-year collection—presented in one hilarious, insightful volume. A favourite with northerners and anyone who has spent time in the north. This book should be required reading for anyone involved in government or resource management.

In 1983, "PAWS" was launched as the first syndicated cartoon strip ever produced in the north. Since then it has appeared as a feature in 34 northern newspapers from Lynn Lake, Manitoba to Dutch Harbour, Alaska. Today, "PAWS" remains the only successful northern cartoon strip in Canada and Alaska. It is carried by about 20 papers on a regular basis.

Skookum ain't hokum.

Charles Lillard, *B.C. Bookworld*

Drawing can be for the dogs.

Alex Taylor, *Yellowknifer*

Of pictures both fun and fantastic.

Dan Davidson, *Whitehorse Star*

Yukon—Colour of the Land

Photography by Richard Hartmier
$29.95 hardcover • 1995 •
ISBN 0-9694612-7-5 • 122 full-colour pages

Poring over the colors of the land...

Dan Davidson, *Whitehorse Star*

Photos capture colours and light of the Yukon.

Kelly Hayes, *The Yukon News*

New book reveals the colour of the land.

Michael Gates, *The Klondike Sun*

The colours are indeed breathtaking.

Patricia Morley, *Northern Review*

A beautiful picture book about the Yukon by Richard Hartmier, the Yukon's leading commercial photographer. Hartmier knows the land and its people. The colourful landscapes, people and places of Canada's Yukon Territory attracted him 20 years ago; they still do. His first book features this land renowned for its breathtaking natural beauty.

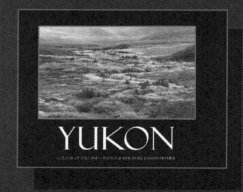

Klondike Ho!

Klondike Ho!
A Cartoon History of the Klondike Gold Rush
by Curtis Vos
$9.95 • 1994 • ISBN 0-9694612-4-0 • 76 pages

... friendly style and appealing cartoon illustrations will be sure to make a favourable impression on even the most reluctant reader.

Sheilagh Martin, *Resource Links*

Adults will like it, too.

The Yukon News

The Klondike gold rush—in a comic book! Author-illustrator Curtis Vos humourously cartoons the world's most famous gold rush through friendly, lovable characters. *Klondike Ho!* covers many of the important events and people of those crazy days in the Yukon 100 years ago.

Each chapter begins with a selection from the famous poet of the north, Robert Service. Clear and detailed maps precede each section.

This primer on the Klondike gold rush is well-suited to children and youth, but everyone will enjoy seeing familiar historical characters come to life.

Edge of the River, Heart of the City
A History of the Whitehorse Waterfront
by Yukon Historical & Museums Association,
prepared by Helene Dobrowolsky and Rob Ingram
$12.95 • 1994 • ISBN 0-9694612-2-4 • 84 pages, maps and B&W photos, index

As on most waterfronts, the survival rate of Whitehorse's historical buildings is not high. The authors compensate by including numerous historic photographs, which recapture the waterfront's past appearance. They also sketch out an intriguing history while arguing for the preservation of the buildings that remain.

Alison K. Hoagland, *Alaska History*

...seeks to remind residents and visitors alike of Whitehorse's vibrant maritime heritage.

Ken Coates, *The Northern Mariner*

For decades, the Whitehorse waterfront teemed with life as trains from the coast met boats bound for the Klondike goldfields. *Edge of the River, Heart of the City* brings to life a town that the construction of the Alaska Highway, post-war developments, and modern urbanization have substantially obscured.

This important addition to Yukon history also provides readers with a historical walking tour of the Whitehorse waterfront, focusing on the small number of remaining historic buildings.

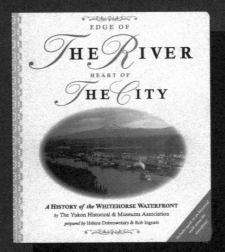

Alsek's ABC Adventure

Written and illustrated by Chris Caldwell
$9.95 • 1996 • ISBN 1-896758-00-2 • 32 pages, full colour

Chris Caldwell creates cool kids' cartoon...

Kelly Hayes, *The Yukon News*

Chris Caldwell's Yukon way of learning things...

Dan Davidson, *The Whitehorse Star*

"Pursued by the persistent pooch, Alsek plows through pines, pelting past petrified ponies..."

from the Pp page

A hungry grizzly bear named Alsek journeys through the Yukon wilderness in high summer, searching for something to eat. Come along on his hair-raising adventure through the alphabet, and hold on tight when Alsek gets too close to people!

Alsek's ABC Adventure can be enjoyed over and over again by youngsters and their parents. It's a great way to learn about the alphabet and something about northern life, too.

Back Pages

Ordering information

For mail orders, contact Lost Moose Publishing, 58 Kluane Crescent, Whitehorse, Yukon, Canada Y1A 3G7
e-mail: lmoose@yknet.yk.ca, phone: 867-668-5076, fax: 867-668-6223 (area code is 403 until October 1997)
Retailers: Order from GDS (Canada) 1-800-387-0172, (U.S.) 1-800-805-1083 or contact Lost Moose Publishing
Visit our website: http://www.yukonweb.com/business/lost_moose

Clear winter night

by Joseph P. Radwanski

You find you don't care where you are
on the highway from Stewart to Cassiar,
And I never saw the stars so bright
like when we stopped by the roadside
on that clear winter night.

The creaking engine cooling down,
the crunch of the snow coming from the ground,
I heard the sky shout with delight
when we stopped by the roadside
on that clear winter night.

Like diamonds in their charcoal glove,
I discovered again this feeling called love,
I've never held something so tight
as when we stopped by the roadside
on that clear winter night.

This long winding road ain't as hard as it seems,
the sky is as big and bright as our dreams,
I've got a feeling we're going to do all right,
just you and me—like a clear winter night.

You feel like life has just begun
on the road to the land of the Midnight Sun,
and nothing has ever felt so right
like when we stopped by the roadside
on that clear winter night.